IN SEARCH OF

PSI

CONTEMPORARY PERSPECTIVES ON EXTRA-SENSORY PERCEPTION, PSYCHOKINESIS, AND SURVIVAL

IN SEARCH OF PSI

CONTEMPORARY PERSPECTIVES ON EXTRA-SENSORY PERCEPTION, PSYCHOKINESIS, AND SURVIVAL

Edited by
ADAM J. ROCK
LANCE STORM

Pari Publishing

First published in Italy in 2014 by Pari Publishing, Sas

A catalogue record for this book is available from the British Library.

ISBN 978-88-95604-22-0

Book and cover design by Andrea Barbieri.

Printed and bound in the United States of America.

Finito di stampare nel mese di settembre 2014
dalla tipografia Bookmasters Inc., Ashland, OH 44805, USA
per conto di Pari Publishing Sas di Eleanor F. Peat & C.

Pari Publishing

Pari Publishing Sas
Via Tozzi, 7
58045 Pari (GR), Italy

To the memory of
Michael A. Thalbourne
1955 - 2010

Table of Contents

PART 2: BELIEF AND CULTURE

PART 3: PSI AND SCIENCE

Preface

In March 2011, a professor of botany at Montana State University, having just read Arthur Koestler's (1972) book *The Roots of Coincidence*, approached one of us, and asked the question: "Can you tell me, from your perspective of having critically reviewed the literature, is there now incontrovertible statistical evidence for psi?"[1] (emphasis added). When statistical evidence is sought, one is tempted (some might say, compelled) to respond from an evidence-based perspective, but unfortunately that approach can often end up in a 'he-said/she-said' exchange that goes nowhere fast. Preferably, to put it briefly and somewhat cautiously, a typical answer should go something like this: There are ongoing disputes over what suffices as statistical evidence in any field of research (such as medicine, or psychology) and, similarly, in parapsychology, many advocates (i.e., believers) are convinced of psi effects purely from the statistical evidence yet, from the very same evidence, skeptics are not so convinced, if at all! It does not seem to matter how much evidence is piled up—believers and skeptics usually maintain their positions. It is unclear just what it would take to convince skeptics that psi exists, but they would wonder what it would take to convince believers that the opposite is true.

Essentially, that was the answer offered to the professor, whose reply was short but sweet—he said he was hoping for a "simple answer". It seemed to him that, after all these years of parapsychological research, scientists should be able to state that at least some of the results obtained were not due to fraud or poor experimental design. Some researchers do state it, but the truth is there are those skeptics who invariably resort to those and other so-called 'explanations' (oftentimes, this attitude masks an agenda, which we will not go into here.[2])

It is in appreciation of this fundamental polarisation in human beings that we find we must speak to, or better, *appeal* to a broader issue when arguing the case for psi. On that note, it was implied, in the introduction of a relatively recent

1. The word 'psi' is used "either as a noun or adjective to identify *paranormal* processes and paranormal causation" (Thalbourne, 2003, p. 92), where 'paranormal' means "outside the realm of human or animal capabilities as presently conceived by conventional scientists" (Thalbourne, 2003, p. 83).

2. For criticisms of this agenda, see Storm (2005, 2008).

article in *Psychological Bulletin* (i.e., Storm, Tressoldi, & Di Risio, 2010), that many of our twentieth-century discoveries and breakthroughs (e.g., the relative properties of 'spacetime', or 'non-local' effects posited in quantum mechanics) would have been rejected as ludicrous in bygone days, yet these phenomena are now met with very little resistance. Sometimes, it does not even seem to be the evidence, pure and simple, whatever form it takes, that wins over the majority of scientists—the phenomena are often still considered to be marvels (magic?) to them, and for that reason alone one would have thought there would still be room for considerable doubt; even Nobel Prize winning physicist Niels Bohr said: "Anyone who is not shocked by quantum theory has not understood it" (cited in Barad, 2007, p. 254). In truth, it simply takes some people longer than others to accept new findings. Is it a drawn-out educational process that explains this conversion, or something simpler than that? In the end, it does not matter—we know the day will come when we will all have to accept seemingly impossible facts about our universe, and the social conventions and prejudices that undermine these newfound facts will simply have to yield.

Taking all this on board, representatives of parapsychology must depend on more than statistics and evidence to argue their case. They must consider their audience; they have to win their hearts as well as their minds. Most parapsychologists know this and agree, but it is almost as if they often forget it for, to reiterate an aforementioned point, they seem to rely heavily, or even exclusively on statistics as evidence when pressed on the topic. Once again, we understand that course of action is the way of the scientist, and we are sympathetic to it, but mountains of evidence can even end up alienating some people—the very thing the scientist might wish to avoid. One explanation for the cause of this alienation, apart from intimidation, is that evidence makes people think, or even think twice, and we know that over-selling can 'queer the deal', to use the vernacular.

In the final analysis, it seems we all have a need to maintain a certain distance from things we do not understand, perhaps out of doubt, or even fear, or both, but (perhaps viewed somewhat more favourably) there is also an inherent mystery behind those phenomena we label 'unexplained', and it is that mystery which acts as a spur to the more adventurous, the more curious among us. Those people know better than anyone what it means to have their hearts and minds won over. This book, *In Search Of Psi*, is a call to the adventurous and the curious who are in search of *more than raw data, proofs, and statistical evidence*, so we leave that material for other authors, and other books, for there is a spate of books out there full of evidence meant to convince, and we do not wish to add to it. *In Search Of Psi* is different. It is a specially prepared compilation of previously published articles that appeared in the *Australian Journal of Parapsychology* from 2001 to 2011 by a diverse group of authors, researchers, experimenters, and theorists. *In Search Of Psi* offers up solutions and innovations, ideas and speculation, and these are the things that stimulate and motivate individuals to entertain the impossible or, just simply, to think for themselves. Our aim is to encourage readers to weigh up the material presented in these pages—we do not wish to win anyone over, or challenge people's doubts and beliefs, or preach to the converted.

To help realise this aim, we have assembled a team of world-renowned and highly respected authors. They are the late William G. Roll, Harvey J. Irwin, the late Montague Keen, Vernon M. Neppe, Pamela Rae Heath, Joan D. Johnstone, Sue-Ellen Kjeldal, the late Simon Harvey-Wilson, the late Michael A. Thalbourne, Peter S. Delin, Ronald Bryan, Richard Blumenthal, Bryan J. Williams, Eric Ouellet, Hannah Jenkins, Colin Mitchell, and of course, the editors of this volume, Adam J. Rock and Lance Storm. To help readers navigate the pages of this book, we have divided the contents into four main sections: Part 1: Extra-Sensory Perception, Psychokinesis, and Survival; Part 2: Belief and Culture; Part 3: Psi and Science, and Part 4: Conclusions.

Part 1 introduces readers to the basic subject matter of the book; namely, extra-sensory perception, psychokinesis, and survival, and in Chapter 1 (Imagery Cultivation and Extra-Sensory Perception), Lance Storm and Adam J. Rock consider the historical factors concerning psi effects that have been linked to altered states of consciousness (ASCs). In this context, arguably the most widely used technique in parapsychology is the Ganzfeld design. However, some scholars have posited arguments that cast doubt on whether the Ganzfeld does, in fact, induce an ASC, and whether it is psi-conducive. Consequently, Storm and Rock argue that it would prove prudent to investigate other conditions that might induce ostensibly psi-conducive ASCs, and it would be wise to get feedback from test participants in these alleged states. Storm and Rock propose that psi is enhanced (i.e., strengthened, or better detected) using a shamanic-like treatment. On that basis, Storm and Rock argue that parapsychologists must go beyond the assumption that psi is optimised under conditions that are inherently passive procedures, and foster techniques that require cognitive action from test participants.

In Chapter 2 (Telepathy as a Process Mediated by Quantum Teleportation Between Remote Neurons), Richard Blumenthal explores the possibility that the quantum state of a given neuron may be teleported to the neuron of a remote brain, thereby initiating normal cognitive activity in that brain and comprising a process known as telepathy, the understanding of which may also help to explain the processing of ordinary sensory stimuli. An attempt is made to relate various aspects of the proposed process to some characteristics of telepathy, such as the apparent ability to transfer information devoid of any discernable movement of mass and/or energy; relating quantum entanglement to the biological similarity of twins and others; and how the introduction of information to neurons ultimately yields cognition within a frame of reference unique to the individual, as reported in cited instances of telepathy.

In Chapter 3 (The Possible Role of Psychokinesis in Place Memory), Pamela Rae Heath entertains the idea that the environment can store recordings made by living beings (i.e., so-called 'place memory')—an idea which has been around for over a century. Pamela's chapter reviews how the term 'place memory' has changed since it was first used by parapsychologists. Her chapter also considers what the research literature says regarding the recording and retrieval of place memory, and suggests that there may be more than one way in which information can be recorded by, or imprinted upon, the environment. The hypothesis is discussed that psychokinesis might be involved in some of these cases, particularly when stress or peak levels of emotion are involved, as is often the case in crisis situations.

In Chapter 4 (Human Levitation), Simon Harvey-Wilson shows how most levitation reports originate from seven main sources or groups: (i) mysticism, (ii) shamanism, (iii) people supposedly possessed by demonic spiritual entities, (iv) those subjected to poltergeist activity, (v) Spiritualism, (vi) people who believe they have been abducted by aliens, and (vii) martial arts such as qigong. So far almost no scientific research appears to have been conducted into levitation. In order to persuade empirical scientists that human levitation warrants further investigation, Simon's study contains two components. First, there is a thematic comparison of historical and modern levitation reports from the seven groups to see what physical, cultural and phenomenological circumstances they may have in common. Second, to assist future researchers in their investigations, Simon's chapter includes a hypothesis-generating exercise that seeks clues from the thematic comparison and interviews as to how human levitation might work.

In Chapter 5 (A Discussion of the Evidence that Personal Consciousness Persists After Death with Special Reference to Poltergeist Phenomena), William Roll explains how human beings have a dual mind, the mind of the left hemisphere and the mind of the right hemisphere. The left hemisphere has an organ for language and when awake can be conscious of things with linguistic labels. The right hemisphere is good at operating with mental images as in dreams. The functions of the right hemisphere include extrasensory perception (ESP) and psychokinesis (PK). However, the findings that have been advanced in favour of the idea that personality survives death have mostly been discussed in terms of the continuation of the left mind. William's chapter explores the pro and cons of this approach.

In Chapter 6 (Is Scientific Investigation of Postmortem Survival an Anachronism? The Demise of the Survival Hypothesis), Harvey Irwin discusses the so-called survival hypothesis. The notion of postmortem survival has been a key domain of parapsychological research since the inception of the Society for Psychical Research in the late nineteenth century. Parapsychologists nevertheless have made no definitive progress toward the verification of the survival hypothesis, and the continued centrality of this issue to parapsychology is a major impediment to the acceptance of the field as a scientific enterprise. Harvey advocates a redefinition of parapsychology and the relegation of the survival hypothesis to minor status.

In Chapter 7 (The Demise of the Survival Hypothesis, or the Errors of Harvey Irwin?), Montague Keen addresses many of the points made by Harvey Irwin in Chapter 6. Harvey argues not merely for the abandonment of the survival hypothesis, but for its specific exclusion from the area of legitimate parapsychological studies, claiming that such study is important, timely, stimulating and challenging. Montague argues that Harvey is wrong, and errs in two ways: One arises from factual errors or misrepresentations when Harvey discusses the strength and nature of evidence which appears to support a survival hypothesis. The second is Harvey's conclusion that survival research can never meet the conditions required for acceptable scientific (i.e., pragmatic) work. After commenting on the disturbing implications of Irwin's thesis for scientific progress in general and psychical research in particular, Montague examines these errors in some detail.

Part 2 (Belief and Culture) follows with investigations into the nature of paranormal belief, and a look at the cultural aspects of paranormal belief. Peter S. Delin starts off this part with Chapter 8 (Scepticism and Credulity). Dr. Delin reminds us that scientific thinking has been in vogue since the seventeenth century, but it represents only a minority view, and is essentially sceptical. The majority of mankind adopts a credulous attitude towards natural phenomena. The extremely sceptical and the extremely credulous have many psychological characteristics in common and both may be unreliable in assessing occasional phenomena.

In Chapter 9 (The John Edward Phenomenon: "I Want To Believe"), Sue-Ellen Kjeldal argues that much international interest has been generated by psychics such as John Edward who purport to communicate with the deceased. In Sue-Ellen's chapter, contemporary decision theory is used as a possible explanatory factor in determining why individuals unquestioningly believe this notion, whilst empirical support against the theory appears overwhelmingly negative at this stage in research into this phenomenon.

In Chapter 10 (The Australian Sheep-Goat Scale: Development and Empirical Findings), Michael A. Thalbourne goes into a technical, but interesting journey into the origins of his so-called "Australian Sheep-Goat Scale" (ASGS), which is a questionnaire measure of belief in various aspects of the paranormal, such as extrasensory perception, psychokinesis, and life after death. The term "sheep" is traditionally used for "believer" in some aspect of psychic phenomena, while "goat" is used for "disbeliever". Paranormal phenomena have in common the fact that they contradict C. D. Broad's (1978) Basic Limiting Principles about the existence and operation of mind in the mathematico-physical world, and are therefore in some sense anti-scientific. Michael provides a summary of relevant empirical findings, both parapsychological and psychological, relating to the ASGS.

In Chapter 11 (Pueblo Parapsychology: Psi and the Longbody from the Southwest Indian Perspective), Bryan J. Williams introduces the concept of the Longbody, which traces its origin to the language and spiritual tradition of Native American tribal cultures, particularly that of the Iroquois Indians. Within these cultures, the concept of the Longbody represents a worldview quite different from that of Western cultures, in that it posits a broad degree of spiritual interconnection between all things in the natural world, living and material alike. From this view, a tribal member's experience of self is not solely limited to their individual living body, but also includes other family and tribal members (both living and deceased), the objects they possess, and the geographical locations that they inhabit or consider sacred. These can all be seen as extensions of the individual small body and the self that, when taken as a whole, comprise the larger tribal "longbody." The concept was first introduced to parapsychology as a metaphorical way to understand the interconnection between mind and matter that is suggested in one form or another by all the known types of psi phenomena. Bryan reviews similar aspects from four Southwest tribes (the Hopi, the Navajo, Laguna Pueblo, and Zuni Pueblo), and he discusses the implications for tribal psi experiences and Roll's longbody hypothesis. It is suggested that tribal oral tradition, which is based in memory, opens the way for psi as a means to ensure the survival of the tribes and their respective longbodies across space-time.

In Chapter 12 (Reincarnation Beliefs of the Gumini People of the Simbu Province of Papua New Guinea), Joan D. Johnstone describes the traditional reincarnation belief system of the Guminis, a small group of people living in the southeast of the Simbu Province of the Highlands of Papua New Guinea.

This system embraces the belief that the spirit of some humans is, after death, reincarnated within the body of another living person of similar age and probably of the same sex as the deceased. This person, a stranger, then represents the continuation of the life of the person who died in terms of his/her social and kinship relationships. Joan demonstrates that this belief system was functional in traditional Gumini society, but may not continue to be so in future due to rapid changes in rural and urban life currently affecting the people of Papua New Guinea.

We round out the main component of our text with Part 3: Psi and Science. This section features a diverse range of innovative and speculative scientific theories pertaining to psi, the future of psi, and beyond.

In Chapter 13 (Why Parapsychology is Amongst the Most Important of the Sciences), Vernon M. Neppe examines the implications for scientific endeavour of a subject that he believes to be of the utmost importance, both philosophically and for its possible practical application. So much and yet so little is known: So much because a vast body of evidence has accumulated over more than a century; and so little, because of this knowledge base's limited ability to withstand critical scientific analysis.

In Chapter 14 (Examining the Evidence for Psi in the Context of Scientific Revolution), Hannah Jenkins presents a chapter that is concerned with the representation of psi in current philosophy texts. She undertakes an analysis of the current status of evidence for psi according to a Kuhnian scientific revolution. This is based on an analysis of the nature of the dispute between those who maintain that psi does not exist (the dominant one expressed in most modern philosophy texts), and those who believe that science will eventually be able to cope with the anomalous phenomena associated with psi effects. An appeal is made for a more even-handed representation in future philosophy texts using this interpretation to help ameliorate the representation of psi phenomena.

In Chapter 15 (Looking into Higher Dimensions: Research with Joseph McMoneagle), a world-class remote viewer, Joseph McMoneagle, offered to work with Ronald Bryan in his particle-physics research program. Ronald thought he might be able to see neutrinos and see into higher dimensions. Joe McMoneagle was asked three things (in sealed envelopes which he did not open): to look inside an electron, examine a radioactive source, and describe a quantum-mechanical wavefunction. He gave credible or useful information on all three targets.

In Chapter 16 (Avoiding the Intervention Paradox), Colin Mitchell aims to show that there are possible models of time for which the Intervention Paradox is not a barrier to the possible existence of a type of precognition in which the event precognised is avoided or changed. The paradox arises as soon as an event is precognised and acted upon to prevent that event from taking place, for what is there to be precognised? Colin uses two different configurations of the 'block model' of space-time to show how this could be done: One with multiple futures, and one with another time dimension.

In Chapter 17 (Social Psi and Parasociology), Eric Ouellet notes how all societies have recorded, in one form or another, anomalies that impacted on life and culture. Whether these anomalies were attributed to the intervention of spiritual entities, magical powers, or a mixture of exotic natural phenomena compounded with superstitious beliefs, the indisputable fact remains that anomalistic events also have a social dimension. Starting with the nineteenth century, a number of serious researchers looked into various forms of anomalies and, during the twentieth century, the discipline of parapsychology emerged to become a more unified research effort to understand anomalies. Yet, most of those who looked into these anomalies were essentially limiting their analysis to the individual experience; the social dimension was often forgotten. Eric's chapter proposes a way forward that bridges the disparities existing between socially-relevant anomalistic events and their rigorous study through approaches that are compatible with the findings of modern parapsychology.

Finally, in Part 4: Conclusions, we wrap up our anthology with Chapter 18 (In Search of Psi: Destination Unknown or Destination Nowhere?), in which we discuss our contributors' various theories and/or research findings. We believe there is much support for a parapsychological dimension that extends beyond the reality we call normal. We argue that researchers must be open to new perspectives, but we extend our argument to mainstream science, not just parapsychology. Most of our contributors address these and other issues, and we concur that there is a place for further research into parapsychological phenomena that may extend our understanding of the world.

We thank our authors for their contributions, and appreciate the time they took to re-read their original articles and, if necessary, make changes that might better clarify their original points. We stress, however, that very few changes were needed, although a few authors added some new material in the form of appendices, etc.

We are proud to present a team of authors whose tireless efforts over the years have resulted in a collection that represents the latest, most innovative of ideas imaginable, even for a field as controversial and far-reaching as parapsychology.

—*The Editors*

» References

Barad, K. M. (2007). *Meeting the universe halfway: Quantum physics and the entanglement of matter and meaning.* Durham, NC: Duke University Press.

Broad, C. D. (1978). The relevance of psychical research to philosophy. In J. Ludwig (Ed.), *Philosophy and parapsychology* (pp. 43-63). Buffalo, NY: Prometheus Books. (Originally published 1949.)

Koestler, A. (1972). *The roots of coincidence.* London: Picador.

Storm, L. (2005). A socioempirical perspective on skepticism about psi. In M. A. Thalbourne & L. Storm (Eds.), *Parapsychology in the twenty-first century: Essays on the future of psychical research* (pp. 275-304). Jefferson, NC: McFarland.

Storm, L. (2008). Preface. In L. Storm (Ed.) *Synchronicity: Multiple perspectives on meaningful coincidence* (pp. xiii-xvi). Pari, Italy: Pari Publishing.

Storm, L., Tressoldi, P. E., & Di Risio, L. (2010). Meta-analyses of free-response studies 1992-2008: Assessing the noise reduction model in parapsychology. *Psychological Bulletin, 136*(4), 491-494.

Thalbourne, M. A. (2003). *A glossary of terms used in parapsychology.* Charlottesville, VA: Puente.

Foreword

Searching for Psi

DEAN RADIN[1]

On a humid planet orbiting a minor star at the ragged edge of an unremarkable galaxy, a bipedal species with a fledgling neural-based intelligence struggles to understand its role in the cosmos. Over roughly a million years, these creatures have sought this understanding through numerous imaginative worldviews, most of which were based on variations of hubris and wishful thinking. A recent invention called 'science' has led to halting progress in understanding a few of Nature's tricks, but the premature developmental stage of this species raises the possibility of self-annihilation before it reaches a more stable adolescence.

Throughout their existence, these organisms have been aware of two puzzling classes of experience. The first suggests that perception has both local and nonlocal components. Local perception they understand, more or less. They are less certain about nonlocal perception, which they label psychic or mystical, and they use quasi-descriptive terms—telepathy, clairvoyance, and precognition—to indicate where in spacetime the information involved in nonlocal perception seems to go to, or come from. The second class of experience implies the existence of meaningful connections between subjective and objective realities; they call such experiences psychokinesis, or mind-matter interactions.

Descriptions of psychic or 'psi' experiences can be found in every language and in every culture on this planet. As historical fashions rise and fall, worldviews evolve and devolve, and depending on where and when the topic is broached, explanations of psi experiences become polarized into divine vs. demonic, grace vs. grit, talent vs. attainment, self-evident vs. impossible, or reasonable vs. anomalous.

For the last 150 years, the 'Western' worldview has regarded psi experiences as anomalous because existing theories cannot easily explain them. This provincial view is not surprising because these creatures have only recently encountered the

1. [Permission to print has been granted by the author.—Editors.]

most elementary aspect of nonlocal Nature through its 'quantum theory', and the import of that slice of reality is still poorly understood, even by those who invented it. The hybrid discipline known as neuroscience has begun to explore connections between mind and matter, but that discipline too is still in its infantile 'hubris and wishful thinking' phase of development. The discipline most closely focused on these phenomena—parapsychology—is making some headway empirically, but it continues to grapple with epistemological puzzles and with hermeneutics.

Is this species destined to remain stalled in a limbo where the mere existence of psi experiences is ensnared in endless skeptical debates and increasingly picayune critiques? Or will it fail to advance beyond the illusion of separation and, in that failure, dissipate into extinction? This volume provides a snapshot of this species' struggle to answer such questions in the second decade of the 21st century BCE.

Meanwhile, we watch and wait.

PART 1: EXTRA-SENSORY PERCEPTION, PSYCHOKINESIS, AND SURVIVAL

Chapter 1

Imagery Cultivation and Extra-Sensory Perception[1]

LANCE STORM AND ADAM J. ROCK

Bem and Honorton (1994) assert that, "Historically, psi has often been associated with meditation, hypnosis, dreaming, and other naturally occurring or deliberately induced altered states of consciousness" (p. 5). Perhaps the most widely used technique in this context is the Ganzfeld ("total field") which may be defined, in broad terms, as a "homogeneous perceptual environment" (Bem, 1993, p. 102). Specifically, the Ganzfeld consists of an undifferentiated visual field created by viewing a red light through halved translucent table-tennis balls taped over a percipient's eyes. Additionally, an analogous auditory field is produced by listening to stereophonic white or pink noise (i.e., a monotonous hissing sound; Bem, 1993). Therefore, as a procedure whereby a 'sender' (agent) is required to "psychically communicate" (Milton & Wiseman, 1999, p. 387) a picture target or movie-film target to an isolated 'receiver' (percipient) who is in the Ganzfeld condition of *homogeneous sensory stimulation*, the Ganzfeld is usually regarded as inducing an altered state of consciousness (ASC)[2] that is considered psi-conducive.

The question of whether the Ganzfeld protocol does in fact induce a psi-conducive ASC is usually answered indirectly in two ways. First, the reasonable and logical assumption is made by Ganzfeld researchers that homogeneous sensory stimulation and relaxation necessarily and favourably help to alter

1. [This chapter was originally published as an article in *Australian Journal of Parapsychology* (2009, vol. 9[1], pp. 5-31). Permission to reprint has been granted by the authors and the journal.—Editors.]

2. It is perhaps noteworthy that Rock and Krippner (2007a,b) argue that "altered states of consciousness" may be more accurately described as "altered patterns of phenomenal properties."

the signal-to-noise ratio (i.e., the psi signal is *enhanced*).[3] Second, and as a consequence of this claim, the subsequent assumption is made that, based on the Ganzfeld meta-analyses, the Ganzfeld design demonstrates consistent, significant, and relatively higher effect sizes compared to its closest parallel, the free-response design, which does not feature an ASC (e.g., see Storm & Thalbourne, 2000).

In regard to the first assumption, the pioneers of the Ganzfeld technique (Braud, Wood, & Braud, 1975; Honorton & Harper, 1974; Parker, 1975) investigated various states such as hypnosis, dreaming, meditation, and relaxation that might be considered psi-conducive. However, it is arguable whether there can be objective evidence (e.g., EEG measures) or subjective evidence (e.g., percipients' self-reports) that, if percipients are in a Ganzfeld altered state of consciousness (Gz-ASC),[4] it is *the* Gz-ASC that is psi-conducive, or some other partial- or sub-condition that is psi-conducive (e.g., relaxation acting alone, or the homogeneous field acting alone).

In regard to the second assumption, Milton (1997) only suggests, in her major meta-analysis of 78 free-response ESP studies, that the Ganzfeld design may deliver a higher effect size compared to the free-response design: "the nonASC [free-response] studies did not obtain a *significantly* lower mean effect than the early ganzfeld studies [see Honorton, 1985] but the lack of significance may have been due to the relatively smaller number of studies involved" (pp. 299-300, italics added). In fact, she adds that "the nonASC studies clearly *outperform* the near-zero mean effect of the new ganzfeld studies [see Milton & Wiseman, 1997]" (p. 300, italics added). Furthermore, although it may be too soon to make such claims, more recent evidence supports Milton's finding that there may not necessarily be a significant effect size difference between Ganzfeld and free-response databases (Storm, Tressoldi, & di Risio, 2010).[5]

---

3. Key pioneers of the Ganzfeld (e.g., Honorton, 1977) have used the term "enhanced" (p. 457) for many years, but William Braud prefers the words, "more readily detected" (W. Braud, personal communication, April 22, 2009).
4. One of the controversial claims concerning the Ganzfeld is that it induces an altered state (for example, see Alvarado, 1998), but we remain impartial on this matter. In the present chapter, we will argue that the Ganzfeld is largely a passive technique that governs the limits of its own psi-conduciveness.
5. In their meta-analysis, Storm, Tressoldi, and di Risio (2010) found that one of their Ganzfeld databases comprised of naïve participants only (n = 17) was not significantly different from a free-response database also comprised of naïve participants (n = 18), though that same Ganzfeld database did have a stronger effect size.

In addition to these criticisms, we argue that the Ganzfeld protocol does not include instruction to *actively* 'target' the target while in the putative Gz-ASC. We acknowledge that in many psi-retrieval studies "there is present an active *intention* or active *expectation* for incorporation of target-relevant information into one's ongoing mentation" (W. Braud, personal communication, April 22, 2009). Braud adds that "such targeting intentions and expectations may be explicit or implicit and may be present in both participants and experimenters." However, we would not use the word 'active' in the same sense to describe 'intentions' and 'expectations', which in and of themselves are not mental actions, but may only precipitate such action.

For these reasons, parapsychologists may have been labouring under the false apprehension that the Gz-ASC facilitates psi like no other ASC, and if the generic Ganzfeld design ever needs procedural changes, it is only insofar as theoreticians might argue that targets should be more interesting (e.g., auditory targets instead of visual, or film instead of stills), or samples should be comprised of test participants who are trained rather than untrained, or selected on the basis of a given trait rather than unselected. These 'modifications' do not address the problems we wish to highlight. We propose that the focus on the signal-to-noise ratio (i.e., noise reduction) has created a paradigmatic block that has blinkered parapsychologists to the degree that they have not entertained alternative, even antithetical, methodologies that encourage fantasy, imagination and other *active* cognitive processes.

It may be the case that a tacit assumption exists whereby Ganzfeld participants are thought to somehow tap into their imagination. This mistaken notion may have come from the belief that participant mentation is a consciously/semi-consciously/unconsciously-influenced fantasy product that has its source in some dimly represented target-as-signal just because said participant, as percipient, is instructed to *visualise* the target image 'sent' by a sender/agent. But as it happens, there is anecdotal evidence that some participants are not only able to perceive trial-specific images, but also (possibly inadvertently) fall victim to expanded or broader domains and perceive incidental events in the laboratory environment and elsewhere (for examples, see Parker, 2005, pp. 78, 81). We hold that the evidence is clear that Ganzfeld experimenters endorse and deploy a primarily passive technique inherent in the various Ganzfeld designs, and it is arguable whether the Gz-ASC somehow encourages any kind of active process on the part of the percipient. Ganzfeld participants are only given instruction to report what they are experiencing (i.e., they give mentation), and there is little or no option after the session to express and discuss fully their subjective experiences during the trial. We stress that in many Ganzfeld studies mentation too was often given *after*, not during the trial,[6] at least until the inception of Parker's (2005) Real-Time Digital Ganzfeld Technique (RTDGT).[7] But in all types of Ganzfeld design, including RTDGT, the fact remains that no rigorous imaginal instruction is given to percipients that seeks to activate a 'journey' into the unconscious to tap psi at its source.

We must be mindful of the fact that the "ESP Ganzfeld studies are probably the most controversial and frequently analysed group of parapsychological studies" (Henry, 2005, p. 43). Indeed, in recent years, many scholars (e.g., Alvarado, 1998; Braud, 2005; Scimeca, Boca, & Iannuzzo, 2001) have presented arguments that cast doubt on whether the ganzfeld induces conditions that facilitate psi.[8]

Alvarado (1998) has brought attention to issues such as "lack of control groups, a variety of design and individual differences problems . . . and an alternative (more general) explanation using expectancy effects of different types" (p. 45).

The question has been asked, Do psi-favorable test conditions such as Ganzfeld procedures really *facilitate* psi? In answer to that question, Braud (2005) has pointed out that:

> ...it is not yet clear to what extent any psi manifested in such conditions might be attributable to psi-enhancing properties of the conditions themselves or to various sampling, demand characteristics, or experimenter effects. In addressing this issue, much more trenchant analyses seem to be in order, rather than taking it for granted that these conditions actually facilitate psi....(p. 48)

---

6. W. Braud (personal communication, April 22, 2009) points out that in many cases, "participants *may verbalize their imagery and impressions throughout the session*" but we argue that, in Braud's own words, "such imagery is recorded and perhaps played back or read to participants *at the end of a session as a memory aid*" (italics added, W. Braud, personal communication, April 22, 2009).

7. RTDGT "automatically enables the real-time recording of the mentation report so as to be synchronous with the film clip" (Parker, 2005, p. 78).

8. We do not intend to deal with the typical criticisms made against the Ganzfeld design, such as fraud, inadequate randomisation, sensory leakage, and other flaws, as these have long been argued as unlikely (see Utts, 1991). Since Hyman and Honorton (1986) produced the so-called *Joint Communiqué*, Ganzfeld practitioners have made sure that the appropriate controls are implemented.

Hyman (2010) argues that "the consistency and reliability of the ganzfeld experiment relies exclusively on meta-analysis" (p. 486). Likewise, Scimeca et al. (2001) have pointed out the failure of independent and neutral scientists to produce successful replications on demand of the Ganzfeld experiment. Scimeca et al. have claimed that it is impossible to observe and positively define the alleged phenomenon (i.e., psi) in the Ganzfeld. They summarised three Ganzfeld meta-analyses and argued that the application of meta-analysis "to synthesize and explain the results of this area of research has been flawed by a misinterpretation of its indices" (p. 13). And they recommend qualitative methods. Consequently, it may be prudent to investigate other test conditions that are ostensibly psi-conducive, though we are not arguing that researchers should deviate too far from the Ganzfeld design. In this context, it is noteworthy that psi effects (PK and ESP) that were induced during shamanic states have been reported extensively in the literature, and we will return to this theme later (e.g., Krippner, 1984; Nelson, Jahn, Dunne, Dobyns, & Bradish, 1998; Nelson & Radin, 2003; Saklani, 1988).

We propose that parapsychologists must meet the psi process head on, and not only accept that psi may be facilitated in a passive state (addressed by the noise-reduction model of the Ganzfeld design), but also regard psi as an effect that can be induced through cognitive action on the part of the participant. We go further by advocating a shift in the experimental paradigm that utilises shamanic-like journeying conditions primarily because the evidence suggests that cognitive action may facilitate psi. In the parapsychological tradition, such evidence comes from the remote-viewing studies. In the anthropological tradition, such evidence comes from the shamanism studies. These bodies of work will be discussed shortly, but it is necessary to first describe the history of the Ganzfeld so that an understanding of its nature can be fully appreciated in the sense that we critique it here.

The Origins and Nature of the Ganzfeld

The pioneer parapsychologist in the United States, J. B. Rhine (1934/1964), once observed that several of his participants "described their ESP experiences as involving a state of 'detachment', 'abstraction', 'relaxation', and the like" (p. 181). He went on to say that any number of his test subjects would go into a "light trance with eyes closed," or "close their eyes when they do not have to keep them open," or "look off with 'a far away look' much of the time" (p. 181). Other participants even "perceive[d]...by hallucination" (p. 181).

Most parapsychologists are familiar with these 'techniques', which are not necessarily instructional components of formal psi procedures, but it is certainly apparent to most parapsychologists that there is much anecdotal evidence that some psi participants attempt to induce in themselves an ostensible ASC that they consider facilitates psi. Certainly there seems to be some degree of focussed attention if it cannot be claimed that an ASC is actually induced. In the next four sub-sections, four states (i.e., hypnosis, dreaming, meditation, and relaxation) will be discussed in terms of either passive process, or psi-conduciveness, or both. While we acknowledge that active processes can undoubtedly define these states, our argument here is that Ganzfeld pioneers endorsed a noise-reduction model and therefore designed the Ganzfeld protocol under the assumption that passive, rather than active, processes in mind constituted the optimum means of increasing the signal-to-noise ratio.

Hypnosis

One of the first to make mention of 'passivity' or a 'passive state' during the psi process was Brugmans (1922, 1924). He based his assumption of a "rapport" between ESP (i.e., telepathy) and the passive state on declines in galvanic skin response. More generally, as with Brugmans, the main focus of researchers came to be the psychic's state of mind—it was thought that ESP was somehow related to degrees of consciousness, such as dissociation brought about by such factors as 'somnambulism', 'absorbing preoccupation', and 'mental fatigue'. Progress proved slow, but it was inevitable that parapsychologists would seriously investigate hypnosis since it was seen as a means of bringing about a passive, dissociative state thought to be conducive to psi (e.g., Honorton & Krippner, 1969; Kumar & Pekala, 2001; Pekala & Cardeña, 2000).

While it was found that "the ability to dissociate was…the strongest predictor of 'anomalous and paranormal experiences',…hypnotizability was a more moderate predictor" (Parker, 2005, p. 71). Parker admits that this conclusion is not clear-cut because anomalous experiences are not necessarily psychic, and can include anything from UFO abduction to belief in fairies. Furthermore, Honorton and Krippner (1969), having reviewed the relevant studies that controlled for waking expectancies, found that nine of 22 studies had significant differences "but sometimes, as well as the psi hitting effect…there could be a so-called *psi-missing effect*" (cited in Parker, 2005, p. 70) in the hypnosis group. Thus, according to Parker, little was achieved in the investigation of hypnosis as a possible psi-conducive variable. Indeed, in the review by Stanford and Stein (1994), results depended on the personality and style of the experimenter. They also noted that participant selection played a part.

These confounding variables only complicated the issue but, as will be seen, the passive aspect of dissociation (induced through techniques such as hypnosis) lived on to influence the design of the Ganzfeld protocol.

Dreaming

Researchers also investigated what is now referred to as 'dream-psi'. This domain had its greatest impact in the work done at the Maimonides Dream Laboratory (Ullman, Krippner, & Vaughan, 1974), and it originated in the idea that many people report telepathic and premonitory dreams, as indeed Rhine's wife, Louisa Rhine, attested on the basis of her vast collection of unexplained anecdotal accounts (L. E. Rhine, 1962). Theoretically, the link to the usually passive condition of the dream state was clear—psi seems to work unconsciously, and imagery was the key. In some sense, the psi process could be encapsulated in the dream process, and the psi target seemed embedded in imaginal form as dream content.

Results from the Maimonides dream studies were mixed and complex, involving a small team of researchers with different methodologies, different statistical testing procedures, and different goals. Nevertheless, it produced a significant mean effect, and a new (post-Maimonides) dataset (Sherwood & Roe, 2003) that also produced a significant mean effect, was not statistically different from the Maimonides dream studies. Not only did that mean that all the dream studies from both sets belonged to a homogeneous set, but the mean effect was highly significant. As Storm (2006) conservatively stated: "These findings do indicate that the 'average' dream-psi study is not likely to elicit evidence of psi, but when the collection is looked at over a 40-year period, there is an extremely strong indication of a correspondence between dream motifs and target material under laboratory conditions" (p. 146).

While most parapsychologists would be cognisant of the phenomenon known as lucid dreaming characterised by *active* involvement of a volitional dream-ego (LaBerge & Gackenbach, 2001), the Ganzfeld design approach seems focussed on only the passive aspect of the dream-psi process.

Meditation

A handful of studies have been conducted that directly investigated the alleged psi-conduciveness of meditation (e.g., Honorton, 1997; Palmer, Khamashta, & Israelson, 1979; Rao, Dukhan, & Rao, 2001; Rao & Puri, 1978; Rao & Rao, 1982; Roney-Dougal & Solfvin, 2006), but results have been variable.

Furthermore, as Steinkamp (2005) has indicated in her meta-analysis of forced-choice studies, the enhanced results after meditation might partly be the result of psychological factors. For example, participants may have greater confidence after meditating, and *their* belief might, in turn, couple with the *experimenter's* belief that meditation will help. In other words, the meditation effect on psi might be conflated with some degree of belief effect from participants and the experimenter (on belief as a psi-conducive variable, see Lawrence, 1993). These findings and assumptions cloud the issue over the psi-conduciveness of meditation *per se*.

Relaxation

Anecdotal and experimental reports of alleged psychic phenomena in meditative or relaxed states suggested an avenue of research for parapsychologists (e.g., Braud & Braud, 1973, 1974). Honorton (1977) cursorily reviewed the relaxation literature and, having found some indication that relaxation could "enhance psi receptivity" (p. 457), advocated relaxation as a psi-conducive condition.

For the period 1946 to 1992, Storm and Thalbourne (2001) collected 21 studies that featured relaxation as a treatment condition. They found that 52% of studies with a relaxation condition (n = 11) produced significantly higher effect sizes compared to the non-relaxation studies (n = 10), and this success rate is about ten times higher than would be expected by chance (where a = 5%).

The relaxation condition is the epitome of the Ganzfeld state for its emphasis on placing participants in a reclining restful position, usually on an appropriately-designed upholstered chair. We can safely assume that a relaxation protocol includes *mental* relaxation, so that percipients in a relaxation condition are not applying some kind of active cognitive process that facilitates psi. We would deem mental relaxation to be a passive state.

The Noise-Reduction Model

As we have seen, the psi-focussed hypnosis, dreaming, meditation, and relaxation literature has produced variable results and a number of assumptions. Although hypnosis was too complex a procedure and not sufficiently understood, dream research, though expensive and time-consuming, did furnish some encouraging results. Notwithstanding the perhaps dubious incorporation of the principles inherent in meditation and seemingly appropriate relaxation techniques, the experimental design that came to be called the Ganzfeld, was simple and inexpensive, and it was Charles Honorton's (1977) work that paved the way for the Ganzfeld as we know it today. Honorton (1977, 1993) had earlier referred to 'internal attention states' and ASCs in ESP research, and he conceptualised psi as a weak cognitive signal usually masked by internal cognitive and external 'noise'. On that basis, he proposed his noise-reduction model (Honorton, 1974, 1993).

Braud (2002) also endorsed a model of mental quietude, and he too described the Ganzfeld as an ASC similar to that obtained in meditation (i.e., stillness of mind or cognitive quietude). We note, in Alvarado's (1998) words, how Braud (1978) had "articulated" the possible sources of noise, including "sensory and perceptual noise, bodily and autonomic activity, *mental activities,*... [and] *excessive striving to obtain ESP information*" (p. 44, italics added). Though these might be considered sources of 'noise' under certain circumstances, we would suggest that mental activity and focus are keys to creativity, and may only be psi-inhibitive when they degenerate into states of anxiety and fervour.

Theoretically, by modifying the "signal-to-noise ratio" (i.e., reducing the noise), using any or all of the above-described treatments (i.e., hypnosis, dreaming, meditation, and relaxation), the presumed psi information could be better detected. Parker (2005) clarifies the Ganzfeld philosophy:

> The common feature, as Honorton described it, is the elimination of "noise" or unwanted sources of stimulation. By "noise" was meant not just external stimulation and sources of distraction but also inner chatter. The objective is to still the mind in order for internal imagery to spontaneously manifest; or, expressed in another way, the brain requires a minimal level of stimulation and in the absence of an external source, it will turn internally for this. (p. 73)

The overall conclusion we must draw about the Ganzfeld is that, by creating a homogeneous field of visual and auditory stimulation, and inducing a meditative relaxed state, the Ganzfeld technique encourages a state in the percipient that is very much akin to the passive state of sleep-onset, even to the degree that there may be hypnagogic effects. In fact, falling asleep requires a winding-down, not a cranking-up of mental activity, and in an EEG study by Wackermann et al. (2002) the restful Ganzfeld state was found to be different from the waking state on alpha-frequency activation only (Ganzfeld alpha was higher). We see here that the Ganzfeld process is very much aimed at putting the percipient in a docile, high-alpha, trance-like or hypnotic state, and these are all passive states. In other words, the Ganzfeld artificially induces a sleep-like state—a lowering of conscious arousal. It is even acknowledged that many Ganzfeld participants can actually fall asleep during their sessions.

We must note that many cases of spontaneous psi seem to involve allegedly passive processes. Braud points out that spontaneous case studies "in everyday life, [and] outside of the laboratory…seem to favor a noise-reduction view (and, perhaps more important, a need-related view), rather than active cognitive factors" (personal communication, April 22, 2009). We reconcile our argument against psi models and theories which propose that psi involves largely passive processes by pointing out that just as many theories and models describe spirit possession and/or channelling for the purposes of eliciting psi (i.e., clairvoyance, telepathy, and precognition), and these are not exclusively passive, and nor do they involve modest expenditures of energy on the part of the psi experient. At this juncture we can only state that there are alternatives to the argument for passive processes, but we also find that adequately addressing these issues is beyond the scope of this chapter and would require exclusive and lengthier treatment by other means.

Regardless of whether or not the Ganzfeld components truly do independently or collectively induce a psi-conducive ASC, we see from Parker's words that the aim of the Ganzfeld is to reduce or eliminate the noise, thereby rendering the psi signal more easily detectable. And when we consider the issue further, we see that the fundamental philosophy of the Ganzfeld technique is the aim of filtering out psi from the noise by inducing a passive state in the percipient. Therefore, strictly-speaking from a procedural perspective, the percipient is never given the opportunity to engage in a process that we would describe as actively cultivating the fertile ground in which psi might be elicited. To do this, we hold that the percipient must be given special instructions (such as the shamanic-like journeying technique discussed later) that foster or encourage psi, by actively creating a suitable environment in which it might emerge.

We hold that noise-reduction itself cannot be the best means by which psi imagery can be cultivated, if at all. One cannot experimentally inculcate two opposing conditions in a participant—promoting noise-reduction necessarily excludes the cultivation of imagery because the former requires mental stillness, whereas the latter requires cognitive activity. Nevertheless, our approach does not necessarily dismiss the notion that the psi process semi-consciously or unconsciously idles away in the background against a peripheral backdrop of noisy and irrelevant contents in consciousness. And we acknowledge that psi images may be made more accessible by some degree of focussed attention towards them (see George, 1981, 1982; George & Krippner, 1984; and White, 1964, for arguments and procedures to that effect). But we maintain that participants can go further and meet psi half-way by being less passive and more active in their search for the psi target. While Rhine's participants perhaps attempted to go into a dissociated, trance-like state—maybe even a state of focussed attention—there is no convincing evidence that they were using any kind of technique that might activate mental imagery. We argue that the way of parapsychology might have been very much different had efforts been made to ascertain what had really transpired in the minds of those early participants, as well as all Ganzfeld percipients since then. However, we acknowledge too that the field is diverse, and researchers have not solely depended on passive techniques but, very occasionally, have given attention to active processes as well. One such example comes in the form of the so-called *remote viewing* protocol which had its origins in the 1970s.

Remote Viewing as an Active Cognitive Process

The first major experimental researches into 'distant seeing' (a variant of clairvoyance)—otherwise known as remote viewing—was by Targ and Puthoff (1974), who actually coined the term remote viewing (RV). Thalbourne (2003) defines RV as "a neutral term for general extrasensory perception [GESP]... especially in the context of an experimental design wherein a percipient attempts to describe the surroundings of a geographically distant agent" (p. 107). Targ and Puthoff were particularly successful with Pat Price, a retired police commissioner, who was able to see objects large and small, such as furniture, and buildings, and concealed text (see Targ, 1996). Neither distance, nor size of target, seemed to influence RV outcomes.

Another key figure in RV research is Joseph McMoneagle (McMoneagle, 1997). He spent twenty years refining his RV skills, and discussed the various methodologies and protocols that facilitate RV (McMoneagle, 2000). RV has been investigated by other researchers (e.g., Dunne, Dobyns, & Intner, 1989; Dunne, Jahn, & Nelson, 1983; Jahn & Dunne, 1987; Schlitz & Gruber, 1981;

Schlitz & Haight, 1984). Schmeidler (1994) concluded that the overall evidence was indicative of a remote viewing procedure that is psi conducive.

It is perhaps noteworthy, as indeed Storm (2003) has pointed out, that a variant of RV—Extended Remote Viewing—consists of dynamic methods aimed at cultivating a semi-trance state or dissociative state, both of which are meant to help establish a connection with the target. Indeed, the RV-state is conceptualised by McMoneagle as a form of 'information retrieval', and thus an active condition. Since the remote viewer reports whatever is being seen, felt, heard, or otherwise perceived, McMoneagle claims that successful RV therefore requires that the remote viewer must learn to respond through writing or relating the RV information directly. Thus, as McMoneagle also points out, RV can be learned, and the basic ability is innate in most people, but may need refining.

The Unconscious Aspect of the Psi Process

Though RV seems largely dependent on a rational conscious process, it is also apparent that unconscious intuitive processes may play a large part in RV, which may be true of psi processes generally. Intuition is one of Jung's four functions in Jungian typology (Jung, 1957/1977), the others being sensation, thinking and feeling. Jung noted that intuition functioned in an unconscious manner, whereby conclusions were arrived at through mental processes for the most part unexplained.

Weiner (1982) argued that psi may be a process assisted by intuition. She viewed ESP as a "two-stage process that involves reception of a message followed by the mediation of that message to awareness through the normal psychological vehicles that transmit unconscious material, such as dreams and intuition" (p. 9). Thalbourne (2004) too, when speaking of anomalous functioning, has referred to a special form of "infallible intuition" that keeps one in "*a condition or state of consciousness*" where "no information is inaccessible" (p. 117). These statements recall the RV condition where the percipient may shift their mental orientation in a way that favors the constellation of imagery from some other (possibly unconscious) source.

Research into other unconscious processes has suggested that intuition may be related to physiological functions. Don, McDonough, and Warren (1998) attempted to elicit 'event-related potentials' in participants that would be greater in 'negative-going amplitude' when participants viewed future targets (graphic images), but not when they viewed future non-targets. Differential brain responses indicated that participants, although they did not consciously recognize the future target when first presented, were responding as if they unconsciously 'knew' that it would be presented later as a target. The results were "interpreted as evidence of unconscious or preconscious psi" (p. 127).

Support for unconscious psi processes has been found in the so-called presentiment effect (e.g., Radin & Lobach, 2007). Radin (1997, 2006), in his reviews of the literature, concluded that there appears to be a future-oriented capacity in human beings that elicits unconscious but measurable physiological reactions to stimuli micro-seconds *before* the stimuli are actually presented. The presentiment effect is most often pronounced when the target images have strong sexual or emotional content.

From all of the above, we maintain that (i) active mental processes access psi signals but not in the same way as the passive Ganzfeld process; and (ii) the unconscious domain of the human psyche is a well-spring of psi images, as indicated in the success of the dream-psi research. We propose that a shamanic-like-journeying state may elicit psi to an equal or greater extent than has been found for the Ganzfeld. However, before we present an experimental protocol designed to test these suppositions it would be prudent to provide some background into the field of shamanism.

Shamanism and Imagery Cultivation

Shamanism may be defined as "a family of traditions whose practitioners focus on voluntarily entering altered states of consciousness in which they experience themselves, or their spirit(s), travelling to other realms at will and interacting with other entities in order to serve their community" (Walsh, 1989, p. 5). While no single definition will appeal to all scholars (Walsh, 1995), this one emphasises several integral features of shamanism. First, it describes shamanism as a set of techniques (e.g., listening to monotonous drumming) designed to facilitate purported ASCs (see Krippner, 2002), rather than a religious tradition (e.g., Eliade, 1964).

Second, the definition highlights the volitional control of the practitioner; that is, the shaman's ability to enter and exit ASCs at will and limited mastery with regards to the phenomenological content of the ASCs.

Third, the definition's reference to the practitioner's spirit "travelling to other realms" (Walsh, 1989, p. 5) underscores the commonly accepted view (e.g., Heinze, 1991; Ripinsky-Naxon, 1993) that an ASC referred to as 'ecstatic journeying' or simply 'shamanic journeying' (i.e., out-of-body experiences or soul flight) constitutes a core aspect of shamanism (Krippner, 2002).

Finally, the practitioner's commitment to serve the interests of the community highlights the social-role function of shamanism (see, for example, Noll, 1983; Wright, 1989).

Shamanism and Psi

The aforementioned social-role aspect of shamanic journeying typically involves the shaman accessing "information that is not ordinarily attainable by members of the social group that gave them privileged status" (Krippner, 2002, p. 962). For example, the shaman may wish to access information regarding the geographical location of a plentiful food source that will provide nourishment for the members of his or her social group. Shamans ostensibly access this information during ASCs using psi (e.g., clairvoyance; Rogo, 1987). For example, Krippner (1984) reviewed psi research concerning tribal shamans, and emphasised that shamans cultivate ASCs with the aim of attempting to "locate lost objects, foretell the future, communicate with someone at a distance, or heal an injured person" (p. 4).

Krippner (1984) concluded that, "the shamanistic tradition can yield information that will be helpful in solving some of the enigmas that currently exist in the understanding and control of *psi*" (p. 4). Indeed, numerous reviews (e.g., Rogo, 1983a, 1983b, 1987) of previous anthropological research suggest that shamanic techniques are associated with psi phenomena such as ESP (e.g., precognition). Furthermore, previous research has also investigated the effect of shamanic techniques on PK. For example, Saklani (1988) tested the PK ability of five adult shamans in Garhwal Himalaya, and reported that the participants were "able to influence plant germination and protect seeds from the deleterious effects of saline" (p. 60).

The abovementioned link between shamanism and psi is particularly salient in light of our earlier contention that active mental processes can facilitate the access of psi signals. Indeed, Walsh (1995) states that shamanic ASCs constitute active states involving the cultivation of mental images whereby the percipient is able to "enter and leave the ASC at will and...partly determine the type of imagery and experiences" (pp. 35-36). Walsh further suggests that this "partial control of experience" is similar to phenomenological reports of lucid dreaming states and various imagery techniques used in a psychotherapeutic context (e.g., Jungian active imagination, Wolberg's 'Theatre Visualisation Technique'). The contention that active processes are an integral feature of shamanic techniques is also emphasised by Noll (1985): "Shamanism is an ecstatic healing tradition which at its core is concerned with the techniques for inducing, maintaining, and interpreting the experience of enhanced visual mental imagery" (p. 45).

Similarly, Peters (1989) highlighted the importance of the cultivation of mental imagery: "In shamanism, the key to the transpersonal is through visualization" (p. 129). Empirical support for these contentions was provided by Houran, Lange and Crist-Houran (1997) who examined the phenomenology of 30 narratives pertaining to shamanic journeying experiences presented in Harner (1990) and reported that 93.3% involved some form of visual phenomena. Thus, it seems reasonable to conclude that shamanic techniques involve active processes or, more specifically, the cultivation, mastery and control of mental imagery.

Shamanic Journeying, Other Worlds, and the Unconscious

The mental imagery content reported during shamanic journeying is typically consistent with the shaman's cosmology (Krippner, 1990; Walsh, 1995), which consists of a multi-layered universe often exemplified by what is technically referred to as the 'lower world' (the underworld or land of the dead), 'upper world' (sky) and 'middle world' (the terrestrial world or Earth).[9] The various worlds are considered to be connected by a 'central axis' that may manifest as, for example, a 'world tree,' 'cosmic mountain' or 'world pillar' (Eliade, 1964). Walsh (1989) asserts that the 'upper world' tends to be associated with spirit guides and teachers and is "perhaps populated with strange animals, plants, and people" (p. 27). Other scholars (e.g., Kalweit, 1988) suggest that while traversing the geography of the 'upper world' the shaman may report light experiences and encounters with celestial beings.

In contrast, the 'lower world's' geography is frequently conceptualised as funerary (e.g., Magar, Tamang, and North Asian shamans routinely report graveyards or cremation grounds; Desjarlais, 1989; Eliade, 1964; Peters, 1990). Furthermore, the 'lower world' often features treacherous landscapes (e.g., rivers,

9. However, it is noteworthy that Rock and Krippner (2008) assert that:

> ...it would be an oversimplification to assume that all shamanic traditions equate the "lower world" with the land of the dead, and the "upper word" with "sky." For example, Lepp (2004, p. 218, 217) stated that Mongolian shamans "travel to the Lower World to talk with the dead" (p. 218) but Na-hki and Moso shamans (in the Tibet area) believed that souls should "rise to heaven" (p. 26).

rocky ravines, mountains) and predatory creatures (e.g., mythical beings, jaguars, bears; Dobkin de Rios & Winkelman, 1989; Peters, 1989; Winkelman, 1986), which constitute "tests and challenges" (Walsh, 1990, p. 147).

Numerous scholars (e.g., Damery, 1997; Halifax, 1979; Layard, 1930; Overton, 1998) have argued that travelling to the various worlds within the shaman's cosmos is interpretable as "symbolic journeys into the unconscious" (Downton, 1989, p. 75). Indeed, Downton (1989) asserts that the middle or terrestrial world is the barrier separating the unconscious (lower world) and conscious (upper world) elements:

> Once the boundary between these realms is broken, the result is a dramatic change as unconscious contents flood into consciousness, transforming it and creating the sense of dismemberment—of being torn to pieces—widely regarded as the first step in the shaman's rebirth. (p. 74)

Consequently, shamanic journeying is an active process that purportedly allows one to access the unconscious domain of the human psyche. If (1) active processes allow the percipient to access psi signals; (2) the unconscious is indeed a wellspring of psi images (as we maintained in the preceding section); and (3) as previously argued, shamanic journeying is an active process of imagery cultivation that allows one to access the unconscious; then (4) the conjunction of (1), (2), and (3) may account, at least in part, for the previously stated link between shamanism and psi.[10]

Experimental Studies on Shamanic-Like Technique

The vast majority of empirical research concerning shamans has been anthropological and, thus, utilised non-experimental methodologies (e.g., naturalistic observation). However, there has been a recent trend towards investigating experimentally the effect of 'shamanic-like' stimulus conditions on non-shamans such as university students (Rock, 2006; Rock, Baynes, & Casey, 2005; Rock, Casey, & Baynes, 2006; Rock, Abbott, Childargushi, & Kiehne, 2008; Rock, Wilson, Johnson, & Levesque, 2008; Woodside, Kumar, & Pekala, 1997). Rock, Abbott, Childargushi, and Kiehne (2008) suggest that, "Techniques

10. Note that we acknowledge the psi-permissiveness of psychological variables such as positive expectations and goal-related intentions that may play a psi-facilitating role in shamanic practices. We simply do not focus on these in this chapter.

may be conceptualised as 'shamanic-like' insofar as they bear some relation to shamanic techniques and yet depart from what may properly be called shamanism" (p. 80). For example, ingesting psilocybin in order to ascend to the 'upper world' and consult one's power animal with the aim of serving one's social group may be considered a shamanic technique, whereas recreationally using psilocybin to enter an ostensible ASC and explore the 'upper world' is merely shamanic-like.

Previous experimental research (e.g., Rock, Abbott, Childargushi, & Kiehne, 2008; Rock, Wilson, Johnson, & Levesque, 2008; Woodside et al., 1997) using non-shamans has found that participants exposed to a shamanic-like stimulus condition (i.e., journeying with the aid of monotonous drumming) report significantly higher amounts of visual imagery compared to controls. These findings support our contention that shamanic techniques, like journeying, involve imagery cultivation processes. The findings also suggest that the imagery-cultivation component of shamanic techniques is perhaps also an integral feature of shamanic-*like* techniques. However, to the best of our knowledge, no published experimental research has investigated the effects of shamanic-like journeying stimulus conditions, and thus shamanic-like imagery cultivation, on psi.

Our aim in this chapter is to argue for, and develop, an innovative technique that involves a cross-cultural incorporation of ideas and findings that have their source in traditions both Western and Eastern, modern and indigenous. We now propose an experimental design that more fully acknowledges the active elements vital to these traditions.[11]

The Shamanic-Like Journeying Experimental Protocol

By way of an introduction, the following description is an outline only of our experimental protocol. Prior to testing a participant, Experimenter #1 randomly selects a four-picture target set (original target picture plus three decoys) from a pool of 45 target sets, and then randomly selects the target picture from that four-picture set. The picture is photocopied, wrapped in aluminium foil, and

11. It may be argued that monotonous drumming used to facilitate shamanic journeying performs a function similar to the monotonous auditory and visual stimulation in the Ganzfeld procedure. However, it should be noted that shamanic journeying facilitates ecstatic states characterised by physiological arousal (Walsh, 1995), whereas the Ganzfeld technique is associated with a relaxed or meditative state (Braud, 2002).

concealed in a light-proof target envelope. The four-picture set is also wrapped in aluminium-foil and concealed in a different light-proof envelope. Since only Experimenter #1 prepares the target-sets, Experimenter #2 remains 'blind' to the targets during the trials. That is, the contents of the target envelope and the four-picture set envelope are never made known to Experimenter #2 prior to, and during, the trial. Each picture-set is randomly assigned to each participant.

Participants are randomly assigned to one of two conditions: (1) the shamanic-like condition; and (2) a control condition.[12] (Experimenters have the option of including a third Ganzfeld group for comparative purposes.) Based loosely on Harner's (1990) protocol, participants in the shamanic-like condition will be instructed to lie on padded floor-mats, placing light-proof eye masks over their eyes. They will each be handed a target envelope, and they will be instructed not to open it. Instead, they are to place it in front of them. Participants in this condition will be required to cultivate specific shamanic-like visual imagery sequences (e.g., journeying to the 'lower world' by visualising entry into an opening in the Earth such as a 'cave' or 'animal burrow') while listening to monotonous drumming.

At the end of the stimulus condition, participants will be required to describe vocally the line drawing that is concealed in aluminium-foil inside the light-proof envelope. Experimenter #2 will take notes of participants' mentations, and read them back, in order to prompt participants' memory, thereby assisting them in the ranking process. Experimenter #2 will offer no personal interpretations as this may mislead participants.

Participants will rank the four pictures from 1 to 4. This ranking procedure follows the preferential ranking method (see Thalbourne, 1981, pp. 55-56), where participants express preferences by assigning rank #1 to the picture 'most likely' to be the target picture concealed in the target envelope, rank #2 to the picture 'second most likely', and so on, until all four pictures are ranked.

Finally, participants will be administered a questionnaire referred to as the *Phenomenology of Consciousness Inventory* (PCI; Pekala, 1991), which purportedly quantifies the phenomenological effects of exposure to a stimulus condition (Pekala, 1985; Pekala & Cardeña, 2000; Pekala, Forbes, & Contrisciani, 1989; Pekala & Kumar, 1984, 1986, 1989). The PCI allows one to determine: (1) if the

12. A control condition consisting of sitting quietly with eyes open has been proposed here because this particular stimulus condition has repeatedly demonstrated phenomenological effects consistent with ordinary waking consciousness in previous experimental studies (see, for example, Pekala, 1991).

shamanic-like stimulus condition induces a subjective sense of an ASC relative to the control condition; and (2) which phenomenological effects (e.g., visual mental imagery, inward absorbed attention, rationality) correlate with psi hitting. (Experimenters have the option of administering other scales and measures for the purposes of their own hypotheses.)

Participants in the control condition will also be handed a light-proof target envelope. Participants in the control condition will be instructed to sit quietly with their eyes open. From this point onwards, the procedure follows that just described in the previous paragraph for picture ranking. (For results of two experiments following the IC protocol, see the Appendix to this chapter.)

CONCLUSION

In this chapter, we have noted that the Ganzfeld procedure is one of the most successful experimental paradigms in parapsychology. In some cases, however, we have questioned the utility of the various primary components of, or influences on, the design of the Ganzfeld protocol (i.e., hypnosis, dreaming, meditation, and relaxation). In critiquing these components and influences we also, to varying degrees, endorse the criticisms of other Ganzfeld commentators (e.g., Alvarado, 1998; Braud, 2005; Scimeca et al., 2001). More importantly, however, we do argue that there may be an opportunity to move beyond the Ganzfeld methodology by implementing a new protocol that encourages active cognitive processes rather than adherence to passive processes. Such an advancement would see the implementation of a shamanic-like journeying protocol, and we have described the experimental parameters of that design.

» Acknowledgements

We thank Professor Stanley Krippner and Dr. William Braud for their helpful suggestions.

» References

Alvarado, C. S. (1998). ESP and altered states of consciousness: An overview of conceptual and research trends. *Journal of Parapsychology, 62*, 27-63.

Bem, D. J. (1993). The ganzfeld experiment. *Journal of Parapsychology, 57*, 101-110.

Bem, D. J., & Honorton, C. (1994). Does psi exist? Replicable evidence for an anomalous process of information transfer. *Psychological Bulletin, 115*, 4-18.

Braud, W. G. (1978). Psi-conducive conditions: Explorations and interpretations. In B. Shapin & L. Coly (Eds.), *Psi and states of awareness* (pp. 1-34). New York: Parapsychology Foundation.

Braud, W. G. (2002). Psi-favorable conditions. In V. W. Rammohan (Ed.), *New frontiers of human science* (pp. 95-118). Jefferson, NC: McFarland.

Braud, W. (2005). The farther reaches of psi research: Future choices and possibilities. In L. Storm & M. A. Thalbourne (Eds.), (2005). *Parapsychology in the 21st century: Essays on the future of psychical research* (pp. 38-62). Jefferson, NC: McFarland.

Braud, W. G., & Braud, L. W. (1973). Preliminary explorations of psi-conducive states: Progressive muscular relaxation. *Journal of the American Society of Psychical Research, 67*, 27-46.

Braud, W. G., & Braud, L. W. (1974). Further studies of relaxation as a psi-conducive state. *Journal of the American Society of Psychical Research, 68*, 229-245.

Braud, W. G., Wood, R., & Braud, L. W. (1975). Free-response GESP performance during an experimental hypnagogic state induced by visual and acoustic ganzfeld techniques: A replication and extension. *Journal of the American Society for Psychical Research, 69*, 105-113.

Brugmans, H. J. F. W. (1922). Une communication sur des experiences télépathiques au laboratore de psychologie à Groningue faites par M. Heymans, Docteur Weinberg et Docteur H. I. F. W. Brugmans. In C. Vett (Ed.), *Le compte rendu officiel du Premier Congres Recherches Psychiches* (pp. 396-408).

Brugmans, H. J. F. W. (1924). "L'état passif" d'un télépathe contrôlé par le phénoméne psychogalvanique. In *L'état actuel des recherches psychiques* (pp. 95-125). Paris: Presses Universitaires de France.

Damery, P. (1997). Shamanic states in our lives and in analytic practice. In D. Sandner & S. H. Wong (Eds.), *The sacred heritage: The influence of shamanism on analytical psychology*. (pp. 71-78). New York, NY: Routledge.

Desjarlais, R. (1989). Healing through images: The magical flight and healing geography of Nepali shamans. *Ethos, 17*, 289-307.

Dobkin de Rios, M., & Winkelman, M. (1989). Shamanism and altered states of consciousness: An introduction. *Journal of Psychoactive Drugs, 21*, 1-7.

Don, N. S., McDonough, B. E., & Warren, C. A. (1998). Event-related potential (ERP) indicators of unconscious psi: A replication using subjects unselected for psi. *European Journal of Parapsychology, 62*, 127-145.

Downton, D. V. (1989). Individuation and shamanism. *Journal of Analytical Psychology, 34*, 73-88.

Dunne, B. J., Dobyns, Y. H., & Intner, S. J. (1989). Precognitive remote perception III. Complete binary data base with analytical refinements. Technical Note PEAR 89002.

Dunne, B. J., Jahn, R. G., & Nelson, R. D. (1983). Precognitive remote perception. Technical Note PEAR 83003. Princeton University Engineering Anomalies Research, Princeton University, School of Engineering/Applied Science.

Eliade, M. (1964). *Shamanism: Archaic techniques of ecstasy*. Princeton: Bollingen Foundation.

George, L. (1981). A survey of research into the relationship between imagery and psi. *Journal of Parapsychology, 45*, 121-146.

George, L. (1982). Enhancement of psi functioning through mental imagery training. *Journal of Parapsychology, 46*, 111-125.

George, L., & Krippner, S. (1984). Mental imagery and psi phenomena: A review. In S. Krippner (Ed.), *Advances in parapsychological research 4* (pp. 64-82). Jefferson NC: McFarland.

Halifax, J. (1979). *Shamanic voices*. New York: Dutton.

Harner, M. (1990). *The way of the shaman* (3rd ed.). New York: HarperCollins.

Heinze, R. I. (1991). *Shamans of the 20th century*. New York: Irvington.

Henry, J. (2005). *Parapsychology: Research on exceptional experiences*. New York: Routledge.

Honorton, C. (1974). State of awareness factors in psi activation. *Journal of the American Society for Psychical Research, 68*, 246-256.

Honorton, C. (1977). Psi and internal attention states. In B. B. Wolman (Ed.), *Handbook of parapsychology* (435-472). New York: Van Nostrand Reinhold.

Honorton, C. (1985). Meta-analysis of psi ganzfeld research: A response to Hyman. *Journal of Parapsychology, 49*, 51-91.

Honorton, C. (1993). Rhetoric over substance: The impoverished state of skepticism. *Journal of Parapsychology, 57*, 191-214.

Honorton, C. (1997). The ganzfeld novice: Four predictors of initial ESP performance. *Journal of Parapsychology, 61*(2), 143-158.

Honorton, C., & Harper, S. (1974). Psi-mediated imagery and ideation in an experimental procedure for regulating perceptual input. *Journal of the American Society for Psychical Research, 68*, 156-168.

Honorton, C., & Krippner, S. (1969). Hypnosis and ESP performance: A review of the experimental literature. *Journal of the American Society for Psychical Research, 63*, 214-252.

Houran, J., Lange, R., & Crist-Houran, M. (1997). An assessment of contextual mediation in trance states of shamanic journeys. *Perceptual and Motor Skills, 85*, 59-65.

Hyman, R. (2010). Meta-analysis that conceals more than it reveals: Comment on Storm et al. (2010). *Psychological Bulletin, 136*(4), 486-490. doi:10.1037/a0019676.

Hyman, R., & Honorton, C. (1986). Joint communiqué: The psi ganzfeld controversy. *Journal of Parapsychology, 50*, 351-364.

Jahn, R. G., & Dunne, B. J. (1987). *Margins of reality: The role of consciousness in the physical world.* New York: Harcourt Brace.

Jung, C. G. (1957/1977). The Houston Films. In W. McGuire & R. F. C. Hull (Eds.), C. G. *Jung speaking: Interviews and encounters* (pp. 276-352). Princeton: Princeton University Press. (Original work published in 1957.)

Kalweit, H. (1988). *Dreamtime and innerspace: The world of the shaman.* Boston, MA: Shambhala.

Krippner, S. (1984). Parapsychological methodology and shamanistic studies. *Psi Research, 3*(3/4), 4-16.

Krippner, S. (1990). Tribal shamans and their travels into dreamtime. In S. Krippner (Ed.), *Dreamtime and dreamwork* (pp. 185-193). Los Angeles, CA: Jeremy P. Tarcher.

Krippner, S. (2002). Conflicting perspectives on shamans and shamanism: Points and counterpoints. *American Psychologist, 57*(11), 962-977.

Kumar, V. K., & Pekala, R. (2001). Relation of hypnosis-specific attitudes and behaviors to paranormal beliefs and experiences. In J. Houran & R. Lange (Eds.), *Hauntings and poltergeists: Multidisciplinary perspectives* (pp. 260-279). Jefferson, NC: McFarland.

LaBerge, S., & Gackenbach, J. (2001). Lucid dreaming. In E. Cardeña, S. J. Lynn, & S. Krippner (Eds.), *Varieties of anomalous experience: Examining the scientific evidence* (pp. 151-182). Washington, DC: American Psychological Association.

Lawrence, T. R. (1993). Gathering in the sheep and goats: A meta-analysis of forced-choice sheep-goat ESP studies, 1947-1993. In *Proceedings of the 36th Annual Convention of the Parapsychological Association* (pp. 75-86). Durham, NC: Parapsychological Association.

Layard, J. T. (1930). Shamanism: An analysis based on comparison with the flying tricksters of Malekula. *Journal of the Royal Anthropological Institute of Great Britain and Ireland, 60*, 525-550.

McMoneagle, J. (1997). *Mind trek: Exploring consciousness, time, and space through remote viewing*. Charlottesville, VA: Hampton Road.

McMoneagle, J. (2000). *Remote viewing secrets: A handbook*. Charlottesville, VA: Hampton Road.

Milton, J. (1997). Meta-analysis of free-response ESP studies without altered states of consciousness. *Journal of Parapsychology, 61*, 279-319.

Milton, J., & Wiseman, R. (1997). Ganzfeld at the crossroads: A meta-analysis of the new generation of studies. *The Parapsychological Association 40th Annual Convention: Proceedings of Presented Papers.* Hatfield, UK: University of Hertfordshire Press.

Milton, J., & Wiseman, R. (1999). Does psi exist? Lack of replication of an anomalous process of information transfer. *Psychological Bulletin, 125*, 387-391.

Nelson, R. D., Jahn, R. G., Dunne, B. J., Dobyns, Y. H., & Bradish, G. J. (1998). FieldREG II: Consciousness field effects: Replications and explorations. *Journal of Scientific Exploration, 12*(3), 425-454.

Nelson, R. D., & Radin, D. I. (2003). FieldREG experiments and group consciousness: Extending REG/RNG research to real-world situations. In W. B. Jonas & C. C. Crawford (Eds.), *Healing, intention, and energy medicine: Science, research methods and clinical implications* (pp. 49-57). Edinburgh, UK: Churchill Livingstone.

Noll, R. (1983). Shamanism and schizophrenia: A state specific approach to the "schizophrenia metaphor" of shamanic states. *American Ethnologist, 10*, 443-459.

Noll, R. (1985). Mental imagery cultivation as a cultural phenomenon: The role of visions in shamanism. *Current Anthropology, 26*, 443-461.

Overton, J. A. (1998). Shamanism and clinical hypnosis: A brief comparative analysis. *Shaman, 6*(2), 117-150.

Palmer, J., Khamashta, K., & Israelson, K. (1979). An ESP ganzfeld experiment with transcendental meditators. *Journal of the American Society for Psychical Research, 73*(4), 333-348.

Parker, A. (1975). Some findings relevant to the change in state hypothesis. In J. D. Morris, W. G. Roll, & R. L. Morris (Eds.), *Research in parapsychology 1974* (pp. 40-42). Metuchen, NJ: Scarecrow Press.

Parker, A. (2005). Psi and altered states of consciousness. In L. Storm & M. A. Thalbourne (Eds.), *Parapsychology in the 21st century: Essays on the future of psychical research* (pp. 65-89). Jefferson, NC: McFarland.

Pekala, R. J. (1985). A psychophenomenological approach to mapping and diagramming states of consciousness. *Journal of Religion and Psychical Research*, *8*, 199-214.

Pekala, R. J. (1991). *Quantifying consciousness: An empirical approach.* New York: Plenum Press.

Pekala, R. J., Forbes, E., & Contrisciani, P. A. (1989). Assessing the phenomenological effects of several stress management strategies. *Imagination, Cognition, and Personality*, *88*, 265-281.

Pekala, R. J., & Cardeña, E. (2000). Methodological issues in the study of altered states and anomalous experiences. In E. Cardeña, J. Lynn, & S. Krippner (Eds.), *Varieties of anomalous experience* (pp. 47-82). Washington DC: American Psychological Association.

Pekala, R. J., & Kumar, V. K. (1984). Predicting hypnotic susceptibility by a self-report phenomenological state instrument. *American Journal of Clinical Hypnosis*, *27*, 114-121.

Pekala, R. J., & Kumar, V. K. (1986). The differential organization of the structures of consciousness during hypnosis and a baseline condition. *Journal of Mind and Behavior*, *7*, 515-540.

Pekala, R. J., & Kumar, V K. (1989). Phenomenological patterns of consciousness during hypnosis: Relevance to cognition and individual differences. *Australian Journal of Clinical and Experimental Hypnosis*, *17*, 1-20.

Peters, L. (1989). Shamanism: Phenomenology of a spiritual discipline. *Journal of Transpersonal Psychology*, *21*, 115-37.

Peters, L. (1990). Mystical experience in Tamang shamanism. *ReVision*, *13*(2), 71-85.

Radin, D. I. (1997). *The conscious universe.* San Francisco, CA: HarperCollins.

Radin, D. I. (2006). *Entangled minds: Extrasensory experiences in a quantum reality.* New York: Paraview/Pocket Books.

Radin, D., & Lobach, E. (2007). Toward understanding the placebo effect: Investigating a possible retrocausal factor. *Journal of Alternative and Complementary Medicine*, *13*(7), 733-739.

Rao, K. R., Dukhan, H., & Rao, P. V. K. (2001). Yogic meditation and psi scoring in forced-choice and free-response tests. In K. Ramakrishna (Ed.), *Basic research in parapsychology* (2nd ed.) (pp. 287-306). Jefferson, NC: McFarland.

Rao, K. R., & Puri, I. (1978). Subsensory perception (SSP), extrasensory perception (ESP) and transcendental meditation (TM). *Journal of Indian Psychology, 1*, 69-78.

Rao, P. V. K., & Rao, K. R. (1982). Two studies of ESP and subliminal perception. *Journal of Parapsychology, 46*, 185-208.

Rhine, J. B. (1934/1964). *Extrasensory perception*. Boston, MA: Bruce Humphries.

Rhine, L. E. (1962). Psychological processes in ESP experiences: Part II. Dreams. *Journal of Parapsychology, 26*, 172-199.

Ripinsky-Naxon, M. (1993). *The nature of shamanism*. Albany, NY: State University of New York Press.

Rock, A. J. (2006). Phenomenological analysis of experimentally induced visual mental imagery associated with shamanic journeying to the lower world. *International Journal of Transpersonal Studies, 25*, 45-55.

Rock, A. J., Abbott, G., Childargushi, H., & Kiehne, M. (2008). The effect of shamanic-like stimulus conditions and the cognitive-perceptual factor of schizotypy on phenomenology. *North American Journal of Psychology, 10*(1), 79-98.

Rock, A. J., Baynes, P. B., & Casey, P. J. (2005). Experimental study of ostensibly shamanic journeying imagery in naïve participants I: Antecedents. *Anthropology of Consciousness, 16*(2), 72-92.

Rock, A. J., Casey, P J., & Baynes, P. B. (2006). Experimental study of ostensibly shamanic journeying imagery II: Phenomenological mapping and modified affect bridge. *Anthropology of Consciousness, 17*(1), 65-83.

Rock, A. J., & Krippner, S. (2007a). Does the concept of "altered states of consciousness" rest on a mistake? *International Journal of Transpersonal Studies, 26*, 33-40.

Rock, A. J., & Krippner, S. (2007b). Shamanism and the confusion of consciousness with phenomenological content. *North American Journal of Psychology, 9* (3), 485-500.

Rock, A. J., & Krippner, S. (2008). Is a realist interpretation of Shamanic "non-physical" worlds logically incoherent? *Transpersonal Psychology Review, 12*(2), 23-31.

Rock, A. J., Wilson, J. M., Johnston, L. J., & Levesque, J. V. (2008). Ego boundaries, shamanic-like techniques and subjective experience: An experimental study. *Anthropology of Consciousness, 19*(1), 60-83.

Rogo, D. S. (1983a). Psi and Shamanism: A Reconsideration I. *Parapsychology Review, 14*(5), 12-15.

Rogo, D. S. (1983b). Psi and Shamanism: A Reconsideration II. *Parapsychology Review, 14*(6), 5-9.

Rogo, D. S. (1987). Shamanism, ESP, and the paranormal. In S. Nicholson (Ed.), *Shamanism: An expanded view of reality* (pp. 133-144). Wheaton, IL: The Theosophical Publishing House.

Roney-Dougal, S. M., & Solfvin, J. (2006). Yogic attainment in relation to awareness of precognitive targets. *Journal of Parapsychology, 70*(1), 91-120.

Saklani, A. (1988). Preliminary tests for psi-ability in shamans of Garhwal Himalaya. *Journal of the Society for Psychical Research, 55*, 60-70.

Schlitz, M., & Gruber, E. (1981). Transcontinental remote viewing: A rejudging. *Journal of Parapsychology, 45*, 233-237.

Schlitz, M., & Haight, J. (1984). Remote viewing revisited: An intrasubject replication. *Journal of Parapsychology, 48*, 39-49.

Schmeidler, G. R. (1994). ESP experiments 1978-1992: The glass is half full. In S. Krippner (Ed.), *Advances in parapsychology research 7* (pp. 104-197). Jefferson, NC: McFarland.

Scimeca, G., Boca, S., & Iannuzzo, G. (2001). Ganzfeld experiment and meta-analysis in parapsychology: Extrasensory perception or experimental mistake? A methodological criticism. *Psychometrics Testing Methodology, 8*(1-2), 13-31.

Sherwood, S. J., & Roe, C. A. (2003). A review of dream ESP studies conducted since the Maimonides dream ESP studies. In J. Alcock, J. Burns, & A. Freeman (Eds.), *Psi wars: Getting to grips with the paranormal* (pp. 85-109). Thorverton, UK: Imprint Academic.

Stanford, R. G., & Stein, A. G. (1994). A meta-analysis of ESP studies contrasting hypnosis and a comparison condition. *Journal of Parapsychology, 58*, 235-269.

Steinkamp, F. (2005). Forced-choice ESP experiments: Their past and their future. In L. Storm & M. A. Thalbourne (Eds.), *Parapsychology in the 21st century: Essays on the future of psychical research* (pp. 124-163). Jefferson, NC: McFarland.

Storm, L. (2003). Remote viewing by committee: RV using a 'multiple agent/multiple percipient' design. *Journal of Parapsychology, 67*, 325-342.

Storm, L. (2006). Meta-analysis in parapsychology: II. Psi domains other than ganzfeld. *Australian Journal of Parapsychology, 6*, 135-155.

Storm, L., & Thalbourne, M. A. (2000). A paradigm shift away from the ESP-PK dichotomy: The theory of psychopraxia. *Journal of Parapsychology, 64*, 279-300.

Storm, L., & Thalbourne, M. A. (2001). Paranormal effects using sighted and vision-impaired participants in a quasi-ganzfeld task. *Australian Journal of Parapsychology, 1*, 133-170.

Storm, L., Tressoldi, P. E., & Di Risio, L. (2010). Meta-analyses of free-response studies 1992-2008: Assessing the noise reduction model in parapsychology. *Psychological Bulletin, 136*(4), 471-485. doi: 10.1037/a0019457.

Targ, R. (1996). Remote viewing at Stanford Research Institute in the 1970s: A memoir. *Journal of Scientific Exploration, 10*, 77-88.

Targ, R., & Puthoff, H. (1974). Information transmission under conditions of sensory shielding. *Nature, 251*, 602-607.

Thalbourne, M. A. (1981). *Some experiments on the paranormal cognition of drawings with special reference to personality and attitudinal variables.* Unpublished Ph.D. thesis, Department of Parapsychology, University of Edinburgh, Scotland.

Thalbourne, M. A. (2003). *A glossary of terms used in parapsychology.* Charlottesville, VA: Puente.

Thalbourne, M. A. (2004). *The common thread between ESP and PK.* New York: The Parapsychology Foundation.

Ullman, M., Krippner, S., & Vaughan, A. (1974). *Dream telepathy*. Baltimore, MD: Penguin Books.

Utts, J. (1991). Replication and meta-analysis in parapsychology. *Statistical Science, 6*(4), 363-403.

Wackermann, J., Pütz, P., Büchi, S., Strauch, I., & Lehmann, D. (2002). Brain electrical activity and subjective experience during altered states of consciousness: ganzfeld and hypnagogic states. *International Journal of Psychophysiology, 46*, 123–146.

Wackermann, J., Seiter, C., Keibel, H., Walach, H. (2003). Correlations between brain electrical activities of two spatially separated human subjects. *Neuroscience Letters, 1*(5), 60-64.

Wackermann, J. (2004). Dyadic correlations between brain functional states: present facts and future perspectives. *Mind and Matter, 2*(1), 105-122.

Walsh, R. (1989). What is a shaman? Definition, origin and distribution. *Journal of Transpersonal Psychology, 21*, 1-11.

Walsh, R. (1990). *The spirit of shamanism*. Los Angeles, CA: J.P. Tarcher.

Walsh, R. (1995). Phenomenological mapping: A method for describing and comparing states of consciousness. *Journal of Transpersonal Psychology*, *27*, 25-56.

Weiner, D. H. (1982). The medium of the message: Information-coding style in psi processes. *Parapsychology Review*, *13*(5), 9-11.

White, R. (1964). A comparison of old and new methods of response to targets in ESP experiments. *Journal of the American Society for Psychical Research*, *58*(1), 21-56.

Winkelman, M. J. (1986). Trance states: A theoretical model and cross-cultural analysis. *Ethos*, *14*(2), 174-203.

Wright, P. A. (1989). The nature of the shamanic state of consciousness: A review. *Journal of Psychoactive Drugs*, *21*(1), 25-33.

Woodside, L., Kumar, V. K., & Pekala, R. (1997). Monotonous percussion drumming and trance postures: A controlled evaluation of phenomenological effects. *Anthropology of Consciousness*, *8*, 69-87.

APPENDIX

Testing the Imagery Cultivation Model

Two studies testing the Imagery Cultivation (IC) model have been conducted since the above chapter was written (see Rock & Storm, 2010; Rock, Storm, Harris, & Friedman, 2012, 2013; Storm & Rock, 2009). In the first of these studies (Storm & Rock, 2009), the number of direct hits (34.5% where *P*MCE = 25%) in the shamanic-like condition produced a significant z score of 1.66 (p = .048) and, as expected, the hit rate for control condition participants was at chance (22.6%).

In a second study (Rock et al., 2012), we decided to test variations of the IC protocol to locate possible specific sources of the psi effect. The three variations of the IC condition were: (i) Voice/Drum (the standard IC protocol); (ii) Voice only, and (iii) Drum only.

Participants in the Voice/Drum condition produced a positive hit rate of 26.9%; participants in the Voice condition produced a positive hit rate of 29.4%; and participants in the Drum condition produced a positive hit rate of 25.9%. None of these hit rates were significant because the sub-samples were deemed too small (ranging from 51 to 54 participants). As expected, the control condition produced a non-significant below-chance hit rate of 23.3%.

To obtain a more up-to-date and reliable indication of the situation as it stands for our IC model, we combined the two sets of data (i.e., the data from Storm & Rock, 2009, and the data from Rock et al., 2012). For the combined shamanic-like group (N = 107), direct hits was high and above chance at 30.8%, though the statistic did not reach significance (p = .101). The corresponding small effect size ES (where ES = $z/\sqrt{n}$) of 0.13 equates with the mean ES for a 10-study Ganzfeld database reported by Bem, Palmer, and Broughton (2001) in their meta-analysis. This ES of 0.13 is also comparable to the ES of 0.16 for the most recent 20-study Ganzfeld database reported by Tressoldi, Storm, and Radin (2010).

In stark contrast, for the combined control group (N = 96), direct hits was below-chance at only 22.9%, and the statistic was not significant. When the direct-hit performances for the two groups (i.e., shamanic-like and control) were compared, the difference approaches significance, $\chi^2(1, N = 203) = 1.61, p = .106$. These findings lend some support to our hypothesis that the ganzfeld paradigm is rivalled by our IC model.

In regard to phenomenological variables, Rock and Storm (2010) found significant differences between the shamanic-like and control groups on three major dimensions of Pekala's (1991) *Phenomenology of Consciousness Inventory* (PCI)—namely, higher Negative Affect, Altered Experience, and Visual Imagery in the shamanic-like group. Also, significant differences between the shamanic-like and control groups were found for four minor PCI dimensions (i.e., higher Anger, Body Image, Perception, and Meaning in the shamanic-like group). In addition, direct hits correlated significantly with the major PCI dimension, Internal Dialogue, for the shamanic-like group, but not the control group.

In the follow-up study (see Rock et al., 2013), the group differences were not replicated, but we did find direct hits significantly and positively correlated with Altered Time Sense, Altered Perception, and Altered Experience; and significantly negatively correlated with Self-Awareness, Volitional Control and Memory. Oddly, the significant direct-hitting/Internal-Dialogue correlation did not replicate. Though we work towards confirmation of our findings, we suggest that phenomenology can be changed using a shamanic-like journeying treatment, and these changes are conducive to the generation of source material that can be an aid to psi processes.

» References

Bem, D. J., Palmer, J., & Broughton, R. S. (2001). Updating the ganzfeld database: A victim of its own success? *Journal of Parapsychology*, *65*, 207-218.

Pekala, R. J. (1991). *Quantifying consciousness: An empirical approach.* New York: Plenum Press.

Rock, A. J., & Storm, L. (2010). Shamanic-like journeying and psi: II. Mental boundaries, phenomenology, and the picture-identification task. *Australian Journal of Parapsychology*, *10*, 41-68.

Rock, A. J., Storm, L., Harris, K., & Friedman, H. (2012). Shamanic-like journeying and psi-signal detection: I. In search of the psi-conducive components of a novel experimental protocol. *Journal of Parapsychology, 76*, 321-347.

Rock, A. J., Storm, L., Harris, K., & Friedman, H. (2013). Shamanic-like journeying and psi-signal detection: II. Phenomenological dimensions. *Journal of Parapsychology, 77*, 249-270.

Storm, L. & Rock, A. J. (2009). Shamanic-like journeying and psi: I. Imagery cultivation, personality, and the picture-identification task. *Australian Journal of Parapsychology*, *9*, 165-192.

Tressoldi, P. E., Storm L., & Radin, D. (2010). Extrasensory perception and quantum models of cognition. *Neuroquantology: An Interdisciplinary Journal of Neuroscience and Quantum Physics, 8*(4), S81-87.

Chapter 2

Telepathy as a Process Mediated by Quantum Teleportation Between Remote Neurons[1]

Richard Blumenthal

In a letter from the White House to his daughter Ethel, American President Theodore Roosevelt (1906) wrote: "I am not in the least surprised about the mental telepathy; there is much in it and in kindred things which are real and which at present we do not understand" (p. 166). A century later, the search for an explanation of telepathy, the apparent transfer of thought from one person to another, devoid of any sensory-based exchange, continues. J. B. Rhine (1937), the pioneer scientist who introduced the phrase 'extra-sensory perception' into English, lamented the limitations of science in his day, which failed to adequately account for the phenomena he studied, including telepathy. He did, however, hold the hope that in the future, discoveries would be made to clarify the physical aspects of thought, which would, in turn, shed light on telepathy. Indeed, great strides have been made since then. For example, machines unknown during the time of Rhine's research, now record brain activity remotely, detecting subtle changes without employing electrodes, implants, or any other invasive apparatus (Harland, Clark, & Prance, 2002).

1. [This chapter was originally published in *Australian Journal of Parapsychology* (2008, vol. 8[1], pp. 29-46). Permission to reprint has been granted by the author and the journal.—Editors.]

The nature of the brain emission measured by this equipment may or may not be that which is responsible for telepathy but, if adequately replicated, a cogent argument can be made that receipt of information emanating from the brain need not require physical contact. Our understanding of how telepathy works may benefit from breakthrough discoveries and theoretical work performed in the cognitive and physical sciences as Rhine had hoped, and is the focus of this discussion. Herein, a theory of telepathy is proposed, beginning with the transfer of information between remote neurons by quantum teleportation and leading to ordinary brain activity, usually described in the context of a sensory-based experience.

Synchronous Neuronal Activity

How activity in remote areas of the brain is gathered together and transformed into cognition is a central question in the study of neuroscience, giving rise to a wealth of research and theory on what has been called the binding problem. Individual neurons seem to show participation by means of their action potential, also called firing, a term used to describe the release of a measurable electrical charge. In any brain activity such as new learning or memory recall, a large number of neurons across various contiguous and non-contiguous brain regions may fire during a given event. When excited by a stimulus such as information collected by the senses or information presented internally, the neurons associated with specific aspects of that stimulus will fire, no matter where they are located in the brain. They have been shown to fire in a rhythm and in concert with other firing neurons, specific to the event (Finkle, Yen, & Menschik, 1998). This relatedness is known as synchronized firing. The repeatable pattern of participant neurons and their firing behavior forms what has been termed a synfire chain (Abeles, 1991).

Singer (1999) provided a view of synchronization as a mechanism for binding together what would otherwise be scattered bits of information and posited that such synchronous discharges are related to elaborate neuronal networks. He (Singer, 2003) later reported that discoveries have shown how cortical neurons engage in synchronous oscillatory activity caused by internal interactions and that neurons within and across cortical areas can synchronize their discharges with a precision in the millisecond range. Synchronization thus helps to explain not only the binding of information from remote areas of the brain but also that it forms a cognitive experience for the individual. Bits of information from various regions of the brain are bound together and make it possible for the person to form a cognition related to an experience. This also implies the transfer of specific information between neurons across the brain. According to Sougné (2004), "To achieve binding it is necessary for neurons to communicate with each other because it has been shown that different aspects of a perceived object are not processed in the same cortical areas". Neurons of one cortical area must communicate with other neurons of a different cortical area.

During a given experience, waves of synfire activity are measurable in a laboratory setting. When the repetition of a specific stimulus or behavioral task is presented to the subject, the associated synfire chain will again engage, each appropriate neuron offering its bit of information to the overall functioning of the brain (Baker, 2003). Since the firing neurons need not be arrayed contiguously to act repeatedly in synchrony, the communication occurs via a signal emitted from one or more neurons that triggers a reaction by other neurons. This stimulates their participatory firing and, in turn, causes other needed neurons to fire. It has been postulated that this signal actually consists of a code comprised of the timing, rhythm, and frequency of the firing (Finkle et al., 1998). This firing code is familiar to, and hence recognized by, other neurons as one which requires their participation. When reacting to external sensory stimuli, according to Jefferys, Traub, and Whittington (1996), "individual neurons do not detect their preferred sensory feature in isolation, but form part of neuronal networks whose emergent properties define the feature-detection properties of the cortical column" (p. 202).

Jefferys (2004) further describes the "coherent rhythms" formed by neuronal firing in this way: "One idea is that they provide a timing reference for a neural code that depends on the phase relationship of individual neurons with the reference oscillation" (p. 13). Singer (1999) found that neuronal networks encode information by modulating both the rate and temporal coordination of distributed responses. Steinmetz (2000) tells us that, "A near axiom in neuroscience is the idea that information is conveyed over distances, both in the peripheral and central nervous systems, by the times of occurrence of action potentials." A code is formed which becomes useful to other, similar neurons, but only if the code is presented to a neuron capable of recognizing it. Then that neuron joins in the orchestrated firing of other neurons, becoming part of an induced synfire chain. Thus we may conclude that neurons across the brain share precisely coded information with other, targeted or 'interested' neurons, and in doing so elicit responsive activity. That activity may involve what Lin, Osan, and Tsien (2006) describes as assemblies of neurons organized into memory coding units called neural cliques. When activated, the neural clique actually recreates an inner version of information previously coded, offering the individual a particular frame of reference for the current experience, as opposed to searching for an exact recording of prior events. If synchronous neural activity occurring in the code-producing brain yields a cognition for person A, then it seems likely do so in the code receiving brain for person B also (Ward, 2003). The second set of reactive neurons would necessarily possess sufficient signal recognition capabilities; close enough to the original to cause native synchronous neuronal assemblies to engage.

In this context, the mechanism of telepathy may involve the neuronal signal stimulating not only a neural clique of the native brain, but that of a remote brain as well; a brain whose organization is similar enough to the original for the information code to trigger cognitive activity. However, though they may be similar, the manifested cognition in both brains may not be identical, or even readily recognizable to the observer, due to differences in the subsequent recreations provided by the neural cliques of the two brains. This would mean that there is a considerable opportunity for distortion in the outcome of telepathy as the information is processed in the brain's peculiar frame of reference, a notion which will also be discussed elsewhere in this chapter. Wackermann (2004) describes brains as having continuously varying functional states.

The disposition of both the sending and the receiving brains at the moment of code sending and arrival are also possible factors in the outcome. In an experimental observation of brain activity, Kittenis and Stevens (2004) showed that when a sensory stimulation (light) produced a measurable EEG response in a sending brain, a measurable, but different EEG was also produced in a remote receiving brain. Though extremely close, the timing (both the start and duration) of the remote activity did not correlate exactly with the timing of the stimulation. Due to this difference between the EEG measurements, Kittenis was reluctant to label the remote activity as an ordinary stimulus-response effect. This difference is to be expected, if the stimulated brain actually sent its coded response to the stimulus and not a replication of the stimulus itself. The remote brain interpreted the coded information independently, thus producing a measurable but different EEG. The remote brain activity in the experiment was related to the receipt of information and not to sensory stimulation. It would seem that the introduction of foreign code will likely have an influence, but the strength and fidelity of that influence compared to the original experience is highly variable.

Quantum Teleportation

While this has been a discussion regarding the firing of neurons, it is important to note that although electrical discharge is produced as neurons fire, the conveyance of the information-bearing code should not be assumed to travel as electricity *per se.* Indeed, a lighthouse signals to passing ships not by electricity but by the light the electricity helps to produce. The ship's pilot, who presumably understands the meaning of the signal code, captures and perceives the light, not electrical current, developing a cognition as a result of the signalled communication. Therefore, the medium by which the neuronal signal is presented may not follow the mechanics which are believed to govern electricity. What is postulated here is not that electricity travels between brains but that neuronal information, the currency of telepathy, is transferred. It is true that research, such as that by Wackermann, Seiter, Keibel, and Walach (2003), has examined the correlation of separated individuals by recording the electrical activity in their brains. The data does show the positive correlation that one might expect in telepathy. However, no electrical activity specifically entering the brain from the outside has been mentioned, which would be necessary if the code were an electrical charge travelling between systems. Still, it is not the action potentials of the neurons that must reach the neurons of the remote brain, it is the information encoded on the neurons that produced the action potentials (as recorded by Wackermann et al.) that needs to find its way to the receiving neurons. Once the code is in place, the receiving neurons produce their own electrical discharge, as also recorded by Wackermann et al. The code seems not to travel and yet reaches a destination. Therefore, it becomes a question of how incorporeal information from one object can be placed into another object in a remote location.

The solution to this paradox may be found in recent experiments in the field of quantum physics. Placement of the code could be the product of quantum teleportation, proposed by Bennett et al. (1993), and first demonstrated in 1998 in the laboratory of the California Institute of Technology (Furusawa, 1998). While the role of quantum theory to explain the physical underpinnings of telepathy has been discussed in other literature, most notably in the work of Shan (2004), this specific action of nonlocality, satisfying so many of the necessary variables outlined in this chapter, has actually been produced and replicated in the laboratory.

Quantum teleportation does not involve the movement of a material object, such as a monkey or a boulder that disappears from one location and reappears suddenly in another, as the term teleport, used copiously in science fiction, would imply. What has actually been shown is the teleportation of information, the measurable attributes of a coherent quantum system, not the receptacle of the attributes. This information refers to the quantum state (Bennet et al., 1993) of the system: "Teleportation of a quantum state encompasses the complete transfer of information from one particle to another" (Riebe et al., 2004 p. 734). Specifically, the quantum state of one quantum system is teleported to a remote system, thereby altering the quantum state of the receiving system to include the teleported information. However, to accomplish the teleportation of the quantum state in the laboratory has first required the preparation of both the sending and receiving systems inducing a quantum entanglement of the systems. They are made to share a small amount of information directly from one object to another, and both systems receive half of an entangled EPR beam of light (named for the Einstein/Podolsky/Rosen paper questioning quantum physics because it implied the nonlocal entangling of spatially separated systems). The beams have the effect of entangling the two previously unrelated quantum systems, forging a relationship between them. When a final procedure of measurement is performed on the sending system, the quantum state is instantly teleported to the receiving system. Though the experiment took place in a laboratory in which the systems were separate but not very far apart, theoretically, they could have been separated over a great distance (Furusawa, 1998).

Apparently, teleportation demonstrated *in vitro,* is accomplished under carefully controlled conditions. However, in the case of telepathy, we are considering the possibility of in vivo biological teleportation. The question arises, could a naturally occurring biological structure, such as a neuron, be seen as a coherent quantum system and, if so, is that system capable of achieving entanglement with another system under *in vivo* conditions? Perhaps the answers are found in the role played by microtubules (Hameroff 1998; Mavromatos, 2000; Mavromatos , Mershin, & Nanopoulos, 2002), which are proteins present in the cell cytoskeleton of the brain's neurons. The microtubules are seen as quantum mechanically isolated cavities and are noted by Mavromatos as showing properties analogous to the cavities used in quantum optics laboratory experiments. If we accept that characterization, then neuronal microtubules may be capable of entanglement and quantum teleportation.

To further support the notion of *in vivo* biological teleportation, Mavromatos calls on the work of Julsgaard, Kozhekin, and Polzik (2001), who experimentally showed that it is possible to maintain entanglement of a large number of atoms, at room temperature. Such a demonstration indicates the possibility of *in vivo* quantum teleportation and the proposition that entangled microtubules may be able to act as mediators for the quantum teleportation of states between neurons. Mavromatos et al. (2002) defines such an instance of biological teleportation as a transfer of the microtubule's coherent state without any direct transfer of mass or energy. The result is that the receiving microtubule possesses an identical state to the sending microtubule. Georgiev (2003), in his work regarding the place in which photons collapse during vision processing, offers further theoretical credence to this scenario, postulating that information in the retina is pre-coded into protein quantum states and then teleported to the neurons in associative areas to eventually become part of a conscious experience. If Georgiev is correct, neuronal teleportation triggers the mental processing that would need to take place for a telepathy experience to ultimately be reported. Though, in these references, entanglement and teleportation has been confined to neurons involved in intrabrain activity, the feasibility of biological teleportation in general and neuronal teleportation in particular, advances the possibility of interbrain neuronal activity.

In the telepathy process, we may view the laboratory entanglement of the systems which precede teleportation as creating the relationship; perhaps a condition analogous to the affinity existing between certain neurons of people predisposed to produce telepathic experiences with each other. Indeed, it bodes well for the notion that twin to twin, mother to child, and other genetically similar people sharing neuronal properties, or even emotionally allied people sharing like neuronal arrays, already are entangled and 'prepared' for the teleportation of their neuronal quantum states. Let us then postulate that the neuronal code so vital to intrabrain processing is part of the quantum state of the neuron. It is, therefore, reasonable to consider that under the right conditions, the code (quantum state) of one system can be teleported to a similar yet remote system, also a repository of code. The sending and receiving neurons are information-carriers. Thus, quantum teleportation may provide the mechanism for telepathy, unbound by the usual constraints of moving mass and energy in a conventional physical channel.

Entanglement

In Broughton's (1988) presidential address to the Parapsychological Association, he pondered a basic assumption found in much of psi research, namely, that psi is a human ability; psi being a broad term including, but not limited to telepathy and defined by Wilson, Morris, Tiliopoulos and Pronto (2004) as interaction through means other than the usual sensorimotor systems. Ability, Broughton reasoned, must have a purpose, which may yield clues as to how it works and is, therefore, worthy of investigation. In this context, Broughton referred to Eisenbud's (1956, cited in Broughton, 1988) concept of psi as serving the goals of survival or psychological need. He also mentioned Stanford (1974a,b, cited in Broughton, 1988), who speculated that while psi is commonplace, the person may be unaware that its influence has been exerted in the accomplishment of a goal. However, Broughton also cited Braude (1986, cited in Broughton, 1988), who cautioned that seeing psi as an ability implies conscious control whereas psi may be more of an involuntary function like digestion. Yet, the two competing ideas of control and function may not necessarily be mutually exclusive. Psi may have once served a vital purpose that placed it at the forefront of satisfying basic needs, but was evolutionarily supplanted by something else, which made survival of the species even more successful. It may have been a consciously controlled ability at one time, now relegated to a different, less conscious status, and making conscious control in modern instances appear more exceptional though still possible. Perhaps modern telepathy is the vestigial remnant of an ancient, purposeful ability, supplanted but not eliminated, and still wielding an influence, though largely out of conscious awareness.[2]

Though telepathic communication may have at one time been an asset, it is possible that, during the course of evolution, personal and/or group survival may have actually depended on the ability to hide brain-stored information from competing individuals and/or groups. Thus, natural selection may have favored less telepathic people. Playfair (2002) relates the story of a particular set of twins who, throughout their lives had numerous spontaneous telepathic communications between them. Yet, on the momentous occasion of one twin's presumed suicide, the surviving twin failed to experience any telepathy. Since they often shared somatic reactions, this would suggest that blocking a particular telepathy might have been a matter of survival because the receipt of suicidal thinking could have triggered similarly lethal action in the mentally healthy twin. A personality trait, valuing survival, seems responsible for placing controls on the completion of telepathy.

Further discouraging selection for telepathy in human evolution is its likely competition with articulate speech, an arguably more precise form of communication than telepathy. As speech and language developed, telepathy

---

2. Note that these ideas are not new. Freud (1933) also believed that telepathy might be an atavistic attribute in human beings, harking back to an early period in human development.

would become less necessary, even less desirable as a means of conveying one's thoughts. More precision, as well as choice, in communication undoubtedly leads to greater survivability and propagation. If telepathy did have its beginnings in group survival, a presumed purpose of any communication, it is likely that genetically similar people, such as members of immediate or extended families, were most proficient in its use with one another. Survival of the family unit and its members would be the obvious benefit.

There is a body of anecdotal and experimental evidence to suggest that spontaneous instances of telepathy occur more often between twins, siblings, parents and children, or amongst other relationships than with unrelated people. It is common for twins to report identical emotions, pain, and even somatic changes, though they may be remotely located from one another (Playfair, 2002), and most often in catastrophic situations such as illness, death, and accident. Ullman, Krippner, with Vaughan (1973) corroborates this, pointing out that most recorded dream telepathy occurs between close relatives. The notion that genetic similarity corresponds to reported spontaneous telepathy leads to the possibility that the attributes of the organic material of the human body is in some way necessary for telepathy to occur. It is logical, therefore, to look to the primary organ of thought, the brain, for an explanation.

The quantum entanglement of two whole brains has been considered by Shan (2004) in a proposed experiment meant to artificially induce telepathy between subjects. In Shan's design, the entire brain is seen as the quantum system and it is the quantum state of the entire brain that would be sent. In actual reports of telepathy, however, descriptions of the telepathy experience seem confined to a particular feeling, or a visual impression, or even a certain storyline, as in a dream. This may indicate that an instance of telepathy involves a particular set of neurons, not the totality of a personality together with all memory and experience as might be expected if every neuron in the entire brain were involved. Even if we took the quantum state of the brain to mean the momentary focus of attention, this would still argue for neuronally mediated telepathy and not of the whole brain because only the neurons participating in the momentary focus would be involved. Therefore, we must consider the information in the code of individual neurons to be the operative quantum state, teleported from a local neuron to a remote counterpart neuron. The individual neurons or perhaps specific neuronal cliques, on either side of the transaction would need to be entangled as well as serving similar functions within their respective brains in order to offer up the teleported information for a somewhat reconstructed mental process and hence producing a chance for a meaningful cognition, recognizable as related to the original cognition. The entanglement and other preparation which makes laboratory orchestrated quantum teleportation possible may actually be a perfectly natural, everyday process.[3]

Distortion in Telepathy

The neuronal view of telepathy not only helps to explain its mechanics, but also its imperfection as a method of communication. Finkle et al. (1998) relates a perceptual experiment devised by Johansson and colleagues at Uppsala University:

> Johansson attached small lights to a subject's joints (elbow, knee, etc.) and viewed the resulting point motions as the subject walked or ran in a dark room. Johansson found that, despite the sparse information provided, it was possible to recognize a human body walking or running, and, in fact, all observers immediately perceived the moving dots as a moving human form. (p. 3)

The correct recognition of just what the lights depicted was largely dependent on previously encoded information (knowledge of what a moving human being looks like) already present in the brain, providing a contextual meaning to the disembodied lights. If we take the lights as a metaphor for the information passed in the quantum teleportation of neuronal code, we can see that it is up to the receiving brain to derive meaning from the teleported code.

Much of the data about telepathy is based on the verbal responses or self reporting of the experimental and anecdotal participants. This information is used to discern the success or failure of the telepathy. However, telepathy seems to obey a variety of normal constraints of personality such as confidence, stress, fatigue, the effects of drugs, etc. (Rhine, 1937). Therefore, constraints which govern more ordinary means of communication should likewise be applied to telepathy. In everyday intercourse verbal miscommunications are prevalent. Conversations often consist of repetition, corrections, qualifications, and other explanations of the intended original message. There is no such opportunity in telepathy. Further, the work of the code-producing brain is imperfect in that the bound

---

3. A reviewer of this chapter commented, "Normal communication across neurons in the brain may take place by a mechanism akin to apprehension of information or events that we see in extrasensory perception…this may not be the only mechanism of such information transfer but…this is suggestive."

neurons undoubtedly approximate the original experience and fill in the rest with related assumptions from prior learning. This may be one reason why human recall represents such an individual version of the experience, differing from the perception of other persons present during the same experience. Thus, the very information to be mediated, the neuronal quantum state, is likely to arrive in a degraded form as compared to the original experience that fostered it.

The accuracy of the teleportation, too, presents the possibility of further degradation inasmuch as the resonating synfire patterns will almost certainly be different to some degree from person to person. Radin (2000) has shown that individuals possess brain signatures that identify them as unique compared to others. This uniqueness is also reflected in the excitation of pertinent neural clique assemblies, a product of experience. The search for meaning of the received code as it is processed, what we might call the conceptual binding, will be moulded by the frame of reference of the recipient, who appears to 'translate' the retrieved information. Evidently, there are a great many obstacles to overcome before the complete success of a telepathy instance is declared. Even when genuine, *in vivo* telepathy has occurred, it may actually elude recognition and the cognition attributed to something else.

A formidable example of this distortion principle is recorded in the work of Upton and Mary Sinclair (Sinclair, 1930). In their experiments, Mrs. Sinclair would attempt to telepathically perceive drawings made remotely by Mr. Sinclair and others. A book showing many of the drawings, both original and received, displays her remarkable ability. However, Mrs. Sinclair would often reproduce the drawings of the senders containing strikingly similar lines and shapes but with changed meaning, according to her own background. Conversely, she also was able to show a substantial portion of the original meaning in some of the drawings, yet distort the lines and shapes. In both instances, the drawings are undeniably recognizable as having originated remotely when compared with the originals.

Dreams show a similar process of formation, beginning with bits of information and resulting in personally referenced cognition. The absence of complex segmentation activity as in sleep or trance may provide a greater opportunity for neurons to be receptive to remote signals. Indeed, if neuronal activity is not occupied with the huge volume of sensory input characteristic of the awake state, it stands to reason that sleep makes more brain resources available to attune to distant neuronal signals. Storm's (2006) review of the dream-psi literature suggests that the sleep state provides conditions favorable for detecting psi and points out that a reduction of sensory noise during sleep is a factor in this.

This finding seems to support the notion that telepathy involves those structures and activities of the brain closely associated with processing sensory information, such as the neurons, even though the input is not from a sensory source. When occupied with the immediacy of waking state necessities demanding attention, the psi signal is perhaps placed in the focal background, last in line to be addressed. The dream state, putting those sensory needs on hold, may allow the signal more ample access to brain functioning. Storm's (2006) meta-analysis examined the statistical results of various psi experiments. Illustrating the possibly superior outcome of dream psi compared to waking psi, the collected dream psi studies (telepathy and clairvoyance combined), produced a mean z score of 1.08, while the waking psi studies of general ESP and remote viewing had a z score of .68, and waking clairvoyance a z score of .60. These scores also tend to support Freud's (1922) earlier, anecdotal observations, from which he concluded that it is an "... incontestable fact that sleep creates favorable conditions for telepathy" (p. 86).

Some years later, Freud (1933) again spoke of the telepathic messages contained in some dreams, as actually being hidden from first view, but subsequently understood through psychoanalysis. Once the dream work had been analyzed and the meaning of the dream was brought to light, the dream's telepathic origins were revealed. To illustrate, Freud offered several examples from his own psychoanalytic practice. Each is an illustration of how the telepathically received material not only translated into the person's frame of reference, but interacted with and incorporated into the person's innermost thinking, all outside of the awareness of the unwitting participant. Only upon analysis was the person made aware of the telepathic nature of the dream. We may surmise, therefore, that telepathy could occur on a completely nonconscious level, perhaps, but not necessarily because it was received during the dream state. It should be noted that elsewhere, Freud (1900/1965) states that the formation of dreams may begin during the awake state, even long before the actual dream is manifested. Pederson-Craig (1947), the prominent psychoanalyst, found that some of the dreams of her patients included accurate depictions of recent events in her personal life. The events were never described to the patients. She was, therefore, convinced that the information had been conveyed between analyst and patient telepathically, ultimately affecting the patients' dreams.

Spontaneous telepathy seems most successful when there is an element of emotional intensity in the information. Early records of telepathic dreams reveal that the vast majority dealt with extremely emotional topics such as death, illness, or an emergency situation (Ullman et al., 1973). It may be easier for a telepathy percipient to bind coherently a strong emotion than to process an exact set of personally meaningless data with precision. Dalkvist and Westerlund (1998) obtained good results in an experiment that elicited the telepathic communication of emotions between subjects. The overall impression of the emotion resides, perhaps, in a more primitive, more universal realm of brain function, closer to an earlier stage of evolution. Neural cliques associated with common human emotional experiences may develop similarly across cultures as a normal part of human personality development. The neurons involved may be more universally placed and of a higher sensitivity to the telepathic process because of survival considerations. The relative universality of emotionally linked neuronal activity probably is likely to be a more successful topic for telepathy than topics with little or no meaning or extremely specific to experience and culture.

It is also reasonable to conclude that receipt of remotely originating neuronal code may often be hidden from the person's awareness in much the same way that other types of brain activity fail to fully reach consciousness. Playfair (2002) reports having designed an experiment in which a pair of adult twins was separated, out of sight and out of earshot. One was exposed to a shocking surprise in the form of a loud, colorful explosion, while the remote twin was monitored for galvanic skin response, brain wave activity, and heart rate. When questioned, the remote twin calmly answered that she thought her sister may have been somewhat anxious. However, the measurements taken at the moment of the explosion showed an extreme nervous reaction. The brain activity of the remote twin barely made it to her awareness and only under direct questioning. This illustrates the possibility of nonconscious neuronal firing due to remote signalling. Indeed, there is a common reference in the neuroscience literature to so-called random, unexplained neuronal firing in the context of what has been termed a generally 'noisy' neural system. It may be that remote neuronal code is received on a fairly constant basis, most of it incapable of inspiring a meaningful synfire reaction, thus never having the opportunity to make its way to awareness.

CONCLUSION

The theory presented above is an attempt to synthesize the remarkable work of scientists the world over, to whom this author is exceedingly grateful. To summarize the model, the following thread is proposed that:

1. telepathy is brain centered;
2. information is passed between neurons via a code;
3. cognition is the result of synchronous neuronal activity;
4. the quantum state of a neuron contains the information code;
5. a biological quantum state may be teleported;
6. the information code of a neuron may be teleported to a neuron of a remote brain;
7. remote neuronal quantum teleportation and the resulting neural processing is known as telepathy.

As with any fledgling theory, initial research may seek to either prove or disprove its validity. It would be helpful if future experiments observing instances of telepathy, such as those concerned with electrical activity in the brain (Kittenis et al., 2004; Wackermann et al., 2003) perhaps can include a method of also ascertaining the quantum states of participating neurons at various stages of the experiment. Perfecting such a method for gathering that information may be the first order of business. In a two-brain experiment, for example, this would present the opportunity to compare the electrical data with the quantum data from neurons in a single brain, and then compare the same data to the data of neurons in the other brain. The resulting correlations could yield an indication of the theory's validity because evidence of neural code teleportation would show the occurrence of telepathy, more clearly than relying on the report of the percipient. Another test of validity is to measure the natural entanglement of the neurons of experimental subjects, using it as a predictor for the degree of telepathic success.

With the notable exception of the brain electricity studies, many (perhaps most) telepathy experiments have measured success and failure on the basis of exact or nearly exact content replication from agent to percipient. If the neuronal theory of telepathy is accurate, this type of experiment would probably yield a fairly unreliable assessment of whether telepathic communication has actually occurred. The excitation of receiving neurons would necessarily call up information previously encoded, dependent on the personal experience and other factors influencing learning. In fact, for the percipient to report absolutely correct information would be extremely unusual, to say the least. A success in such a case would probably indicate that either the content is so universal as to require virtually no interpretation, or that the neuronal structures of the subjects are nearly identical. Perhaps the most appropriate measure of telepathy based on subject reporting would somehow account for individuality on a neuronal level. Two markedly successful experiments with such an individualistic approach, the

Maimonides telepathic dream study (Ullman et al., 1973) and the Sinclair (1930) drawings both used art as the telepathic content. In doing so, they allowed for the idiosyncratic differences between individuals when judging the results.

Another experimental venue which may make the behavior of neurons and their quantum properties more accessible is the use of cultured neurons, even if the donors are of non-human origin. Cultured neurons have been shown to thrive and fire synchronously (Stepanova et al. 2003), self-organizing into arrays. In an experiment to test the validity of some aspects of the current theory, neurons from a cultured array demonstrating synchronous firing could be physically separated from the original array. One may predict that the separated neurons are likely to continue some synchronous or other reactive activity with the original culture, even after physical separation. In other scenarios, observing cultured neurons from different donors could yield valuable data about remote neuronal interactivity, and examining individual neurons from a cultured environment may also lead to a method of determining entanglement.

A medical phenomenon that may offer promise in the research of how remote neurons interact is the occurrence of phantom limb pain following amputation in as many as 60-80% of patients (Nikolajsen & Jensen, 2001). In light of the current theory, it is possible that a residual entanglement between the neurons of the separated limb and the neurons of the amputee's brain enable the teleportation of some information such as that which triggers the cognition of pain.

References

Abeles, M. (1991). *Corticonics: Neural circuits of the cerebral cortex.* New York: Cambridge University Press.

Baker, S. N., Pinches, E. M., & Lemon, R. N. (2003). Synchronization in monkey motor cortex during a precision grip task. II. Effect of oscillatory activity on corticospinal output. *Journal of Neurophysiology, 89,* 1941-1953.

Bennett, C. H., Brassard, G., Crépeau, C., Jozsa, R., Peres, A., & Wootters, W. K. (1993). Teleporting an unknown quantum state via dual classical and Einstein-Podolsky-Rosen channels. *Physics Review Letters, 70,* 1895-1899.

Broughton, R. S. (1988). If you want to know how it works, first find out what it's for. (Presidential address to the Parapsychological Association), In D. H. Weiner & R. L. Morris (Eds.), *Research in Parapsychology 1987* (pp. 187-202). Metuchen, NJ: Scarecrow Press.

Dalkvist, J., & Westerlund, J. (1998). Five experiments on telepathic communication of emotions. *Journal of Parapsychology*, *62*, 29-59.

Finkle, L. H., Yen, S., & Menschik, E. (1998). Synchronization: The computational currency of cognition. ICANN 98, *Proceedings of the 8th International Conference on Artificial Neural Networks Skövde*, Sweden, 2-4 September 1998.

Freud, S. (1900/1965). *The interpretation of dreams*. New York: Avon Books (Originally published 1900).

Freud, S. (1922). Dreams and telepathy. In G. Devereux (Ed.), (1974). *Psychoanalysis and the occult* (pp. 69-86). London: Souvenir Press.

Freud, S. (1933). Dreams and the occult. In G. Devereux (Ed.), (1974). *Psychoanalysis and the occult* (pp. 91-109). London: Souvenir Press.

Furusawa, A., Sørensen, J. L., Braunstein, S. L., Fuchs, C. A., Kimble,H. J., & Polzik, E. S. (1998). Unconditional quantum teleportation. *Science, 282*, 706-709.

Georgiev, D. (2003). Where do the photons collapse: In the retina or in the brain cortex? http://arxiv.org/ftp/quant-ph/papers/0208/0208053.pdf.

Harland, C. J., Clark, T. D., & Prance, R. J. (2002). Remote detection of human electroencephalograms using ultrahigh input impedance electric potential sensors. *Applied Physics Letters, 81*(17), 3284-3286.

Hameroff, S. (1998). Quantum computation in brain microtubules? The Penrose-Hameroff 'Orch OR' model of consciousness. *Philosophical Transactions of the Royal Society of London A*, *356*, 1-28.

Jefferys, J. G. R., Traub, R. D., & Whittington, M. A. (1996). Neuronal networks for induced '40 Hz' rhythms. *Trends in Neurosciences*, *19*(5), 202-208.

Jefferys, J. (2004). Recordings of neurons. University of Birmingham Neuroscience Unit website. Retrieved November 2, from http://medweb.bham.ac.uk/neuroscience/jefferys/waves/record.htm.

Julsgaard, B., Kozhekin, A., & Polzik, E. (2001). Experimental long-lived entanglement of two macroscopic objects. *Nature, 413*, 400-403.

Kittenis, C. P. G., & Stevens, P. (2004). Distant psychological interaction effects between related and unrelated participants. *Proceedings of Presented Papers* (pp. 67-76). Parasychological Association Convention.

Lin, L., Osan, R., & Tsien, J. Z. (2006). Organizing principles of real-time memory encoding: Neural clique assemblies and universal neural codes. *Trends in Neurosciences*, *29*(1) 48-57.

Mavromatos, N. E. (2000). Cell Microtubules as Cavities: Quantum Coherence and Energy Transfer? Invited talk at the 2000 International Conference on Mathematics and Engineering Techniques in Medicine and Biological Sciences, Monte Carlo Resort, Las Vegas (USA), June 26-29 2000, published in the proceedings.

Mavromatos, N. E., Mershin, A., & Nanopoulos, D. V. (2002). QED-Cavity model of microtubules implies dissipationless energy transfer and biological quantum teleportation. *International Journal of Modern Physics B, 16*(24), 3623-3642

Nikolajsen, L., & Jensen, T. S. (2001). Phantom limb pain. *British Journal of Anaesthesia, 87*(1) 107-116.

Pederson-Craig, G. H. (1947). Telepathy and repression. In G. Devereux (Ed.), (1974). *Psychoanalysis and the occult* (pp. 277-282). London: Souvenir Press.

Playfair, G. L. (2002). *Twin telepathy*. London: Vega.

Radin, D. I. (2000). Neural network analyses of consciousness-related patterns in random sequences. *Neural Networks, July*, 1-19.

Riebe, M., Haffner, H., Roos, C. F., Hansell, W., Benhelm, J., Lancaster, G. P. T., Korber, T. W., Becher, C., Schmidt-Kaler, F., James, D. F. V., & Blatt, R. (2004). Deterministic quantum teleportation with atoms. *Nature, 429*, 734-737.

Rhine, J. B. (1937). *New frontiers of the mind*. New York: Farrar & Rinehart.

Roosevelt, T. (1906). Attic delights. In B. J. Bishop, (Ed.), (1919). *Theodore Roosevelt's letters to his children*. New York: Charles Scribner's Sons. Retrieved May 11, 2004 from http://www.bartleby.com/53/86.html.

Shan, G. (2004). A primary quantum model of telepathy. *Proceedings of presented papers. Parasychological Association Convention* (pp. 413-421).

Sinclair, U. (1930). *Mental radio*. Charlottesville: HamptonRoads.

Singer, W. (1999). Neuronal synchrony: A versatile code for the definition of relations? *Neuron, 24*, 49-65.

Singer, W. (2003). Synchronization, binding and expectancy. In M. A. Arbib (Ed.), *The handbook of brain theory and neural networks* (2nd ed.) (pp. 1136-1143). Cambridge, MA: The MIT Press.

Sougné, J. (2004). The binding problem and the problem of multiple instantiation. Retrieved November 2, 2004 from http://www.ulg.ac.be/cogsci/jsougne/jsresbind.html.

Steinmetz, P. (2000). Temporal coding and synchronous neuronal firing. Retrieved November 2, 2004 from http://www.bml.umn.edu/Research/TemporalCoding.html.

Stepanova, T., Slemmer, J., Hoogenraad, C. C., Lansbergen, G., Dortland, B., De Zeeuw, C. I., Grosveld, F., van Cappellen, G., Akhmanova, A., & Galjart,

N. (2003). Visualization of microtubule growth in cultured neurons via the use of EB3-GFP (end-binding protein 3-green fluorescent protein). *Journal of Neuroscience, 23*(7), 2655-2664.

Storm, L. (2006). Meta-analysis in parapsychology: II. Psi domains other than ganzfeld. *Australian Journal of Parapsychology, 6*, 135-155.

Ullman, M., Krippner, S., with Vaughan, A. (1973). *Dream telepathy.* New York: Macmillan Publishing Company.

Wackermann, J. (2004). Dyadic correlations between brain functional states: Present facts and future perspectives. *Mind and Matter, 2*(1), 105-122.

Wackermann, J., Seiter, C., Keibel, H., & Walach, H. (2003). Correlations between brain electrical activities of two spatially separated human subjects. *Neuroscience Letters, 1*(5), 60-64.

Ward, L. M. (2003). Synchronous neural oscillations and cognitive processes. *Trends in Cognitive Sciences, 7*, 553-559.

Wilson, S., Morris, R. L., Tiliopoulos, N., & Pronto, E. (2004). Psi and associational processes. *Journal of Parapsychology, 68*, 129-155.

Chapter 3

The Possible Role of Psychokinesis in Place Memory[1]

Pamela Rae Heath

Parapsychologists have long been aware that the environment sometimes appears to hold the memory of past events, which can be variously 'viewed', 'heard', 'tasted', 'smelled', or 'felt' at a later time by a person with sufficient sensitivity to the information. Place memory is typically considered to be a possible factor in hauntings, along with the usual factors of fraud, hallucination, misperception, malobservation, retrocognition, discarnate entities, and environmental factors. According to some, place memory may represent over ninety percent of haunting cases (Graves, 1986). Furthermore, it can apparently exist as layers of recordings, which can be separately 'read' and 'interpreted'.

The idea that objects and locations could hold such recordings is not a new one. In fact, it has been discussed by parapsychologists since virtually the inception of the field. The initial notion was a simple one, as Lodge (1920) stated:

> Here is a room where a tragedy occurred, where the human spirit was strung to intensest anguish. Is there any trace of that agony present still and able to be appreciated by an attuned or receptive mind? If it happened, it may take many forms; vague disquiet perhaps, or imaginary sounds or vague visions, or perhaps a dream or picture of the event as it occurred….

1. [This chapter is based on an article that was originally published in *Australian Journal of Parapsychology* (2004, vol. 4[2], pp. 63-80). Permission to reprint has been granted by the author and the journal.—Editors.]

> Relics again: is it credible that a relic, a lock of hair, an old garment, retains any trace of a deceased friend—retains any portion of his [*sic*] personality. Does not an old letter? Does not a painting? (p. 95)

In order to make sense of what could be holding this information, parapsychologists speculated on the presence of some kind of unseen 'ether' or 'medium' (Tyrrell, 1953). Tyrrell (1953) reported:

> In the fifth Myers Memorial Lecture, Dr. C. A. Mace outlined a suggestion of what he called a 'substantival medium' capable of receiving and re-rendering ''patterns of events'...With regard to it he says: 'Personally I am of the opinion that we can, with good scientific conscience, postulate the existence of a medium which records impressions of all sorts of patterns of events.' (p. 104)

It is unclear from the literature whether the expression 'place memory' actually originated with Sir Oliver Lodge or H. H. Price. However, it is plain that Price (1939) popularised the idea and placed his own spin on it, defining place memory as images that, "permanently, and collectively constitute the memory of the place" (p. 332). Tyrrell (1953) explained Price's beliefs as follows:

> Such images he supposed to be originated by a mental act, but not to be themselves mental...He then supposed these images, neither mental nor material, to be endowed with telepathic charges and illustrated his theory by applying it to haunting. Such a persistent image might, he suggested, be tied down in some particular way to a physical place or object, might act telepathically on a percipient near this place and might cause him to see an apparition. (p. 105)

This would seem to suggest that Price felt that the objects provided an anchor for active telepathic agents that were both non-corporeal and non-conscious. Thus, although Price did much to advance the term, his version of place memory differed considerably from that with which we are more familiar, as Roll (2003) has pointed out:

> Price's concept of place memory should not be confused with the conventional meaning of the term, the tendency to remember events by revisiting the place where they took place. In Price's sense, you "remember" events that have been experienced by others. Like familiar

> memories, events that are recent, frequent, and emotionally significant may be more likely to come to mind than others. (p. 201)

Sometimes there has been the suggestion that such recordings could even take on something of a life of their own, manifesting as a 'pseudo-haunting.' McCue (2002) wrote:

> Denning (op. cit.) suggests that some cases, which she calls pseudo-hauntings, do not entail the active intervention of spirit entities, but rather an "energy form created by traumatic events [that] seems to be charged with a powerful energy that continues to exist…for a considerable length of time." (p. 12)

This appears to take Price's original view a bit further, suggesting the possible formation of something that occultists refer to as thought forms.

During the years since it was introduced, place memory has often been lumped in the same category with retrocognition—which literally means "backward knowing" (Irwin, 1994, p. 128). In essence, this is the opposite of precognition, with the ESP extending back in time instead of forward. For example, the 'playback theory' of haunting apparitions proposed that experients "are simply witnessing a playback of a past scene or scenes. Perhaps that scene is somehow imprinted or recorded on the physical locality in which it happened; perhaps there is a reoccurring kink or loop in space-time" (Gauld, 1983, p. 248). Thus, in speaking of this theory Gauld is combining two possibilities—present-day environmental imprints (place memory) with alterations in time that might let you literally see the past (retrocognition).

Let us pause for a moment to distinguish retrocognition from place memory. This is critical because present thought suggests that they involve different mechanisms of action. Guiley (1991) characterised the typical retrocognitive experience as follows:

> Spontaneous retrocognition usually manifests as a hallucination or vision. The present surroundings are abruptly replaced by a scene out of the past. Although the vision usually is fleeting, some last for minutes and generally feature movement, sounds, and smells.
>
> Retrocognition is a phenomenon of some hauntings and apparitions that seem to be continual replays of events, such as murders or suicides. Psychologist Gardner Murphy theorized that most ghosts are cases of

> retrocognition, in which an individual becomes momentarily displaced in time and can perceive scenes from the past. (pp. 509-510)

It should be noted that an individual would not have to literally travel back in time, or be in a 'time slip' where two time periods exist simultaneously, for retrocognition to occur. ESP might be sufficient.

Retrocognition cases are said to be rare (Irwin, 1994). They are often described as: 1) beginning and ending abruptly; 2) having a dream-like character; 3) focusing on some sensory modalities while excluding others; and 4) being specific to a particular object or location. Irwin (1994) observed that, when reported, retrocognition frequently (but not always) involves battle scenes. Rogo (1975) also noted that experients may report an altered sense of time (suggesting a shift in their state of consciousness) and that:

> In each case the experiencer feels himself to be completely engrossed within the experience and, in fact, often mistakes it as reality until some inconsistency jolts him into the realization that he is witnessing something paranormal. Sometimes this realization does not occur until after the experience has been completed, and often the discovery is accidental. (pp. 142-143)

Retrocognition has not been formally investigated both because of the scarcity of documented cases and because there appears to be no way to separate it from other forms of ESP (Irwin, 1994). Although both retrocognition and place memory seem to be place-oriented events, they differ in three ways. First, people who experience place memory typically describe it as a far less intense experience than retrocognition—more often a 'knowing' than a re-living or cinematic vision of the past. Second, with place memory there is the assumption that both the percipient, and the information that they are receiving, exist in the same present time period—which may not be the case with retrocognition. Finally, there may be little, if any, alteration in consciousness with place memory as opposed to the 'dream-like state,' altered sensory modalities and altered sense of time associated with retrocognition, and which would all seem to indicate a distinct shift in consciousness.

Place memory is most often thought of today as the apparent energetic imprint of information, produced by living beings and somehow stored by the environment, which some individuals may be able to retrieve through paranormal means. It is interesting to note that while some individuals may sometimes dispute the existence of ghosts, the notion that, under the right conditions, locations can record and hold impressions of the people, places, and events that occurred there appears to be generally accepted by the populace, perhaps in part due to our comfort and familiarity with camcorders.

Place memory is most often discussed in the research literature in association with haunting cases. McCue (2002) wrote of its possible role:

> Another approach to understanding hauntings is to suppose that events occurring in a particular place, such as a house, can leave a trace, impression or record that can influence subsequent occupants or visitors, causing them to experience the characteristic phenomena. From this perspective, experiencing a haunting is similar to watching a video-recording or listening to a tape-recording of past events, and arguably this approach could help to explain cases, such as the Cheltenham ghost (Collins, 1948; MacKenzie, 1982), in which apparitions act in a rather stereotyped way. Such a theory might also make sense of some of the auditory phenomena reported in cases of haunting. If, for example, furniture had been dragged about in a particular room at some point in the past, and if some sort of trace or record of that event had been made, occupants of the haunted building might be able to hear (either physically or via some other process) the sound of furniture being moved. If the laying down of the 'trace' is a hit-and-miss business, dependent at any given point on a concurrence of various physical and emotional factors, the 'playback' might yield a telescoped and disjointed sequence of sounds, perhaps giving the manifestations a bizarre and frightening character. (p. 15)

To avoid confusion, it should be noted that in recent years the terms 'residual haunting' and the 'stone tape' theory have both been used to refer to place memory, although the latter appears to refer primarily to buildings (Cornell, 2002). Cornell (2002) explained:

> The reader may recall that this theory was put forward some time ago as the cause of recurrent visual and auditory paranormal phenomena in old buildings. It suggests that there is a mechanism whereby the emotions of the living become absorbed and retained by the fabric of a building. Thus, so the theory goes, these recordings either lie in wait for whatever it is that causes them to be replayed for an individual who is sensitive to their continued presence. (p. 391)

Unfortunately, as Cornell (2002) noted, the stone tape theory is more speculation than explanation. He stated:

> How and why human emotions should become embedded in the material of a building has never been investigated nor theorized further, nor have the mechanics of their replaying been explored further. Even allowing that psychometry might provide an instance of a similar phenomenon, there is nothing in physics nor any recorded data which might support or allow us to develop this theory further. Unless we were concerned here solely with crisis events, the problem of why only a few fragmentary snippets of a few seconds or minutes of a former life should be absorbed—rather than longer periods—poses an as yet unanswerable question. (Cornell, 2002, p. 391)

Thus, stone tape theory does not advance our understanding of the process. Moreover, since it seems to look at a limited subset of what may be occurring, it appears to serve no advantage over the original term. Unfortunately, the same could also be said of place memory. As McCue (2002) noted in echo of Cornell's comment, "without some specification of a mechanism (or mechanisms) by which the 'recording' and 'playback' occur, much remains to be explained" (p. 15).

McCue's point is well taken. We do indeed understand little about the 'how's' and 'why's' of place memory. Part of the difficulty is that place memory is essentially a subjective, experiential event. It is perceived within the brain and even if there are objective, environmental variables that can be measured—like the geomagnetic field—they do not really get at the heart of the experience. Furthermore, place memory is difficult, if not impossible, to isolate for study. The experimenter must first rule out all the normal causes for the experience, plus some paranormal ones, as well. This can be particularly difficult because as Brugger (2001) noted, there is a "pervasive tendency of human beings to see order in random configuration" (p. 196). People may see patterns where there are none, and attribute them to discarnate entities or other causes. When there is a belief in the paranormal, this may be even more true, making it extremely difficult to separate out real findings from those of the imagination. Worse still, we currently have no way of distinguishing between sources of ESP information—whether the environment, living minds, the future, the past, discarnate sources, or even other dimensions of existence.

It would seem likely that place memory (when real, and not a subjective experience generated by normal, if misunderstood, means) is retrieved through anomalous cognition. However, little is known about how place memory initially comes about, or what factors might act as modifiers for it. And like many who speak of place memory, McCue (2002) made an assumption that may not be correct—that place memory is recorded by the environment. Another possibility is that this information could be imprinted or stamped onto the environment by the living.

Known Variables in Place Memory

Before we discuss hypothetical possibilities, let us look first at those few things that we believe to be true regarding place memory. Parapsychologists noted early on that the living seemed to be involved. In his Presidential Address, Price (1939) stated that, "We ordinarily think that memory-images can only be *generated* in connection with some sort of brain or nervous system…that they acquire a more or less complete independence afterwards" (p. 332). This suggests that living beings may be one of the factors in the development of place memory, which, once recorded, may remain for a period of time. Furthermore, it is the living who are responsible for the haunting, as Price indicated in the following passage:

> Moreover, in haunting the *immediate* agent is not a mind, but only an image: though the *ultimate* agent is the mind which originated and projected the image long ago. So it is a case of *deferred* telepathy, resulting in the production of a "post-dated" telepathic phantasm…in haunting it has long since got dissociated from the mind which originally owned it, and indeed that mind (if the Anti-Survivalists are right) may long ago have ceased to exist. (Price, 1939, p. 340)

Emotion is another factor that seems to play a role in place memory. Emotionally-charged events appear to be more apt to be recorded and/or retrieved. Sometimes this may relate to crisis situations. Alvarado (2000) noted that:

> Bozzano presents statistics on the frequency of some features of hauntings and poltergeists. One is the relationship of haunting phenomena and tragic events: "So, for example, in an initial group of 180 cases…the origin of the haunting coincided with a tragic event that occurred in the same place…." Regarding death, Bozzano wrote that: "from a total of 374, in 304 there is, coinciding with the haunting, the precedent of a case of death." (p. 163)

Not all researchers agree with Bozzano. Alvarado (2000) observed that Maher (1999) did not find a relationship between hauntings and a preceding death. This may not be surprising given the existence of place memory, where the dead may not be involved. Somewhat amusingly, at least some ghosts would seem to agree that strong emotions can directly impact the environment and be responsible for a 'haunted' locale. Evans (2002) reported:

> Many theories about hauntings speak of traces left by emotions, which do not necessarily have to be the result of violent death. Ghost-hunter James Wentworth Day reports: 'Mr. Clay [a ghost witness] gave me the most logical explanation I have ever heard of why some people see ghosts and others do not. His view was that certain happenings in life—murder, suicide, extreme agony of mind or infinite kindness to others—can leave an impression on what one might describe as "the cinema screen of time." The result is that at certain periods the episodes of the past are thrown up and repeated on, say, the anniversaries of their happening'. (pp. 209-210)

In cases where death does precede a haunting, it may not be so much because a ghost is created, but because the event was an emotional one. This would be particularly true when that death is violent or tragic. Furthermore, emotion itself may aid place memory retrieval, since it could make the information stand out from other recordings. Price (1938-1939) explained:

> We can now see that it must stand out in two different ways, *both* in respect of quality *and* in respect of intensity. To use the same sort of analogy as before: if a lot of signatures were written all over a small piece of paper, one on top of the other, you could not read any of them. You would see only a confused blur. But if one were written in red ink and all the rest in black, you might be able to read the red one quite well. And you would be more likely to do so if the ink in which it was written had been particularly strong and lasting....
>
> It may, however, be that great intensity in the telepathic charge can compensate for otherwise unsuitable quality. Conversely, if the *quality* is exactly right (if there is the maximum degree of telepathic affinity between the persisting image and the mental contents of the percipient) this may compensate for feeble intensity. (p. 340)

Thus, we see that the best known variables for place memory appear to be that: 1) a living agent is somehow involved; and 2) strong emotion appears to be a factor that enhances the recording and/or retrieval of place memory. It is unclear whether the latter can entirely account for the fact that crisis situations (which may, or may not, include a being's death), are more likely to create place memory.

Possible Physical Variables in Place Memory

A number of physical variables have been proposed to affect the anomalous experiences reported in hauntings, which could possibly impact place memory recording or retrieval, as well. Perhaps foremost among these are environmental factors, such as local geomagnetic fields, geologic factors, and weather conditions. For example, Graves (1986) felt that quartz crystals (in stone or bedrock), underground water, and atmospheric water—such as a damp, misty day—could all enhance place memory retrieval. Unfortunately, it is unclear whether these factors would affect the reporting of anomalous experiences via an effect on the experiences themselves or through normal physical or psychological variables causing an increased number of normal experiences that are only mistaken for anomalous. Such cases of pseudo-place-memory could be induced by hearing odd sounds from underground water, being psychologically primed by a foggy day, or hallucinating due to standing waves of sound or temporal lobe dysfunction.

A more intriguing correlation is the one between geomagnetic fields and purportedly paranormal experiences. As Wiseman, Watt, Greening, Stevens, & O'Keefe (2002) reported,

> Persinger (1985) argued that changes in geomagnetic fields (e.g., created by tectonic stresses in the Earth's crust) could stimulate the brain's temporal lobes and produce many of the subjective experiences associated with hauntings. In a preliminary test of this theory, Gearhart and Persinger (1986) examined a collection of alleged poltergeist experiences and reported finding significant relationships between the time of onset of unusual phenomena and sudden increases in global geomagnetic activity.... More recent support has come from several on-site investigations of alleged hauntings that have reported a high degree of local magnetic activity in locations associated with eyewitness reports of unusual phenomena.... Some of the work arguing for a link between magnetic fields and unusual experiences has noted that the effect seems to be associated with high levels of geomagnetic activity...whereas other researchers have related the effect more to gradients in static magnetic fields. (pp. 389-390)

Likewise, Maher (1999) commented regarding a haunted Japanese restaurant in Georgia, that:

> Electromagnetic field strengths collected by Maher at the restaurant were significantly higher at sites of reported phenomena than at control sites, suggesting to her that conventional electromagnetic fields were implicated in the phenomenology of the participants. A subsequent test…gave null results, however, suggesting that electromagnetic fields are likely to explain only selected reports of ghostly phenomena. (p. 64)

Persinger and Koren (2001) have suggested that such factors could explain all hauntings and be the process behind both apparitional sightings and place memory. They stated:

> There is not a single case of haunt phenomena whose major characteristics cannot be accommodated by understanding the natural forces generated by the earth, the areas of the human brain that are stimulated by these energies, and the interpretation of these forces by normal psychological processes. (Persinger & Koren, 2001, p. 179)

Persinger and Koren based this statement in part on research that showed that stimulating the parietal and temporal lobes of the brain can elicit sensations, smells, and feelings similar in content to that which people report in hauntings. However, to say that such experiences can be duplicated or mimicked through artificial exposure to electric or geomagnetic fields is not to say that is why such experiences are always reported. Nonetheless, it is a likely component of many such events and may hint at what part of the brain processes this kind of information.

Another possibility is that there may be a variable interaction between geomagnetic fields and psi. Roe, Holt, & Simmonds (2003) noted that other factors may act as modifiers for whatever effect the geomagnetic field may have:

> Past research has often shown a relationship between the state of the geomagnetic field and both success in psi tasks and the frequency of spontaneous psi experiences….a negative correlation has typically been found between the magnitude of the geomagnetic field fluctuations and psi success/experience…. However, there is some evidence to suggest that this relationship may be affected by other factors. For example, Spottiswoode (1997) reported a suggestive overall negative correlation but found the effect to be restricted to only a limited window of local sidereal time. (p. 349)

Thus, whatever effect the geomagnetic field has, if any, on anomalous cognition and hauntings, it may be inconsistent. Wiseman et al. (2002) summed up the issue best in their discussion of the correlation of the magnetic fields at Hampton Court Palace with reports of anomalous experience. They concluded:

> The experiment provided no support for the notion that the experiences could be explained by suggestion alone, and only modest evidence that magnetic fields caused the experiences. However, it is clear that believers tended to report significantly more experiences than disbelievers, and those reports tended to cluster or focus in certain areas. (Wiseman et al., 2002, p. 404)

One of the problems with relying on the haunting literature for information about place memory, is that the reports may involve a wide mixture of factors, including (but not limited to) both non-psychic phenomena—such as standing waves of infrasound at 19Hz, hallucinations, temporal lobe dysfunction, malobservation, misinterpretation—and apparently psychic phenomena, such as apparitions that interact with the living and can be tracked as isolated moving electromagnetic fields (i.e., ghosts), and place memory (McCue, 2002). It is very difficult, if not sometimes impossible, to adequately differentiate between this combination of possible causes for a percipient's experience. Because of this, it may be difficult to determine the precise connections in haunting investigation cases between weather, geologic conditions, the geomagnetic field and place memory *per se*. To investigate place memory properly, we would first have to rule out a wide range of normal causes of apparently anomalous experiences and other paranormal causes, such as ghosts.

The Creation of Place Memory

We have little understanding about the actual creation of place memory—what conditions are required, what could play a role as modifying variables, exactly how the information is stored, and the specifics of how that information storage is accomplished. Often theories on place memory have mimicked the technologies of the time in which they were proposed. The first such suggestion was reminiscent of still photography. Price (1939) wrote:

> Now it has often been suggested that such apparitions are due to some sort of localised trace or vestige or impress left in the matter of the room.

> These traces would be the quite automatic result of the emotions or other experiences of some person who formerly inhabited the room, much as finger-prints result automatically from our handling of a wine-glass or a poker. Thus on this view the apparition is not a *revenant*, as popular superstition supposes—not a deceased personality revisiting the scenes of its former experience nor yet an "earth-bound spirit" lingering on in them—but is something more like a photograph or a cinematograph picture. (The physical trace would correspond to the photographic negative; and it would be as it were "developed" when anyone with a suitable mind and nervous system enters the room.) This is what Signor Bozzano calls "the Psychometrical Theory" of Haunting. For in Psychometry too we seem to find that a material object retains traces of the past experiences of a person who was formerly in physical contact with it. (p. 324)

With videotape and motion film development, there appeared to be even more acceptance of the idea of an imprint. Johnson (1983) referred to place memory as, "the problem of whether mental events are accompanied by the induction or creation of traces in surrounding animate and inanimate matter" (p. 178). He discussed W. G. Roll's theory of a 'psi-field' as one possibility for how place memory works. Key factors of this theory include: (1) the importance of spatial proximity; (2) the "*frequency hypothesis* which states that a more efficient communication of psi can be obtained via a token-object which has often and over a longer period of time been in touch with the target person than a token-object which rarely and briefly has been in contact with the target person" (Johnson, 1983, p. 178); and (3) the recency of the contact between the inductor and the target. This theory would seem to be equally valid for psychometry or place memory in the environment. The notion of a passive left-over residue of energy might well explain instances where a set of actions that were repeated in identical fashion (such as a man walking on the castle ramparts) over a long period of time could become recorded by the environment. Under the right conditions, or with someone sufficiently gifted, this place memory can be 'played back' so to speak.

With greater awareness of subtle energy fields, Maher (1999) theorized that place memory could derive from contact with the aura of a living person:

> The psychometric energy that I'm speaking about may be the same as a person's life force or stream of life energy.... It may simply be the unbroken flow of energy that animates the organism from conception to death.... The energy itself is not ordinarily visible while a person is alive,

> but it can on occasion manifest to an observer as an aura, from which information regarding the person may be derived. (p. 56)

It may not be surprising that, with our increasing understanding of laser technology, Persinger and Koren (2001) have come up with a different theory of place memory. They suggested that geomagnetic fields might record events in a similar way to the creation of a hologram, stating:

> In this context, local geomagnetic activity would be the working and reference beams, and the interaction between the local static geomagnetic field and composition of the earth's surface would be the equivalent of the exposure plate. If an event occurs during a geomagnetic storm with a specific pattern whose local signatures are matched with the inductance of the local crust, then a small representation might be maintained within the crystalline structure of the rock. The presence of human beings and objects during the event might generate interference patterns by distorting the ongoing geomagnetic activity (the working beam) as it is superimposed upon the static field. (Persinger & Koren, 2001, p. 192)

As with Roll's 'psi-field' theory, this is an interesting idea that would seem to hold some promise for explaining at least some cases of place memory. Certainly, those who routinely perform haunting investigations believe it is possible to erase place memory through the use of strong magnets or a bulk videotape eraser, which would disrupt any static electromagnetic fields (L. Auerbach, personal communication, 2004). However, unlike Roll's 'psi-field,' Persinger and Koren's holographic method would not seem to explain why small objects, regardless of composition, seem also to be able to hold 'memories' that can be picked up by those sensitive to such information.

This author would like to suggest that if we consider that living beings are involved and that this form of place memory involves emotionally charged events, then it is not only possible, but likely, that psychokinesis (PK) is the means by which this form of place memory is recorded.[2] This would go beyond what parapsychologists have typically thought of as the role of PK in hauntings where,

---

2. [The author now uses the terms 'mind-matter interaction' and 'MMI' instead of 'psychokinesis' and 'PK', respectively, but the terms 'psychokinesis' and 'PK' remain in this chapter, as in the original. The author (P. R. Heath, personal communication, December 4, 2011) explains that:

> the term psychokinesis translates to 'mind/soul movement'. However, many forms of MMI do not involve movement at all. Because of this, I prefer mind-matter

as with poltergeist phenomena, apparitions are artificially created, lights and sounds created, or objects moved (Auerbach, 1986).

There are two lines of evidence that would seem to support the idea of PK as a possible active agent in the recording of some forms of place memory. First, that spontaneous extra-sensory perception (ESP) and PK appear to be more prevalent when an individual is under stress (Gurney, Myers, & Podmore, 1962; Rhine, 1961). This would seem to be true for both poltergeist phenomena and crisis situations, where there is a greatly increased incidence of spontaneous case reports. Furthermore, others, like Radin (2001), have mentioned a possible role of PK in haunting when "intense subjective experiences…intrude upon the physical world, as postulated in poltergeist activity" (p. 167). Certainly some of the cases where place memory appears to be particularly strong, such as the locale of violent murders, would qualify for someone having such an "intense subjective experience." It seems likely that PK can occur, not only as poltergeist phenomena, but in other ways.

The second line of evidence is phenomenological. It is well known that peak levels of emotion are associated with all forms of spontaneous PK (Heath, 2003). Spoons bend. Objects break. Computers go haywire. Humans can and do affect the environment around them when under stress. Thus, in a high-emotion situation—whether death results or not—it does not seem unreasonable that the living person could emit signals that actively impress the environment, perhaps through affecting the local electromagnetic fields of the environment or items within it.

If PK is involved, it could explain part of the variability in why the environment sometimes picks up some memories of crisis situations but not others. Not all individuals would have talent at recording their impressions. Furthermore, there could be considerable variation at the time of the event in key factors involved in the production of PK, such as the individual's state of consciousness, feeling of connection or dissociation, level of emotion, use of intellect, degree of focus, physical state, and investment (Heath, 2003).

It should also be noted that what kind of psi a person develops spontaneously appears to be need-related. In other words, it serves a need that the organism cannot otherwise meet. For those individuals who have no conventional means for telling others what happened to them, the recording of place memory through

---

interaction (MMI) as a more accurate and inclusive term that covers the entire range of PK phenomena.

—Editors.]

PK would seem to serve a similar need for expression as that which is reported with poltergeist agents. This could include a wide range of crisis situations where a victim might wish to leave some record of their passing, or communicate how they died. If unable to connect through ESP to another individual, they might imprint the information instead onto the environment around them. That it can work is shown by some of the 'cold cases' solved by psychics who go back and 'read' what really occurred, allowing crimes to be solved years later.

One of the greatest difficulties with the hypothesis that PK is involved in some forms of place memory is how to test it properly. It must be falsifiable. This would require finding a way to separate PK-created place memory that is 'read' by ESP, from other normal and paranormal elements—clearly not an easy task. Nonetheless, if PK is involved, then it might be possible to use intentional PK to create place memory—which was previously considered a random or uncontrollable event.

McCue (2002) commented that one of the problems with designing haunting experiments in the past was that, "to the extent that hauntings arise in settings of unhappiness or trauma, it might not be possible, within the scope of ethical practice, to reproduce all the necessary conditions occurring in spontaneous cases" (p. 19). This, of course, presupposes that death or trauma are required—which may not be the case if PK is involved. Certainly, as mentioned earlier, some haunting investigators have reported place memory involving positive emotions or situations (L. Auerbach, personal communication, 2004). If spontaneous PK is involved, it should be possible to ask a PK performer to try, intentionally, to imprint an emotion, sound, or set of images onto a location, and then take a combination of skeptics, psi-believers, and individuals with psychic sensitivity to that location along with 'control' locations to see whether they are able to 'pick up' on that feeling or information. Whoever interacted with the participants trying to receive that information would have to be blind to what others had attempted to record on those locations. However, there would still be the problem of trying to differentiate between telepathy between the living PK agent (or the experimenter) to the participants, general ESP, retrocognition, precognition (if they received future feedback as to whether they had been correct or not), normal (if misunderstood) causes in the environment, and what is being 'stored' paranormally as place memory.

Future investigations need not be limited to quantitative studies. The fact that place memory is a subjective experience brings up another possible avenue of research. Phenomenological inquiry is a form of qualitative research designed for dealing with this kind of situation. Thus, a detailed phenomenological study on place memory that compares and contrasts it to other forms of psi, such as retrocognition, or even with non-paranormal experiences such as the artificial stimulation of the brain described by Persinger and Koren (2001) might lead to some valuable insights.

In conclusion, it is easy to see why many researchers would become discouraged with the idea of investigating place memory, and move on to easier topics. Isolating place memory is a daunting task for the investigator. Nonetheless, this is an aspect of psi that appears to literally surround us, and there are numerous possible areas that could be investigated. One concept that might be useful to experimenters is to look at place memory not as a solitary kind of phenomenon, but rather as something by which there could be two methods of creation—one active, involving PK, and the other a more passive phenomenon relating, as W. G. Roll noted, to repetition, proximity to the object/place, and recency. It is hoped that by looking at place memory in this way, it can improve our understanding of the topic and open up new avenues of research.

» References

Alvarado, C. S. (2000). Introduction to Ernest Bozzano's analysis of hauntings and poltergeist cases. *International Journal of Parapsychology, 11*(2), 161-168.

Auerbach, L. (1986). *ESP, hauntings, and poltergeists: A parapsychologist's handbook.* New York: Warner Books.

Brugger, P. (2001). From haunted brain to haunted science: A cognitive neuroscience view of paranormal and pseudoscientific thought. In J. Houran & R. Lange (Eds.), *Hauntings and poltergeists: Multidisciplinary perspectives* (pp. 195-213). Jefferson, NC: McFarland.

Cornell, T. (2002). *Investigating the paranormal.* New York: Helix Press.

Evans, H. (2002). *Seeing ghosts: Experiences of the paranormal.* London: John Murray.

Gauld, A. (1983). *Mediumship and survival: A century of investigations.* London: Paladin Books.

Graves, T. (1986). Ghosts and ghouls. In *Needles of stone* (2nd ed., chap. 6). Gothic Image. Retrieved September 11, 2004, from http://www.isleofavalon.co.uk/GlastonburyArchive/ndlstone/00contnt.html.

Guiley, R. E. (1991). *Harper's encyclopedia of mystical and paranormal experience.* Edison, NJ: Castle Books.

Gurney, E., Myers, F. W. H., & Podmore, F. (1962). Phantasms of the living. In E. Sidgwick (Ed.), *Phantasms of the living: Cases of telepathy printed in the Journal of the Society for Psychical Research during thirty-five years and phantasms of the living* (pp. iii-518). New Hyde Park, NY: University Books. (Original work published in London in 1886).

Heath, P. (2003). *The PK zone: A cross-cultural review of psychokinesis.* New York: iUinverse.com.

Irwin, H. J. (1994). *An introduction to parapsychology (2nd ed.).* Jefferson, NC: McFarland.

Johnson, M. (1983). A technique for testing of the psi-field theory with some implications for survival research. *Journal of the Society for Psychical Research, 52*, 177-188.

Lodge, O. L. (1920). *The survival of man: A study in unrecognized human faculty* (enlarged edition). New York: George H. Doran.

Maher, M. C. (1999). Riding the waves in search of the particles: A modern study of ghosts and apparitions. *Journal of Parapsychology, 63*, 47-80.

McCue, P. A. (2002). Theories of hauntings: A critical overview. *Journal of the Society for Psychical Research, 66*, 1-21.

Persinger, M. A., & Koren, S. A. (2001). Predicting the characteristics of haunt phenomena from geomagnetic factors and brain sensitivity: Evidence from field and experimental studies. In J. Houran & R. Lange (Eds.), *Hauntings and poltergeists: Multidisciplinary perspectives* (pp. 179-194). Jefferson, NC: McFarland.

Price, H. H. (1939). [Presidential Address.] *Proceedings of the Society for Psychical Research, 1938-1939, 45*, 307-343.

Radin, D. (2001). Seeking spirits in the laboratory. In J. Houran & R. Lange (Eds.), *Hauntings and poltergeists: Multidisciplinary perspectives* (pp. 164-178). Jefferson, NC: McFarland.

Rhine, L. E. (1961). *Hidden channels of the mind.* New York: William Morrow and Company.

Roe, C. A., Holt, N. J., & Simmonds, C. (2003). Considering the sender as a PK agent in ganzfeld ESP studies. *Journal of Parapsychology, 67*, 129-145.

Rogo, D. Scott. (1975). *Parapsychology: A Century of Inquiry.* New York: Taplinger Publishing Company.

Roll, W. G. (2003). Book review. *Journal of Parapsychology, 67*, 187-203.

Tyrrell, G. N. M. (1953). *Apparitions.* New York: Pantheon Books.

Wiseman, R., Watt, C., Greening, E., Stevens, R., & O'Keefe, C. (2002). An investigation into the alleged haunting of Hampton Court Palace: Psychological variables and magnetic fields. *Journal of Parapsychology*, *66*, 387-408.

Chapter 4

Human Levitation[1]

Simon Harvey-Wilson

In 2005 I completed an interdisciplinary (religious studies/anthropology) PhD with a thesis on human levitation at Edith Cowan University in Perth, Western Australia. For many years I have had an interest in research into what is colloquially called the paranormal, but which academics refer to as parapsychology. There are no parapsychologists at any of the five universities (four public and one private) in Perth and I do not have any formal parapsychology qualifications, so I was effectively obliged to do my research from a social sciences perspective. I picked the topic of human levitation (which I define as the whole physical body inexplicably lifting into the air) because virtually no serious research has been done into this phenomenon and in my opinion it would be one of the least ambiguous paranormal events that one can witness. I do not doubt the existence of phenomena such as telepathy, remote viewing or clairvoyance, but skeptics frequently claim that, because they are largely internal experiences, they are hard to define or measure. Human levitation, on the other hand, would be clearly visible and hard to fake.

I have only come across two serious books (in English) on levitation. The first is by the French Catholic researcher Olivier Leroy (English edition, 1928). This is by far the most comprehensive book on this subject, but suffers from significant religious bias. Leroy documents a large number of historical levitation reports including Christian saints and Spiritualists but, in my opinion, rather irrationally concludes that divine forces levitate those of high moral standing while demonic forces levitate everyone else.

The second book on levitation (Richards, 1980) is not a scholarly analysis, but does discuss the subject in a fairly comprehensive fashion. Most books on the

1. [This chapter was originally published in *Australian Journal of Parapsychology* (2006, vol. 6[1], pp. 21-34). Permission to reprint has been granted by the journal.—Editors.]

paranormal or parapsychology mention human levitation, but have little to say about it other than referring to well-known levitators such as the Spiritualist D. D. Home, or the seventeenth-century Catholic monk Saint Joseph of Cupertino. Some books even assert that all levitation claims are probably fictitious.

Although my research was done from a social sciences perspective, I wanted it to be as close to a parapsychological perspective as I could get it. Because human levitation appears to have been almost completely ignored by the academic community, the purpose of my qualitative study was to persuade empirical researchers (e.g., parapsychologists) that the phenomenon of human levitation is sufficiently credible to warrant further investigation, and to provide them with enough relevant information to commence their research.

Because my research methodology does not fall into any precise category, I was often rather embarrassed when people would ask me what my methodology was, so I would attempt jokingly to claim that I was studying human levitation using grounded theory. In his book *An Introduction to Parapsychology*, Dr. Harvey Irwin (2004) claims that parapsychology's three basic concerns are "authenticity, underlying process and phenomenology" (p. 7). By 'authenticity' he means whether the phenomenon being investigated is "ontologically real" (p. 7). In his opinion, because parapsychology is a scientific discipline, the authenticity issue "properly can only be resolved in the scientific laboratory" (p. 7), although he believes that it is appropriate to investigate how a so-called paranormal phenomenon might work even if its authenticity has not yet been proven (p. 8). However, it is unlikely that anyone would receive funding or be motivated to research human levitation within a laboratory unless preliminary research elsewhere had demonstrated that it is reasonable to believe that the phenomenon exists, with suggestions as to how the laboratory research might proceed.

My research project does not attempt to prove that any individual levitation report is genuine. It only addresses the authenticity question to the degree required to persuade empirical researchers that the phenomenon is sufficiently convincing to warrant further investigation. Instead of ignoring the slowly increasing body of human levitation reports, as the empirical sciences are doing, my project is a study of these reports primarily to seek information that relates to Irwin's underlying process and phenomenology components.

Irwin's three issues can be adopted for the study of human levitation, asking about its authenticity, how it works and what the experience of levitation is like. The main thrust of my research focuses on Irwin's second parapsychological issue, which he describes as "*process-oriented* research…designed to ascertain the processes by which parapsychological experiences are enacted" (Irwin, 2004, p. 8).

Irwin further claims that, "like other behavioural scientists parapsychologists seek to understand the bases of human experience" (p. 8). This leads to his third issue, phenomenology, which "focuses on the description of parapsychological phenomena from the *experient's* point of view; that is, investigators seek to establish the characteristics of the phenomena as actually experienced and the impact such experiences have upon the individual" (p. 8). Irwin asserts that "phenomenological research should set the research agenda in parapsychology, because it has the function of specifying the essential characteristics of the phenomenon to be explained" (2004, p. 9). His justification for this claim is that:

> although it certainly is possible to study phenomenological characteristics of the experiences without the slightest concern for underlying processes, such study often does suggest ideas about the nature of underlying processes. In other words, phenomenological research is useful in generating hypotheses for investigation in process-oriented research. (Irwin, 2004, p. 8)

Human levitation has often been regarded as a religious or miraculous phenomenon, but a wider examination reveals that the main groups that have traditionally produced levitation reports are:

1. Shamans.
2. People supposedly possessed by demonic spiritual entities.
3. Those subjected to poltergeist activity.
4. Spirit mediums (Spiritualism).
5. People who believe that they have been abducted by aliens (abductees).
6. Practitioners of Eastern martial arts traditions such as *qigong* (sometimes spelt *qigong*, *qi kung* or *ch'i kung*).
7. Mystics from all major religions.

I have referred to these people as belonging to particular 'groups', but this word is being used merely for convenience. By providing seemingly relevant details about the groups that traditionally produce levitation reports my research is meant to assist parapsychologists find someone who can levitate, and provide them with some helpful research hypotheses. In summary, the two main components of my levitation research project are:

1. A thematic comparison of historical and modern human levitation reports, and of the groups that have traditionally produced them, to see what physical,

cultural and phenomenological circumstances the levitators and their groups may have in common.

2. A hypothesis-generating exercise that seeks clues that might begin to explain what causes human levitation. This information may assist future researchers investigate the dynamics of levitation from a more empirical perspective.

I also conducted interviews with a selection of people from three of the seven groups, (1) Christian priests and pastors; (2) Spiritualists; and (3) *qigong* instructors, all of whom were asked whether they have experienced or witnessed levitation and what their opinions are about miraculous or psi events such as human levitation. Members of these so-called groups may vary significantly in their beliefs and behaviour. For example, while the Spiritualists whom I have interviewed mostly live in Western Australia, they come from a variety of Spiritualist churches, and some of the interviewed *qigong* instructors also teach yoga and other traditions. Information from some of these interviews has been used to enhance both the thematic comparison and the hypothesis-generation exercise. I have interviewed six people who claim to have levitated, and received email and phone reports from two others who claim to have levitated and from two who said they almost levitated while participating in the lifting game or Transcendental Meditation (TM). All of these people fit into one or more of the seven groups that traditionally produce levitation reports. Although few interviewees claim to have levitated or to have seen someone else do it, their beliefs are important because they represent the particular spiritual and cultural environment surrounding levitators or potential levitators within these groups.

It has not been possible to conduct interviews with representatives of all the groups that have traditionally produced levitation reports. Instead of interviewing samples of indigenous shamans and mystics from around the world, I have used levitation reports from anthropological, religious and paranormal literature. For ethical and availability reasons, I have been unable to interview people who are or have been spiritually possessed or have suffered from poltergeist activity. These people are rare indeed and may not be able to provide informed consent to be interviewed.

Thematic Comparison

The thematic comparison of the seven groups that have traditionally produced human levitation reports constitutes the main body of my thesis and is split into five thematic sections. Within those sections, I also quote numerous levitation reports and, as part of the hypothesis-generating exercise, discuss ideas that might reveal how human levitation works.

Spirits and Spirit Realms

The first thematic section demonstrates that, to varying degrees, most members of the seven groups believe that various types of spiritual entities exist, such as spirits of the dead, gods, demi-gods, angels, demons, or inter-dimensional beings. Sometimes—especially in *qigong*—spiritual powers are perceived not as personal entities, but as impersonal energies such as *chi* or *prana*. Some mystics claim that it is possible for the mind to create independent or semi-independent spiritual entities, such as Tibetan *tulpas* (David-Neel, 1965). Spirit realms are invisible to the normal person; they have no precise geographical location, but are generally claimed to interpenetrate physical reality in a multi-dimensional manner. All the groups attribute divine, magical, or psi abilities to spiritual entities or powers and treat them with great reverence or, in the case of demons, attempt to banish or avoid them.

Similarly, some abductees are fearful of aliens—whom they may regard as spiritual entities—although others welcome their attention. In all seven groups, the power of spiritual entities or energy is the most common explanation for spontaneous or involuntary human levitation, although some members claim that with sufficient meditative training one can learn to levitate voluntarily by accessing this power oneself without the assistance of spirits. Whether couched in personal (e.g., spirits) or impersonal (e.g., *chi*) terms, this first theme is the most popular way to explain how levitation works, and the subsequent four themes are dependent on the apparent existence of the psi powers that originate from these hypothesised spiritual realms. The primary question that this theme raises is whether there really exists an invisible, multi-dimensional realm that is somehow linked to consciousness and which contains discarnate entities and/or powers that at times facilitate psi events. It seems unlikely that all seven groups would invent a similar explanation for levitation if it was completely untrue. A second question is whether this explanation largely just replaces one mystery with another.

Spirit Possession

The second thematic comparison section discusses spirit possession. Many members of the seven groups engage in activities such as prayer, contemplation, meditation, or trances that they hope will bring them closer to spiritual beings or powers. This may be done to seek protection, spiritual guidance, clairvoyant information, contact with the dead, improved martial arts abilities, or psi results such as healing. To varying degrees these activities lead practitioners to claim that spiritual entities can intrude into or completely take over their consciousness, although many modern researchers believe that these are merely psychological disturbances.

In some, such as spirit mediums and shamans, this intrusion may be voluntary and temporary, but in spirit possession, poltergeist activity and some alien abductions it is involuntary and difficult to stop. Levitation and other psi events may occasionally occur during voluntary or involuntary spirit possession. As an extension of the first theme, the possession theme is believed to explain some levitations and suggests that consciousness interfaces with the hypothesised spirit realm, although claiming that spiritual entities cause levitation explains little about how levitation works.

Within most of the seven groups there is evidence that practitioners who are highly trained in their group's conceptual map of these realms are the least likely to become involuntarily possessed and the most likely to be able to levitate at will, which again suggests a link between consciousness and psi abilities.

Altered States of Consciousness and Breath Control

In the third thematic section it is claimed that everyone who levitates does so while in some form of altered state of consciousness (ASC), such as trance or religious ecstasy. ASCs may vary significantly among the groups; a mystic may sit impassively in deep meditation, whereas entranced shamans can display intense physical activity and psi abilities that are completely different from their normal behaviour.

Among those that employ the technique, breath control is frequently used to enter ASCs and is believed to assist in accessing universal or life energies, such as *prana* or *chi* which, like spirits, are claimed to facilitate psi abilities. Like the theme of spirit possession, this third theme of ASCs and breath control is linked to a belief in spirit realms because many group members believe that certain ASCs enable one to access these realms and the powers or entities they contain.

The ASC theme is only partially explanatory because, although almost all levitators enter ASCs, these states are not seen as the cause of levitation, but as a means of accessing its cause(s), which are believed to be spirits or spiritual energies. Because consciousness and ASCs are already the subject of several academic disciplines, from a scientific perspective this theme may perhaps be the most fruitful one from which to research levitation. Although they are uncertain about the reason, parapsychologists are aware of a correlation between ASCs and psi events (Radin, 1997, p. 105). Science has only a limited understanding of the nature of human consciousness. Nevertheless this theme, like the previous two, suggests a link between psi abilities such as levitation and what appear to be transpersonal dimensions of the mind.

Levitators' Other Paranormal Abilities

Within the seven groups there are a small number of people who seem to have a remarkable range of psi abilities in addition to the ability to levitate. These include healing, fire invulnerability, clairvoyance, teleportation, radiance, weather control and extrasensory interaction with animals. There are no psi abilities that are exclusive to any one of the groups. This seems to confirm that some aspect of the groups' members' behaviour triggers or enhances psi abilities and that these powers are not culturally dependent: they cross geographical and religious boundaries with ease, although useful abilities such as healing are more prevalent than less productive ones like levitation.

The young age at which some people develop psi abilities suggests that they may have a genetic component. Not all group members welcome all psi events; demonic spirit possession and poltergeist activity are certainly not sought after, although shamans and mediums often seek a variety of psi powers. There often seems to be a complex, human-like intelligence behind psi abilities, especially in cases of poltergeist activity, which appears to strengthen the suggestion of a link between these abilities and consciousness. This fourth theme is closely linked to the previous themes. Group members generally propose the same explanations for other psi abilities as they do for levitation and these abilities can overlap or occur simultaneously, which suggests that at some level they may be powered by the same energy. Learning how one psi ability works may therefore help explain some of the others.

Taboos and Obstacles

In the fifth thematic section, it is noted that most of the seven groups have either longstanding or more recent cultural taboos against developing and demonstrating psi abilities. There are also numerous practical difficulties that researchers need to overcome if they wish to investigate these abilities. These result largely from the fact that psi abilities are so often unpredictable, involuntary and supposedly caused by invisible entities. Most religions accept that some advanced mystics have healing or other psi abilities that they claim are divinely inspired but, with little justification, they tend to demonise reports of similar abilities from members of other groups.

This fifth theme is the most varied among the seven groups—for example Spiritualists may seek psi powers while mystics do not—and does not reveal very much about how levitation works. But most of the taboos against developing or displaying psi powers have a religious origin, which implies that in those circles it has long been known that activities such as meditation and ASCs will produce psi abilities in some practitioners that may subvert their spiritual progress or produce unfavourable publicity. This appears to strengthen both the probability that psi abilities such as levitation exist and that they are linked to consciousness. It also links the taboo theme to the previous four themes and suggests that there may be more people who can levitate voluntarily than the groups have traditionally acknowledged.

Almost Levitating

Additionally, seemingly related topics or groups might provide information for the hypothesis-generation exercise because they could be seen as either precursors to human levitation or they have produced a few levitation reports. These are *lung-gom*; hypnosis, mesmerism and animal magnetism; witchcraft; mass control and excessive gravitation; the lifting game; and Transcendental Meditation.

Alexandra David-Neel (1965) describes encountering a monk indulging in *lung-gom* in Tibet. As Blofeld (1974) writes, *lung-gom* "enables people in a state of trance to cover great distances at amazing speed leaping like a ball and negotiating obstacles with supernormal dexterity" (p. 223). It is interesting to note that *lung-gom* trainees have to spend many years meditating. There exist reports of shamans in other parts of the world, including Australia, doing 'fast walking' which resembles *lung-gom*.

A few references in the literature on mesmerism and animal magnetism (e.g., Leroy, 1928) claim that a small number of deeply entranced patients would spontaneously levitate.

There are also claims that some traditional witches confessed to being able to fly or levitate through the air. However, witches' confessions produced under torture cannot be relied upon, and the witchcraft literature is rather inconsistent. Nevertheless, witchcraft is at times supposedly linked to spirit possession and some of its activities derive from shamanism.

'Mass control' is a term that some researchers use to describe the anecdotal observations that, for example, some ballet dancers seem able to stay in the air slightly longer than gravity should allow. Nandor Fodor (1933/1966) writes that Vaslav Nijinsky possessed this ability.

'Excessive gravitation' refers to reports of a few spiritually possessed people who suddenly become very heavy or appear to be stuck to the ground. This ability is sought after by some martial arts practitioners, as well as the capacity to make themselves lighter. Is the cause of excessive gravitation just levitation in reverse or are the two unrelated?

The lifting game normally involves four standing people lifting a seated subject by putting both forefingers, or the first two fingers of one hand, under the subject's knees and armpits. There are claims that the lifted person often feels unusually light. Some researchers assert that breathing exercises produce the weight loss during the lifting game. The psychical researcher Dr Hereward Carrington conducted experiments where he put four lifters and a seated subject on a large weighing scale. The technique required the lifters to "bend forward several times in unison, inhaling and exhaling deeply together. The person seated in the chair also inhales and exhales at the same time. On the fifth count all five persons hold their breath" and the seated person is lifted (in Fodor, 1933/1966, p. 37). Although the combined weight of the lifters, chair and subject was 712 pounds (323 kg), on each of five successive lifts, a weight loss of between 50 and 60 pounds (23-27 kg) was recorded (p. 37). The weight loss "slowly returned to normal as the subject was held for some considerable time in the air" (in Fodor, 1933/1966, p. 37). Apart from the suggestion of mass control, no conventional scientific explanation has been proposed for the lifting game.

Because of the publicity it has received in previous years, a link between TM and levitation, or at least hopping while sitting cross-legged, exists in the minds of many Westerners. Although they have been largely secularised, most of the beliefs and practices of TM derive from Hindu and yogic traditions and are closely linked to the breathing exercises and mantra repetition of *pranayama*.

The *pranayama* tradition claims that advanced practitioners may start hopping or jumping about like a frog and some may eventually levitate. The TM organization has produced videotapes of its students hopping around with tremendous vitality, but they have not proved that any of them can genuinely levitate. Although there is no guarantee that all the activities described in the 'Almost Levitating' section are related to or are precursors to levitation, they may be worth investigating in case they are. For example, researching the lifting game, which uses normal people as sitters, would probably be much easier than finding a genuine levitator to study.

DISCUSSION

Although the thematic comparison cannot verify any particular levitation report, it appears to demonstrate that there are two main variable factors in levitation cases: (i) they are either voluntary or involuntary in nature, and (ii) the levitator either hovers in one place, or flies through the air. Joseph of Cupertino did both on different occasions. Some people from groups such as shamanism, *qigong* and mysticism, appear able to levitate at will, while people who are supposedly possessed by demonic entities, those affected by poltergeist activity and most alien abductees, appear to have no control over their levitations and are often thrown through the air. Some Spiritualists who levitate appear to have a slight amount of control while others have no control, whether they hover or fly a trajectory. People who are levitated by others generally hover. Another interesting feature involves demoniacs being involuntarily levitated upside down without their clothes (e.g., skirts) falling down.

Thematic comparison suggests that, from a future research perspective, the link between human levitation and ASCs is the most important similarity between the groups. Everyone who levitates appears to do so while in an ASC. Some may be in a deep trance while others may be in such a shallow trance that witnesses do not realise it. People who are levitated by others always seem to be in a trance. Further research into human consciousness and the ASCs that levitators experience seems to be an important pathway to investigate how levitation works. To varying degrees, all the groups believe that ASCs enable people to access spiritual realms containing entities and/or powers that can transcend the known laws of physics. This suggests that the empirical sciences need to continue the investigation into whether there is an unknown, transpersonal force that links some aspect of human consciousness and physical reality.

Several hypotheses have been generated from this research. These ideas are not formal scientific findings—they are merely suggestions or qualitative findings that may be of relevance to any subsequent parapsychological investigation of human levitation. The first point is that the consistency of worldwide human levitation reports over the centuries suggests that the phenomenon may be genuine. Minor differences in beliefs about the causes of levitation can be explained by varying cultural influences, but descriptions of the phenomenon and the circumstances under which it occurs appear to remain reasonably consistent.

It is unlikely that similar levitation reports are the product of mistaken observations because human levitation is so different from other physical activities. It is difficult to mistakenly observe a person hovering half a metre off the ground, which Leroy (1928, p. 180) claims is the height of the average levitation. Leroy (p. 184) also notes that most levitations last for several minutes and that Joseph of Cupertino and some others were reported to have remained in the air for over an hour. These heights and durations provide ample opportunity for witnesses to observe the phenomena. For example, Sister Anne testified that she observed Teresa of Avila levitate in religious ecstasy about 50 centimetres off the ground for half an hour and that she passed her hands under Teresa's feet (in Leroy, 1928, p. 72).

If all levitation reports are delusional, surely they would vary considerably more than they do and would not be as confined to members of the seven groups. Mental illness is not limited to these groups, so there would be people from all walks of life making delusional levitation claims, but I have not found any such reports. If the reports are produced by spiritual groups attempting to prove that their gods are more powerful, the levitation descriptions would, over the centuries, probably have become increasingly exaggerated, which is not the case. Despite the extraordinary nature of the phenomenon, the most likely explanation for the thematic consistency of the worldwide body of levitation reports is that genuine psi events are being described.

The dominant themes that distinguish the seven groups from the public at large are a belief in and an attempt to get to know, to interact with, to tap into, to merge, or resonate with unknown spiritual powers which some members personify and others do not. The most common way of doing this is by entering voluntary or involuntary ASCs, and almost all levitators do so while in these states. Given that parapsychologists accept that there is a correlation between ASCs and psi events, it seems probable that what distinguishes levitators from other members of their groups is a rare combination of three factors: (i) a belief in spiritual entities or powers; (ii) physical activities such as prayer, meditation, or séances; and (iii) certain ASCs.

There is a difference, however, between whatever might cause levitation and its actual mechanism. For example, if an entranced physical medium successfully requests to be levitated by a spirit, we can conclude that that behaviour caused the levitation, but, from an empirical perspective, it does not prove that spirits exist; it does not explain the force or energy that lifts the person into the air; and it does not eliminate the possibility that other levitations may occur under different circumstances. But, whatever the mechanism or force, the evidence suggests that it is reasonable to conclude that ASCs and communicating with or tapping into spiritual powers are activities that significantly increase the probability of levitation. Heath (2003, p. 21), too, concludes that "an altered state of consciousness (ASC) seems to be a helpful, and perhaps necessary, condition" for levitation. The capacity to enter certain ASCs, therefore, seems to be the most likely explanation for such a small percentage of the groups' members levitating, despite many of them having the same spiritual beliefs and regularly carrying out the same physical activities.

Each part of the hypothesis-generation sections seems to point towards an open model of the human mind that asserts that consciousness is somehow capable of transcending the biological brain. Mainstream science largely adopts the theory of materialistic monism, which claims that "matter causes mind, that the mind is essentially a function of the activity of matter in the brain. The basic stuff of the universe is matter and energy" (Radin, 1997, p. 255). But this limited model can only be accepted if numerous psi anomalies are ignored or rejected. The beliefs of the seven groups examined would make more sense, and psi phenomena would be more easily explained, if an open model of the mind were correct, but at this stage the theory has not been verified conclusively despite having been in existence for several thousand years.

In general terms the groups' beliefs and their anecdotal psi reports postulate the existence of a multi-dimensional realm or field that interfaces or interpenetrates our physical universe. The hypothesised qualities of this realm are that it stores information in a non-local manner, and appears capable of controlling or overriding what physicists claim are the four basic forces of nature. The human brain is believed to be an interface device between this realm of transpersonal consciousness and physical reality. The realm seems accessible only by using certain ASCs. Because of their lack of appropriate training, and possibly their genetic inheritance, most people, therefore, do not seem to have voluntary or conscious access to this realm.

As the thematic comparison reveals, the activities and beliefs of all seven groups contain elements of mysticism, which can be seen as the art of attempting to transcend these barriers. The belief that certain people can transcend the physical body to access this realm assumes that humans have what religions call a soul or spirit but, as Braude (2003, p. 292) asks, what is the nature of the 'stuff' that survives death? This research cannot answer that question, but if this realm is able to sustain clairvoyant information, spirits, Taoist immortals, *tulpas* and other seemingly intelligent entities, then it would surely need to be composed of a substance that has highly sophisticated information storage and processing capacities, to use computing terminology. In addition, if this realm can facilitate human levitation and other PK phenomena, it would need to contain large amounts of energy as well as being connected to human consciousness.

In my research, I interviewed eleven people who were Spiritualists, ten Christian priests and pastors, and nine *qigong* instructors. Six actually claimed to have levitated, but all six said it was spontaneous and involuntary, so they were unable to provide a demonstration. The Spiritualists produced three levitators and three levitation witnesses; one of the Catholic pastors claims to have levitated; and two of the *qigong* instructors have witnessed someone levitate. In addition, I interviewed an abductee who claims to have levitated, and a woman who says she levitated twice during yoga classes while doing breathing exercises. This suggests that human levitation is more common than parapsychologists appear to believe.

Levitation probably occurs most often among Spiritualists because they deliberately attempt to interact with spiritual forces and entities, and normally welcome psi phenomena as confirmation of their belief in an afterlife. All my interviewees come from Perth, Western Australia, which has a population of nearly one and a half million, only a small percentage of whom are priests, pastors, Spiritualists, or *qigong* teachers. This suggests that worldwide there may be many people who have either levitated or seen someone do it, but whose experiences have not been publicised or researched. Spiritualism may thus be the best field for future levitation researchers to investigate.

» References

Blofeld, J. (1974). *The tantric mysticism of Tibet.* New York: Causeway.

Braude, S. E. (2003). *Immortal remains: The evidence for life after death.* Lanham, MD: Rowman & Littlefield.

David-Neel, A. (1965). *Magic and mystery in Tibet*. New York: University Books.

Fodor, N. (1933/1966). *Encyclopaedia of psychic science*. New York: University Books.

Heath, P. R. (2003). *The PK zone: A cross-cultural review of psychokinesis (PK)*. New York: iUniverse, Inc.

Irwin, H. J. (2004). *An introduction to parapsychology* (4th ed.). Jefferson, NC: McFarland.

Leroy, O. (1928). *Levitation*. London: Burns Oates & Washbourne.

Radin, D. (1997). *The conscious universe*. New York: HarperEdge.

Richards, S. (1980). *Levitation*. London: The Aquarian Press.

Chapter 5

A Discussion of the Evidence that Personal Consciousness Persists After Death with Special Reference to Poltergeist Phenomena[1]

William Roll

Following the lead of Frederic Myers (1903), the possibility of survival has been discussed in terms of the survival of *personality*, but with little attention to the organ where the idea of personality originates. Studies of the brain reveal that humans possess two very different personalities: the personality of the left-brain hemisphere and the personality of the right-brain hemisphere. Physiologically and psychologically each of us has a split personality. In the healthy individual the two sides of the brain work together. In the simple act of walking, now it is the right hemisphere and the left leg, then the left hemisphere and the right leg. Similarly the right hemisphere is in charge of the left arm and hand, and the reverse for the left hemisphere. Our eyes and ears also come in pairs, each primarily controlled by the opposite hemisphere.

1. [This chapter was originally published in *Australian Journal of Parapsychology* (2006, vol. 6[1], pp. 5-20). Permission to reprint has been granted by the journal.—Editors.]

The two hemispheres are bridged by the corpus callosum, a large bundle of neurons. If it were not for this bridge, the left hand would not know what the right hand is doing. For a person whose corpus callosum has been cut, usually to relieve epileptic symptoms, neither side of the body knows about the other.

Poltergeist Phenomena

Poltergeist phenomena (e.g., Roll, 2004a; Roll & Storey, 2004) mainly consist of the movement of household objects and pieces of furniture and of loud percussive sounds. The occurrences have been questioned because as a rule they are only investigated after they have taken place, which may leave room for fraud. But in two of our cases (Roll, 2004a, ch. 10; Roll & Storey, 2004, ch. 17), we set up experiments and observed the incidents when fraud and other familiar causes could be ruled out. In fact, RSPK tests are not rare: In a survey (Roll, 1977) of 116 cases from the professional literature, 48 investigators performed minor tests of which 46 succeeded. For instance, the observer would throw an object somewhere, hoping that it would be thrown back, which then occurred.

Poltergeist is German for rowdy ghost, but most researchers are convinced that the incidents are due to psychokinesis by the living people who are at the centre of the turmoil. This view has been questioned by well-known investigators, Ian Stevenson (1972), and Alan Gauld and Tony Cornell (1979). Both parties believe that some cases may be due to discarnate entities. The term RSPK, for recurrent spontaneous psychokinesis, which is commonly used, allows for either interpretation.

Stevenson (1972) lists several features that he believes may indicate discarnate agency. He expects heavy objects to be affected, over great distances and in complicated trajectories. He expects little breakage, but that objects will be deposited gently as if carried. Moreover, the occurrences will express the purpose and intelligence of the departed, for instance, by injuring or inconveniencing a living person or persons. There may be intelligible communication by raps, collectively seen apparitions, and auditory communication from ostensibly discarnate entities. The living person at the center may enter a mediumistic trance and be of any age. Finally, the phenomena may abate after exorcism.

Conversely, Stevenson predicts that cases, which are due to PK from living agents, will tend to involve light objects, travelling short and simple trajectories, with forceful landings and much breakage. There would be no communication by raps, no collectively seen apparitions, no auditory communications, and no mediumistic trance for the subject. The phenomena would mainly serve to release psychological tension, would occur around someone below 20 years of age and may cease with psychotherapy.

While some RSPK is *prima facie* suggestive of spirits, insofar as apparitions are seen or raps spell out intelligible messages, the other characteristics mentioned by Stevenson do not suggest spirit involvement. The more violent cases and those where heavy pieces of furniture are moved about, as seen near 12-year-old Roger Callihan (Roll, 2004a, ch.11) and 14-year-old Tina Resch (Roll & Storey, 2004, ch. 6), showed no evidence of spirits. Objects that moved around corners were frequently reported near Tina.

Gauld and Cornell (1979) debate another feature of Stevenson's distinction:

> The totally blind and purposeless poltergeist is perhaps a rarity even among obvious 'living agent' cases... There is...a good deal of evidence that living agents can produce not just mere whirlwind-like explosions of energy around them, but, for example, communicative rappings through which pseudo-personalities manifest themselves. (pp. 351-352)

Gauld and Cornell propose a modified version of Stevenson's spirit hypothesis:

> If there are indeed both living agent cases and discarnate agent cases we should surely expect, not the absence of intelligence and purpose in the former, but different kinds of purposes and different degrees of intelligence in the two sorts of case. (p. 351)

They advance four criteria (p. 355) for discarnate agency:

> 1. The phenomena are wholly or partially independent of the presence of any living person. This condition would obtain if the incidents...linger on for some while after his departure, occur in his absence, occur inside a locked empty room away from him, and so on. A particularly curious form of the latter is when 'arrangements' of objects into patterns are made inside empty rooms or in empty houses.... It is as though some intelligent entity is present which can store and make use of some form of energy even in the absence of those who may have generated it. (p. 353)

I do not think that momentary independence of the phenomena from the living agent suggests a discarnate one. The focusing effect found in most cases, where the same object or area is affected when the agent is absent, may indicate that the agent transmitted energy to the object or area when he or she was near which was then released as object movement when the person was away. I now turn to Gauld and Cornell's three other criteria for discarnate agency:

> 2. The purposes exhibited by the phenomena appear quite alien to the known aims and purposes of the poltergeist agent, or, in the absence of an obvious agent, of any other person in the household. (Gauld & Cornell, 1979, p. 354)

All cases I have investigated at first sight seemed foreign to the motives of the central person as these were known at the time. But in all our five cases (Roll, 2004a, ch. 4, 6, 13 & 14; Roll & Storey, 2004, ch. 20) where psychological or psychiatric examinations were made, the agents showed signs of anger, usually repressed, in relation to parents or the parental figures on whom they depended. The parent figures seemed harsh or uncaring for their charges, usually children in their teens, an age that in any case may be emotionally unstable. It should be emphasized that the anger was not general but directed only at parent figures.

The anger theory does not apply to all occurrences in a case. While anger may ignite RSPK, once underway the phenomena may be elicited by visitors who are solicitous to the agent. Positive attention no less than the negative sort may facilitate RSPK. When the visitors are scientists, they may be rewarded with occurrences that take place when the agent is under full observation (Roll, 2004a, ch.10 & 11; Roll & Storey, 2004, ch.18).

I discuss Gauld and Cornell's (1979) two last points together:

> 3. On more than one occasion several witnesses simultaneously see, or failing that, a series of separate witnesses not knowing of each other's experiences see the same phantasmal figure or figures, or similar misty shapes, etc., in association with, or better still actually bringing about, certain of the phenomena. (pp. 354-355)

> 4. Phenomena take place which…so far as is known exceed the capacities of any living agent, however powerful his repressed emotions and however saturated he may be with 'psychic force' or 'RSPK energy'…. Perhaps certain forms of 'apport' phenomena belong here, e.g., the ostensible 'eating' of fruit by invisible beings in the Poona [case], or cases in which objects have

> 'materialized' in mid-air or in which 'direct voices' have spoken fluently or direct writing been received, or in which objects have become 'animated' in characteristic ways. (p. 355)

Gauld and Cornell support their position with two remarkable cases from Sandfeldt and Poona. Sandfeldt is a village in Germany that was the scene of a violent RSPK outbreak in 1722. Poona is a town in India that was the scene of RSPK in 1920 and 1923-1930. In Sandfeldt the five children of a farming family were closely involved, one perhaps being the RSPK agent. The Poona phenomena first centered on one boy and then on his younger brother. In Sandfeldt as well as Poona, the supposed spirits exhibited intelligence and also responded appropriately to the people who were present. Sometimes apport-type incidents took place that suggested intelligence. For instance, in Poona, the shoe polish belonging to the boy's home teacher had disappeared when she needed it. She asked that it be returned and it at once landed at her feet (Gauld & Cornell, 1979, p. 109).

The children in both cases described apparitions. In Sandfeldt the children said they saw ghostly animals and an apparition of a child or angel causing some of the incidents. In Poona the boy reported seeing his deceased brother, nurse and father, identifying who was responsible for which incidents.

The Sandfeldt farm was the scene of peculiar "arrangements" in empty rooms. At one time a servant of the man, who was investigating the phenomena on behalf of the owner, was in the kitchen with the children when they heard noises from the empty living room. When he looked in:

> To his astonishment he found that objects in the room were gradually being arranged into a little scenario. Each time he looked, more objects had been added.... A cloth was spread on the floor, and on it were laid numerous dishes and various kinds of foodstuffs. The figures of two picnickers were made out of clothes ingeniously put together. (Gauld & Cornell, 1979, p. 110)

The two cases differ along cultural lines. The Sandfeldt incidents may have been shaped by German folk tales, and the Poona occurrences may have reflected Indian beliefs.

You have to agree with Gauld and Cornell (1979) that simple RSPK energy is insufficient to account for cases like these. Nevertheless there were physical occurrences, which means that energy was expended. The question is, 'By whom?' Gauld and Cornell suggest that the intelligence belonged to discarnate entities

(p. 359). This proposal comes with a disclaimer, "we are not attempting to decide whether or not the supposed discarnate entities are to be identified with surviving portions of formerly incarnate human beings" (p. 360). Without explicitly saying so, Gauld and Cornell seem to leave open the possibility that the agents produced person-like entities, which in turn performed the phenomena. None of my cases are as complex as Sandfeldt and Poona, but stories from Tibet, if they can be believed, tell of human-like figures created to perform various tasks.

Stevenson (1972) suggests that if RSPK could be terminated by exorcism, this would suggest spirit agency. The phenomena around one of the boys in Poona ceased after religious intercession. However, this was conducted after more than two months of activity when the phenomena in any case may have died down. In my survey of RSPK (Roll, 1977), the median duration was two months.

Exorcism was attempted in 30 cases. The phenomena ceased in four cases, but continued in 21 cases, sometimes intensifying during the religious intervention. It is uncertain if the four cases that ceased did so because of the ritual; in two of the four, the phenomena had gone on for two and three months so the RSPK may already have run its course; in the two others the duration of RSPK was not reported. In the Tina Resch case (Roll & Storey, 2004, ch. 6), which came after the survey, there were two attempts at exorcism. One was by the family's Lutheran minister, the other was by a Mormon elder brought in by one of their sons. During each exorcism, the couch on which the clergyman was seated scooted out from the wall. The Lutheran gave up when this happened, but the Mormon, being more persistent, repeated the ceremony when the same thing happened and he too gave up. I thought that the exhibit of strong RSPK during the exorcisms was due to the added mental stress on the girl because of the implication that she was possessed.

While exorcism seems to be ineffective, other courses of action may reduce or terminate the phenomena. In several cases in the survey, the incidents stopped after the family dismissed the servant or employee who was the center of activity or, if a member of the family, after he or she was sent away to stay with relatives. Occasionally the whole family moved; at times the phenomena continued in the new location, but sometimes they ceased.

To determine whether a move actually tended to shorten RSPK, I examined the duration of the cases in relation to moves. In 31 cases where the ostensible agent or someone else moved and where duration was recorded, the median duration was 1.13 months, versus 2 months for all the cases, and the averages were 52.4 versus 115.6 days. The difference was significant ($p < .05$, one-tailed), and may suggest that the moves tended to shorten duration.

As shown by psychological tests, tense family relations may contribute to RSPK. A move by the central person or by other members of the household changes the social situation and may thereby attenuate tension and thereby RSPK. In summary, there is little evidence that RSPK is due to spirits other than the corporeal spirit of the RSPK agent.

The Psychic Brain

Frederic Myers (1903, vol. I) identified psychic functions with the subliminal mind. In contrast, the supraliminal mind guides ordinary perception and behavior. He spoke of a "subliminal uprush" as "an emergence into waking consciousness of ideas matured below the threshold" (p. 20). The sudden manifestation of the subliminal mind in supraliminal awareness includes creativity, telepathy, telestaesia (clairvoyance), and telekinesis (PK). It can now be seen that the subliminal mind is essentially the same as the mind of the right hemisphere, and that the supraliminal mind is the mind of the left hemisphere.

Myers (1885), as Broughton (1984) has noted, in fact saw a role for the right hemisphere in psychic functions and was the first to do so. Myers noticed that the automatic writing of trance mediums, which often showed psychic awareness, was characterized by word blindness, repetitiveness, and swearing, tendencies typical of people who had lost the use of their left hemisphere and were now relying on the right.

There is experimental evidence that ESP may be a function of the right brain. Braud and Braud (1975) found an advantage of borderline significance in free-response ESP trials after the subjects had listened to a tape intended to elicit right hemispheric mentation as compared to trials following a left mentation tape. They called the right hemisphere, "the psi conducive syndrome" (p. 17).

In a study designed to determine if the left hemisphere interferes with ESP, Broughton (1976) compared conditions where the subjects were occupied with reading, a left hemispheric activity that may distract this hemisphere from blocking ESP, with trials without reading. The tests also addressed the laterality issue by having the subjects record their responses with either the left or right hand. There were tendencies for higher ESP scores when the left hemisphere was occupied with reading, and for greater divergence from chance when the left hand was used. After publication of his results, Broughton (1978) learned about the discovery that hemispheric differences are less pronounced for females than for males, which has been attributed to the fact that the corpus callosum has more connections in the female brain. A re-examination of his data showed that the interference effect was in fact only present for the male subjects. However, the interference effect and the sex difference did not show up in two later studies (Broughton, 1978).

Broughton (1977) pointed to the proclivity for ESP to take the form of visual images as indicating right hemispheric mentation. He referred to White (1964) who had found that most of the psychics in her survey relied on visual images, and Kelly, Kanthamani, Child, & Young (1975) who had observed that the ESP responses to cards by the psychic, Bill Delmore, were encoded in the form of 'fleeting visual images'.

Broughton (1976, 1977, 1978) also noted that dreaming, which seems conducive to ESP, may be a function of the right hemisphere. He mentioned findings by Johnson (1968) and Honorton (1972) that people with frequent dream recall may have an ESP advantage over those who only occasionally remember their dreams. The indications that visual images, and therefore the right hemisphere, may be important for ESP is suggested also by the relative ease of obtaining experimental evidence of ESP in dreams (Van de Castle, 1977), in the ganzfeld (Honorton, 1977; Honorton & Harper, 1974), and in remote perception (Jahn & Dunne, 1987, pp. 151-173).

Ehrenwald (1979) noted that the drawings of patients with injuries to their left parieto-occipital region, including one of his own patients, were strikingly similar to drawings from telepathy experiments. He wrote:

> The world of the patient suffering from optical agnosia closely resembles the telepathic or clairvoyant percipient's impression of his target—psi phenomena, lacking as they do, the precise spatio-temporal ordering and organizing qualities of the dominant hemisphere, are processed in the right side of the brain. (p. 221)

He applied the same reasoning to PK, the motor counterpart of ESP. Ehrenwald (1979) had seen films of Nina Kulagina and other subjects performing macro-PK and was struck by the similarity of their efforts to the attempts by paralysed patients to move an affected limb:

> Here, too, it appears that the PK subject is lacking the fine-tuned motor controls provided by the left hemisphere, to say nothing of the modulating effects of the cerebellum and its corticothalamic and subcortical feedback loops. (p. 221)

In contrast to this work, Maher (1986) did a study, which suggests that ESP may utilise either hemisphere depending on the task at hand. Her test focused on the apparent tendency for the right hemisphere to process emotional stimuli by presenting two types of tapes to the subjects under sensory and ESP conditions, a video tape designed to elicit emotion and a tape showing architectural views which presumably generated little emotion. The tapes were displayed repeatedly and in random order. Since the abundance of alpha in one hemisphere as compared to the other is negatively related to that hemisphere's engagement in the task (less alpha; more task involvement), EEG recordings were used to determine which hemisphere was predominantly occupied with the task in question. For the subjects who showed the most evidence of ESP, their alpha activity under sensory and ESP conditions was significantly correlated in the predicted direction. In other words, the subjects seemed to process sensory and ESP stimuli the same way, whether by the right or left hemisphere as determined by the nature of the material (see also Maher & Schmeidler, 1977; Maher, Peratsakin, & Schmeidler, 1979). Except for Maher's work, the findings point to the right hemisphere as the hemisphere primarily responsible for ESP and PK.

If the right hemisphere is the psi-sensitive hemisphere, then conditions that facilitate right hemispheric dominance should increase the probability of ESP. The most conspicuous periods of right hemispheric dominance occur during REM dreams, and natural ESP is found most frequently in dreams. It may also be pointed out that the phenomenological themes of dreams, which emphasise displacement of the dreamer in space and time, the sense of a presence (the other or the stranger), and feelings of anxiety, reflect the functional characteristics of the right hemisphere. Conditions that facilitate right hemispheric dominance during waking, should also increase the likelihood of detecting ESP stimuli. These conditions, which would be associated with periods of relaxation, absence of thinking, and other indications of disengaged left hemispheric functioning, including linguistic processing, have been associated with ESP of emotionally important events occurring to significant others.

Since ESP does not depend on the familiar senses, such as vision and hearing, it also does not result in a characteristic sensory experience. Vision results in visual images, hearing in auditory experiences, and so on for the other senses. But ESP has no experience to call its own. When ESP appears in consciousness, it comes in borrowed garb. The brain has a storehouse of used apparel in the hippocampus where ESP chooses whatever fits the occasion. When the ESP target is a visual scene, the response may be a visual image or it may be an auditory impression. Or ESP may take the form of a string of words or guesses. ESP is multi-modal.

But there is little doubt that the evidence for ESP is best when it takes the form of visual images. 'A picture is worth a thousand words,' an additional factor that places ESP in the right hemisphere under most circumstances.

Evidence for Survival from Mediums and Rebirth Subjects

Several assumptions about personality have guided survival research: (1) Personality is inviolable and impenetrable; (2) it is non-biological and may survive bodily death; and (3) it is the seat of consciousness. Evidence for the existence of personality after death would therefore be evidence for the survival of the person's consciousness. Each of these assumptions needs to be examined.

1. Personality is Inviolable and Impenetrable

Stevenson (1977) argued eloquently against the assumption that personality is an entity separate from others: "Once considered about as well defined as an orange by its peel, human personalities now appear to be much more extensible and penetrable than they were thought to be" (p. 166). He referred to two types of evidence for this, the evidence for ESP and the evidence for survival after death. With respect to ESP, in telepathy images or thoughts from one personality, as it were, penetrates another personality, and in clairvoyance, personality extends to a remote physical object. In precognition and retrocognition, personality also extends in time. As we have noted, these observations are consistent with the view that ESP is a function of the right brain hemisphere.

Apparent mediumistic communications and rebirth memories also indicate that personality is extensible and penetrable, now from the body of a deceased person to the body of a living person. The medium momentarily seems to absorb the personality of a departed individual while the rebirth subject does the same but permanently.

When the argument that personality is extended and penetrable is applied to the evidence for survival after death, it turns out to be a two-edged sword. One edge undercuts the argument that personality is necessarily restricted to one body; the other edge turns out to be Occam's razor. Occam's razor is the scientific principle which requires that explanations of unknown phenomena first be sought in terms of known phenomena. Occam's razor shaves theories to bare essentials.

Skeptics who seek to explain ESP in terms of sensory cues, chance coincidence, or other familiar processes attempt to use Occam's razor, but in this case the razor does not cut. ESP requires more than sensory cues, chance and the like to be understood.

Occam's razor is more effective when it comes to the evidence for the survival of personality after death. In this context, the known phenomenon is the fact that people may use ESP to access physical objects (clairvoyance) or the minds of the living (telepathy); the unknown phenomenon is survival after death.

If we are to conclude that a medium or a rebirth subject incorporates the personality of someone deceased, we have to be certain that the information about the deceased could not have been derived by ESP from the minds of living survivors or from physical sources, such as obituaries. This has not been done.

On the contrary, an examination (Roll, 1982) of the evidence for survival shows that the data exhibit the same features as this-world ESP. For instance, a child who seems to remember a previous life, as a rule recalls a life that ended by accidents or violence and not from natural causes. Similarly, spontaneous ESP is often about a crisis befalling a remote person though the crisis does not necessarily end in death. However, were new discoveries to be made about data suggestive of survival that are different from what is known about ESP, unaided ESP would not cover the evidence; it would no longer be the simpler theory.

The theory that ESP may explain the evidence for survival is sometimes called the super-ESP or super-psi theory, but there is nothing super about the idea—it is common scientific sense.

2. Personality May Survive Bodily Death

This statement represents the core of the survival hypothesis as it is most frequently expressed and investigated. Among the various aspects of personality, the search for surviving memories has played a central role in determining whether deceased personalities continue after death. Stevenson's (1977) paper is a vivid account of the important role memory plays in establishing evidence for identity in studies of mediumistic communication and reincarnation. He leaves open the question where memories may exist: "Memories may exist in the brain and also in a 'somewhere else' that may endure after physical death" (p. 153).

The possibility that memories can be transferred by means other than learning, and may exist in places other than central nervous systems, has emerged in the biological sciences. We have been told that memory in planaria have been transferred to other planaria by cannibalism (Hartry & Keith-Lee, 1964) and that learning in rats to fear the dark has been transferred by injecting peptides from one animal to another (Ungar, Desiderio, & Parr, 1972).

The apparent connection between matter and memory has a parapsychological parallel in psychometry (not to be confused with the usage of this term as mental measurement). In psychometry, the subject apparently gains information about a past event by handling an object that was part of the event. Important studies of psychometry have been made by Barrington (2005), Osty (1923; Roll, 2005), Pagenstecher (1922), and Sidgwick (1915; Roll, 2004b). This type of ESP has also come up in card experiments (Roll, 1966; Ryzl, 1982).

According to Hans Driesch (1933), psychometry is evidence that physical objects other than brains can hold memories. Driesch was a German embryologist and President of the Society for Psychical Research. The possible relationship between physical objects and memory has often come up in survival studies. Mrs. Piper frequently obtained information about deceased persons by contact with their personal belongings although the objects provided no sensory information (James, 1909; Sidgwick, 1915). In the studies of 'drop in' communicators by Gauld (1972), the unexpected visitors usually had a geographic connection to the experimenters (Roll, 1982, pp. 178-180). This may also be a feature of Stevenson's reincarnation cases—the memories of the deceased sometimes reappeared in a child in the geographic or social surrounding of the departed (Roll, 1982, pp. 197-201; Stevenson, 1974). Memories are connected to the brains of their owners before death and may be connected to other physical objects after death.

3. Personality is the Seat of Consciousness

Nearly all research on survival assumes that if there is evidence after a person has died of the continued existence of the person's memories, this means that the consciousness of the person also continued. We know from ordinary living that complex tasks, such as driving a car may be performed while we think about other matters. In psychometry, memories even operate at a distance in time and space from their owner without awareness by this person that his/her memories may now be recalled by others. A similar process seems to have been at work in mediumistic communications where messages with veridical information were received from people who turned out to be neither dead nor evidently trying to communicate. Stevenson (1977) refers to a case from World War I, when L. P. Jacks, Principal of Manchester College, Oxford, had an anonymous session with the medium,

Mrs. Leonard during which Jacks' son, who was at the front, apparently came to bring news of his death to his father. The medium gave an accurate description of the young man, and of the supposed circumstances of his death, as well as family names and initials. He then departed and the medium commented that he "was glad to come. He's alright, he says, getting on splendidly" (Salter, 1922, p. 143). As it turned out, this was also true not for the man's life in the next world but in this: The young man had not died. There are several such cases in the literature, such as the famous Gordon Davis communication (Soal, 1925), which involved another medium and investigator, and another young soldier who was feared dead.

The word personality comes from the Latin term, *persona*, meaning actor's mask. The mediumistic material is a lively reminder of the origin of the word and of the dramas, which can be produced by the familiar as well as the psychic reach of humans, but the dramas are mute as to whether there is consciousness behind the masks. Studies of persons who have experienced altered states of consciousness, such as terminal cancer patients undergoing LSD-supported therapy, suggest that there may be an inverse relation between vividness and 'expansion' of consciousness on the one hand, and identification with the patient's memories and personality characteristics, on the other (Grof, 1972). The latter do not necessarily disappear, but may be experienced as part of a larger matrix, which includes other people and places. Experiences of individuals who have been declared clinically dead and are then resuscitated are sometimes of this type (Moody, 1975; Osis, 1961). Occasionally there is evidence for ESP. For instance, the patient may report a conversation from a part of the hospital that is beyond their sensory range.

The possibility has come up from studies of psychometry that something like memories may persist in physical objects other than the brains where they were formed. Like brain memories, psychometric memories are often about recent, frequent and emotionally significant events.

Haunting apparitions, including bystander cases, where the apparition is seen near a person who knew the departed, as well as the more familiar apparitions seen in the homes of the departed, suggest that memory-like structures may persist after death, but not necessarily that the memories are animated by the consciousness that formed them.

CONCLUSION

The findings we have examined may be important not for what they show about life after death but for what they show about the world of the living. The world, it seems, is permeated by the memories of the departed and also by the memories of the living. If such memories may be remembered or perceived in ESP, this may suggest that they have an energetic charge that may affect people also in unknown ways. Our lives may have causal effects not only in familiar physical and social fashions, but also because they may affect others who enter our places or come in contact with our objects. Similarly, our lives may be impacted by those who have gone before. These possibilities lend credence to the idea of karma—that is, to the idea that our actions may affect others long after the actions and their physical aftermath have run their course. Memories may be infectious.

» References

Barrington, M. R. (2005). *The clairvoyance of Stefan Ossowiecki.* Jefferson, NC: McFarland.

Braud, W. G., & Braud, L. W. (1975). The psi conducive syndrome: Free response GESP performance following evocation of "left-hemispheric" vs. "right-hemispheric" functioning. In J. D. Morris, W. G. Roll, & R. L. Morris (Eds.), *Research in Parapsychology 1974* (pp. 17-20). Metuchen, NJ: Scarecrow.

Broughton, R. S. (1976). Possible brain laterality effects on ESP performance. *Journal of the Society for Psychical Research, 48,* 384-399.

Broughton, R. S. (1977). Brain hemisphere specialization and ESP: What have we learned? *Proceedings of the 26th Annual Convention of the Parapsychological Association,* 373-384.

Broughton, R. S. (1978). *Brain hemisphere differences in paranormal abilities: With special reference to the influence of experimenter expectancies.* PhD thesis, University of Edinburgh.

Broughton, R. S. (1984). Brain hemisphere specialization and ESP: What have we learned? In R. White & R. S. Broughton (Eds.), *Research in Parapsychology 1983* (pp. 2-3). Metuchen, NJ: Scarecrow.

Driesch, H. (1933). *Psychical research.* London: G. Bell and Sons.

Ehrenwald, J. (1979). The right hemisphere: Pathway to psi and creativity. In B. Shapin & L. Coly (Eds.), *Mind/brain and parapsychology* (pp. 221-232). New York: Parapsychology Foundation.

Gauld, A. (1972). A series of "drop in" communicators. *Proceedings of the Society for Psychical Research, 55*, 273-340.

Gauld, A., & Cornell, A. D. (1979). *Poltergeists.* Boston, MA: Routledge & Kegan Paul.

Grof, S. (1972). Varieties of transpersonal experiences: Observations from LSD psychotherapy. *Journal of Transpersonal Psychology, 4*, 45-80.

Hartry, A. L., & Keith-Lee, P. (1964). Planaria: Memory transfer through cannibalism reexamined. *Science, 146*, 274-275.

Honorton, C. (1972). Reported frequency of dream recall and ESP. *Journal of the American Society for Psychical Research, 66,* 369-374.

Honorton, C. (1977). Psi and internal attention states. In B. B. Wolman (Ed.), *Handbook of parapsychology* (pp. 435-472). New York: Van Nostrand Reinhold.

Honorton, C., & Harper, S. (1974). Psi-mediated imagery and ideation in an experimental procedure for regulating perceptual output. *Journal of the American Society for Psychical Research, 68*, 156-168.

Jahn, R. G., & Dunne, B. J. (1987). *Margins of reality.* New York: Harcourt Brace Jovanovich.

James, W. (1909). Report on Mrs. Piper's Hodgson-control. *Proceedings of the Society for Psychical Research, 23,* 1-121.

Johnson, M. (1968). Relationship between dream recall and scoring direction. *Journal of Parapsychology, 32*, 56-57.

Kelly, E. F., Kanthamani, H., Child, I. L., & Young, F. W. (1975). On the relation between visual and ESP confusion structures in an exceptional ESP subject. *Journal of the American Society for Psychical Research, 69*, 1-31.

Maher, M. (1986). Correlated hemispheric asymmetry in the sensory and ESP processing of 'emotional' and 'nonemotional' stimuli. *European Journal of Parapsychology, 6*, 217-257.

Maher, M., Peratsakin, D., & Schmeidler, G. R. (1979). Cerebral lateralization effects in ESP processing: An attempted replication. *Journal of the American Society for Psychical Research, 73*, 167-177.

Maher, M., & Schmeidler, G. R. (1977). Cerebral lateralization effects in ESP processing. *Journal of the American Society for Psychical Research, 71*, 261-271.

Moody, R. L. (1975). *Life after life.* Atlanta, GA: Mockingbird Press.

Myers, F. W. H. (1885). Automatic writing. *Proceedings of the Society for Psychical Research, 8*, 1-63.

Myers, F. W. H. (1903). *Human personality and its survival of bodily death* (two volumes). London: Longmans, Green.

Osis, K. (1961). *Deathbed observations by physicians and nurses*. New York: Parapsychology Foundation.

Osty, E. (1923). *Supernormal faculties in man*. London: Methuen.

Pagenstecher, G. (1922). Past events seership: A study in psychometry. *Proceedings of the American Society for Psychical Research, 16*, 1-136.

Roll, W. G. (1966). Token object matching tests: A third series. *Journal of the American Society for Psychical Research, 60*, 363-379.

Roll, W. G. (1977). Poltergeists. In B. B. Wolman (Ed.), *Handbook of parapsychology* (pp. 382-413). New York: Van Nostrand Reinhold.

Roll, W. G. (1982). The changing perspective on life after death. In S. Krippner (Ed.), *Advances in parapsychological research 3* (pp. 147-291). New York: Plenum.

Roll, W. G. (2004a). *The poltergeist*. New York: Paraview.

Roll, W. G. (2004b). Early studies on psychometry. *Journal of Scientific Exploration, 18*, 711-720.

Roll, W. G. (2005). Review of *Supernormal Faculties in Man*, by Eugene Osty. *Journal of Scientific Exploration, 19*, 615-624.

Roll, W. G., & Storey, V. (2004). *Unleashed of poltergeists and murder: The curious story of Tina Resch*. New York: Paraview.

Ryzl, M. (1982). Mental imprints: An overlooked breakthrough in parapsychology? *Psi Research, 1*, 14-26.

Salter, W. H. (1922). A further report on sittings with Mrs. Leonard. *Proceedings of the Society for Psychical Research, 32*, 1-143.

Sidgwick, H. (1915). A contribution to the study of the psychology of Mrs. Piper's trance phenomena. *Proceedings of the Society for Psychical Research, 28*, 1-657.

Soal, S. G. (1925). A report on some communications received through Mrs. Blanche Cooper. *Proceedings of the Society for Psychical Research, 35*, 471-594.

Stevenson, I. (1972). Are poltergeists living or are they dead? *Journal of the American Society for Psychical Research, 66*, 233-252.

Stevenson, I. (1974). *Twenty cases suggestive of reincarnation* (2nd ed.). Charlottesville, VA: University Press of Virginia.

Stevenson, I. (1977). The evidence of man's survival after death. *Journal of Nervous and Mental Disease, 165*, 152-170.

Ungar, G., Desiderio, D. M., & Parr, W. (1972). Isolation, identification and synthesis of a specific-behaviour-inducing brain peptide. *Nature*, *238*, July 28.

Van de Castle, R. L. (1977). Sleep and dreams. In B. B. Wolman (Ed.), *Handbook of parapsychology* (pp. 473-499). New York: Van Nostrand Reinhold.

White, R. A. (1964). A comparison of old and new methods of response to targets in ESP experiments. *Journal of the American Society for Psychical Research*, *58*, 21-56.

Chapter 6

Is Scientific Investigation of Postmortem Survival an Anachronism? The Demise of the Survival Hypothesis[1]

HARVEY IRWIN

Parapsychology, the investigation of ostensibly paranormal phenomena through conventionally scientific methods, has three classical domains of inquiry: extrasensory perception (ESP), psychokinesis (PK, or mind-over-matter effects), and the survival hypothesis (Irwin, 2004). This chapter addresses the viability of research into the last of these three domains.

The survival hypothesis proposes the occurrence of postmortem survival, that is, the notion that "a disembodied consciousness or some such discarnate element of human personality might survive bodily death at least for a time" (Irwin, 2004, p. 144). This hypothesis is of course a tenet of most systems of religion, but as a scientific discipline parapsychology does not embrace hypotheses either as self-evident dogma or as assumptions defensible solely on philosophical grounds; rather, parapsychologists seek to subject the survival hypothesis to rigorous scientific scrutiny and to gauge the extent of strictly empirical support for the hypothesis.

This approach to the survival hypothesis has been endorsed in parapsychology since the establishment of 'psychical research' as an empirically oriented activity in the late nineteenth century. Much of the early work of the (English) Society for

1. [This chapter was originally published in *Australian Journal of Parapsychology* (2002, vol. 2[1], pp. 19-27). Permission to reprint has been granted by the author and the journal.—Editors.]

Psychical Research (SPR) was concerned principally with the issue of discarnate survival (Beloff, 1993; Inglis, 1977). That is, members of the SPR investigated phenomena of the séance room and documented the occurrence of spontaneous psychical experiences with an explicit aim of providing data upon which the survival hypothesis might be assessed. Today there is a substantial empirical literature on a number of parapsychological experiences that appear to bear on the hypothesis. An analysis of the viability of scientific investigation of the survival hypothesis therefore might usefully begin with a brief (and necessarily selective) examination of this body of evidence.

The Study of Specific Parapsychological Experiences

Among the principal parapsychological experiences that have been advocated in support of the survival hypothesis are séance phenomena, near-death experiences, out-of-body experiences, poltergeist and apparitional experiences, and reincarnation experiences. Each of these is considered in turn.

Séance Phenomena

Spiritualistic mediums reportedly have elicited many phenomena in the séance room that suggest the intervention of entities from the spirit world. The reported evidence here includes *mental* phenomena, that is, communications from spirits of information to which the medium evidently had no normal access, and *physical* phenomena such as materialisation of a spirit, levitation of objects (e.g., the séance table) by spirit forces, production of sounds (raps) by unseen spirit hands, and the delivery of exotic objects (apports) by courtesy of a spirit entity. These diverse phenomena nevertheless have proved to be scientifically inconclusive for the survival hypothesis. Thus, the mental phenomena could feasibly be the product of the medium's extrasensory awareness of relevant information from mundane sources such as the sitter, people outside the séance room, and written records.

These non-survivalist accounts of mental séance phenomena may appeal to some extraordinary extrasensory processes and thus they are commonly dubbed the 'super-ESP hypothesis' (Braude, 1992; Gauld, 1961), but as the operation of such processes is seemingly impossible to exclude, mental séance phenomena cannot be conclusive for the survival hypothesis. I must admit I am not in irrevocable despair of séance research on this ground, as I see no reason *in principle* why the limits of ESP (or super-ESP) will not be ascertained at some future time. Another methodological constraint is, however, rather more problematic. Specifically, the detection of fraudulent activity by mediums is so common, and researchers' prevention of such activity so difficult and open to criticism, that there appears to be no possibility of the controlled investigation of séance phenomena ever generating universally persuasive, scientifically rigorous evidence of postmortem survival. The same conclusions may be seen to obtain in the case of some contrived experimental 'tests' of survival such as the cipher test (Thouless, 1946) and the combination lock test (Stevenson, 1968) that rely on postmortem communication of information (for a review see Irwin, 2004).

Near-Death Experiences

In a near-death experience (NDE) people faced with a life-threatening situation may have the impression of leaving their physical body and proceeding to an otherworldly environment in which they may encounter religious figures and the spirits of deceased friends and relatives. Superficially, therefore, the NDE seems to constitute descriptive evidence of a postmortem state of human existence. On the other hand, many commentators have formulated theoretical explanations of the NDE in purely psychological or neuropsychological terms (for a review see Irwin, 2004).

What is particularly noteworthy about the NDE literature is that proponents of the survival hypothesis (e.g., Sabom, 1982) essentially have sought to establish their case by demonstrating the insufficiency of the psychological and neuropsychological accounts. Clearly this does not constitute direct testimony to the survival hypothesis. Thus, the NDE remains an experience to be explained; in itself the content of the experience does not represent a scientifically acceptable source of evidence for the survival hypothesis, in part because this content may ultimately be hallucinatory. In addition, even a successful demonstration that a nonphysical self may persist at the moment of biological death would not constitute proof of postmortem existence as an enduring state.

Out-of-Body Experiences

An out-of-body experience (OBE) is one in which a person has the impression that consciousness temporarily is outside the physical body. At first blush this experience appears to indicate that there is an element of human existence that is distinct from our status as a biophysical entity. Some parapsychologists (e.g., Osis, 1975) have even attempted experimentally to show that the accuracy of perceptual impressions during an OBE cannot be explained by (in-the-body) ESP, but again this research has been plagued by an inability to specify with confidence the limitations of ESP.

Similarly, experimental attempts to detect the presence of an exteriorised self at some place outside the body (for reviews see Alvarado, 1982; Irwin, 1985) have not been able to exclude possible psychokinetic influences over the detection apparatus. More fundamentally, even if there were some way to document objectively the exteriorisation of the self during an OBE, this would not demonstrate that this element of existence actually survives physical death; it must be remembered that the person is physically alive during an OBE, and the viability of the hypothetical exteriorised self could well depend on the physical integrity of the individual. On this ground the OBE is unable to provide definitive support for the occurrence of postmortem survival.

Poltergeist and Apparitional Experiences

Spontaneous cases in which spirits' activity reportedly is witnessed (poltergeists) or spirit forms reportedly are seen and heard (apparitions) are widely interpreted by the general public as evidence of spirit entities. There is no doubt that people do have poltergeist and apparitional experiences, and in this regard there are phenomena here that require research and explanation. On the other hand, no human experience in itself can properly be construed as objective evidence for spirit entities. Again, it has proved difficult for scientific investigators to obtain objective recordings of such entities under rigorously controlled conditions, and the methodological elimination of all opportunity for fraud among the principals of the case is problematic.

In addition, various commentators have suggested the possible role in these experiences of psychological and parapsychological (ESP and PK) mechanisms that do not require any assumption of postmortem survival, and some evidential support for these approaches has been educed (for reviews see Houran & Lange, 2001; Irwin, 2004). For these diverse reasons the study of poltergeist and apparitional experiences has not been productive for the survival hypothesis.

Reincarnation Experiences

The notion of reincarnation is that a nonphysical element of human existence not only survives biological death but subsequently is reborn in another body. In the parapsychological context the principal source of evidence for this putative phenomenon comes from documented cases of people (usually children) who seemingly recall detailed memories of a previous existence (e.g., Stevenson, 1966). Reincarnation experiences are particularly intriguing for the survival hypothesis because they prompt a more careful consideration of just what it is that is deemed under the hypothesis to survive death (Edwards, 1996). It must be said that the documented experiences certainly are consistent with the survival hypothesis, and parapsychologists such as Stevenson (1966) have made impressive efforts to establish the inapplicability of alternative accounts of the cases, but still there is no satisfactory demonstration that postmortem survival necessarily must have occurred. Thus, even Stevenson himself prefers to designate these reports as "cases of the reincarnation type" rather than more definitively as "cases of reincarnation".

In summary, there are various parapsychological (i.e., ostensibly paranormal) experiences that appear superficially to be compatible with the survival hypothesis. The survivalist interpretation of these experiences nevertheless remains a hypothesis; in itself the mere occurrence of the experiences is not evidence for the hypothesis, in part because alternative explanations are available which do not posit postmortem survival and indeed, in some instances there is encouraging empirical support for these alternatives.

Is Scientific Investigation of the Survival Hypothesis Viable?

A fundamental assumption of contemporary parapsychology is that its hypotheses are accessible to empirical scrutiny; such access is of course a defining characteristic of a scientific enterprise (Popper, 1963). Arguably the major contribution by J. B. and Louisa Rhine to this field (see Mauskopf & McVaugh, 1980) was to show that both the ESP hypothesis and the PK hypothesis are empirically testable and amenable to a sustained program of scientifically rigorous investigation.

The same status has not been achieved for the survival hypothesis. As indicated above, the investigation of parapsychological experiences with a putative bearing on the survival hypothesis typically has not succeeded in subjecting the survival hypothesis to critical scrutiny but rather, it has merely involved the documentation of the occurrence and phenomenological content of the experiences and the empirical evaluation of testable alternatives to the survival hypothesis rather than the survival hypothesis itself. Occasional declarations to test the survival hypothesis in a direct manner have been ill-conceived and ineffectual.

At present it seems fair to say that the scientific investigation of the survival hypothesis strictly speaking is not viable because the hypothesis has not been shown to be empirically testable in any direct sense. The inaccessibility of the survival hypothesis to definitive empirical scrutiny in turn raises the fundamental issue of whether this hypothesis warrants retention as one of the key domains of parapsychological research. There are three major potential justifications for its retention; each of these will be enunciated and then countered.

First, retention of the survival hypothesis would serve to maintain for the field of parapsychology a sense of conceptual continuity from the early days of psychical research. In response to this view, I would readily acknowledge the values of appreciating the history of one's discipline (see Irwin, 2004), but a sense of history also entails an eye for progress and development. In short, if an objective of the field is proving inefficacious its retention is actually an obstacle to conceptual progress and this is a greater danger than that of neglecting the objective's historical significance. Parapsychology should not be allowed to become stagnant because of a reluctance to abandon futile aspirations.

Second, the survival hypothesis may be held to provide at least a nominal rationale for the study of OBEs, reincarnation, and other experiences under the rubric of parapsychology. Without the imputation of postmortem survival there would seem to be little reason to construct these experiences as "paranormal" or scientifically impossible, and in the absence of this construction in mainstream psychology there appears to have been little sense of a need to investigate these experiences. There is certainly a grain of truth in the latter observation: although some researchers (including myself) think the above experiences deserve study in their own right, most people who think this way are self-declared parapsychologists or else scientists (e.g., medical NDE researchers) with at least a nominal interest in the viability of the survival hypothesis.

At the same time the fact that research into these experiences may largely be undertaken only by parapsychologists does not require parapsychologists to justify such research in terms of the survival hypothesis. In this regard there is a strong case to be made for redefining parapsychology more in terms of the study of scientifically *anomalous* experiences instead of the study of scientifically impossible events. Such redefinition would not only legitimise the continued study of reincarnation experiences, NDEs, and like experiences by parapsychologists, but would also facilitate the timely acceptance of the demise of the survival hypothesis as a major impetus to parapsychological research.

A third possible rationale for the retention of the survival hypothesis is that while this hypothesis may currently be empirically inaccessible, it would be injudicious to claim that this will always be the case. Perhaps scientific progress will create future opportunities for direct empirical investigation of the hypothesis, and in any event current inaccessibility to investigation should not be used to prohibit researchers from continuing their pursuit of such access. In response to this position I would not wish to deny anyone another opportunity to show that the survival hypothesis is empirically testable, but both the feasibility of this aspiration and the need for its nominated centrality to the discipline are moot. It is not unduly pessimistic to note that after more than one hundred years of research effort parapsychology has made no decisive progress in garnering support for the survival hypothesis. Further, at present there do not appear to be any indications of the prospect of scientific measurement of the nonmaterial dimension in which postmortem survival is hypothesised to take place. Thus, if only by default, it is becoming increasingly feasible that postmortem survival will always be a matter of faith (whether belief or disbelief) rather than a testable scientific hypothesis. In this circumstance it is highly tenuous to retain the survival hypothesis as a major conceptual framework for the field of parapsychology, in essence for the following reason.

Although the domains of ESP and PK have been shown to be open to empirical evaluation, the fact that this has not been satisfactorily demonstrated for parapsychology's third domain, postmortem survival, signifies a clear limitation to parapsychology's claim to be a science. Contemporary survival research is *proto-scientific,* that is, it may well embrace scientific methodology but it has yet to establish conclusively that its subject matter is accessible to direct empirical scrutiny. In light of the failure of considerable past research effort to redress this problem and in the absence of any contemporary indications that the problem is imminently likely to be resolved, it is foolhardy to persevere with this intractable and severe compromise to the standing of parapsychological research as a legitimate scientific endeavour. The survival hypothesis needs to be substantially set aside as a provocative but ultimately unproductive facet of the history of parapsychology.

In summary, it seems the current compromise position in parapsychology is to retain two somewhat conflicting items on the research agenda: first, to undertake rigorously scientific study of the *psychology and neuropsychology* of

OBEs, NDEs, apparitional experiences, reincarnation experiences, and the like; and second, to seek a means to test the survival hypothesis by direct empirical means. As argued above, I have little optimism for the second of these objectives and indeed, I deem it a major impediment to the acceptance of parapsychology among mainstream scientists. Among my principal recommendations are the displacement of the survival hypothesis from its central conceptual position in parapsychology and the redefinition of parapsychology in terms of the study of anomalous experiences. Thus, in no sense am I proposing that research on NDEs, reincarnation experiences, OBEs, and like experiences be abandoned. On the contrary, these parapsychological experiences are thoroughly worthy of empirical study in their own right. What is suggested here is that parapsychologists (and the readers of parapsychological research) should not be driven to expect such research to illuminate the survival hypothesis.

As long ago as 1974 J. B. Rhine himself declared spirit communication to be an "untestable hypothesis" and proposed that parapsychology should cease "its long and wasted preoccupation with unsolvable questions without necessarily dismissing them with finality" (Rhine, 1974, p. 137). A similar stance should now be taken in regard to the survival hypothesis as more generally conceived.

» References

Alvarado, C. S. (1982). Recent OBE detection studies: A review. *Theta, 10*(2), 35-37.

Beloff, J. (1993). *Parapsychology: A concise history.* London: Athlone Press.

Braude, S. E. (1992). Survival or super-psi? *Journal of Scientific Exploration, 6,* 127-144.

Edwards, P. (1996). *Reincarnation: A critical examination.* Amherst, NY: Prometheus Books.

Gauld, A. (1961). The "super-ESP" hypothesis. *Proceedings of the Society for Psychical Research, 53,* 226-246.

Houran, J., & Lange, R. (Eds.) (2001). *Hauntings and poltergeists: Multidisciplinary perspectives.* Jefferson, NC: McFarland.

Inglis, B. (1977). *Natural and supernatural: A history of the paranormal from earliest times to 1914.* London: Hodder & Stoughton.

Irwin, H. J. (1985). *Flight of mind: A psychological study of the out-of-body experience.* Metuchen, NJ: Scarecrow Press.

Irwin, H. J. (2004). *An introduction to parapsychology* (4th ed.). Jefferson, NC: McFarland.

Mauskopf, S. H., & McVaugh, M. R. (1980). *The elusive science: Origins of experimental psychical research*. Baltimore, MD: Johns Hopkins University Press.

Osis, K. (1975). Perceptual experiments on out-of-body experiences. In J. D. Morris, W. G. Roll, & R. L. Morris (Eds.), *Research in parapsychology 1974* (pp. 53-55). Metuchen, NJ: Scarecrow Press.

Popper, K. R. (1963). *Conjectures and refutations: The growth of scientific knowledge*. London: Routledge & Kegan Paul.

Rhine, J. B. (1974). Telepathy and other untestable hypotheses. *Journal of Parapsychology, 38,* 137-153.

Sabom, M. B. (1982). *Recollections of death: A medical investigation*. New York: Harper & Row.

Stevenson, I. (1966). Twenty cases suggestive of reincarnation. *Proceedings of the American Society for Psychical Research, 26,* 1-362.

Stevenson, I. (1968). The combination lock test for survival. *Journal of the American Society for Psychical Research, 62,* 246-254.

Thouless, R. H. (1946). A test of survival. *Proceedings of the Society for Psychical Research, 48,* 253-263.

Chapter 7

The Demise of the Survival Hypothesis, or the Errors of Harvey Irwin?[1]

Montague Keen

Harvey Irwin's Chapter 6 above (see also Irwin, 2002), in which he argues not merely for the abandonment of the survival hypothesis but for its specific exclusion from the area of legitimate parapsychological studies, is important, timely, stimulating, and challenging. It is also wrong.

Dr. Irwin errs in two ways. One arises from factual errors or misrepresentations when he discusses the strength and nature of evidence which appears to support a survival hypothesis. The second is his conclusion that survival research can never meet the conditions required for acceptable scientific (i.e., pragmatic) work. After commenting on the disturbing implications of Irwin's thesis for scientific progress in general and psychical research in particular, I examine these errors in some detail below.

Irwin's major contribution to the subject has been as boil-lancer. The embarrassment of the survival hypothesis, and work on it, has long been an incubus for most professional psychologists. Many of them would welcome a clear message that parapsychology is concerned solely with what goes on in the minds of living people, individually and collectively, and has no connection with occult mysteries and the fate of dead souls. In that way, the attitude of suspicion and obstruction which characterises orthodox science towards the paranormal investigator can be appeased. The painful ascent begun by J. B. Rhine towards the summit of the mountain of scientific respectability will near attainment, albeit posthumously.

1. [This chapter was originally published in *Australian Journal of Parapsychology* (2003, vol. 3[1], pp. 36-42). Permission to reprint has been granted by the journal.—Editors.]

The association with séances, mediumistic frauds and dubious physical antics in darkened rooms could thenceforth be repudiated, not simply ignored. Such would be the pathway enabling full entry into the scientific community, without prejudicing prospects of academic advancement or incurring the odium of one's peers. Hence Irwin's tantalising rationalisation of his wish to be rid once and for all of an area of research which can never satisfy the stern scientific mistress in a way that parapsychologists regularly demonstrate by their single and double blind tests and their obedience to probability calculations: areas forever beyond the aspiration of the survivalist.

By articulating so clearly what constitutes the divide between psychical research (which embraces all aspects of the paranormal) and parapsychology (which does not, and does not want to), Irwin has performed a valuable service from which I trust the harshness of my criticisms will not detract.

There are four areas of research bearing on survival listed by Irwin, and all of which he finds wanting. Probably the most important, and one which has occupied more time and space than all the rest, he classifies as séance phenomena. Both the physical and the mental aspects he dismisses as scientifically inconclusive. That means that if a large number of scientists declare themselves dissatisfied with the validity of the phenomena, or simply retain doubts about their authenticity, regardless of whether they have studied the evidence or subjected it to intelligent criticism, it is unworthy of further consideration. Applying any such criterion to many of the greatest discoveries of the past two centuries would leave us in medieval ignorance. That physical phenomena occur has been repeatedly demonstrated. *How* it occurs remains uncertain, and a proper province for scientific investigation. Scientific investigation simply involves the application of methods of thorough, dispassionate, intelligent and critical examination. It no more presupposes dedication to replication than does work in the fields of astronomy or geology, where replication may be impossible.

The more important reservation Irwin expresses, however, relates to mental séance phenomena. Here he sees no end of the seemingly interminable debate between the protagonists of super-ESP and the survival hypotheses. It is true that neither theory holds prospect of scientific proof, but one is founded on an indefinite extension of macro-telepathic and clairvoyant precognitive powers, of whose existence there is not one whit of demonstrable evidence; while its alternative is based on cases which strain the super-psi hypothesis well beyond the limits of human credulity. The survival advocates base their conviction on inference from a huge assembly of evidence. They cannot send expeditions of scientists to the next world to report on their findings and return with specimens susceptible to analysis in human laboratories, but inference is a perfectly respectable scientific tool. If it is not, then what of medical diagnosis? If I am convinced that all around me plot my downfall and spy on my every move, the medical inference is that I am afflicted with paranoia, but it can be neither replicated, smelled, measured, seen, felt, touched nor heard.

The fact is that the evidence for the existence of intelligent communications which cannot reasonably be attributable to any form of ESP among the living, is both overwhelming and thoroughly neglected. It is regrettable, but hardly surprising, that Irwin's chapter exemplifies that neglect. His failure to mention the cross-correspondences,[2] for example, equates with the essayist who analyses Hamlet without referring to the Prince of Denmark. It would unduly extend the length of this comment were I to attempt to list all the examples which make the super-psi hypothesis an affront to commonsense. I would refer doubters to the exchanges on super-psi and survival between Professor Stephen Braude and others, disseminated by the International Survivalist Society;[3] or to Professor Archie Roy's (Roy, 1995) challenge to skeptics to confront some (or all) of the 20 best cases, which he listed in the Society for Psychical Research's *Psi Researcher* (later, the *Paranormal Review*), a challenge that has been ignored ever since.

I have singled out three varied cases. All are in theory susceptible to an explanation which confines a psychic faculty to the living mind, but only by postulating the most improbable, speculative and evidentially unsupported extensions of psi. The first comprises the responses of the deceased Frederic Myers to George Dorr's and Oliver Lodge's invitation via Mrs. Piper in Boston, Massachusetts, and Mrs. Willett in England, respectively, to say what the word Lethe conveys to his mind (Lodge, 1911; Piddington, 1910); the second is the most recent and striking case of communication from a newly murdered woman via an unknown medium of very large numbers of specific, accurate and relevant statements relating to the murder and the murderer, and some of them not confirmed until many years later (Playfair & Keen, 2004). The third is the Edgar Vandy case, which has been recently re-examined (Keen, 2002).

2. [Cross-correspondence is defined as "a highly complex series of independent communications delivered paranormally (and ostensibly from one or more discarnate entities) to two or more geographically separate mediums such that the complex message is not clear until the separate fragments are pieced together into a meaningful whole" (Thalbourne, 2003, p. 24).—Editors.]

3. See www.survivalafterdeath.org [This website was not accessible at the time of publication.—Editors.]

I accept that the evidence from mediumistic communications for survival of consciousness is not conclusive; but it is the only viable alternative to a super-psi explanation which for most informed observers would be considered less persuasive. If that is enough to warrant its rustication from the University life, it is founded on the same misapprehensions that afflict other arguments advanced by Irwin. One of them is that mediumistic statements are inherently incapable of submission to orthodox disciplines, i.e., quantification through measurement and probability calculations. No doubt Irwin's chapter was written before he was aware of the contents of recent accounts of two quite distinct but equally important methods of disproving that widely held assumption. They are contained in the several papers published in the SPR's Journal in 2001/2 by Professor Gary Schwartz and his several associates in the University of Arizona at Tucson, and the papers of Professor Roy and Mrs. Robertson describing their MIA (Medium Information Analysis) experiments. The former shows how controlled, recorded blind readings by five mediums of subjects who have suffered bereavements can be conducted in a fashion which conforms to the rigorous requirements of scientific orthodoxy, and presented analytically as probability calculations. The Roy/Robertson experiments, now in their fourth or fifth year at the time of writing, have tested and thoroughly trounced the hypothesis that information from mediums to recipients is acceptable and relevant equally to the intended recipient as to non-recipients. There may be holes to be picked in the protocol, as there continue to be in conventional ganzfeld tests, despite adherence to the Hyman/Honorton communiqué reached some ten years ago; but parapsychologists are well aware that there is no limit to the ingenuity and obduracy displayed by the determined critic when prejudice has priority over reason.

I comment more briefly on Irwin's three other parapsychological experiences appearing to support survival. The first relate to poltergeists and apparitions. True, these errant entities remain unsusceptible to the disciplines of a laboratory test. But even if it had thus far proved impossible to obtain objective records amenable to scientific examination (which it has not), this is no reason to disbar investigation, especially when the evidence favours a discarnate origin over a psychological explanation. Thus when the child Janet, as the human epicenter of the Enfield Poltergeist, produced *basso profundo* messages from false vocal chords (*plica ventricularis*), it was later discovered that the coarse and degenerate communicating entity gave correct but hitherto unknown information about his identity and his life and fatal illness many years earlier in the family's house (Playfair, 1980). That for scientists counts for more than the independent confirmatory testimony of some thirty witnesses over a period of a year, since it appears to be an essential part of the official scientific credo, to which Irwin and others wish to do obeisance, to discount any witness evidence as the product of imagination, exaggeration, self-delusion or plain lies, no matter how numerous or normally reliable the observers.

True, the Enfield case provides far stronger evidence of discarnate intrusion than does the equally famous and probably more typical 1967 Rosenheim poltergeist reported by Bender (1969), and Karger and Zicha (1967). But this simply emphasises the importance of continuing scrupulous investigations of such cases, where the psychological implications (regardless of the origin of the phenomena) are of such outstanding importance in understanding the nature and operation of psi.

Still less worthy are the reasons given for abandoning investigation of those cases suggesting reincarnation which clearly presuppose survival of some sort, however brief the duration of transfer. To cite Stevenson's prudent preference for the non-committal phrase "cases of the reincarnation type" in support of the claim that there is no evidence that reincarnation has necessarily occurred, dodges the question: What alternative explanation is there to offer?

Irwin affirms that contemporary psychology makes the fundamental assumption that its hypotheses are accessible to empirical scrutiny, "a defining characteristic of a scientific enterprise" (p. 103). He appears to equate this with replicable experiments. But empirical simply means evidence based on observation, not theory: it relates to the derivation of knowledge from experience alone. Thus the several critics of the Scole Report (Keen, Ellison, & Fontana, 1999) based all their criticisms on the theory of fraud, without producing the slightest evidence that there was any; whereas the protagonists, Professor Ellison, Professor Fontana and I produced overwhelming empirical evidence. The fact that an event cannot be repeated, or declines to exhibit itself in accordance with the requirements and to the satisfaction of experimenters under controlled conditions, neither detracts from the reality of the event nor excuses parapsychologists from investigating it.

It is dumbfounding to read Irwin's statement that the "investigation of parapsychological experiences with a putative bearing on the survival hypothesis typically has not succeeded in subjecting the survival hypothesis to critical scrutiny" (pp. 103-104). Is he not aware of the volumes of analyses and debates on this very issue in the *Proceedings* and *Journal of the Society for Psychical Research*, and its American sister publication?

Based on this misinterpretation of empiricism, and with apparent lack of familiarity with the literature, Irwin gives three reasons to suggest that retention of the survival hypothesis is no longer viable. The first is that retaining the hypothesis has proved an obstacle to conceptual progress. But if, by eliminating all the evidence supporting survival, we concentrate on constructing theories based entirely on the laboratory type experimentation promoted so effectively by the Rhines, we are in the position of the theorist attempting to explain in terms of electromagnetism the operation of the dowsing twig, without acknowledging the evidence of map-dowsing which effectively torpedoes the theory.

To construct theories of psi based on the fundamental rule that it must be a product of and limited by the human psyche, disappearing with human death, is arbitrary and irrational, unwarranted by the evidence, contemptuous of the rules of free scientific investigation, and ultimately self-defeating, by reducing the parapsychologist to the role of medieval seamen mapping out the contours of a continent they are too timid to circumnavigate.

Second, Irwin advances an interesting but questionable linguistic device which, by outlawing anything touching on survival, could make the phenomena investigated by parapsychologists no longer "paranormal" or "scientifically impossible" (p. 104). If all the aspects of ESP which come within the parapsychologist's current purview are to be redefined as normal, *Hey Presto*!, the doors of academia are flung open and all is forgiven. But Irwin's definitions are not mine; nor is his world. ESP is by current definition, paranormal, in that its evidence breaches current scientific orthodoxy. Crawling under the door of the palace of Establishment Science by ostentatious repudiation of any connection with the tawdry bunch of relatives who stare into crystal balls and commune with spirits is not going to do the trick, because the Establishment does not accept that telepathy and clairvoyance, let alone precognition and psychokinesis, are compatible with their immutable philosophy.

Perhaps I have misunderstood Irwin's second reason for jettisoning the survival hypothesis. He appears to argue that it may become scientifically acceptable, and no longer considered paranormal, to continue to study reincarnation, among other matters, so long as one talks only of anomalies and abandons any suggestion that it may be connected to survival. That sounds like studying sailing without allowing for the possibility of floating. Irwin is eager to ensure that we continue to research subjects traditionally accepted as appearing to favour the survival hypothesis so long as the researchers do not expect their work to illuminate it. To make sure that our critics will not suspect anything so dangerous and damaging, call it the study of anomalous experiences. That'll fool 'em. Euphemisation always does.

There is a deeper malaise underlying Irwin's plea. He takes psychical research to be a branch of parapsychology instead of the other way round. This leads him to argue that, no matter how persuasive the evidence for discarnate communication may be, it will transgress the rules if it is not somehow explained as a manifestation of the living mind, fitted into some form of the super-ESP hypothesis. A century of argument has shown how extravagant and evidentially ill-supported this belief is; but it is an essential requirement so long as psychical research is shoe-horned into the ill-fitting boot of parapsychology, which allows nothing beyond the living psyche.

Parapsychologists have had to struggle long and hard to gain a tenuous foothold on the scientific rock-face. There have been marked successes, notably in the UK where parapsychologists now breed in a dozen or more university psychology departments. It is unquestionably true that recognition continues to be made more difficult by the contamination of occult association. It is also true that anyone foolish enough boldly to declare his conviction in the truth of some aspect of the paranormal, particularly if it hints at let alone embraces survival, is henceforth relegated to the realm of the intellectually unstable and scientifically unreliable.

The answer is not to kow-tow to bigotry, but to challenge the ignorance and expose the prejudice of those unwilling to study the evidence and unready to engage in open debate. Our fault lies not in the poverty of the material but in failure to proclaim its existence.

» References

Bender, H. (1969). New developments in poltergeist research. In *Proceedings of the Parapsychological Association*, *6*, 81-102.

Irwin, H. (2002). Is scientific investigation of postmortem survival an anachronism? The demise of the survival hypothesis. *Australian Journal of Parapsychology, 2*, 19-27.

Karger, F., & Zicha. G. (1967). Physikalische untersuchungen des spukfalls in Rosenheim [Physical investigations of the Rosenheim Incident]. In: *Zeitschrift für Parapsychologie und Grenzgebiete der Psychologie* [*Journal for Parapsychology and Border Areas of Psychology*]. Freiburg im Breisgau: Aurum.

Keen, M., Ellison, A., & Fontana, D. (1999). The Scole Report: An account of an investigation into the genuineness of a range of physical phenomena associated with a mediumistic group in Norfolk, England. *Proceedings of the Society for Psychical Research, 58*, 151-452.

Keen, M. (2002). The case of Edgar Vandy: Defending the evidence. *Journal of the Society for Psychical Research, 66*, 247-259.

Lodge, O. (1911). Evidence of classical scholarship and of cross correspondence in some new automatic writings. *Proceedings of the Society for Psychical Research, 25*, 113-175.

Piddington, J. G. (1910). Three incidents from the (Piper) Sittings, Part 1, Lethe. *Proceedings of the Society for Psychical Research, 24*, 86-144.

Playfair, G. L. (1980). *This house is haunted*. London: Souvenir Press.

Playfair, G. L., & Keen, M. (2004). A possibly unique case of psychic detection. *Journal of the Society for Psychical Research, 68*(1), 1-17.

Roy, A. E. (1995). An open letter to the sceptic. *Psi Researcher, 18*, 3-7.

Thalbourne, M. A. (2003). *A glossary of terms used in parapsychology (2nd ed.)*. Charlottesville, VA: Puente.

PART 2: BELIEF AND CULTURE

Chapter 8

Scepticism and Credulity[1]

PETER S. DELIN

Technology has existed, as far as we can tell, for as long as man has existed. Although we can find, almost as far back as written records extend, individuals who show signs of a scientific approach to the world, scientific thinking did not really come into its own until the seventeenth century, with the writings of Francis Bacon and René Descartes, and the researches of such men as Galileo, Hooke, and Boyle.

Science has only had a firm hold on the tiller of technology for about the last century, during which time it has been responsible for fantastic changes in the mode of living of a considerable proportion of the world's population.

Considerable though this proportion is, however, it is by no means as great as we who are the most affected tend to suppose. There are still hundreds of millions of people whose world is bounded by their capacity for walking, and for whom the day ends when the sun goes down. Furthermore, relatively few of those whose lives are affected by the products of science are in any important way infected with scientific thinking.

Scientists, then, represent a minority view among mankind, and even among their own countrymen. They must always be on the defensive against more popular and more traditional ways of viewing and handling the universe. The end of this long-term confrontation is still in doubt. Newspapers, for instance, are prepared to devote more space to astrology, graphology, or spiritualism than to science, and they do this on the basis of their knowledge of popular tastes.

1. This chapter is based on a talk delivered at the symposium 'The Unidentified Flying Object Problem' organised by the South Australian Division of ANZAAS, and held in Adelaide, 30 October 1971. [This chapter was originally published as an article in *Australian Journal of Parapsychology* (2002, vol. 2[1], pp. 28-36). Permission to reprint has been granted by the author and the journal.—Editors.]

In view of these observations, the deference accorded to scientists seems a little surprising until one recalls that men have always feared or revered the powers they did not understand. Remarkable too, is the way in which scientists so obviously see themselves as representing the sane, 'normal', viewpoint. This is perhaps explicable, at least in part, as a defensive response to the state of being committed to an unpopular position. The opposition is perceived as being a handful of 'odd' people instead of what it happens to be, namely, the majority of people.

Science can be seen as having two main aspects. There are, on the one hand, processes concerned with the discovery and demonstration of phenomena, and, on the other, processes of organising and collating information about the universe once it has been attained. The latter kind of process is relatively well established and understood, and no great commitment to a particular point of view is necessary. It does not hurt a scientist to agree that someone may come along later and organize his findings differently, around a different set of concepts, although individuals may develop commitment to a particular viewpoint as a result of the investment of a great deal of time and effort.

With regard to the establishing of phenomena the situation is entirely different. Both the scientists and the philosophers are unclear about the status of scientific induction. Logical consideration of the scientific technique of establishing generalisations by collecting positive instances leads to a series of paradoxes. No agreed techniques exist for the setting of criteria for evidence. The accepting of new phenomena may enforce the reorganisation of whole areas of theory in initially incalculable ways. In short the scientist is likely to be strongly motivated towards scepticism in relation to new phenomena.

Scepticism is in any case academically respectable. It has a long tradition stemming from Descartes, and has become a part of the scientist's image. The sceptical posture is one which requires no special training. It will then be no surprise to find it being worn as a badge of merit by those scientists who are least sure of their other qualifications for that title and its status. We may also expect it to characterise those people who have little scientific training or aptitude, but who, for reasons related to their personality structure, wish to think of themselves as being scientific.

Clearly other mechanisms leading to scepticism could be envisaged. Not all sceptics are scientific sceptics. But we do not have to comprehend all of the mechanisms involved in order to recognize that there are people for whom scepticism has become a habitual mode of response. The so-called 'authoritarian personality' was recognised by Adorno and his colleagues (1950) through the observation that people holding one 'authoritarian' belief tend to hold other, and unrelated, 'authoritarian' beliefs. Thus the belief that homosexuality is a serious crime, and should be severely punished, is more likely to be held by someone who assents to the statement that foreigners are not to be trusted than by someone who disagrees with this statement.

In the same way one might identify a 'sceptical personality' through observation of a correlation between sceptical beliefs with unrelated content. A scale could be constructed consisting of statements such as, 'Flying saucers are extra-terrestrial vehicles' and, 'Some people can obtain information directly from the minds of others', and some people would probably score very low in terms of their tendency to agree with these statements.

Conversely some people would probably score very high on such a scale. We might call such people 'credulous' as opposed to 'sceptical'. Anyone who has ever had any contact with 'fringe' areas such as psychical research, or the investigation of UFOs will have encountered people who, like Lewis Carroll's White Queen, try to believe at least one impossible thing before breakfast.

One would expect such people to come out very high on the scepticism/credulity scale. In the case of the authoritarianism scale it appears that people who have scores at opposite extremes have some important characteristics in common. Thus they both tend to be high on independent measures of rigidity. It would not be surprising if we found that there were other measures which were related in a similar way to our scepticism/credulity scale, so that people who were at opposite poles of the scepticism/credulity dimension were similar in their positions on other dimensions. Certainly my own history of interaction with the extremely sceptical and the extremely credulous leaves me with the feeling that the similarity between the two types is far greater than either would care to acknowledge.

The speculative analysis so far has suggested that the sceptical and the credulous are at opposite ends of a continuum. Very often, however, in public discussion of contentious material, the middle of the continuum is not represented. People at the two extremes tend to be highly vocal, not to say vociferous, in response to each other. The area of their dispute tends to be one in which a phenomenon is being recognised by one and denied by the other. The dispute itself tends to become highly acrimonious, with all sorts of personal comments and accusations being levelled at each side by the other.

The sceptic is accused of bolstering up a system in which he has high status, of pandering to the repressive demands of governmental authority, of wilful blindness. The believer is accused of fabricating data; of pretending to believe in order to jump onto a financial bandwagon; of striking back at the scientific 'club' he has not been able to join; of being a deliberate agent for chaos. The atmosphere becomes charged with personal descriptions ranging from pig-headedness through stupidity to insanity.

The content of these accusations is quite often justified. There are 'nuts' on both sides. Some of the sceptics are clearly more than a little obsessional, while some of the believers are clearly classifiable as paranoid schizophrenics. Data do get fabricated. Unscrupulous people do capitalise on the credulity of others. Governments do try to exercise control of the beliefs of the public, and sometimes they use scientists in this endeavour. However justified may have been the negative conclusions of the Condon Report on UFOs (1969), there can be little doubt that the study was conceived and executed with a strong bias towards reaching such negative conclusions, and that the governmental institution of the project and selection of its personnel was intended to produce this bias.

Irrespective of the frequent justifiability of such accusations it is clear that they usually predate the evidence. The disputes are operating at an emotional level that has little in common with the state appropriate to the dispassionate establishment of facts. Qualitatively the emotional atmosphere resembles that which accompanies a clash of attitudes or of tastes rather than of beliefs. The disputants evidently find each other incomprehensible in the same way that we find people incomprehensible who dislike the foods we like. It is interesting to note that in that situation too we often find ourselves suspicious that the other person does not really believe what he is saying.

The foregoing implies a similarity in state of mind between the credulous and the sceptical. Some similarity may also be observed when one comes to consider the specific theoretical and methodological errors which they make. Thus both show a tendency to confuse and amalgamate theoretical and observational issues. Thus one man may see a lenticular formation moving in the sky in a particular way, and interpret this as an extra-terrestrial vehicle. Another man, deeply sceptical about extra-terrestrial vehicles and the like, may set out to prove that he did not see anything, when all he has to prove to maintain his position of scepticism is that whatever was seen it was not an extra-terrestrial vehicle. Similarly, J. B. Rhine (1948) puts forward evidence suggesting that some subjects in ESP experiments obtain information that is difficult to account for their obtaining through any well-recognised sensory modality. Rhine makes it clear that he believes that the phenomena are outside the explanatory scope of science. Many sceptics behave as if Rhine's observations and his beliefs about them were inseparable, and therefore find it necessary to argue, not just that the phenomena can be explained in scientific terms, but that there are no phenomena.

This error can arise in a more subtle way, taking advantage, as it were, of one of the weakest links in the chain of scientific reasoning. One might have thought that to the scientist, striving to obtain an objective view of the universe, a piece of evidence for a proposition would have a status independent of his previous opinions, but this is not so. What he in fact does is to weight the evidence according to his current state of belief about the phenomenon or theory it relates to. In other words he attaches a certain probability to the phenomenon or theory, and demands stronger or weaker evidence in accordance with this a priori probability. The philosophical status of this procedure is not clear, although attempts have been made to justify it in terms of the varying degrees of reorganisation of previous concepts that may become necessary upon the acceptance of new phenomena or theories.

However justifiable the procedure may be it is clear that it provides a broad avenue for the entry of subjectivism into science. Many examples can be found of the attaching of particular a priori probabilities on the most flimsy, or mysterious, of grounds. Very often the low probability is attached to a theory simply because it is not in keeping with the spirit of the times. Sometimes it is difficult, looking back, to account for the scepticism with which a particular hypothesis was greeted. What, for instance was so very unlikely about Wegener's (1915) theory of continental drift as to justify its forty years in the wilderness?

Let us return to our consideration of Rhine's experimental reports and his anti-materialistic interpretation of them. The sceptic who does not go so far as to confuse the phenomenon with the interpretation may nevertheless place an unrealistically low a priori probability on the phenomenon by transferring to it the incredulity which the interpretation arouses in him. He may then find himself in a position to say that the evidence is weak. Thus he may point out that three researchers in cahoots could have faked a particular set of results. So, perhaps, they could, but one wouldn't demand that this possibility be obviated if one didn't regard the results as incredibly unlikely.

This brings us to another, but related, way in which the credulous and the sceptical are often similar. They both seem to have a penchant for innocently putting forward hypotheses of strikingly low intrinsic probability. Thus the believer in flying saucers may suggest that the earth has been under observation and guidance from outside over a period of millennia. One of his cases may be that of a trio of astronomers who spent some hours observing the antics of a UFO over the Sahara in daylight. This case is explained by the sceptic as a confusion on the part of the astronomers, who were really observing the planet Venus. Both hypotheses would seem to me to be of vanishingly small a priori probability.

Their anxiety to explain away phenomena rather than to explain them often prevents sceptics from noticing that they too have theories about the nature of the field of events they are dealing with, and that their theory may be inconsistent with some of the facts available to them. Thus the person who is sceptical about ESP may have an implicit theory that all of the positive results in this area reflect, through one psychological mechanism or another, the folk belief in these phenomena. This person may not notice that the general failure to find positive results in precognition experiments, and the relative abundance of positive results in telepathy experiments, do not reflect the relative frequencies of belief in these phenomena.

The fact is that a position of scepticism is one that stands in need of justification as does a position of belief, and there is often as capricious a basis for the sceptic's disbelief as for the believer's credulity. In exactly the same way as the credulous person sometimes seems to go out of his way to find extraordinary things to believe in, the sceptical person often seems to be trying very hard to find things in which to disbelieve, and to modify his perceptions accordingly.

A good example of this can be seen in the response of many sceptics to the claims of ESP researchers that ESP does not obey the inverse square law for the propagation of energy. The evidence for this proposition is that a number of ESP subjects have scored at about the same level over a variety of distances. This is clearly very poor evidence for the claim. A similar case could be made for the proposition that radio does not obey the inverse square law. Yet many sceptics seem to be prepared to accept this finding as a basis for rejecting ESP because it is scientifically impossible. This reasoning is as zany as anything the most cranky believer is likely to come up with.

Here again we find the sceptic selecting items from the information available to him in ways not essentially different from those of the believer. He is not trying to account for observations, but to find support for a particular world-view. An interesting example of such selection can be seen through a comparison of observations relevant to witness credibility in relation to psychical phenomena and to flying saucers. Numerous sceptics, for example D. J. West (1962), have pointed out that if one tabulates claims for spontaneous psychical phenomena in relation to the qualifications of those making them one finds that the most detailed claims come from the people whose credibility as witnesses is lowest. If one does the same for UFO reports one finds, in fact, leaving aside those claims which fall down on grounds of internal consistency alone, that the most detailed claims come from just those people whose status as observers of aerial phenomena should be highest; pilots, astronomers, meteorologists, and so on. UFO sceptics do not draw attention to these facts. A similar observation can be made about the variability of the claims in the two areas. That is, the bigger the sample of internally consistent psychical event claims one considers, the more different phenomena there seem to be, whereas most of the internally consistent UFO claims seem to fall in one of a very limited number of categories.

To sum up, a consideration of the people expressing belief and disbelief in a wide range of fringe phenomena and speculations suggests that the extremely credulous and the extremely sceptical are brothers under the skin, displaying similar faults of reasoning, biased observation, and capricious assignment of a priori probabilities. They also display similar evidence of strong internal motivation unrelated to the subject-matter under discussion, but predisposing them to the point of view they take up.

Science may have made enormous strides in recent years, but we are still a long way from being able to assign confident a priori probabilities to occasional phenomena. We may never be in a position to do this. This being so, any claim to have observed a new phenomenon must be judged by a procedure independent of our immediate ability to make it cohere within the structures that appear already to have been elucidated. The credibility of witnesses must be assessed as it is in a court of law, with the same scrupulous separation of the witness's report from his interpretation of that report.

It is in fringe areas like psychical research and the investigation of UFO claims that our ability as a species to make sense of our universe is under test, and it is my belief that if we are unable to prevent our psychological weaknesses from muddying the water we will fail that test.

» References

Adorno, T. W., Frenkel-Brunswick, E., Levinson, D. J., & Sanford, R. N. (1950). *The authoritarian personality.* New York: Viking.

Condon, E.U. (1969). *Scientific study of unidentified flying objects.* USAF Contract No. F44620-67-C-0035. New York: Bantam Books.

Rhine, J. B. (1948). *The reach of the mind.* London: Faber and Faber.

Wegener, A. L. (1915). *Enstehung der Kontinente und Ozeane.* Braunschweig: F. Vieweg.

West, D. J. (1962). *Psychical research today.* London: Penguin Books.

Chapter 9

The John Edward Phenomenon—"I *Want* To Believe"[1]

SUE-ELLEN KJELDAL

It is no secret that John Edward, the self-styled 'psychic medium', has enjoyed phenomenal success since he began stating publicly that he could act as an intermediary between the living and the dead. His website refers to him as an 'internationally acclaimed psychic medium'.[2] The Macquarie Dictionary refers to psychic ability as "pertaining to super- or extra-sensory mental functioning, such as clairvoyance, telepathy" (1990, p. 762). Edward purports to be able to communicate, in some way, with the deceased, and has received widespread support for his contentions from an uninformed public. According to his website:

> John Edward has brought a fresh, honest and thought-provoking attitude to the world of psychic phenomena. As a psychic medium, author and lecturer, he has, over the last fifteen years, helped thousands with his uncanny ability to predict future events and communicate with those who have crossed over to the Other Side.

Such claims as these are indeed 'larger than life', and through such media as television shows, newsletters and books, Edward has convinced many that there is, in fact, life after death. He freely asserts that he is communicating with the deceased and this assertion and the behaviour he exhibits publicly, *ipso facto*,

1. [This chapter was originally published in *Australian Journal of Parapsychology* (2003, vol. 3[2], pp. 123-139). Permission to reprint has been granted by the journal.—Editors.]
2. John Edward website: http://www.johnedward.net/

demonstrate his belief that he is, in fact, communicating with the deceased. This claim is taken seriously by those who seek to investigate the notion of the survival of some form of consciousness after death, such as Susan Blackmore (1993), who has written a comprehensive and well-researched book on the subject entitled *Dying to Live* in which she explores the many theories that have been put forward to explain the near-death experience.

The near-death experience has been reported by many individuals who, on the verge of death (but who subsequently live through the experience), purport to experience such things as lights at the ends of tunnels, a life review (which is a rapid 'scan' through the events of one's life), and being able to tell doctors performing emergency surgery on their bodies about things they could not have known unless their soul had somehow left their body. Many discuss the fact that they seem to have a 'bird's-eye' view of the emergency procedures, as though they were actually floating near the ceiling. After an exhaustive review of studies conducted in this area, Blackmore has been forced to conclude that the data best fit a 'dying brain' hypothesis rather than the more publicly accepted 'after life' hypothesis. That is to say, consciousness (what some might call the soul) does not continue after death.

This evidence has been seriously challenged by a series of studies conducted by Schwartz (2003a) which were subsequently the subject of a book entitled *The Afterlife Experiments* (Schwartz, Simon, & Chopra, 2003). The book describes a series of research studies conducted with famous mediums such as Edward and George Anderson. The results of these studies, which *may* be counted as evidence in support of the afterlife hypothesis, have been strenuously debated by those scientists who place themselves on one side of the argument or the other. An article by Schwartz (2003b) provides a very suitable example of the type of debate that is ongoing. A critique of the work of Schwartz by Wiseman and O'Keefe (2001, cited in Hyman, 2003a) stating that his work is not compelling evidence to support the afterlife hypothesis has increased the controversy surrounding this topic. Schwartz contends, however, that his studies *are* supportive of the afterlife hypothesis, and he further asserts that Wiseman and O'Keefe, who critique his work, have a duty to practice what they preach: even-handed skepticism (Schwartz, 2003a). Hyman (2003a,b) also critiques the work of Schwartz, and so it goes on (e.g., Wiseman, 2002)—claims for paranormal phenomena by distinguished academics critiqued by researchers with a wealth of research expertise.

At this point it is timely to define the purpose of those such as Michael Shermer (2003) who takes the debate very seriously and strenuously denies that skeptics are engaging in selective perception in finding evidence to use against paranormal experiences. As is stated in every issue of *Skeptic* magazine (2003):

> With regard to its procedure of examination of all claims, the Skeptics Society uses the scientific method first developed in the 16th and 17th centuries. While it recognises the limitations and socio-cultural influences on science, it adopts the philosophy of Albert Einstein: "All our science, measured against reality, is primitive and childlike—and yet it is the most precious thing we have." (*Skeptic*, 2003, p. 4)

The point here is that those members of the Skeptics Society in the US and abroad have no other tools to measure paranormal phenomena apart from the scientific method, and it is their intention to honestly evaluate any claims of paranormal experiences by utilising the scientific method. The appearance of the Schwartz experiments appear to be 'muddying the waters' in this regard. It is the intention of the present author to use contemporary decision theory in an attempt to understand why Edward's ideas are so easily accepted amongst the general public and, perhaps too, to understand some of the controversy surrounding the phenomena.

This approach is not unlike that taken by Blackmore in attempting to find a parsimonious explanation for paranormal phenomena. In this instance, purely psychological theories are advanced to explain why some individuals wholeheartedly believe in the afterlife, which is arguably an irrational act. The Macquarie Dictionary defines rationality as: "agreeable to reason; reasonable, sensible; having or exercising reason, sound judgement, or good sense" (p. 786) and its definition of reason: is "sound judgement or good sense", or "to draw conclusions or inferences from facts or premises" (p. 790). Hammond states that rationality is similar to analysis, and analysis is defined by Macquarie as: "the ascertainment of the kind or amount of one or more of the constituents of a substance, whether actually obtained in separate form or not" (p. 29).

It can be argued from these definitions, therefore, that rational analysis of belief in a claim (such as the existence of life after death) that has to date, a great deal of empirical support against it and very little research or data to support it, leads one to the compelling conclusion that, at this point, the data supports the former rather than the latter view. If the evidence is weighed, it can be stated that, on balance, a belief such as life after death is not entirely rational in nature. It must be restated however, that the author believes that paranormal research is in an embryonic stage and that, although it would appear that there is overwhelming evidence that all constituents of the self cease to be at the moment of death, the present chapter is not primarily concerned with joining the debate. It is the simple wish of the author to attempt to explain why individuals might believe in a phenomenon that has, to date, so little research to support it. Interestingly, and as alluded to above, the theories discussed below can be extrapolated to understand more fully the above-mentioned debate by those on either side of the 'paranormal fence'—that is to say, an attempt at rational analysis of the data is overwhelmed by a more intuitive decision process.

Contemporary Decision Theory

Contemporary decision theorists stress the need to view the decision process in a holistic manner. The work of these researchers points to the importance of a wide range of information that impacts on decisions, including a complex array of sensory stimuli as well as information from memory. Many cognitive psychologists discuss the notion of the interaction of rational and intuitive cognitive processes in a decision mode (see Hammond, 1996, for a review of research in this area). They posit that information relevant to a decision is likely to include, on the one hand, knowledge that is semantic/analytic/factual in nature and, on the other hand, knowledge that is episodic/experiential or personally meaningful to the individual decision-maker. There is a need to embrace decision models that are cognisant of the complex array of "information gathered using their five major senses as well as upon information reconstructed from their memory systems" (Cooksey, 1996, p. xi).

The work of neuropsychologists and cognitive psychologists is leading to the construction of a template of the brain structures implicated in these processes, as well as a general theory of the way that knowledge is cognitively stored. It is only through a thorough investigation of these cognitive processes that researchers can begin to unpack the complexity of the decision-making process, a process that is no less relevant to an understanding of why Edward is so readily accepted than to why the space shuttle Challenger was launched under the circumstances that it was.

Hammond's Ideas

The work of decision theorists such as Hammond (1996) is relevant to the above ideas on dual-processing memory structures, in the following way. It appears that both decision theorists and cognitive psychologists are cognisant of the need to treat the information-processing mechanisms of humans other than in a unitary fashion, as was the case for much of the twentieth century. Rather, these theorists are beginning to understand the complexity of the cognitive system, with its concomitant dependence on several types of information, including factual and episodic data. It would seem that researchers such as Tulving (Tulving & Schacter, 1990) and Paivio (1983) are concentrating upon the specific mechanisms of information processing, including storage of, and access to qualitatively distinct knowledge. Decision theorists such as Hammond (1996) and Epstein (1994), on the other hand, focus on the cognitive system in a more global manner, and attempt to understand how the brain uses this qualitatively distinct information to make decisions.

To elaborate on the ideas of contemporary decision theorists, Hammond (1996) suggests that humans process information on a 'Cognitive Continuum' anchored at one end by pure intuition and at the other by analysis. Depending upon the task to be performed and the conditions surrounding the decision-maker, an individual will use a cognitive process along this continuum. Hammond explains the Cognitive Continuum thus:

> Consider the behaviour of persons attempting to cope with a highly structured task, a problem in physics, say, or mathematics, that they expect to solve by analytical means. It is common to observe that problem-solvers proceed by trying an analytically derived solution, discovering failure, and, at that point, making a new attempt. When all analytically derived efforts fail, the subject's cognitive activity moves away from analysis to quasirationality; that is, the subject's cognitive activity begins to acquire elements of intuitive cognition. "Hunches" begin to guide behaviour; undefended, perhaps indefensible, ideas spontaneously appear and affect decisions about what to do. If the problem is so difficult that "hunches" refined by analysis fail to provide a solution, then the subject's cognitive activity will move far enough along the cognitive continuum to become predominantly intuitive; cognition may consist almost entirely of pictorial imagery.... But if the problem-solver finds that intuition provides an idea to be tested and is therefore sufficient to move him or her to an analytical mode..., the subject may be said to move, not necessarily continuously or smoothly, from analysis through quasirationality to intuition and then back again to analysis. The path from the context of discovery to the context of verification is a cyclical one. (Hammond, 1996, p. 193)

Elements of the information environment that influence cognition along the continuum include time pressure, confusing circumstances and information overload. Thus, an intuitive mode of cognition is likely to be induced whenever there is limited time to make a decision, the circumstances surrounding the decision are confusing (such as attempting to determine the death experience, a process wherein lies little consensus) and there is a great deal of information to be processed (Hammond, 1996). Hammond further suggests that information presented in pictorial form (such as Edward being broadcast through television as well as appearing live in some instances) will induce intuition, whereas verbal or numerical information induces analysis. His ideas are supported by research findings reviewed by Epstein (1994).

At this point, it is also timely to discuss the fact that Hammond's (1996) notion of quasirationality might be useful in explaining the ongoing and sometimes heated debate between those who are skeptical of paranormal phenomena and those who are not. It was stated above that confusing circumstances and information overload can move an individual towards the intuitive end of the continuum and it is suggested by the present author that these two criteria are most definitely in existence with regard to paranormal research. Might it be the case that skeptics and non-skeptics alike find themselves shifting along the Cognitive Continuum as more information appears? In addition, the circumstances surrounding life after death are certainly one of the more confusing questions posed by individuals throughout history. Hammond's theory (1996) would seem to suggest that this (shifting along the Continuum) is indeed the case.

Hammond's ideas are valuable in understanding the ability of humans to process information both analytically and intuitively. Historical attempts to understand these processes have assumed an either/or view of intuition and analysis; that is, that when an individual is faced with a decision situation, they will behave either rationally or intuitively. These researchers have, furthermore, attached value judgements to these two forms of cognitive activity. Some have stated that intuition is best, whereas others have argued forcefully for the superiority of analysis (see Hammond [1996] for a comprehensive discussion of this debate).

Hammond refutes the superiority of one form of cognition over another, stating that, given sufficient time, individuals will 'oscillate' between analysis and intuition when making a single decision, and that both of these forms of information processing are necessary in everyday problem-solving. He states that 'quasirationality', which includes elements of both intuition and analysis is the predominant mode of information processing, and that it combines the best of both worlds: relative precision is gained from analysis, and generalisability (of the solution) occurs from intuition. It is argued that this notion of 'quasirationality' is responsible for the widespread support that Edward enjoys. That is to say, many factors coalesce to induce a less-than-rational analysis of Edward's ability. Our rational minds question his ability; however, our intuition 'takes over' and we are left thinking that interacting with deceased persons is a reality. This phenomenon may also assist in an explanation of why investigators in this area of research are not able to reach any degree of consensus. It may be the case that some of their attempts to analyse data relating to life after death are quasirational in nature.

Hammond's ideas present a solid framework into which can be comfortably placed many current ideas relating to knowledge systems (presented below), such as those of Epstein (1994), Loewenstein (1996) and Damasio (1994) (who postulate the existence of two interacting forms of cognition, one rational, the other experiential or intuitive). As discussed below, although the terminology used by these authors differs, similarities in the ideas presented point towards a consensus relating to the relative actions of intuitive and rational cognitive processes. As is discussed in the following section, the work of these authors provides a holistic approach to human decision making which is compatible with the ideas of cognitive psychologists, such as Tulving (Tulving & Schacter, 1990) and Paivio (1983), who are interested in these processes at a finer level of analysis.

The complexity of human information-processing has only recently begun to be fully appreciated, and the onus now is on researchers to be cognisant of the dual-code perspective and Hammond's (1996) notion of a Cognitive Continuum, and to begin to research cognitive structures in more depth. If it is the case that humans utilise multiple information processing systems, and that the information contained therein has differential effects on behaviour, it is important for researchers to attempt to tap into these, and to measure, more precisely, their relative behavioural impacts.

Epstein's Ideas

Epstein (1994) has reviewed multiple-memory theory and decision theory and has, in addition, discussed supporting evidence for these views in his seminal article. Epstein (1994) discusses the notion of interactive modes of cognitive processing, the rational (a verbal-analytical, deliberative, rational process) and the experiential (a largely preconscious, nonverbal, automatic process based on experience and which is emotionally-laden). According to Epstein, individuals possess three conceptual systems: namely, a rational, an experiential, and an associationistic system (1991). These systems constitute levels of awareness, and these, in turn, affect our feelings, behaviour and conscious thinking. The rational system operates primarily at a conscious level, and its actions are governed by socially prescribed rules of inference. The associationistic system is similar to Freud's unconscious system, and the experiential system is a relatively old system, due to its long evolutionary history (evolving over at least seven million years), its direct link to emotions suggesting a strong biological component, and its intractability relating to moderation by cultural training.

Epstein (1991) states that, by contrast, the rational system has been developed over a mere 5000 years, and that it has a lesser effect on everyday decisions and behaviours because "it would be inefficient to be conscious of all of one's interpretive and decision making processes" (p. 7). That is, much behaviour is determined by preconscious cognitions that allow individuals to manoeuvre through life's course without continually bringing thoughts (cognitions) to awareness, thus allowing rapid assessment and decisive action. An advantage of the rational system is that it is well suited to analysis and for evaluating long-term consequences of particular decisions.

The experiential system, by contrast, takes into account emotional consequences of decisions (thereby attending to possibly significant 'emotive' sources of data that are not considered by the rational system). This system appraises a situation according to certain feelings aroused (e.g., emotions surrounding the grieving process)—if the feelings are positive, behaviours are enlisted to enhance this state. However, if feelings are negative, behaviours will act to terminate it. That is, individuals will attempt to counteract their negative emotions surrounding a loved one who is deceased by terminating these feelings, perhaps via consulting a psychic. Thus, these feelings influence both thoughts and behaviours in specific ways. Loewenstein (1996) discusses human decision-making, and takes particular note of so-called visceral factors (emotionally-driven ideas) that affect our behaviour. Loewenstein's ideas are described later.

According to Epstein (1991), the experiential system also affects conscious thoughts. The rational system can override the experiential system when there is a perceived conflict between the two. However, the experiential system will win out when the individual is not aware of any such conflict and also when the individual is under stress. Epstein states that "it is important to note that the consideration here is of a distinction between two cognitive systems that operate in parallel, and not between a cognitive system and a presumably noncognitive emotional system, which I do not believe exist" (p. 14). These two cognitive systems, the experiential and the rational, have been associated with left- and right-hemispheric functions, respectively (Fox, 1995). That is, the functions of these two systems appear to mimic the actions of the two hemispheres of the brain.

Evidence for the existence of these two primary systems comes from a number of sources. Fazio (1986) and Bargh, Chaiken, Governer and Pratto (1992) have posited two ways of processing information, one that is purposeful and deliberative, the other being relatively automatic and heuristic. Fazio (1986) and Bargh et al. (1992) propose a system whereby attitudes can be automatically activated. These authors state that, furthermore, "attitudes can affect behaviour without any effort or intention on the part of the individual, that is, in a spontaneous, automatic manner" (Bargh et al., 1992, pp. 893-894). There exists much research support for this contention, namely through sequential priming experiments (Bargh, 1992; Bargh et al., 1992; Fazio, 1986, 1993a,b).

In addition, Fazio has conducted a number of studies showing that there is a stronger attitude/behaviour relationship when a subject has had *direct experience* with the attitude object (in this case, Edward himself), which might be an instance of experiential knowledge affecting behaviour. For example, in a study involving campus housing (Regan & Fazio, 1977; cited in Fazio & Zanna, 1981) it was found that the attitudes of students having direct experience with a housing shortage (which resulted in these students experiencing temporary housing before being moved into permanent housing) were more predictive of behaviour than the attitudes of students not having personally experienced the campus housing crisis. Furthermore, it has been shown that attitudes based upon direct experience with the attitude object are more accessible from memory (Fazio, Powell & Williams, 1989). Sappington et al. (reported in Epstein, 1994) also conducted experiments, the results of which showed that emotionally-based beliefs predicted subsequent behaviour more strongly than intellective beliefs. Reber (1993) also discusses implicit and explicit knowledge systems, which equate to experiential and rational systems, respectively.

The use of vignettes to determine when subjects will make irrational judgements (Epstein et al., cited in Epstein, 1994; Miller, Tversky & Kahneman, cited in Epstein, 1994) shows that when subjects are asked specifically to make rational judgements, they can, but that these conflict with more emotionally-laden judgements. That is, when asked about the proper response, they admit that the intellectual one is more rational, but that they still prefer the experiential one.

Damasio's Ideas

This discussion about two interacting, parallel systems of information-processing is directly relevant to the ideas of Damasio (1994), Vogel (1997) and Bechara et al. (1997), who posit the existence of two systems of knowledge, one that is largely factual, and which proposes response options and possible outcomes relating to these and applies reasoning strategies to the activated facts and options; and another, which contains information related to past, emotional experiences and the rewards and punishments attached to these behaviours. When faced with a sensory representation of a particular situation or object, it is thought that the latter (experiential) system is accessed prior to the former (factual) system, and that the information contained therein biases, or influences how information in the factual system is dealt with. The authors suggest that the ventromedial frontal cortices of the central nervous system are involved in the storage of experiential information.

These conclusions were reached after extensive research with brain-damaged patients who experienced difficulty in making decisions. These patients appeared to lack the ability to trigger, in the decision process, the "nonconscious emotional responses that normal people may register as intuition or a 'hunch'" (Vogel, 1997, p. 1269). In other words, a nonconscious, emotionally-oriented central nervous system mechanism, possibly processed in the ventromedial prefrontal cortex, which is responsible for guiding reasoning, is dysfunctional in some individuals, so that, when faced with several options in a decision task, they have no emotional guide as to which options would be better. Wrangham and Peterson (1996), in explaining why some individuals have difficulty in deciding which option is best, paraphrase Damasio's ideas thus:

> their brains are unable to connect an emotional value to the intellectual menu of possible options. Without being able to feel which solution they like, they have no way to choose. These patients seem to demonstrate that pure reason is inadequate for reaching a decision, a hypothesis that Damasio applies to all of us. Reason generates the list of possibilities. Emotion chooses from that list. (Wrangham & Peterson, 1996, p. 189)

The work of Damasio and his colleagues provides support for the existence of multiple memory systems, namely an emotional, intuitive system, and another that is factually-oriented, and that involves rational/analytic cognitive processes. The interaction of these two systems appears to mediate decision processes and, as the research of Vogel (1997) and Bechara et al. (1997) demonstrates, failure of the emotionally-oriented system to influence the actions of the factual system leads to sub-optimal decisions.

Jaynes's Ideas

In a similar vein, Jaynes (1990) suggests that the conscious mind is a relatively recent development in human history and that, prior to this, mental language did not exist, and initiation of action occurred via cognitive, or internal voices, believed by the individual to be externally-generated, instructing the individual on how to behave. These voices were interpreted by earlier civilisations as religious entities speaking to the individual. Jaynes interprets humans' predisposition towards introspection and problem-solving, on the one hand, and intuitive, action-based cognitive processes in terms of influences of the right- and left-hemisphere of the central nervous system, and suggests that the right hemisphere, which is involved with creativity, non-verbal ideation, and spatial and pattern construction was dominant in earlier civilisations. The left-hemisphere, specialised for language, has only become an important influence on behaviour in more recent times and may be compromised by an intuitive thought process in certain circumstances. Jaynes' ideas are compatible with the ideas of Epstein (1994), Hammond (1996), Damasio (1996) and others in postulating the existence of multiple cognitive systems which underlie particular behaviours, and whose processes are not available for conscious consideration.

Jaynes marshals an impressive array of support for his theory, including a discussion of the notion that ideas, intellectual insights, and suchlike are not arrived at through conscious deliberation. Jaynes suggests that consciousness is not the seat of reason. That is, when individuals find a solution to a problem, it tends to burst into consciousness and we are at a loss to explain how this conclusion was reached. Jaynes (1990) describes the well-known anecdotes of: (a) Einstein's greatest ideas coming to him so suddenly while he was shaving that he was forced to move the razor blade carefully each morning lest he cut himself, (b) a well-known British physicist stating that "we often talk about the three B's, the Bus, the Bath, and the Bed. That is where the great discoveries are made in our science" (p. 44), and (c) Poincaré (reported in Jaynes, 1990) describing how his mathematical theories suddenly erupted into consciousness during a geological excursion. Similar examples are provided by Hammond (1996), who describes the cognitive styles of both Einstein and Richard Feynman, demonstrating their use of both intuition and analysis. It would appear that these great thinkers used both pictorial and analytical modes of cognition and that they were at a loss to explain the mechanisms of the former. This discussion relates to the present argument in highlighting the notion that humans may, in fact, possess multiple processing capabilities, and that the system responsible for some of the most brilliant ideas is not conscious, and not capable of being made conscious.

Loewenstein's Ideas

Loewenstein (1996) discusses the area of decision behaviour, and suggests that visceral factors influence behaviour. His theory relates to the observation that individuals frequently behave in a manner that runs counter to their self-interest. An example of this phenomenon is the fact that individuals will follow religious 'rules' even to the detriment of their personal financial circumstances. Some church-goers regularly pay sometimes quite substantial sums to their particular denominational church. The more extreme of 'suicide bombers' also attests to this phenomenon.

Loewenstein (1996) suggests that, when individuals behave in a manner that is counter to their self-interest (addictions, and so on), that *visceral factors*, such as the craving for chemical substances to which they have become addicted, or the craving for food when hungry and liquid when thirsty, are at least partially responsible. He states that visceral factors entail:

> a direct hedonic impact,...and an influence on the relative desirability of different goods and actions. Hunger, for example, is an aversive sensation that affects the desirability of eating. (Loewenstein, 1996, p. 273)

Loewenstein (1996) states that, furthermore, when the intensity of a visceral factor reaches a certain threshold, this will lead individuals to behave in a manner that is counter to their self-interest, even though they may be aware, at a conscious level, of behaving thus. For example, in many cases the craving for overindulging in alcohol consumption will override rational, analytic considerations relating to the utility of this (self-defeating) behaviour, and individuals will find themselves participating in such activities despite their awareness of the negative consequences that will follow. An example that is more pertinent to the present chapter relates to individuals engaging in the act of adultery despite the reservations of society (and perhaps the individual) that this behaviour is irrational.

This theory might help to explain the finding that traditional decision theories flounder in predicting behaviour from attitudes because they assume rational deliberation (that is, they emphasise 'cool' behaviour), rather than examining the effects of 'hot', emotionally-driven behaviour (Loewenstein, 1996, p. 274). That is, while individuals know at an 'intellectual' and rational level that continuing to take drugs will harm them, or that having unsafe sex has the potential for serious health risks, perhaps death, their behaviour in these contexts is driven by less rational, emotionally driven visceral factors.

Loewenstein (1996) states that the action of visceral factors overwhelms individuals temporarily, so that, while they are able, at an intellectual level, to envisage the negative effects of their actions, these ideas lack any visceral factor, and individuals therefore do not experience (in their imaginings) the full emotional impact of behaving in a manner that is congruent with their self-interest. That is, when we imagine how we will feel if we leave a fun party early, this cognitive picture consists of a scenario that is not accompanied by the corresponding emotional state and, when contrasted with the emotion present when the craving for fun and gaiety arrives, the battle between acting in accordance with our self-interest and not acting in this manner is won over by the activation of visceral factors. That is, we decide to over-consume alcohol due to the existence of visceral factors urging us on, and the concurrent lack of emotion relating to how we will feel if we follow our consciences. These ideas closely resemble those of Hammond (1996), as Loewenstein (1996) is clearly alluding to the existence of two cognitive decision styles, one that is analytical and one that is intuitive.

These ideas are readily able to explain the John Edward phenomenon. When a close relative or friend dies, it is very likely that visceral factors will be active to the detriment of more rational thought processes. The notion that we can communicate in some way with our dearly deceased would naturally elicit strong emotional responses (i.e., visceral factors) that overwhelm our ability to think rationally. It must also be stated at this point that the fear of death, which is almost universal, can be alleviated if visceral factors are readily available to overwhelm our willingness to thoroughly study the evidence of life after death and therefore, positive outcomes from dealings with those such as John Edward are very likely to block the action of more factual, rational cognitive styles.

As stated, Loewenstein's theory is congruent with that of Hammond (1996) but is also remarkably similar to the ideas of Epstein (1994), Bechara et al. (1997), and other theorists discussed above, in postulating the existence of two information-processing systems, one that is rational, and one in which cognitions are driven by emotional factors (largely derived from past experiences).

Specifically, Loewenstein's ideas on visceral factors temporarily overwhelming individuals (1996) are not unlike those of Damasio (1994) and Epstein (1994) in suggesting that an emotional system that is initially triggered in response to a particular stimulus object affects the subsequent functioning of a rational system, leading to certain information and options being explored at the expense of others.

These findings relate to the present chapter in drawing attention to the notion that researchers investigating parapsychological phenomena cannot continue to use (exclusively) models of individual behaviour that do not encompass these purported multiple systems in their theoretical underpinnings.

CONCLUSION

The conclusion to be drawn from the work of Hammond (1996), Fazio (1986), and Epstein (1994), as well as that of others positing a dual-processing cognitive structure is as follows: human knowledge is not only context-specific, it derives from many sources and there is evidence to suggest that there exist at least two systems for processing this knowledge which, in turn, engender two behavioural outcomes: namely, knowledge which is influenced by emotionally-significant past experience, that is emotionally-laden, and is encoded in the form of concrete exemplars and narratives; and knowledge which is based upon analytical, conscious reasoning and is factual and relatively affect-free in nature. These theories can be of enormous assistance in helping researchers understand behaviour more fully, such as an individual's willingness to believe that Edward can 'communicate' with deceased persons, despite the lack of research findings to support this notion (Skeptic, 2003; see also Blackmore for a comprehensive review of data in this field). A notable exception is the findings by Schwartz (2003a) which are at present being vigorously debated by interested parties, the debate of which may also, in fact, be explained using the above ideas on decision theory.

Furthermore, why go to all the trouble of attempting to explain human decision-making in this context? Despite the obvious benefits of contributing to a body of knowledge that helps us to understand behaviour (such as paranormal beliefs), there is the very real notion that psychics such as Edward are blocking the grieving process, leaving individuals with little or no closure regarding the death of loved ones (Skeptic, 2003). There is a well-established body of research to support the notion that the grieving process is complex and consists of stages through which an individual must move in order to accept the death of a loved one (Kubler-Ross, 1997). Use of mediums to 'communicate' with deceased loved ones arguably blocks successful transition through these stages.

Finally, and as alluded to above, the decision theories discussed in this chapter may be useful in explaining, to some degree at least, the heated debate surrounding paranormal phenomena. Researchers in this area who profess to be entirely analytical in their approach to science may, in fact, find that, like all other humans, they too are capable of moving along the 'Cognitive Continuum' (Hammond, 1996) for various reasons. This last point is certainly worth pondering.

Future research will be conducted by administering to individuals a decision-styles inventory (e.g., Rational Emotive Inventory—Pacini & Epsterin, 1999) and by asking them to demonstrate their decision-making propensity via properly designed decision vignettes.

» References

Bargh, J. A. (1992). The ecology of automaticity: Toward establishing the conditions needed to produce automatic processing effects. *American Journal of Psychology, 105*, 181-199.

Bargh, J. A., Chaiken, S., Governer, R., & Pratto, R. (1992). The generality of the automatic attitude activation effect. *Journal of Personality and Social Psychology, 62*, 893-912.

Bechara, A., Damasio, H., Tranel, D., & Damasio, A. (1997). Deciding advantageously before knowing the advantageous strategy. *Science, 275*, 1293-1294.

Blackmore, S. (1993). *Dying to live: Near-death experiences.* Buffalo, NY: Prometheus Press.

Cooksey, R. W. (1996). *Judgment analysis: Theory, methods and applications.* San Diego, CA: Academic Press.

Damasio, A. R. (1994). *Descartes' error: Emotion, reason, and the human brain.* New York: Grosset Putnam.

Epstein, S. (1991). Cognitive-experiential self-theory: An integrative theory of personality. In R. C. Curtis (Ed.), *The relational self: Theoretical convergences in psychoanalysis and social psychology* (pp. 111-137). New York: Guilford.

Epstein, S. (1994). Integration of the cognitive and the psychodynamic unconscious. *American Psychologist, 49*, 709-724.

Fazio, R. H. (1986). How do attitudes guide behavior? In R. M. Sorrentino & E. T. Higgins (Eds.), *Handbook of motivation and cognition, Vol 1* (pp. 204-243). New York: Guildford Press.

Fazio, R. H. (1993a). Addendum: Reply to Chaiken & Bargh by Russell H. Fazio. *Journal of Personality and Social Psychology*, *64*, 764-765.

Fazio, R. H. (1993b). Variability in the likelihood of automatic attitude activation: Data reanalysis and commentary on Bargh, Chaiken, Govender & Pratto (1992). *Journal of Personality and Social Psychology*, *64*, 753-758.

Fazio, R. H., Powell, M. C., & Williams, C. J. (1989). The role of attitude accessibility in the attitude-to-behavior process. *Journal of Consumer Research*, *16*, 280-288.

Fazio, R. H., & Zanna, M. P. (1978). On the predictive validity of attitudes: The roles of direct experience and confidence. *Journal of Personality*, *46*, 228-243.

Fox, D. (1995). Neurodynamics and analytic foundations for Epstein's paradigm. *American Psychologist*, *50*, 798-799.

Hammond, K. R. (1996). *Human judgment and social policy: Irreducible uncertainty, inevitable error, unavoidable injustice.* New York: Oxford University Press.

Hyman, R. (2003a*).* How not to test mediums (1): critiquing The Afterlife Experiments. *Skeptical Inquirer*, *27*(1), 20-31.

Hyman, R. (2003b). Hyman's reply to Schwartz's "How not to review mediumship research". (Follow-up). (Response to article by Gary E. Schwartz.) *Skeptical Inquirer*, *27*(3), 61-65.

Jaynes, J. (1990). *The Origin of consciousness in the breakdown of the bicameral mind.* London: Penguin.

Kubler-Ross, E. (1997). *On death and dying*. New York: Scribner.

Loewenstein, G. (1996). Out of control: Visceral influences on behavior. *Organisational Behavior and Human Decision Processes*, *65*, 272-292.

Macquarie Dictionary. (1990). Macquarie University: Sydney, Australia.

Pacini, R., & Epstein, S. (1999). The relation of rational and experiential information processing styles to personality, basic beliefs, and the ratio-bias phenomenon. *Journal of Personality and Social Psychology, 76*, 972-987.

Paivio, A. (1983). The empirical case for dual coding. In J. C. Yuille (Ed.), Imagery, memory and cognition: Essays in honour of Allan Paivio (pp. 307-332). Hillsdale, NJ: Lawrence Erlbaum.

Reber, A. S. (1993). *Implicit learning and tacit knowledge.* New York: Oxford University Press.

Schwartz, G. E. (2003a). After-death communications: A misleading critique. (Follow-Up). (Response to Wiseman and O'Keeffe.) *Skeptical Inquirer, 27*(3), 58-62.

Schwartz, G. E. (2003b). How not to review mediumship research: Understanding the ultimate reviewer's mistake. *Skeptical Inquirer, 27*(3), 64.

Schwartz, G. E., Simon, W. L., & Chopra, D. (2003). *The afterlife experiments.* Simon & Schuster: Africa House, UK.

Shermer, M. (2003). *How we believe: Science, skepticism, and the search for God.* London: Holt.

Tulving, E., & Schacter, D. L. (1990). Priming and human memory systems. *Science, 247*, 301-306.

Vogel, G. (1997). Scientists probe feelings behind decision-making. *Science, 275*, 1269-1270.

Wiseman, R., & O'Keefe, C. (2001). Accuracy and replicability of anomalous after-death communication across highly skilled mediums: A critique. *The Paranormal Review, 19*, 3-6.

Wiseman, R. (2002). Wiseman replies to Schwartz. (Follow-Up). (Response to "After-death communications: A misleading critique," by Gary E. Schwartz, in September/October 2002 issue) *Skeptical Inquirer, 26*(6), 65-66.

Wrangham, R., & Peterson, D. (1996). *Demonic males: Apes and the origins of human violence.* Boston: Houghton Mifflin.

Chapter 10

The Australian Sheep-Goat Scale: Development and Empirical Findings[1]

Michael A. Thalbourne

Further research . . . unfortunately must await the development of a psychometrically satisfactory measure of paranormal beliefs.
(Irwin, 2009, p. 47)

Australian psychologist and parapsychologist Harvey Irwin (2009) once opined:

> ...strictly speaking, the term 'paranormal belief' should apply only to belief in events that in mainstream science are generally deemed to be scientifically *impossible*, that is, belief in phenomena that are widely viewed as contravening the 'basic limiting principles' of current scientific thinking.... In this sense paranormal beliefs pertain to the subject matter of scientific parapsychology: psi processes (ESP and PK) and ostensibly psi-dependent phenomena (e.g., divinatory arts) as well as the notion of a non-material element of human existence (viz., the spirit) and associated spiritist constructs (e.g., apparitions, reincarnation, astral projection). (p. 109).

Regardless of what we as scientists think of claims that paranormal, or psychic, phenomena occur, it is accepted that belief in the paranormal is widespread

1. [This chapter was originally published in *Australian Journal of Parapsychology* (2010, vol. 10[1], pp. 5-39). Permission to reprint has been granted by the journal.—Editors.]

throughout the population (Dossey, 2009). Such belief requires a scientific explanation rather than mere rejection as 'obviously' unfounded: no theory of human behaviour can be complete that does not take paranormal belief into account (Ross & Joshi, 1992).

It was the clinical psychologist Gertrude Schmeidler who borrowed from a New Testament simile the imagery of the sheep and the goat. Originally, a goat was someone who rejected the possibility that ESP could be demonstrated in the experiment in which they found themselves, while a sheep was someone who did *not* reject this possibility (Schmeidler, 1943, p. 107). Over time, the terms 'sheep' and 'goats' have evolved to mean, in general, believers and disbelievers, respectively, in some aspect of psychic phenomena conceived of broadly or narrowly. Two obvious questions arise from this separation: (1) do sheep and goats differ in paranormal performance when tested under impeccable laboratory conditions?; and (2) do sheep and goats differ in any *other* aspects of their psychology?

In order to answer these questions we need to have well-developed tools for categorising persons as sheep or as goats (or for placing people along a continuum of sheep-goat attitude). The psychologist is likely to use a questionnaire of some description, single-item or multi-item, allowing a participant to self-report their views on the paranormal. Unfortunately, what has been considered 'paranormal' has included all manner of topics such as astrology, Ufology, cryptozoology, graphology and palmistry (Thalbourne & French, 1997), which could be said, perhaps, to concern potential *anomalies* but are not paranormal, at least not as parapsychologists would define their field.

Prior to the devising of the first version of the Australian Sheep-Goat Scale there were at least two sheep-goat scales in existence which were restricted to the paranormal as defined above and as specified in the second quote given from Irwin (2009): these were the Sentence Completion Test of ESP Belief (Van de Castle & White, 1955), and Bhadra's Attitude to ESP Scale (Bhadra, 1966). The first of these required some clinical judgment in scoring the completed sentences. The second scale was multiple-choice but was directed towards performance in a card-guessing test. Something more suitable for *any* ESP test was desired.

Construction of the Australian Sheep-Goat Scale

The ASGS had a very modest beginning as a simple list of multiple-choice questions devised jointly by the author and his then-supervisor, Dr. Peter S. Delin. The list covered belief in, and ostensible experiences of, ESP, as well as belief in life after death and in the possibility of contact with the deceased.[2] The questionnaire was administered to all participants prior to a free-response drawing ESP test (Thalbourne, 1976). Initially, the focus of interest was merely in tabulating and reporting the responses to each question and comparing between the experimental and control groups (emotionally close, and not emotionally close to anyone, respectively). In the following year, however, it was decided to combine the answers to these questions into a 10-item scale, which turned out to have some interesting correlates, including ESP-score in some subgroups—the so-called Sheep-Goat Effect.

At the same time, some researchers were developing an interest in the issue of whether there might exist psychological differences between believers and disbelievers in psychic (and other anomalous) phenomena, irrespective of whether such phenomena actually existed. An example is the extensive research programme initiated by Tobacyk and Milford (1983). Irwin (2009) has recently produced an excellent book reviewing what has become an extensive literature. The 10-item Australian Sheep-Goat Scale has been used in a number of examinations of such psychological differences (e.g., Richards, 1990; Roig, 1992), and we shall study these differences systematically later in this review.

By 1982, an expansion of the ASGS was contemplated, and carried out in two steps. First, the 10 items were augmented with three asking about the theoretical possibility (not just personal experience) of, specifically, precognition and active and receptive telepathy. Some research was conducted with this 13-item scale (e.g., Irwin, 1985; Thalbourne, 1985). At the same time, and for the purposes of a large-scale survey of beliefs and experiences (Thalbourne, 1994b) and a psychokinesis experiment (Thalbourne, 1996a), it became desirable to have in the scale items pertaining to psychokinetic phenomena as well. Five items explicitly about belief in and ostensible experience of PK were therefore constructed. Thus was born the 18-item Australian Sheep-Goat Scale.

This assessment instrument is available in a number of formats: (1) The forced-choice format, which presents a statement (such as *I believe in ESP*) and then provides three alternative responses, *true*, *uncertain*, and *false*;[3] responses attract 2, 1, or zero points respectively, and these are summed across the 18 items to provide a total score (Thalbourne, 1995a; see also Irwin [2009, Appendix 11]); (2) The visual analogue format, in which the respondent is asked to mark a point

2. For the wording of these items see either Thalbourne and Haraldsson (1980, Table 1) or Thalbourne (1981a, Appendix A).

3. Sometimes *yes*, *unsure* and *no* (e.g., Goulding, 2004).

on a horizontal line anchored at one end by complete conviction of a goat belief and at the other end by complete conviction of a sheep belief; marks are converted to scores ranging from 1-44 for increasing 'sheepishness' and transformed across items to give a total score (Thalbourne & Delin, 1993); (3) A six-point Likert scale ranging from *strongly disagree* to *strongly agree* (Roe, 1998, objected to the visual analogue scale and replaced it with this six-point scale.[4] For the purposes of his [Roe, 1998] study, he also reduced the number of items from 18 to 6; see a discussion of the merits of the various approaches in Roe, 2002; and Thalbourne, 1998c; 2003b); (4) A Rasch-scaled version of the ASGS where Rasch scaling fixes response bias that comes from age or gender (see Lange & Thalbourne, 2002)—the visual analogue scale is presented but the 1-44 metric is collapsed into three categories, scored zero, 1 and 2 points (this scale can be downloaded from the AIPR website: aiprinc.org/resources.asp); these scores are then summed for the ESP/PK items (the two afterlife items are a separate factor) and converted to interval-level (scaled like temperature) Rasch scores, which were found to be independent of gender and age.

The Factor Structure of the ASGS

The dimensionality (or underlying factor structure) of the ASGS items has been investigated on a number of occasions. Thalbourne and Haraldsson (1980) applied principal components analysis with so-called 'quartimax rotation' (to minimize factors) to the 10-item ASGS and obtained three factors, viz., general experience and telepathy, precognition and apparition, and otherworldliness, accounting together for 59% of the variance in ASGS scores (i.e., scores vary because of these factors).

Thalbourne (1981a) performed the same analysis with an expanded dataset for the 10-item ASGS and found two factors which were approximately (1) ESP belief and experience, and (2) an afterlife factor, this solution accounting for 49% of the variance.

For the 18-item visual analogue scale, Thalbourne and Delin (1993), subjected data from 241 students first to a principal components analysis to determine how many factors could be extracted using a principal factors analysis. Using the so-called 'Kaiser criterion', which singles out the most important factor(s), three factors were identified. Principal axis analysis was then applied,

4. Later, a 7-point Likert scale (e.g., Roe, Sherwood, Farrell, Savva, & Baker, 2007).

using an oblique rotation because the factors showed high inter-correlations ranging from 0.34 to 0.63.

The three factors jointly accounted for a total of 60% of the variance. The first factor accounted for 49% of the variance. The items that loaded on it consisted of all but one of those having to do with belief in and experience of ESP. The second factor, accounting for 7% of the variance, contained all of the items to do with experience of psychokinesis. And the third item, though accounting for relatively little of the variance (4%), contained the conceptually important items on life after death and in the possibility of contact with spirits.

The high correlations between these factors allow us to differentiate three traditional strands of interest to parapsychologists—ESP, PK and life after death—but at the same time to see them as essentially related and thus to be able to use the total score meaningfully as a measure of attitude towards parapsychological phenomena.[5] The results are consistent with Lange and Thalbourne's (2002) later finding that the ESP and PK findings may be considered, together, as a New Age Philosophy factor (e.g., psychic phenomena, reincarnation, astrology), and the life after death items as a Traditional Paranormal Beliefs factor (e.g., the devil, heaven and hell, witchcraft), the two of which positively correlate (Lange, Irwin & Houran, 2000). Consequently, the practice of, for example, Roe and his colleagues (e.g., Roe, Davey & Stevens, 2003) of subdividing the total ASGS score into as many as three components is unnecessary: there is either one orthogonal (independent) component or two oblique (correlated) components. In what follows we shall assume the uni-componential approach (the approach that has been taken on the vast majority of occasions), but it should be pointed out that a bi-componential approach, which is arguable, might well lead to different analytic outcomes.

Reliability

As regards internal reliability (i.e., whether the ASGS measure is consistent within itself), Thalbourne and Delin (1993) report a high Cronbach's alpha of 0.94 (maximum alpha = 1.00) for the 18-item visual analogue scale. Goulding (2005)

5. Willson (2009) performed an analysis of these data, and while remaining undogmatic as to the number of factors produced, pointed out that a graphic representation of the data (a so-called scree-plot) suggested that only one factor should conceptually define paranormal belief.

reports an alpha of 0.91 for a Swedish version of the ASGS. Thalbourne, Silva and Razente (2006) report an alpha of 0.82 for a Portuguese version of the ASGS. Dagnall, Parker and Munley (2008) give an alpha of 0.92 for the forced-choice 18-item ASGS. A value of 0.91 was reported by Storm and Rock (2009) for the Rasch ASGS.

Related to the issue of internal reliability is the fact that the correlations among the 18 ASGS items tend to be all positive and substantial, and this is reinforced by the Kaiser-Meyer-Olkin measure of sampling adequacy of 0.91 (Willson, 2009, p. 77), which is much larger than the 0.60 suggested as a minimum for performing factor analysis.

Thalbourne and Delin (1993) measured test-retest reliability for the scale over a time interval of approximately 11 months for 29 participants: the coefficient was 0.66 ($p < .001$). If the forced-choice and the visual analogue versions of the ASGS may be considered in some sense parallel, then the reliability is 0.85 for 301 participants (Thalbourne, 2004a).

Response Bias

Four investigations have looked at the possible influence on the ASGS of social desirability responding. Thalbourne (1981a) administered the Eysenck Lie Scale (Eysenck & Eysenck, 1964) in a classroom setting, and found no association with the 10-item ASGS; nor was there any association between a later Lie Scale (Eysenck & Eysenck, 1991) and the 18-item ASGS (Thalbourne, 1998a).

Roig (1992) argued that a better measure of this response bias was the Marlowe-Crowne Social Desirability Scale (Crowne & Marlowe, 1960), but nevertheless found a zero correlation (as did Thalbourne, Dunbar & Delin, 1995). He remarked that "whether some experimental situations that demand close one-to-one interactions between subject and experimenter elicit social desirability, still remains unclear and needs to be explored further" (Roig, 1992, p. 162).

Validity Issues

Content Validity

This form of validity can be said to be established if the frequencies obtained for each item match those intuitively thought by rational people to be appropriate for that item. Thus, Thalbourne and Delin (1993) found that the most commonly endorsed item was about hunches (viz., 59% said "true"), the next most endorsed item was life after death (viz., 50%: a 2009 poll of the Australian population yielded a percentage of 53%), precognitive dreams were reported by 35%, belief that one is psychic was a low 10%, and just 3% of participants professed to have marked psychokinetic ability.

Convergent Validity

The correlation between the ASGS and other scales purporting to measure paranormal belief has been reported by a number of researchers. Table 10.A1 lists these findings (see Appendix A in this chapter), giving the source references, the names of the scales, the number of items in the version of the ASGS used, and the correlations obtained. It can be seen, when expressly investigated that, in every case convergent validity has been demonstrated, usually with a high degree of correlation. It can be concluded that despite the heterogeneous content of the other paranormal belief scales, they and the ASGS tend to be tapping into the same variance. This gives us confidence that results obtained with the other scales are likely to generalise to the ASGS.

Predictive Validity: The Sheep-Goat Effect

Comments Richards (1989), "In parapsychology, the eventual concern is with predictive validity: whether subjective experiences reflect actual psi and can be used to predict performance on objective tests" (p. 53). Independently of the ASGS there is evidence that variables such as belief in ESP show a positive relationship to guessing-scores in well-controlled laboratory experiments (see, e.g., Palmer, 1971). Is the ASGS efficacious in empirically bringing about this relationship? In this section are discussed the considerable number of studies which have utilised one or other form of the ASGS to predict performance in

ESP or PK tasks. In Table 10.A2 (see Appendix A in this chapter) can be found a summary of these results, citing source, mode of psi tested, number of items in the ASGS, number of participants, direction of effect (a positive sign indicates that sheep scored higher than goats), and the statistical outcome if available.

Table 10.A2 shows a number of facts. First of all, it shows that a significant Sheep-Goat Effect (SGE) was found in 7 out of 28 cases (25%).[6] Very clearly, use of the ASGS does not guarantee that an SGE will be found—the effect is by no means 100% replicable, and this might be an issue if the scale measures two rather than just one components. However, despite this, the direction of the sheep-goat difference is slightly more often found in favour of sheep than of goats (22 positive differences as opposed to 19 negative differences); and when the difference is *significant*, Table 10.A2 shows that it has been such that sheep have always had the higher scores, as indicated by the correlations in the last column—there is not a single reversal of the effect.

It could be argued that significant reversals of the effect have been obtained but not published,[7] so as to maintain, in the literature, the integrity of the sheep-goat hypothesis. However, parapsychologists in fact show eagerness to publish significant results whatever their direction, and a few significant reversals of the SGE have indeed been reported in the literature, involving other sheep-goat measures (e.g., Haraldsson, 1993; Moss, Paulson, Chang & Levitt, 1970; Thorisson, Skulason & Haraldsson, 1991). Selective reporting of significant positive results may therefore not be a great problem.

Looking at Table 10.A2 there *appears* to be at least one evident pattern in the results: significant outcomes seem to be more often obtained when the test is one of telepathy than of clairvoyance, precognition, or psychokinesis (see Table 10.1). The data are too few to permit fine-grained analysis, but a comparison of the telepathy studies (6 significant, 8 nonsignificant) with the other three modes combined (1 significant, 14 nonsignificant) suggests an excess of significant telepathy studies (a chi-square test would be invalid owing to small expected frequencies). In other words, when using the ASGS, the SGE is most reliably found in experiments using pairs of people attempting to transmit information to each other. Future studies might compare (let us say) a clairvoyance condition with a telepathy condition, in circumstances where the receiver subject is blind to

6. This total omits the two studies (Thalbourne et al., 1982, and Evans & Thalbourne, 1999) where, respectively, goats scored significantly below chance and sheep above, but where there was no significant group-difference.

7. There are statistical tests for this.

sending condition. Analyses should relate the sender's ASGS data to the receiver's production as well as the receiver's ASGS data.

Table 10.1: Breakdown of Significance of Outcome by Mode of Psi Tested

	Telepathy	Precognition	Clairvoyance	Psychokinesis
Significant	6	1	0	0
Non-Significant	8	1	7	6
Not reported	4	6	5	0
Total studies	18	8	12	6

Moreover, item analyses should be conducted: belief items may show correlations different from experience items. Indeed, Thalbourne (1981b, p. 225) found that the item that correlated strongest with telepathy-score was 'Have Had a Telepathic Experience', for senders: $rs(51) = 0.59$, $p < 0.001$ (two-tailed), as one might expect if predictive validity holds.

Median splits could also be made for the ASGS total score, and this should show that goats tend not to score *at* chance but significantly below, avoiding the target information, in the phenomenon known as psi-missing. Thus goats are (probably to their surprise) like sheep in that *both* groups have ESP, but they differ in how they use it. The present reviewer has suggested that the underlying mechanism is a need to produce an apparent reality that accords with one's metaphysical paradigm or worldview in relation to the claim that telepathy exists: one does this by paranormally producing information-correspondence in the case of sheep, and lack of information-correspondence in the case of goats (Thalbourne, 1981b, 1983). The work of Storm and Thalbourne (2005) on 'conversion effect' is also relevant to this hypothesis. Certainly, Table 10.A2 stands as a testament to the reality of the SGE, weak and difficult to demonstrate though it may be.

Non-Parapsychological Correlates of the ASGS

The ASGS has sometimes been used simply to describe the average level of paranormal belief in a given sample (e.g., Roe et al., 2007; Sherwood, Roe, Holt, & Wilson, 2005; Thalbourne et al., 2006). However, in addition, there is a large database of studies examining the correlation between the ASGS and a great variety of non-parapsychological variables. In order to render our account of these correlates somewhat more systematic, the approach adopted here for the most part was that used by Irwin (1993, 2009). He grouped his data under four main theoretical depictions of paranormal belief: the social marginality hypothesis, the worldview hypothesis, the cognitive deficits hypothesis, and the psychodynamic functions hypothesis. We define each of these in turn, and tabulate the evidence for them from studies using the ASGS.

The Social Marginality Hypothesis

According to this view:

> the people most susceptible to paranormal belief are members of socially marginal or disadvantaged groups, for example, the poorly educated or the unemployed who have characteristics or roles that rank low among dominant social values.... It is held that the privation, loss of control over life and alienation associated with marginal social status encourage such people to appeal to magical and religious beliefs, presumably because these beliefs bring some emotional compensation to their lives. (Irwin, 2009, p. 51)

The primary indices of social marginality include (old) age, (female) gender, (low) socioeconomic status, (minority) ethnicity and (gay) sexual orientation.

There are a number of studies in which women have scored higher on the ASGS than have men (Goulding, 2004; Irwin, 1985; Thalbourne, 1994b; Thalbourne, Dunbar & Delin, 1995; but note an exception: Thalbourne, 1981a).

As to age, Thalbourne (1994b) found no age-differences, but one recent study (Storm & Rock, 2009) found a correlation with the Rasch ASGS, $r(104) = +0.26$, $p = .008$. Note, however, that analysis using the Rasch scores of a much bigger sample ($N = 1{,}822$: Lange & Thalbourne, 2002), controlling for differential item functioning, showed only negligible age and sex differences.

As regards marital status, persons coming from 'broken' relationships (in this case, separated, divorced or widowed) had a higher mean on the ASGS than did those from 'unbroken' situations (single or married), confirming two previous findings (Thalbourne, 1994b; see Thalbourne, 2001a). In this study also, which was a survey of members of the Society for Psychical Research, there was a small but significant tendency for members with higher degrees to prove more sceptical according to the ASGS.

No studies have been reported looking at socioeconomic status or ethnicity and the ASGS. However, one study (Thalbourne, 1997b) compared the level of paranormal belief between heterosexual and homosexual men and found no differences.

Clearly the problem in evaluating the social marginality hypothesis from the perspective of the ASGS is that relatively few relevant data have been collected, and this leaves open a wide scope for future research, perhaps combining sociological variables, although Irwin concludes that the outlook is not promising.

The Worldview Hypothesis

According to the worldview hypothesis:

> paranormal belief is simply one facet of a broader worldview, a view that is primarily characterised by a highly subjective and esoteric perspective on humanity, life and the world at large. For example, under this worldview events may be interpreted more in terms of intangible mental and metaphysical processes than in relation to observable or physical factors. (Irwin, 2009, p. 67)

Irwin (2009, p. 68) goes on to say that under this hypothesis the esoteric orientation should be reflected in behaviour, such as psychic activities of various sorts. If paranormal beliefs are nothing more than abstractions, there is little merit in seeking to interpret them as a component of a 'worldview' that underlies the believer's fundamental approach to the world at large.

Evidence pertinent to this theme comes from at least two studies. In the first (Thalbourne, 1998-1999b), attendees at an adult education course on psychic experiences had ASGS scores that were extremely high compared with those of a group of university students. In a second study, participants were required to read accounts of coincidences and rate them for degree of perceived paranormality. The ASGS was a good predictor of level of paranormality-rating awarded to the coincidences (Moore, Thalbourne, & Storm, 2010). In other studies, sheep were more inclined to read about paranormal or psychic phenomena (Irwin, 1985; Thalbourne et al., 2006). There is also fairly abundant evidence that high scorers on the ASGS report other psychic beliefs and experiences (Thalbourne, 1994b; Thalbourne & Delin, 1993; Thalbourne & French, 1997) or mystical experiences (Thalbourne, 1994b; Thalbourne, 1998a; Thalbourne, 1998-1999b; Thalbourne & Fox, 1999). Thus, the ASGS measures something that evidently has some influence on behaviour. Does it impact upon *other* domains of behaviour?

We first consider religious beliefs and practices. Using the Haraldsson (1981) 8-item non-sectarian Religiosity Scale with the ASGS, significantly positive correlations have been observed in a variety of studies (Thalbourne, 1994b; Thalbourne, 1995b; Thalbourne, 1998a; Thalbourne & Hensley, 2001; Thalbourne & Houtkooper, 2002; Thalbourne & O'Brien, 1999). Irwin (1985) achieved a significant positive correlation of 0.20 between the 13-item ASGS and a single religiosity item. Thalbourne (1994c, 1995b) found a significant correlation between this ASGS and religion-puritanism (Wilson, 1975). A study by Thalbourne (2003a) showed sheep were more inclined to be theists. Sheep tend to read about religion, to pray, to self-report being religious, and to read the Bible in some studies but not in others (Thalbourne, 1994b; Thalbourne et al., 2006). The present database thus shows a clear trend in favour of sheep being more likely to be religious in a general sense. Further research might examine whether this is indeed true for a variety of faiths, and perhaps denominations. However, religious affiliation "appears to have only weak links with the intensity of paranormal belief" (Irwin, 2009, p. 71; see Thalbourne, et al., 1995, p. 222). Even so, the evidence canvassed here suggests some support for the worldview hypothesis. We may note in addition that sheep are more likely to report a vivid religious or spiritual experience, and to read about Eastern religions or theosophy (Thalbourne, 1994b, 1995b, 1998a).

Further support for this hypothesis comes from studies where the ASGS has been correlated with belief in a dualist (mind/body) philosophy of human nature (Stanovich, 1989; Thalbourne, 1999a). The belief held by sheep of an extra-corporeal component of human existence is reflected in their beliefs about their fate following death: ASGS scores are significantly higher in persons who believe in reincarnation (Thalbourne, 1996b; 1998-1999a; Thalbourne et al., 2006), who believe in Heaven and in reunion with loved ones after death (Thalbourne, 1995a), who believe in the Resurrection of the dead (Thalbourne et al., 2006), who report past lives (Thalbourne, 1994b; Thalbourne et al., 2006), and who believe in survival of death generally (Irwin, 1985). The subjectivity of the sheep's stance on life is further evidenced by greater dream recall and particularly by a tendency to engage in dream interpretation (Irwin, 1985; Thalbourne, 1994b; Thalbourne, 1995b; Thalbourne, 1998a; Thalbourne & Delin, 1999), though exactly what aspects are examined in such scrutiny deserves further research.

Another relevant domain may be the belief in a just world, "the fanciful notion that good people will tend to fare well in life and bad people one day will inevitably get their just desserts" (Irwin, 2009, p. 73). The present reviewer was unable to obtain evidence confirming a relationship with the sheep-goat scale (Thalbourne, 1995a).

As a last word in this section, it may be mentioned that sheep have demonstrated an external locus of personal control (Thalbourne et al., 1995), implying that believers in parapsychological phenomena think that their fate tends to be determined by forces outside their own control.

The Cognitive Deficits Hypothesis

According to Irwin (2009), under this view "the believer in the paranormal is held variously to be illogical, irrational, credulous, uncritical and foolish" (p. 77). Thalbourne and Nofi (1997) administered the Raven's Progressive Matrices (Raven, 1965) to university students, along with a measure of superstition and the ASGS. Lack of intelligence was correlated with a specially devised measure of superstitiousness, but not with the sheep-goat scale. However, it should be mentioned that there is a low-to-moderate correlation between the ASGS and superstition (Thalbourne, 1997a). In a very large sample, tolerance of ambiguity was positively but not significantly correlated with the 10-item ASGS (Thalbourne et al., 1995).

Thalbourne (2005a) provides a narrative meta-analysis of five out of six studies in all of which the ASGS has positively and significantly correlated with a measure of creative personality (Thalbourne & Delin, 1994, 1995; Thalbourne, Bartemucci, Delin, Fox & Nofi, 1997; Thalbourne, 1998a; Thalbourne, Keogh, & Crawley, 1999), omitting a further positive confirmation (Thalbourne, 2000a). One normally assumes that creativity is a positive trait rather than one that detracts. Comments Irwin (2009): "...this finding [therefore] does not sit well with the cognitive deficits hypothesis, although the implacable sceptic might seek to interpret it in terms of suggested associations between creativity and psychopathology" (p. 89).

Do sheep tend to have a richer imagination? Thalbourne (1995a) devised a Conceivability Scale, consisting of 26 items that were preceded by the following instructions:

> Listed below are a number of unusual notions. These notions may be quite unlikely or perhaps even impossible. Your task is not to say whether they are possible or impossible, likely or unlikely. You simply have to say how easily you, personally, can imagine them being true.

Three illustrative items are: (4) Lunar influence on human emotions; (5) The complete elimination of war; and (7) Discovery of the Loch Ness Monster. Sheep scored significantly higher on this Conceivability Scale, suggesting that goats suffer from a lack of imagination.

Finally we consider the construct of fantasy proneness, measured by the Inventory of Childhood Memories and Imaginings (Myers, 1983). Three studies have looked at this measure in relation to the ASGS, and all have found significant positive correlations (French, Santamauro, Hamilton, Fox and Thalbourne, 2008; Thalbourne, 1998a; Thalbourne et al., 1997). A related variable, absorption, correlates moderately with the ASGS (French et al., 2008; Thalbourne, 1998a; Thalbourne et al., 1997).

The Psychodynamic Functions Hypothesis

Irwin (2009) states that:

> The general view that paranormal beliefs are need-serving will be termed the *psychodynamic functions hypothesis*. Sceptics usually take this hypothesis to mean that paranormal believers are in some respects psychologically deviant or dysfunctional[8] and although this is not a necessary implication of the hypothesis, the personality correlates of paranormal belief clearly are data to be taken into account in this regard. (Irwin, 2009, p. 91)

Work with the ASGS has contributed to understanding the social dimension of personality: there has been a consistent tendency for sheep to be more extraverted than goats (Thalbourne & Haraldsson, 1980; Thalbourne, 1981a, 1998a; Thalbourne, Beloff & Delanoy, 1982; Thalbourne, Beloff, Delanoy, & Jungkuntz, 1983; Thalbourne & Jungkuntz, 1983; but note a non-significant difference in Thalbourne, Dunbar & Delin, 1995). On the whole this seems to confirm the statement made by Eysenck (1967) to the effect that…

> …introverts tend to be characterized by scientific, cautious and doubting tendencies which would seem to predispose them to become 'goats', while extraverts are more characterized by artistic tendencies and to be

8. Since creativity is found amongst the "deviant and/or dysfunctional" (e.g., bipolar disorder amongst poets) there would therefore be some overlap between this Hypothesis and the Cognitive Deficits Hypothesis.

> less resistant to such group pressures as often exist (or may be imagined to exist) in ESP experimental circles (Eysenck, 1967, p. 63)

The evidence for a link with neuroticism is much more tenuous, a significant positive correlation being found by Thalbourne et al. (1995) but not by Thalbourne (1981a, 1998a). (The literature *not* using the ASGS is similarly quite mixed: see, for example, Francis, Williams & Robbins, 2009, p. 341, and Irwin, 2009, p. 93).

On at least two occasions the ASGS has been administered together with Antonovsky's (1993) measure of well-being, the Sense of Coherence Scale (Goulding, 2005; Holt, Simmonds-Moore & Moore, 2008). Re-analyses of each study yielded non-significant correlations.

We now move on more clearly to the topic of psychopathology. The ASGS has been used in a large number of studies of this kind. For example, the 18-item ASGS correlates significantly with history of manic experience and with history of depressive experience (Thalbourne & Delin, 1994, 1995; Thalbourne et al., 1997; Thalbourne, 1998a; Thalbourne & French, 1995; Thalbourne, Keogh, & Crawley, 1999). Narrative meta-analyses for each variable can be found in Thalbourne (2004b, 2005b).

There is also evidence that sheep are more likely to report hallucinatory predisposition (Thalbourne, 2006; French, et al. 2008), dissociation (replicated by Dagnall et al., 2008; French et al. 2008), schizotypal personality (the STA scale),[9] and psychoticism (Thalbourne, 1998a). Goulding (2004) found that ASGS scores were higher in participants who were high on the Unusual Experiences scale of the Oxford-Liverpool Inventory of Feelings and Experiences—a multi-dimensional measure of schizotypy.

Turning back in time, to the early 1980s, Thalbourne (1985) was interested in the Magical Ideation Scale (MIS) of Eckblad and Chapman (1983), because about a third of its items had a direct link to parapsychological themes. Yet it was claimed that the scale could be used to indicate proneness to psychosis. So were sheep more likely to become psychotic? Thalbourne (1985) administered the 13-item ASGS and the MIS to 99 students, and obtained a positive correlation of 0.62. Thinking the high correlation might be due to the inclusion in the MIS of paranormal items these were removed and the correlation re-performed. Still there was a significant positive correlation between the ASGS and the 'purified' MIS was 0.40, suggesting that sheep may indeed be more prone to psychosis. This correlation has been replicated in a large number of samples (Thalbourne, 1994a,

---

9. However, it should be pointed out that there are paranormal belief items in the STA scale of schizotypy (Claridge & Broks, 1984, p. 648).

1998a; Thalbourne et al., 1995; Thalbourne et al., 1997; Thalbourne & Delin, 1994; Thalbourne & French, 1995.) So are believers simply deranged?

Irwin argues that with a typical correlation of 0.60 the majority of the variance is still to be accounted for. The author argues that this is not so. If the correlation were as high as 0.71, the amount of variance in common between the two measures would be 50%, and this would traditionally be taken as *evidence* of the identity of the two variables. Thus, while 36% of the variance is accounted for by magical ideation, just 14% more is needed to effectively explain it all.[10] So there seems to be a major connection between paranormal belief and psychological disturbance.

Irwin speaks strongly against the psychopathological interpretation but neglects to encourage researchers to use better measures of psychopathology. Goretzki, Thalbourne and Storm (2009) published a study in which, amongst other things, they correlated what is essentially a sheep-goat scale (called the Psychic Opening Subscale) with a validated measure of experience of psychotic symptoms, obtaining a significant positive result, $r(107) = 0.67$, $p < .001$. Since even higher correlations have been found in later studies, it is difficult to avoid the suggestion that sheep are indeed prone to experiencing psychotic symptoms.[11] These findings are currently being followed up using a newly constructed 26-item version of the ASGS,[12] which is philosophically founded on the basic limiting principles of Broad (1978), utilises a Likert scale and alternate positive and negative wording to avoid acquiescence response bias, improves the wording of the old items, and has nine additional items—four on mind-body dualism, three on paranormal healing, and two on clairvoyance (see Appendix B in this

---

10. One reviewer rejected utterly this reasoning, arguing that 100% of the variance needed to be in common before identity of variables could be posited. Further debate seems to be required in order to resolve the differences of opinion. Perhaps both sides could agree that at least 30-40% of the variance is in common, and that this is a substantial amount.
11. There are of course further questions that need to be asked, such as (1) are traditionally psychotic traits totally without redeeming qualities (McCreery & Claridge, 1995)?, and (2) even if paranormal believers are more psychotic in a truly pathological sense does this imply anything about their psi abilities? (Greyson, 1977; Rogo, 1975).
12. Note that the item on hunches has been dropped partly due to the difficulty of translating the word into other languages (e.g., German: Thalbourne & Houtkooper, 2002).

chapter). This new instrument—tentatively named the Basic Limiting Principles Questionnaire (BLPQ)—has not been psychometrically tested as yet.[13]

The author additionally proposes an updated version of Goretzki's (Goretzki et al., 2009) Experience of Psychotic Symptoms Scale (EPSS; see Appendix C in this chapter), likewise not yet psychometrically tested. Together the two instruments might prove to be the most incisive method yet of testing for a genuine positive relationship between paranormal belief and psychosis.

Special Groups of Participants

Thalbourne (1998b) compared the ASGS scores of participants with manic-depression or schizophrenia with those from a sample drawn from the wider community, and found the two clinical groups to be significantly higher. A group of persons suffering from panic attacks scored similarly to the two psychiatric groups.

Next, there exists a minority of individuals who report that they have never, in their lifetimes, formed an extremely close personal and emotional relationship with another human being. Research indicates that, compared with persons who report that they *have* at some time entered into such a relationship, these 'non-close-relaters' tend to be more shy, more lacking in trust, more introverted and more lacking in social skills (e.g., Thalbourne, 1976). In addition, non-close-relaters score lower on the 10-item ASGS: the difference between the scores of close-relaters was significant in four out of five samples (Thalbourne, 2001c). This difference could be explained in a variety of ways, psychological or parapsychological: for example, being closely associated with another person may give rise to a greater possibility of experiencing coincidences of thought, and these coincidences are erroneously interpreted as paranormal communication; or a close relationship may in fact facilitate the occurrence of telepathic experiences with one's partner.

Basterfield and Thalbourne (2002) administered the 18-item ASGS to 21 self-selected ostensible UFO abductees and compared their responses with those of a control group of 301 students. Abductees scored significantly higher on the sheep-goat scale. This finding was confirmed by French et al. (2008) using a less strict criterion for abduction status (only observation of UFO craft was required,

13. A high priority would be to correlate the 18-item ASGS and the BLPQ to see whether they may be regarded as yielding approximately the same *z* scores.

not abduction), and gave the highest effect size of a number of psychological variables.

Miscellaneous Correlates

Hypnotisability

Richards (1990) administered the 10-item ASGS along with the Harvard Group Scale of Hypnotic Susceptibility and obtained a low positive but non-significant correlation.

The Feeling of Being Stared At

Thalbourne and Evans (1992) presented to 59 students a simple 10-item survey to explore attitudes and beliefs about, and reactions to, phenomena having to do with staring and being stared at: significantly higher scores on the 13-item ASGS were obtained by respondents who (1) reported that they liked being stared at intensely by people they knew; (2) said that they liked being stared at intensely by strangers; (3) said they would not be suspicious of someone staring for no apparent reason; (4) believed that gaze could inflict harm or bring about bad luck; (5) believed that some people possess a 'magnetic gaze'; (6) believed that "Sometimes *I* can make someone turn towards me just by looking at them"; and finally (7) reported sensing that they were being stared at "by someone even though they were situated a considerable distance behind me" (p. 382). In short, sheep take a positive attitude towards the phenomena of staring and detection of the unseen gaze.

Type 'A' Behaviour Pattern

McBeath and Thalbourne (1993) investigated whether the ASGS was related to various aspects of the coronary-prone Type A Behavior Pattern (Friedman & Rosenman, 1974). In all of five studies, goats were no more likely than sheep to display hurried impatience (as measured by the Jenkins Activity Survey of Krantz,

Glass, and Snyder, 1974) or suspiciousness (as measured by Factor L of the Cattell Sixteen Factor Questionnaire of Cattell, Eber, and Tatsuoka, 1970).

Hypersensitivity to Sensory Stimulation

Sheep obtain higher scores than do goats on measures of hyperaesthesia, that is, reported hypersensitivity to sensory stimulation (Thalbourne, 1998a; Thalbourne & Delin, 1994; Thalbourne et al., 1997).

Other Correlates

Thalbourne (1995b) found no significant correlation with the ASGS and non-religious conservatism (Wilson, 1975), nor with having a religion in one's upbringing or now (cf., Thalbourne, 1995a), or with the Mosher Sex-Guilt Scale (Mosher, 1966). However, there was a significant positive correlation with the Ås Experience Inventory (Ås, O'Hara & Munger, 1962), suggesting that sheep reported more experiences presumably related to hypnotic susceptibility.

Thalbourne, et al. (1995) found non-significant correlations between the ASGS and interpersonal locus of control and socio-political locus of control, dogmatism, and independence of judgment.

The reviewer has earlier contended that the term 'paranormal' should be used as a synonym for 'parapsychological'. Nevertheless, sheep show statistically significant tendencies to endorse not only non-ASGS paranormal items (such as out-of-body experiences: see Thalbourne, 1994b; Thalbourne & Delin, 1993; Thalbourne & French, 1997),[14] but also items to do with astrology and UFOs (Thalbourne & French, 1997).

Kundalini is the Sanskrit term for a hypothetical yogic energy that is said to travel up the spine and throughout the body (Krishna, 1970). Thalbourne and Fox (1999) constructed a 32-item scale to measure manifestations of this energy, and found that it correlated 0.36 with the visual analogue ASGS. The researchers

14. A reviewer commented that "the reference to 'non-ASGS paranormal items' surely raises questions about the breadth of items comprising the ASGS and the dimensionality of paranormal belief had such items been included." This is one reason why the author believes it urgent to expand the number of items from 18 to 26.

also found that persons who suffered from panic attacks scored significantly higher on the ASGS than did control participants.

Wilson and French (2006) found that 36% of respondents falsely claimed to have seen footage of the Bali bombings. Participants reporting false memories of this kind scored higher on the ASGS. Dagnall et al. (2008) sought to determine whether this effect was moderated by news-item order, some of the items having actual footage of them, others not. Level of paranormal belief had no effect on clarity rating when the Princess Diana car crash question was presented first (that is, in the same experiment as other questions), but sheep gave significantly higher clarity ratings when the question was posed fifth. Thus, in some instances, sheep reported more vivid false recollections of non-existent footage. Do they have a more liberal criterion of 'clarity'? Further analyses indicated...

> ...a significant positive correlation between false memory and belief in the paranormal...when the false memory item is not preceded by events for which footage exists. However, no relationship was found between false memory and belief in the paranormal...when the false memory item was presented after events for which there was known footage. (Dagnall et al., 2008, p. 183)

The findings of Rogers, Davis and Fisk (2008) suggested that moderate believers in the paranormal are more susceptible to the conjunction fallacy, i.e., they are especially prone to misperceiving the co-occurrence of two independent events as being more likely than either constituent event alone. Surprisingly, believers' susceptibility to this fallacy was *less* pronounced when one constituent was portrayed as an ostensible paranormal event.

Roe and Morgan (2002) had their participants complete the Narcissistic Personality Inventory along with the ASGS and found a significant correlation due apparently to ESP and PK belief rather than belief in an afterlife. Moore et al. (2010) administered the Rasch-scaled ASGS along with the Selfism Scale of Phares and Erskine (1984) to measure narcissism or egocentricity. The correlation was very low and non-significant. Thus, the findings here are inconclusive.

In a psychophysiological study, Voracek (2009) correlated a German version of the ASGS (alpha = 0.94) with the 2D:4D digit ratio, which putatively measures pre-natal androgen levels. A higher (feminised) 2D:4D correlated with stronger beliefs in men, even when controlling for age, education, adult height and weight, and birth length and weight. Shorter birth length (in men and in women) and lighter body were associated with stronger beliefs. This evidence may be informative for narrowing down possible developmental pathways of paranormal belief. Says Voracek: "Propensities contributing to sex and individual differences in these beliefs probably arise in utero…" (p. 105). Note that it is the women who had the higher beliefs, confirming much previous research. Note also that Voracek replicated Willson's (2009) single-factor solution for the ASGS. However, note finally that the observed associations with physiology were very low (< .15).

Transliminality

Transliminality is defined as the hypothesised tendency for psychological material to cross the threshold into consciousness (Thalbourne, 2010). It is relevant to the present review because paranormal belief as measured by the ASGS is one of the nine variables that load on the transliminality factor (the others include mystical experience, creative personality, manic experience, magical ideation, absorption, fantasy proneness, hyperaesthesia, and attitude to dream interpretation—Thalbourne, 1998a; Wiseman & Watt, 2006). Indeed, it has been shown that transliminality is an index of the sheep-goat variable, to such an extent that correlates of one tend to be correlates of the other (Thalbourne & Houran, 2003), and this is not an artefact produced by the fact that there are items on paranormal belief in the Revised Transliminality Scale (Lange, Thalbourne, Houran, & Storm, 2000). The implication for this review is that whatever is the mechanism underlying the threshold-crossing tendency, this mechanism may account for the sheep-goat variable as well. Moreover, research on the ASGS could be extended in scope by examining reported correlates of transliminality, such as openness to experience (Thalbourne, 2000b), sensation-seeking (Thalbourne & Cochrane, 2002), and thin boundaries (Thalbourne & Maltby, 2008). These variables have already to some extent been researched using non-ASGS measures. Likewise, research on transliminality could be informed by work on the sheep-goat variable, e.g., with regard to hypnotisability (Thalbourne, 2009).

CONCLUSION

In this review we have followed the development of the ASGS from a 10-item scale to an 18-item scale (and looked ahead to a possible 26-item scale, which, it is proposed, be called the BLPQ). We have examined the evidence for the reliability and validity of the ASGS, and have reported the multitude of uses of the scale in work such as frequency and especially correlational studies, both in parapsychology and orthodox psychology. The sheer quantity of findings and the widespread use of the test instrument should encourage researchers who are looking for a measure of belief in the paranormal to consider strongly an appropriate version of the Australian Sheep-Goat Scale.

» References

Antonovsky, A. (1993). The structure and properties of the sense of coherence scale. *Science and Medicine*, *36*, 725-733.

Ås, A., O'Hara, J. W., & Munger, M. P. (1962). The measurement of subjective experiences presumably related to hypnotic susceptibility. *Scandinavian Journal of Psychology*, *65*, 204-214.

Basterfield, K., & Thalbourne, M. A. (2002). Belief in, and alleged experience of, the paranormal in ostensible UFO abductees. *Australian Journal of Parapsychology*, *2*, 2-18.

Bhadra, B. H. (1966). The relationship of test scores to belief in ESP. *Journal of Parapsychology*, *30*, 1-17.

Broad, C. D. (1978). The relevance of psychical research to philosophy. In J. Ludwig (Ed.), *Philosophy and parapsychology* (pp. 43-63). Buffalo, NY: Prometheus Books. (Originally published 1949.)

Cattell, R. B., Eber, H. W., & Tatsuoka, M. M. (1970). *Handbook for the Sixteen Personality Factor Questionnaire (16PF).* (2nd ed.) Champaign, IL: Institute for Personality and Ability Testing.

Claridge, G., & Broks, P. (1984). Schizotypy and hemisphere function: I. Theoretical considerations and the measurement of schizotypy. *Personality and Individual Differences*, *5*, 633-648.

Crowne, D. P., & Marlowe, D. (1960). A new scale of social desirability independent of psychopathology. *Journal of Consulting Psychology*, *24*, 349-354.

Dagnall, N., Parker, A., & Munley, G. (2008). News events, false memory and paranormal belief. *European Journal of Parapsychology*, *23*, 173-188.

Dossey, L. (2009). Foreword. In M. A. Jawer with M. S. Micozzi, *The spiritual anatomy of emotion. How feelings link the brain, the body, and the sixth sense* (pp. ix-xii). Rochester, VT: Park Street Press.

Eckblad, M., & Chapman, L. J. (1983). Magical ideation as an indicator of schizotypy. *Journal of Consulting and Clinical Psychology, 51*, 215-225.

Evans, L., & Thalbourne, M. A. (1999). The feeling of being stared at: A parapsychological investigation. *Journal of the American Society for Psychical Research, 93*, 309-325.

Eysenck, H. J. (1967). Personality and extrasensory perception. *Journal of the Society for Psychical Research, 44*, 55-71.

Eysenck, H. J., & Eysenck, S. B. G. (1964). *Manual of the Eysenck Personality Inventory.* London: University of London Press.

Eysenck, H. J., & Eysenck, S. B. G. (1991). *Manual of the Eysenck Personality Scales (EPS Adult).* London: Hodder & Stoughton.

Francis, L. J., Williams, E., & Robbins, M. (2009). Christianity, paranormal belief and personality: A study among 13- to 16-year-old pupils in England and Wales. *Archive for the Psychology of Religion, 31*, 337-344.

French, C. C., Santamauro, J., Hamilton, V., Fox, R., & Thalbourne, M. A. (2008). Psychological aspects of the alien contact experience. *Cortex, 44*, 1387-1395.

Friedman, M., & Rosenman, R. H. (1974). *Type A behavior and your heart.* New York: Knopf.

Goretzki, M., Thalbourne, M. A., & Storm, L. (2009). The questionnaire measurement of spiritual emergency. *Journal of Transpersonal Psychology, 41*, 81-97.

Goulding, A. (2004). Schizotypy models in relation to subjective health and paranormal beliefs and experiences. *Personality and Individual Differences, 38*, 157-167.

Goulding, A. (2005). Participant variables associated with psi Ganzfeld results. *European Journal of Parapsychology, 20*, 50-64.

Greyson, B. (1977). Telepathy in mental illness: Deluge or delusion? *Journal of Nervous and Mental Disease, 165*, 184-200.

Haraldsson, E. (1981). Some determinants of belief in psychical phenomena. *Journal of the American Society for Psychical Research, 75*, 297-309.

Haraldsson, E. (1993). Are religiosity and belief in an afterlife better predictors of ESP performance than belief in psychic phenomena? *Journal of Parapsychology, 57*, 259-273.

Holt, N. J., Simmonds-Moore, C. A., & Moore, S. L. (2008). Benign schizotypy: Investigating differences between clusters of schizotype on paranormal belief, creativity, intelligence and mental health. Paper presented at the

51st Annual Convention of the Parapsychological Association, Winchester, England.

Irwin, H. J. (1985). A study of the measurement and the correlates of paranormal belief. *Journal of the American Society for Psychical Research, 79*, 301-326.

Irwin, H. J. (1993). Belief in the paranormal: A review of the empirical literature. *Journal of the American Society for Psychical Research, 87*, 1-39.

Irwin, H. J. (2009). *The psychology of paranormal belief. A researcher's handbook.* Hatfield, Herts: University of Hertfordshire.

Krantz, D. S., Glass, D. C., & Snyder, M. L. (1974). Helplessness, stress level, and the coronary-prone behavior pattern. *Journal of Experimental Social Psychology, 10*, 284-300.

Krishna, G. (1970). *Kundalini: The evolutionary energy in man.* Boston, MA: Shambhala.

Lange, R., Irwin, H. J., & Houran, J. (2000). Top-down purification of Tobacyk's Revised Paranormal Belief Scale. *Personality and Individual Differences, 29*, 131-156.

Lange, R., & Thalbourne, M. A. (2002). Rasch scaling paranormal belief and experience: The structure and semantics of Thalbourne's Australian Sheep-Goat Scale. *Psychological Reports, 91*, 1065-1073.

Lange, R., Thalbourne, M. A., Houran, J., & Storm, L. (2000). The Revised Transliminality Scale: Reliability and validity data using a top-down purification procedure. *Consciousness and Cognition, 9*, 591-617.

Lawrence, T. (1993). Gathering in the sheep and goats: A meta-analysis of forced-choice sheep/goat ESP studies, 1947-1993. *Proceedings of the Parapsychological Association 36th Annual Convention*, Toronto, Canada, pp. 75-86.

McBeath, M. K., & Thalbourne, M. A. (1993). A technical note: The relationship between paranormal belief and some variables relevant to Type A Behavior Pattern. *Journal of Parapsychology, 57*, 411-415.

McCreery, C., & Claridge, G. (1995). Out-of-the-body experiences and personality. *Journal of the Society for Psychical Research, 60*, 129-148.

Moore, T., Thalbourne, M. A., & Storm, L. (2010). A study on coincidences. *Australian Journal of Parapsychology, 10*, 154-176.

Mosher, D. I. (1966). The development and multitrait-multimethod matrix analysis of three measures of three aspects of guilt. *Journal of Consulting Psychology, 30*, 25-29.

Moss, T., Paulson, M. J., Chang, A. F., & Levitt, M. (1970). Hypnosis and ESP: A controlled experiment. *American Journal of Clinical Hypnosis, 13*, 46-56.

Myers, S. A. (1983). The Wilson-Barber Inventory of Childhood Memories and Imaginings: Children's form and norms for 1,337 children and adolescents. *Journal of Mental Imagery, 7*, 83-94.

Palmer, J. (1971). Scoring in ESP tests as a function of belief in ESP. Part I. The Sheep-Goat Effect. *Journal of the American Society for Psychical Research, 65*, 373-408.

Palmer, J. (1999). Covert psi in computer solitaire. *Journal of Parapsychology, 63*, 216-217.

Parker, A., Grams, D., & Pettersson, C. (1998). Further variables relating to psi in the Ganzfeld. *Journal of Parapsychology, 62*, 319-337.

Pérez-Navarro, J. M., Lawrence, T., & Hume, I. (2009). Personality, mental state, and procedure in the experimental replication of ESP: A logistic regression analysis of a successful experimental condition. *European Journal of Parapsychology, 24*, 68-92.

Phares, E. J., & Erskine, N. (1984). The measurement of selfism. *Educational and Psychological Measurement, 44*, 597-608.

Raven, J. C. (1965). *Advanced Progressive Matrices: Plan and use of the scale.* London: H. K. Lewis.

Richards, D. G. (1989). Measures of subjective psi experiences: Consistency, reliability, and validity. In L. A. Henkel & R. E. Berger (Eds.), *Research in parapsychology 1988* (pp. 49-53). Metuchen, NJ: Scarecrow.

Richards, D. G. (1990). Hypnotic susceptibility and subjective psychic experiences: A study of participants in A.R.E. conferences. *Journal of Parapsychology, 54*, 35-51.

Roe, C. A. (1998). Belief in the paranormal and attendance at psychic readings. *Journal of the American Society for Psychical Research, 92*, 25-51.

Roe, C. A. (2002). Further ruminations on the Australian Sheep-Goat Scale. *Journal of the American Society for Psychical Research, 96*, 99-101.

Roe, C. A. (2003). Revisiting false memories as a vehicle for psi. *Journal of the Society for Psychical Research, 67*, 281-295.

Roe, C. A., Davey, R., & Stevens, P. (2003). Are ESP and PK aspects of a unitary phenomenon? A preliminary test of the relationship between ESP and PK. *Journal of Parapsychology, 67*, 343-366.

Roe, C. A., Davey, R., & Stevens, P. (2004). Arousal and performance at ESP and PK tasks using a common protocol. *European Journal of Parapsychology, 19*, 29-43.

Roe, C. A., Davey, R., & Stevens, P. (2005). Are ESP and PK aspects of a unitary phenomenon? The effects of deception when testing the relationship between ESP and PK. *Journal of the Society for Psychical Research*, *69*, 18-32.

Roe, C. A., & Morgan, C. L. (2002). Narcissism and belief in the paranormal. *Psychological Reports*, *90*, 405-411.

Roe, C. A., Sherwood, S. J., Farrell, L., Savva, L., & Baker, I. S. (2007). Assessing the roles of sender and experimenter in dream ESP research. *European Journal of Parapsychology*, *22*, 175-192.

Rogers, P., Davis, T., & Fisk, J. (2008). Paranormal belief and susceptibility to the conjunction fallacy. *Applied Cognitive Psychology*, *23*, 524-542.

Rogo, D. S. (1975). Psi and psychosis: A review of the experimental evidence. *Journal of Parapsychology*, *39*, 120-128.

Roig, M. (1992). Belief in psi and social desirability. In L. A. Henkel & G. R. Schmeidler (Eds.), *Research in parapsychology 1990* (pp. 161-162). Metuchen, NJ: Scarecrow Press.

Ross, C. A., & Joshi, S. (1992). Paranormal experiences in the general population. *Journal of Nervous and Mental Disease*, *180*, 357-361.

Sanders, R. E., Thalbourne, M. A., & Delin, P. S. (2000). Transliminality and the telepathic transmission of emotional states: An exploratory study. *Journal of the American Society for Psychical Research*, *94*, 1-24.

Schmeidler, G. R. (1943). Predicting good and bad scores in a clairvoyance experiment: A preliminary report. *Journal of the American Society for Psychical Research*, *37*, 103-110.

Sherwood, S. J., Roe, C. A., Holt, N. J., & Wilson, S. (2005). Interpersonal psi: Exploring the role of the experimenter and the experimental climate in a ganzfeld telepathy task. *European Journal of Parapsychology*, *20*, 150-172.

Stanovich, K. E. (1989). Implicit philosophies of mind: The Dualism Scale and its relation to religiosity and belief in extrasensory perception. *Journal of Psychology*, *123*, 5-23.

Storm, L., & Barrett-Woodbridge, M. (2007). Psi as compensation for modality impairment: A replication study using sighted and blind participants. *European Journal of Parapsychology*, *22*, 73-89.

Storm, L., & Rock, A. J. (2009). Shamanic-like journeying and psi: I. Imagery cultivation, paranormal belief, and the picture-identification task. *Australian Journal of Parapsychology*, *9*, 165-192.

Storm, L., & Thalbourne, M. A. (2005). The effect of a change in pro attitude on paranormal performance: A pilot study using naïve and sophisticated skeptics. *Journal of Scientific Exploration*, *19*, 11-29.

Thalbourne, M. A. (1976). *Closeness of relationship, and telepathy, personality, and social intelligence.* Unpublished B.A. Honours thesis, University of Adelaide, South Australia.

Thalbourne, M. A. (1981a). Extraversion and the sheep-goat variable: A conceptual replication. *Journal of the American Society for Psychical Research, 75*, 105-119.

Thalbourne, M. A. (1981b). *Some experiments on the paranormal cognition of drawings, with special reference to personality and attitudinal variables.* Unpublished Ph.D. thesis, University of Edinburgh, Scotland.

Thalbourne, M. A. (1983). A proposed mechanism for the sheep-goat effect and its relationship to psi-missing, experimenter effect, and the problem of repeatability. In W. G. Roll, J. Beloff, & R. A. White (Eds.), *Research in parapsychology 1982* (pp. 89-92). Metuchen, NJ: Scarecrow Press.

Thalbourne, M. A. (1984). The SPR Centenary Census: I. The ESP test. [Abstract] *Journal of Parapsychology, 48*, 238-239.

Thalbourne, M. A. (1985). Are believers in psi more prone to schizophrenia? In R. A. White, & J. Solfvin (Eds.), *Research in parapsychology 1984* (pp. 85-88). Metuchen, NJ: Scarecrow Press.

Thalbourne, M. A. (1989). On the psychology of belief in life after death. In G. K. Zollschan, J. F. Schumaker, & G. F. Walsh (Eds.), *Exploring the paranormal: Different perspectives on belief and experience* (pp. 215-236). Bridport, Dorset, United Kingdom: Prism.

Thalbourne, M. A. (1994a). Belief in the paranormal and its relationship to schizophrenia-relevant variables: A confirmatory study. *British Journal of Clinical Psychology, 33*, 78-80.

Thalbourne, M. A. (1994b). The SPR Centenary Census: II. The survey of beliefs and experiences. *Journal of the Society for Psychical Research, 59*, 420-431.

Thalbourne, M. A. (1994c). Conservatism and its relation to various aspects of belief in the paranormal. *Journal of the Society for Psychical Research, 60*, 86-94.

Thalbourne, M. A. (1994d). Are believers in psi more prone to manic-depression? *Proceedings of the 37th Annual Parapsychological Association Convention* (pp. 382-389).

Thalbourne, M. A. (1995a). Further studies of the measurement and correlates of belief in the paranormal. *Journal of the American Society for Psychical Research, 89*, 233-247.

Thalbourne, M. A. (1995b). Psychological characteristics of believers in the paranormal: A replicative study. *Journal of the American Society for Psychical Research, 89*, 153-164.

Thalbourne, M. A. (1996a). Technical note: A caution regarding the Knowles apparatus for psi dexterity. *Journal of Parapsychology, 60*, 251-256.

Thalbourne, M. A. (1996b). Varieties of belief in life after death: A factor analytic study. *Journal of the American Society for Psychical Research, 90*, 268-291.

Thalbourne, M. A. (1996c). An attempt to predict precognition scores using transliminality-relevant variables. *Journal of the Society for Psychical Research, 61*, 129-140.

Thalbourne, M. A. (1997a). Paranormal belief and superstition: How large is the association? *Journal of the American Society for Psychical Research, 91*, 221-226.

Thalbourne, M. A. (1997b). Testing the McBeath hypothesis: Relation of sexual orientation and belief in the paranormal. *Psychological Reports, 81*, 890.

Thalbourne, M. A. (1998a). Transliminality: Further correlates and a short measure. *Journal of the American Society for Psychical Research, 92*, 402-419.

Thalbourne, M. A. (1998b). Technical note: The level of paranormal belief and experience among psychotics. *Journal of Parapsychology, 62*, 79-81.

Thalbourne, M. A. (1998c). On the Australian Sheep-Goat Scale. *Journal of the American Society for Psychical Research, 92*, 308-309.

Thalbourne, M. A. (1998-1999a). Belief in life after death and its relationship to transliminality-relevant variables. *European Journal of Parapsychology, 14*, 16-30.

Thalbourne, M. A. (1998-1999b). The sheep-goat variable and mystical experience: Their relationship and their levels in a special population. *European Journal of Parapsychology, 14*, 80-88.

Thalbourne, M. A. (1999a). Dualism and the sheep-goat variable: A replication and extension. *Journal of the Society for Psychical Research, 63*, 213-216.

Thalbourne, M. A. (1999b). On the psychology of belief in the paranormal. *The Skeptical Intelligencer, 3*(3), 17-27.

Thalbourne, M. A. (2000a). Transliminality and creativity. *Journal of Creative Behavior, 34*, 193-202.

Thalbourne, M. A. (2000b). Relation between transliminality and openness to experience. *Psychological Reports, 86*, 909-910.

Thalbourne, M. A. (2001a). Broken relationships and claims of psychic phenomena. *Australian Journal of Parapsychology, 1*, 56-60. [Spanish version in *Revista Argentina de Psicologia Paranormal, 12*, 171-175.]

Thalbourne, M. A. (2001b). Measures of the sheep-goat variable, transliminality, and their correlates. *Psychological Reports*, *88*, 339-350.

Thalbourne, M. A. (2001c). The paranormal and its place in human relationships: Some hypotheses. *Australian Journal of Parapsychology*, *1*, 72-85.

Thalbourne, M. A. (2003a). Theism and belief in the paranormal. *Journal of the Society for Psychical Research*, *67*, 208-210.

Thalbourne, M. A. (2003b). The way forward for the Australian Sheep-Goat Scale. *Journal of the American Society for Psychical Research*, *97*, 88-89.

Thalbourne, M. A. (2004a). A note on paranormal belief and paranormal experience: Their levels, absolute and relative. *Journal of the Society for Psychical Research*, *68*, 115-121.

Thalbourne, M. A. (2004b). Mania and its relationship to the sheep-goat variable. *Australian Journal of Parapsychology*, *4*, 109-113.

Thalbourne, M. A. (2005a). Research note: Creative personality and belief in the paranormal. *European Journal of Parapsychology*, *20*, 79-84.

Thalbourne, M. A. (2005b). Depression and the sheep-goat variable: Is there a relationship? *Journal of the Society for Psychical Research*, *69*, 143-147.

Thalbourne, M. A. (2006). Hallucination proneness and experiences related to survival. In L. Storm & M. A. Thalbourne (Eds.), *The survival of consciousness: Essays on the possibility of life after death* (pp. 94-106). Jefferson, NC: McFarland.

Thalbourne, M. A. (2008). Predicting the ostensible paranormal experiences canvassed in the Inventory of Childhood Memories and Imaginings (Form C). *Australian Journal of Parapsychology*, *8*, 180-191.

Thalbourne, M. A. (2008). The effect of closeness of relationship on interpersonal psychopraxia. A free-response study evaluated by both response-ranking and target-ranking methods. *Journal of the Society for Psychical Research*, *72*, 146-163.

Thalbourne, M. A. (2009). Transliminality, anomalous belief and experience, and hypnotizability. *Australian Journal of Clinical and Experimental Hypnosis*, *37*, 45-56.

Thalbourne, M. A. (2010). Transliminality: A fundamental mechanism in psychology and parapsychology. *Australian Journal of Parapsychology*, *10*, 70-81.

Thalbourne, M. A., Bartemucci, L., Delin, P. S., Fox, B., & Nofi, O. (1997). Transliminality: Its nature and correlates. *Journal of the American Society for Psychical Research*, *91*, 305-331.

Thalbourne, M. A., Beloff, J., & Delanoy, D. (1982). A test of the "extraverted sheep vs. introverted goats" hypothesis. In W. G. Roll, R. L. Morris & R. A. White (Eds.), *Research in Parapsychology 1981* (pp. 155-156). Metuchen, NJ: Scarecrow Press.

Thalbourne, M. A., Beloff, J., Delanoy, D., & Jungkuntz, J. H. (1983). Some further tests of the extraverted sheep vs. introverted goats hypothesis. In W. G. Roll, J. Beloff, & R. A. White (Eds.), *Research in parapsychology 1982* (pp. 199-200). Metuchen, NJ: Scarecrow Press.

Thalbourne, M. A., & Cochrane, M. (2002). Relation of transliminality and sensation seeking. *Psychological Reports, 90*, 685-686.

Thalbourne, M. A., & Delin, P. S. (1993). A new instrument for measuring the sheep-goat variable: Its psychometric properties and factor structure. *Journal of the Society for Psychical Research, 59*, 172-186. [Translated into Spanish in *Revista Mexicana de Psicologia Paranormal,* 1996, *1,* 35-50]

Thalbourne, M. A., & Delin, P. S. (1994). A common thread underlying belief in the paranormal, creative personality, mystical experience and psychopathology. *Journal of Parapsychology*, *58*, 3-38.

Thalbourne, M. A., & Delin, P. S. (1995). *Correlates of belief in the paranormal: A partial replication.* Unpublished manuscript.

Thalbourne, M. A., Dunbar, K. A., & Delin, P. S. (1995). An investigation into correlates of belief in the paranormal. *Journal of the American Society for Psychical Research, 89*, 215-231.

Thalbourne, M. A., & Evans, L. (1992). Attitudes and beliefs about, and reactions to, staring and being stared at. *Journal of the Society for Psychical Research, 58*, 380-385.

Thalbourne, M. A., & Fox, B. (1999). Paranormal and mystical experience: The role of panic attacks and Kundalini. *Journal of the American Society for Psychical Research*, *93*, 99-115.

Thalbourne, M. A., & French, C. C. (1995). Paranormal belief, manic-depressiveness, and magical ideation: A replication. *Personality and Individual Differences, 18*, 291-292.

Thalbourne, M. A., & French, C. C. (1997). The sheep-goat variable and belief in non-paranormal anomalous phenomena. *Journal of the Society for Psychical Research*, *62*, 41-45.

Thalbourne, M. A., & Haraldsson, E. (1980). Personality characteristics of sheep and goats. *Personality and Individual Differences, 1,* 180-185.

Thalbourne, M. A., & Hensley, J. H. (2001). Religiosity and belief in the paranormal. *Journal of the Society for Psychical Research*, *65*, 47.

Thalbourne, M. A., & Houran, J. (2003). Transliminality as an index of the sheep-goat variable. *European Journal of Parapsychology, 18*, 3-14.

Thalbourne, M. A., & Houtkooper, J. M. (2002). Religiosity/spirituality and belief in the paranormal. *Journal of the Society for Psychical Research, 66*, 113-115.

Thalbourne, M. A., & Jungkuntz, J. H. (1983). Extraverted sheep vs. introverted goats: Experiments VII and VIII. *Journal of Parapsychology, 47*, 49-51.

Thalbourne, M. A., & Maltby, J. (2008). Transliminality, thin boundaries, Unusual Experiences, and temporal lobe lability. *Personality and Individual Differences, 44*, 1617-1623.

Thalbourne, M. A., Keogh, E., & Crawley, S. E. (1999). Manic-depressiveness and its correlates. *Psychological Reports, 85*, 45-53.

Thalbourne, M. A., & Nofi, O. (1997). Belief in the paranormal, superstitiousness and intellectual ability. *Journal of the Society for Psychical Research, 61*, 365-371.

Thalbourne, M. A., & O'Brien, R. (1999). Belief in the paranormal and religious variables. *Journal of the Society for Psychical Research, 63*, 110-122.

Thalbourne, M. A., Silva, C. F., & Razente, S. R. (2006). Belief in, and alleged experience of, the paranormal in the Portuguese population. *Australian Journal of Parapsychology, 6*, 155-165.

Thorisson, K. R., Skulason, F., & Haraldsson, E. (1991). Effects of belief in ESP and distorted feedback on a computerized clairvoyance task. *Journal of Parapsychology, 55*, 45-58.

Tobacyk, J. [J.], & Milford, G. (1983). Belief in paranormal phenomena: Assessment instrument development and implications for personality functioning. *Journal of Personality and Social Psychology, 44*, 1029-1037.

Van de Castle, R. L., & White, R. A. (1955). A report on a sentence completion form of sheep-goat attitude scale. *Journal of Parapsychology, 19*, 171-179.

Voracek, M. (2009). Who wants to believe? Associations between digit ratio (2D:4D) and paranormal and superstitious beliefs. *Personality and Individual differences, 47*, 105-109.

Willson, R. (2009). *Data analysis using SPSS version 15*. School of Psychology, University of Adelaide.

Wilson, G. D. (1975). *Manual for the Wilson-Patterson Attitude Inventory.* Windsor, England: NFER Publishing Co.

Wilson, K., & French, C. C. (2006). The relationship between susceptibility to false memories, dissociativity, and paranormal belief and experience. *Personality and Individual Differences, 41*, 1493-1502.

Wilson, S., & Hamlin, I. (2007). Implicit learning in a card prediction task. *European Journal of Parapsychology, 22*, 3-29.

Wiseman, R., & Watt, C. (2006). Belief in psychic ability and the misattribution hypothesis: A qualitative review. *British Journal of Psychology, 97*, 323-338.

APPENDIX A

Table 10.A1: Studies of Convergent Validity for the ASGS

Source	Scale	ASGS	*r*
French et al. (2008)	Anomalous Experience Inv. Exper.	18	0.86
French et al. (2008)	Anomalous Experience Inv. Belief	18	0.88
French et al. (2008)	Anomalous Experience Inv. Able	18	0.85
Irwin (1985)	Tobacyk Paranormal Belief Scale	13	0.69
Irwin (1985)	Sheils & Berg	13	0.74
Richards (1989)	Psychic Experiences Questionnaire	10	0.69
Richards (1990)	Psychic Experiences Questionnaire	10	0.62
Roe & Morgan (2002)	Tobacyk Paranormal Belief Scale	18	0.53
Thalbourne (1981a)	Icelandic Sheep-Goat Scale	10	0.55
Thalbourne (1995a)	Tobacyk Paranormal Belief Scale	18	0.73
Thalbourne (1995b)	Icelandic Sheep-Goat Scale	13	0.67
Thalbourne (2001b)	New Age Philosophy	18	0.77
Thalbourne (2001b)	Traditional Paranormal Beliefs	18	0.46
Thalbourne (2001b)	Anomalous Experience Inv. Exper.	18	0.72
Thalbourne (2001b)	Anomalous Experience Inv. Belief	18	0.66
Thalbourne (2001b)	Anomalous Experience Inv. Able	18	0.68
Thalbourne & Delin (1993)	Paranormality Scale	18	0.72
Thalbourne, Dunbar & Delin (1995)	Tobacyk Paranormal Belief Scale	10	0.68
Thalbourne & French (1995)	Windholz/Diamant SOBEP	18	0.74
Thalbourne & Houtkooper (2002)	Honorton's belief in psi rating	17	0.70

Table 10.A2:

Summary of Sheep-Goat Results from Psi Studies Utilising the ASGS

Source	Psi mode	ASGS	*N*	Direction	Outcome
Evans & Thalbourne (1999)	Te	11	28	+	(Sheep sig. above chance)
Goulding (2005)	Te	18	64	+	n.r.
Palmer (1999)	Cl	?	48	?	n.r.
Parker, Grams, & Pettersson (1998)	Te	10	28	+	$r = 0.38^*$
Pérez-Navarro, Lawrence & Hume (2009)	Te	18	90	?	n.r.
Roe (2003)	Cl	18	98	?	n.r.
Roe, Davey & Stevens (2003)	Cl_{true}	18	40	–	$rs = 0.06$
	$Cl_{disguised}$	18	40	+	$rs = -0.23$
	PK_{true}	18	40	+	$rs = -0.10$
	$PK_{disguised}$	18	40	–	$rs = 0.05$
Roe, Davey & Stevens (2004)	Cl_{true}	18	40	–	$rs = 0.23$
	$Cl_{disguised}$	18	40	–	$rs = 0.10$
	PK_{true}	18	40	–	$rs = 0.12$
	$PK_{disguised}$	18	40	+	$rs = -0.01$
Roe, Davey & Stevens (2005)	Cl_{true}	18	40	–	$rs = 0.13$
	$Cl_{disguised}$	18	40	+	$rs = -0.05$
	PK_{true}	18	40	–	$rs = 0.06$
	$PK_{disguised}$	18	40	–	$rs = 0.14$
Sanders, Thalbourne & Delin (2000)	Te	18	87	+	$r = 0.23^*$
	Te	18	87	+	$r = 0.32^{**}$
Storm & Barrett-Woodbridge (2007)	Cl	18	76	–	n.r.
Storm & Rock (2009)	Cl	16	55	–	$r = -0.07$
	Cl	16	53	–	$r = -0.19$

Table 10.A2 (Cont'd):
Summary of Sheep-Goat Results from Psi Studies Utilising the ASGS

Source	Psi mode	ASGS	N	Direction	Outcome
Thalbourne (1981b, 2008)	Te	11	18	+	$r = 0.11$
	Te	11	13	+	$r = 0.58^*$
	Te	11	18	+	$r = 0.24$
	Te	11	13	+	$r = 0.80^{***}$
	Te	11	30	–	$r = -0.04$
	Te	11	30	–	$r = -0.14$
	Te	11	13	+	$r = 0.47$
	Te	11	14	+	$r = 0.49^*$
	Te	11	13	+	$r = 0.00$
	Te	11	14	–	$r = -0.27$
	Te	11	14	–	n.r.
	Te	11	14	+	n.r.
Thalbourne, Beloff & Delanoy (1982)	Pr	10	101	+	Goats sig. < MCE
	Pr	10	86	+	$r = 0.30^{**}$
Thalbourne, Beloff, Delanoy & Jungkuntz (1983)	Pr	10	135	–	n.r.
	Pr	10	152	+	n.r.
	Pr	10	246	–	n.r.
	Pr	10	14	–	n.r.
Thalbourne & Jungkuntz (1983)	Pr	10	144	+	n.r.
	Pr	10	62	–	n.r.
Wilson & Hamlin (2007)	Cl	18	61	?	n.r.
	Cl	18	44	+	n.r.

Key: Te = telepathy; Cl = clairvoyance; Pr = precognition; PK = psychokinesis; *: $p < .05$; **: $p < .01$; ***; $p < .001$; n.r. = not reported

APPENDIX B

The Basic Limiting Principles Questionnaire

Note: the responses are on a 5-point Likert scale ranging from "strongly disagree" to "strongly agree"

1. I do not believe in the *existence* of ESP (extrasensory perception, such as telepathy, clairvoyance, or precognition).
2. I believe I have had *personal experience* of ESP.
3. I do not believe *I am psychic.*
4. I believe it is possible *to obtain knowledge of hidden situations* such as the location of underground water or of deceased persons.
5. I do not believe that I have ever *obtained knowledge of hidden situations* such as the location of underground water or of deceased persons.
6. I believe it is possible to *predict the future* in ways that do not depend upon reason or the normal sense organs.
7. I have had not had any *premonitions* about the future that came true and which (I believe) were not just a coincidence.
8. I have had at least one *dream* that came true and which (I believe) was not just a coincidence.
9. I have not had any *visions* that were not hallucinations and from which I received information that I could not have otherwise gained at that time and place.
10. I believe that what we call *"mind" is different from the brain.*
11. I do not believe that *the minds of some people can leave their bodies,* travel around, and return.
12. I believe that on at least one occasion *my own mind has left my body,* travelled around, and returned.
13. I do not believe in *life after death.*
14. I believe that *some people can contact spirits of the dead.*
15. I believe *I have never myself contacted the spirit of a dead person.*
16. I believe that it is possible to *gain information about* the thoughts, feelings or circumstances of another person in a way that does not depend on reason or normal sense organs.
17. I do not believe that it is possible to *send a "mental message"* to another person, or in some way influence them at a distance, by means other than the normal channels of communication.

18. I believe I have had at least one experience of *telepathy* between myself and another person.
19. I do not believe in the existence of psychokinesis ("PK", or mind-over-matter), that is, *the direct influence of mind on a physical system*, without the mediation of any known physical energy (e.g., psychically bending metal).
20. I believe I have *personally exerted PK* on at least one occasion (e.g., willed dice to come up a given face).
21. I do not believe that *I have marked psychokinetic ability*.
22. I believe that, on at least one occasion, an inexplicable (but *one-off*) physical event of an apparently psychokinetic origin (such as someone bending metal) has occurred in my presence.
23. I believe that *persistent inexplicable physical disturbances*, of an apparently psychokinetic origin (as, for example, a poltergeist) have *never* occurred in my presence.
24. I believe that *psychic healing* occurs.
25. I believe that I have *never exercised* psychic healing myself.
26. I believe that *I have benefited* from psychic healing.

APPENDIX C

The Experience of Psychotic Symptoms Scale—Revised

Note: the responses are on a 5-point Likert scale ranging from "strongly disagree" to "strongly agree"

1. I have sometimes found that the familiar boundaries between people, events, time and space were blurred or not as accessible as they once were.
2. I have never experienced distressing voices inside my head that didn't seem to belong to me.
3. I have experienced a period of time when my sentences were unclear or didn't make sense.
4. I have never felt strange and cut off from the world with everything moving in slow motion.
5. I have sometimes been really convinced of something being real even though no one else shared the same belief.
6. I have never found myself desperately trying to make sense of an unfamiliar environment.
7. I have sometimes experienced someone outside of myself controlling my body or actions.
8. I have never heard voices as distinct from my own coming from inside my head.
9. I have sometimes experienced significant difficulties in keeping up with social and/or occupational obligations.
10. I have never believed that my thoughts were being interfered with in some way.
11. I have sometimes felt that my internal world was being played out in the external communication of those around me.
12. I have never found my everyday thoughts becoming confused or not joining up properly.
13. I have sometimes experienced seeing, hearing, feeling, smelling or tasting something that no one else could.
14. I have never experienced enormous difficulty in organising my thoughts.
15. I have sometimes found myself laughing inappropriately or becoming angry or upset without a reason.
16. I have never believed for a while that I was someone who in fact I was not.

Chapter 11

Pueblo Parapsychology: Psi and the Longbody from the Southwest Indian Perspective[1]

Bryan J. Williams[2]

Although it has not been widely recognized in recent years, it seems that the worldviews of Native American tribal cultures may offer perspectives about the relationship between humans, nature, and the physical world that could lead to new insights about psi phenomena. William G. Roll (1981b) was among the first to recognize the potential value of worldviews from tribal and Third World societies, pointing out that, within such views, there is often no individual distinction between humans and the objects and locations associated with them. From the viewpoint of these cultures, everything that exists in the natural world—living and material alike—is interconnected in some fundamental way. Psi phenomena seem to suggest interconnections of a similar sort. For example, telepathy suggests interconnection between two or more human minds, clairvoyance suggests interconnection between the human mind and a physical object or location, and psychokinesis (PK) suggests a sort of interconnection that allows interaction between mind and matter. This worldview is quite different

1. [This chapter was originally published as an article in *Australian Journal of Parapsychology* (2007, vol. 7[2], pp. 134-163). Permission to reprint has been granted by the author and the journal.—Editors.]
2. My deep gratitude goes to Dr. William G. Roll for his guidance, many discussions on the longbody, and comments on an earlier version of this chapter.

from that of most Anglo-Western cultures, which tend to put a lot of emphasis on distinct individuality. This may be one reason why psi is often perceived as anomalous or 'strange' within these cultures.

Based on its interconnected worldview, it would seem that concepts derived from Native American tradition might be useful in describing and thinking about psi functioning. One concept that has been used in this manner within parapsychology is the longbody, first introduced to the field by Christopher Aanstoos (1986) as a means of advancing the phenomenology of psi experiences. The concept itself has its origins in the language and spiritual tradition of the Iroquois Indian tribe, found in the area surrounding the Northeast United States and Southeastern Canada. Within this culture, a tribal member's sense of self is not limited only to the familiar boundaries of their small living body. Through shared cultural and ancestral bloodlines, the self is extended to include a larger tribal body that consists of other family and tribal members, both living and departed. The extended self can also include the various physical objects and geographical locations that have particular spiritual significance to the tribe, usually because they are perceived as having sacred ceremonial value or as having aided in the tribe's survival. In addition to the individual body, the tribal member's self is viewed as part of an elongated living body which encompasses all the things in nature and spirit that have come to shape and define their tribe's existence, providing a basis for the member's own existence.

Building upon the work of the French phenomenologist Maurice Merleau-Ponty, Aanstoos (1986, 2005) had shown that even people in modern Western societies sometimes incorporate other people and objects into their own embodiment, not unlike the ties reflected in Native American tradition.[3] He therefore suggested that the longbody concept could reflect these familiar connections between people and objects, as well as reflect psi connections. William Roll (1987, 1989, 2005) soon adopted the concept as a metaphorical way to picture the deep, yet subtle, interconnection between mind and matter that is inherently suggested by all forms of psi.

In Roll's usage of the concept, the longbody may be seen as the larger web that connects people, object, and place across space and time. According to Roll (2005), the mind is embodied within the living brain and body of the individual

3. Aanstoos (1986, 2005) offers several familiar examples of this from everyday life: a person winces in pain when witnessing someone close to them being poked with a needle, some people have a tendency to perceive the traits of certain individuals in their offspring, and golfers may exhibit a kind of "body English" in relation to the movement of their putted ball.

person, and the body is emplaced along with other people and material objects in space. The mind includes implicit memories of other significant people, objects, and places, which often come easily to mind as images when called forth. This suggests that the mind within the emplaced body of the individual person is also linked through memory to the emplaced minds and bodies of these significant others, as well as their own objects and places. This memory linkage between people, object, and place may open the way for psi as a way to maintain these meaningful relationships at a distance. If one goes further, they may eventually find a grander universal web of interconnection, or 'Big Mind', that ties all people, objects, and places together at the most fundamental level of existence (Roll, 1997).

The tradition of the longbody, as held by the Iroquois, does not seem to be unique only to this particular tribe. Some Indian tribes of the American Southwest have aspects in their primarily oral-based tradition that seem to reflect something very similar to the longbody. In this chapter, those aspects from four Southwest tribes (the Hopi, the Navajo, Laguna Pueblo, and Zuni Pueblo;[4] collectively referred to hereafter by the acronym "HNLZ") are reviewed,[5] and their possible implications for tribal psi experiences and for Roll's longbody hypothesis are discussed. Possible directions for further research on these aspects are also offered.

Unity Among People, Place, and Spirits

One aspect from HNLZ tradition that reflects something like the longbody consists of the references that are suggestive of a collective unity among tribal people, places, and the spiritual beings inherent in the religious beliefs of the culture.

Tribal unity is often expressed in verbal ways. Large tribes like the Navajo often collectively refer to themselves as nations as a way to reflect the fact that

4. The ancestral homeland of the Hopi tribe is located in the central and southeastern parts of Arizona. The Laguna Pueblo is found in the west-central portion of New Mexico, east of the city of Grants. The Navajo Nation and the Zuni Pueblo can both be found on the border between New Mexico and Arizona, with the Navajo being north of Zuni.

5. In addition to being based on documented accounts from the anthropological literature, the information provided on the relevant aspects from the Laguna tradition is also based to a lesser degree on my own personal knowledge as I have come to understand it based on traditions related to me by my family. For the reader's knowledge, I am full-blooded Pueblo Indian, being 3/4 Laguna and 1/4 Zuni (the latter comes from my maternal grandfather).

all of their members share a common bloodline.[6] Another way observed among the Navajo people is the referral to themselves by their ancestral tribal name of *Diné* (pronounced 'dee-nay'), which means 'The People'. The plural of this, *Dine'é* (roughly pronounced 'dee-nay-eh'), is often considered the full and more correct term, and also means 'tribe', 'people', and 'nation' synonymously (Kluckhohn & Leighton, 1962, p. 23). Thus, when Navajo people refer to themselves and their origin, they do not perceive themselves as individuals, but as part of a collective tribal unit that includes their family and tribal ancestors.

This type of verbal reference is also meant to reflect the importance of kinship within a given tribe in order to preserve ancestral relations. Within the Navajo and Laguna tribes, the basic unit of kinship is the family or the clan, called *dóone'é* (roughly pronounced 'doo-o-ne-eh') in Navajo (Pratt, 1993, p. 154) and *hano* in Laguna (Parsons, 1923, p. 206). The individual self and its origin are defined by group identity to a clan and all the family members that comprise it, whether they be direct relation or extended family (the latter is often declared through spiritual rite), living or deceased. Relationships between clans in turn help to structure and define the tribe as a whole, particularly in the way of clan functions in ceremonialism.[7] In addition, the clan also helps to define a given tribe's past (described more below).

Within the Laguna Pueblo, tribal unity is displayed overtly through the behavior of tribal members with respect to one another. Though tribal members live as separate families within villages, many of them respect the tradition of their shared bloodline, and this underlies the social unity of unrelated members.[8] Thus, many unrelated tribal members and families may closely interact, support, and openly help each other on a frequent basis, as if they were immediate family. This unity is more overtly displayed during times of ceremony, when an entire village or even larger parts of the tribe comes together to take part.

A given tribe may also claim unity with a given location, leading to the concept of sacred sites. This is not only meant to reflect an ancestral and spiritual tie to the land for planting and harvesting, but can also reflect tribal origins and places of mystical significance. For example, the Navajo trace part of their origin

---

6. This usage of 'nation' is in addition to its other meaning as a political symbol of the tribe's self-governing nature.

7. The relations between family members and individual clans can become quite complex within a tribe given that there is less emphasis on individuality. Parsons' (1923) detailed monograph on Laguna genealogy provides a clear reflection of this.

8. This respect to bloodline tradition is one of the things that sets the foundation for extended family relations within a clan.

to a place known as *Dinétah*, an area of canyons, mesas, and mountains located southeast of Farmington, New Mexico. Navajo mythology holds that *Dinétah* was the site where the first tribal people had emerged from an underworld existence, along with the deity-like spirits inherent in the tribal religion (Marriott & Rachlin, 1968). For this reason, it is seen as the source of all aspects of Navajo life: their history, language, ceremonies, and beliefs (Tapahonso, 2001). It is also thought to have curing powers. Whenever a healing ceremony is held, some reference to *Dinétah* is always made in the ceremony, if it cannot be directly held there (Kluckhohn & Leighton, 1962; Pratt, 1993).

Among the Hopi, unity is held with a small point in the ground called the *sipapu*, to which they trace their own origin. Like the Navajo, Hopi mythology dictates that the tribal members emerged from an underworld existence (Marriott & Rachlin, 1968), and the *sipapu* represents the point of emergence. Similarly, when Hopi people die, it is thought that they return to the underworld through the *sipapu*. Spiritual beings known as kachinas are also thought to enter the physical world through the *sipapu* during times of ceremony. Typically, an entire Hopi village ties itself to a central *sipapu* located toward the centre of the village, although individual families often reflect the tradition themselves by having a smaller *sipapu* in one room of their home (Hieb, 1992). The Laguna have their own loose interpretation of the *sipapu*, represented by a cave in the foothills of the tribe's sacred mountain[9] that the deceased journey to at death in order to re-enter the underworld (Mails, 1983, p. 280).

Across HNLZ tradition, there is often a tribal tie to the land on which the *kiva* (ceremonial room) is built. The usual significance of the *kiva* is that it houses the village *sipapu* (Waters, 1963, p. 129), but it can also have other spiritual significances, such as being a place of natural healing power, or a place where spiritual visions have been reported in the past (Hieb, 1992).

Pueblo houses and *kivas* are thought to have tribal significance because of their symbolic connections to tribal people, to the underworld afterlife, and to the natural world. According to one perspective by Rina Swentzell (2001) of Santa Clara Pueblo, the structure of houses and *kivas*...

> ...emulated the low hills and mountains in their connectedness to the earth. The adobe structures flowed out of the earth, and it was often difficult to see where the ground stopped and where the structures began. The house structures were, moreover, connected to each other, enclosing

9. This sacred mountain is Mount Taylor, located approximately 15 miles northwest of the pueblo in New Mexico.

> an outdoor space from which we could directly connect with the sky and focus on the moving clouds. Connectedness was primary. The symbolic flowed into the physical world as at the nansipu [the Santa Clara word for *sipapu*] where the *po-wa-ha* (the breath of the cosmos) flowed out of the underworld into this world (p. 87).

Spiritual unity is the aspect within HLNZ tradition that often seems most reflective of the longbody. Each tribe believes that interrelatedness and interconnection also extends to the spiritual beings of the underworld existence, which are thought to continuously help guide tribal life and survival. Within the Hopi, Laguna, and Zuni cultures, this belief has led to the concept of the kachinas (David, 1993; Parsons, 1920; Waters, 1963, pp. 165-173, 198-209). In these cultures, the spirits of the underworld consist not only of deity-like beings that are tied to natural phenomena, but also of the spirits of deceased tribal members. Among their various symbolic purposes (others to be mentioned below), kachina figures are meant to represent the deceased in their temporary earthbound form as they return to the physical world to aid in tribal ceremony (Kealiinohomoku, 1989, p. 53; Mails, 1988/2003, pp. 76-77; Ricks & Anthony, 1993, p. 7; Waters, 1963, p. 165-166). This has led some scholars to view kachina religion as ancestor worship and as a cult of the dead (Adams, 1991, pp. 9, 11-12). Since the longbody is thought to encompass both living and deceased people (Roll, 1989, 2005), kachina ceremonies may be viewed as ceremonies held to honour the tribal longbody. An indirect (and literal) symbol of this among the Zuni may be the existence of the *Shalako*s, towering kachina figures appearing in winter that have elongated bodies (Scully, 1975, p. 271).

Since spiritual unity includes ties to the deceased, it is also used to define the past of the tribe. It seems that for tribes "…[w]here there is an oral tradition, the emphasis is on the need to remember the past and to teach it. This is basically for survival" (Pratt, 1993, p. 154). Oral traditions are inherent in HLNZ, being sustained primarily through personal memory, and they are passed to others based on the recounted actions of deceased tribal ancestors and relatives. One poem by Navajo writer Luci Tapahonso (1990, cited in Pratt, 1993, p. 152) well reflects the tribal definition of past through its oral tradition:

> *It has been this way for centuries among us [the Navajo]*
> *This is our history and way of raising children.*
> *It has worked well for centuries.*
> *You are here, your parents are here, your relatives are here.*
> *We are all here.*

In encompassing all those that one is related to, this poem suggests that longbody connections are vital not only to defining the Navajo's past, but also to defining their own identity. From this, it may be argued that one reason it is important for tribal members to remember their past is that doing so may help ensure the survival of the tribal longbody over time.

A second, much broader reference to unity among people, nature, and spirits can be found in Navajo tradition relating to the concept of *Diyin*. The concept itself relates to a kind of 'sacred wholeness' that is believed to be fundamental to human life. According to Navajo professors Nancy Maryboy and David Begay (2004), *Diyin* is a dynamic and ongoing process encompassing all things existent in the universe through a pattern of complex interrelationships, and this process constantly changes as the living and natural elements which make it up change. Since human behavior changes frequently and humans often manipulate their surroundings in various ways, it is thought that humans can greatly affect the flux of *Diyin*, as can the underworld spirits through their influence on nature. These effects are thought to generate both positive and negative relationships between all things, and in turn, positive and negative 'energy' within the flux of *Diyin*. The accumulation of negative energy is often associated with the occurrence of harmful events such as human sickness and tribal conflict, necessitating the preparation of the healing ceremony (discussed later).

The Cognitive and the Conative in Pueblo Society

Another aspect from HNLZ tradition that seems to reflect the longbody is the reflection of both the cognitive and the conative within tribal culture. The two terms, cognitive and conative, are used here with respect to Roll's (2005) intended use of them, where they define the two forms of meaning attributed to either an animate (e.g., another person) or inanimate object. According to Roll (p. 150), an object's cognitive meaning reflects its measurable aspect, whereas its conative meaning reflects its emotional or affective quality.

An object's existence within physical reality is largely defined by its material properties: it has certain dimensions (e.g., length and width), a certain mass, and a certain composition, and these things usually change little over time. These properties are what localize the object in a certain place at a certain time, giving it physical being. In short, they are the things that make an object an object. They are also measurable, and give rise to the object's cognitive meaning by the people measuring them, leading to knowledge in science and technology.

People also often ascribe personal, affective quality to an object according to the significance it has in their lives, whether functional (i.e., utilitarian) or sentimental. This affective quality can be quite important because it can either draw us towards or away from certain objects based on the perceived effect that they may have on our survival and well-being. The degree of affective quality we ascribe to a certain object based on its perceived effect can give rise to its conative meaning, and this meaning can change frequently over time. In ESP, a person nonlocally perceives the conative meaning of another person or inanimate object whose physical form is absent, according to Roll (2005, p. 151). The sensibility of this notion can be seen when one looks at certain features of spontaneous psi experiences (Feather & Schmicker, 2005; Rhine, 1961). For example, telepathic experiences seem to occur most often among persons that share a meaningful relationship.[10] The event which seems to precipitate the experience (as in crisis cases) also seems to carry a great deal of emotional meaning for one or both of the persons involved. In psychometry (Roll, 1978, 2004; Schwartz, 1978/2001, Ch. 2, 4-6), a person seems to perceive meaningful details about the person or events that have been associated with the handled object. Similarly, in PK experiences, the objects affected often have some degree of meaningful significance to either the person witnessing the PK event, or the person that it is attributed to.[11]

Within pueblo society, the cognitive and conative aspects of objects are often seen as being intertwined when it comes to ceremonial observation. Regarding kachina religion, Hopi scholar Barton Wright (1977, cited in Ricks & Anthony, 1993) writes: "The basic concept of the katsina cult is that all things in the world have two forms, the visible object and a spiritual counterpart, a dualism that balances mass and energy" (p. 7). This concept sets a basis for kachina representation during ceremonial dances, which has its own dual nature. On the one hand, human impersonation of a kachina spirit brings a cognitive construct into material form (i.e., by wearing a kachina costume, a tribal member brings a mythical being inherent in the tribal religion into visual form). On the other hand, the elaborate details of the costume bring out the spiritual significance of the kachina, expressing its spiritual nature, and thus, its conative meaning.

Other activities in Hopi life have a similar dual nature. During the farming season, the processes of planting and harvesting each have their own cognitive

10. This meaningful relationship can involve people who are emotionally close, or who are biologically related. This feature is also reflected in some experimental results (e.g., Broughton & Alexander, 1997; Rice & Townsend, 1962; Stuart, 1946).

11. For more extensive discussion about ESP as the nonlocal perception of conative meaning, see Roll (2005).

aspects in where to grow crops, how deep to place their seeds, and how they should be irrigated, for example. Yet these processes also have conative aspects, in that they have strong underlying spiritual meaning, as well. When these processes are carried out, they are often done with ritual prayers to the spirits who are believed to have an influence on crop growth and rain cycles. One function of the kachina ceremony is to honor and pray to these spirits so that they may bring the tribe a bountiful harvest. In relation to Hopi crop farming, Native American historian Thomas Mails (1988/2003) writes:

> In its essence, the central pathway walked by the Hopi has been an annual cycle of rituals that are preparatory in nature and go hand in hand with specific planting, cultivating, and harvesting tasks. These rituals include acts having to do with the continuance and heightening of their spiritual awareness of everything needful to life and survival. In other words, *both the material and the spiritual sides of life are addressed in the central pathways, although in truth the Hopi sees no distinction between the two, for the material life is itself infused with spirituality.* (p. 73, emphasis added)

In other words, the cognitive (reflected by the material side) and the conative (reflected by the spiritual side) are both involved in the process.

Another clear suggestion of cognitive and conative within kachina religion is the way in which tribal people regard the kachina mask worn in ceremonies. In the eyes of non-Indians, a kachina mask is often seen as a wonderfully simple piece of cultural art made of wood, pine boughs, and bird feathers, among other natural materials. In the eyes of Pueblo Indians, the mask represents something much more than just art. In addition to its material form, a tribe gives the mask conative meaning that embodies the mask with strong spiritual significance, in that they equate the mask with the spirit of the kachina itself. This is most evident in the tribal accounts of how it is cared for and perceived among the pueblo people. When a pueblo man dons the mask in ceremony, it is believed that he becomes instilled with the spirit of the kachina, and that rather than being a simple man impersonating a kachina, he becomes the kachina in every way (Adams, 1991; Ricks & Anthony, 1993; Waters, 1963, p. 167). When not in ceremonial use, a kachina mask is carefully stored and is ritually fed every day, with certain songs and prayers expressed to the mask during them (Mails, 1988/2003, p. 79; Waters, 1963, p. 167). During ceremonial dances, pueblo villagers display a similar ritual by symbolically 'feeding' the kachinas through offerings of cornmeal while making prayers to them. Mails (1988/2003) notes in this ritual that, of the offerings made, "...the spirits only eat the soul of the food" (p. 76). Roll (personal communication, 2004) has previously noted the cognitive and conative aspects of this ritual, which is present in many other tribal cultures of the world.

The way in which pueblo people approach the ceremony seems to offer another suggestion of cognitive and conative. Historian Edward Dozier (1970/1983) notes: "Pueblo ceremonialism is best understood as an aspect of the general Pueblo concept of the interrelatedness and cooperative nature of the universe. Ceremonial activity is the Pueblo's contribution to maintaining a harmonious balance which is believed to be the natural state of affairs" (p. 200). In relation to the pueblo's contribution, Thompson and Joseph (1944, cited in Dozier, 1970/1983) further note: "The rules of ceremonial observance have two aspects, the spiritual and the psychical. If either aspect is neglected or any regulation is broken, failure will result" (p. 200). This suggests that the ceremonial process as a whole has cognitive aspects (reflected in its ritual activity, which must be carried out in a precise manner) and conative aspects (reflected in the higher spiritual significance that is believed to result from that activity) to it that complement each other. This is also the viewpoint in Navajo healing ceremonies with regard to *Diyin*, examined further in the next section.

One last suggestion comes from the clan rituals and customs observed when a tribal member has died (Parsons, 1923, pp. 216-219). Though their viewpoints slightly differ, the HNLZ each hold the belief that the soul departs from the body upon death and makes a spiritual journey back to the underworld (Erdoes, 1976, p. 202) to live on as part of the larger tribal longbody. The Laguna also believe that the deceased continue to spiritually interact with the physical world, helping to bring rain (Mails, 1983, p. 280), in addition to being guiding spirits for the tribe through longbody ties. The Hopi believe that upon death, the deceased become kachina spirits (Kealiinohomoku, 1989, p. 53; Mails, 1988/2003, pp. 76-77; Ricks & Anthony, 1993, p. 7; Waters, 1963, p. 167), forming the basis for viewing the kachina religion as a cult of the dead (Adams, 1991). Burial rituals done by the Hopi, Laguna, and Zuni symbolize this belief: the Hopi cover the deceased's face with cotton or place cotton tiers along the top of the head, which is meant to symbolize the kachinas as cloud spirits (Mails, 1983, p. 280; 1988/2003, p. 77).

In Zuni and Laguna, if the deceased was a kachina impersonator, the face is painted with a certain pattern indicative of this, and the body may be sprinkled with water as ritual song that places the deceased among the storm clouds is chanted (Parsons, 1923, pp. 217-218). Feathers and other sacred animal objects are also commonly placed on the corpse to symbolize the tribe's spiritual connection to nature and the tribal land, both of which bring rain and life. Food, filled water jugs, and other material belongings are buried along with the deceased, reflecting the belief that the deceased's spirit needs to take what they need to make the journey back to the underworld, which is often thought to be a long process.[12]

The ritual of burying objects with the deceased apparently dates back to the time of the ancient Anasazi Indians (the historical ancestors of modern Pueblo people), as evidenced from the archaeological record dating from the Mimbres period (1000-1150 A.D.). Pottery artifacts found at Anasazi burial sites that date from this period often had holes punched into them. It is thought that the Anasazi believed that upon moulding the piece, a pottery 'spirit' became embodied within it,[13] and that when the pottery was buried with the deceased, a break in the piece (called a 'kill hole') had to be made so that the embodied 'spirit' could then be released and accompany the deceased's spirit to the afterlife (Erdoes, 1976, p. 202; Peckham, 1989). This ritual is still done in modern times by tradition, and one tends to find many pottery shards littering pueblo cemeteries.

Rituals carried out following the burial further suggest cognitive and conative aspects. The Laguna and Zuni believe that after the burial, the spirit of the deceased lingers for a short time (usually 2-4 days) in their home before beginning the journey back to the underworld. The day after the burial, the spirit is invited into the home, and food and drink are offered to it (Erdoes, 1976, p. 202). Food may be taken to the deceased's grave in the few days following to 'feed' the lingering spirit (Parsons, 1920, p. 219). Once this short period has elapsed, the deceased's home is then spiritually cleansed by washing its walls and repainting them (Mails, 1983, p. 280). Any remaining belongings are similarly washed and fumigated with cedar wood smoke as a means of spirit release (Parsons, 1920, p. 129; 1923, p. 219).

These are only but a few of the many possible examples from pueblo life that seem to reflect Roll's (2005) idea of the cognitive and the conative.

12. Although the journey between them is long, it is believed in some tribes like Laguna that the actual metaphoric 'distance' between the physical world and the underworld is very short, which allows the spirits of the deceased to continue interacting with the physical world and helping to guide tribal life.

13. Most often this pottery 'spirit' was an animal spirit, given the frequency of animal designs on Mimbres pottery (Fewkes, 1914/1990; Peckham, 1989).

Ceremony, Healing and Psi

> *"When you put a thing in order, and give it a name,*
> *and you are all in accord, it becomes"*
> (From the Navajo tradition, Waters, 1950)

Among the Navajo, the cognitive and the conative are reflected most often in the healing ceremony. Navajo spirituality primarily focuses on achieving a balance between the positive and negative relationships between everything in the universe that is inherent in the flux of *Diyin*.[14] As mentioned previously, it is thought that humans can have a great effect on *Diyin*, not only by manipulating their environment, but also by holding negative thoughts and dabbling in magical powers.[15] Such acts tend to upset the balance by creating more negative 'energy' within *Diyin*, and an excessive amount of this energy is thought to lead to negative consequences like human sickness and social or intertribal conflict. In order to cure an ill person and/or restore the balance to *Diyin*, the healing ceremony is carried out (Kluckhohn & Leighton, 1962; Maryboy & Begay, 2004).[16]

Healing ceremonies among the Navajo (and other tribes) are often communal events that can involve entire families or even an entire village. Central to the ceremony is the medicine man, who acts both as a spiritual healer and as the Indian equivalent of a psychotherapist, hearing the patient's guilty acts that led to the *Diyin* imbalance and forgiving them. As a result of this trusting relationship, both healer and the patient form a bond analogous to kinship that remains for life (Kluckhohn, 1939, p. 58; Kluckhohn & Leighton, 1962, p. 198). The families and larger sections of the tribe that are participating in the ceremony often aid each other in performing its rituals, and this large-scale cooperation with a shared focus on healing may facilitate the formation of a temporary healing longbody.

---

14. In other words, the focus is on achieving homeostasis, which the Navajo call *hozhoo*, loosely translated as meaning 'harmony' (Maryboy & Begay, 2004, p. 28).
15. A strong belief in witchcraft exists in Navajo culture. For detailed discussion, see Kluckhohn (1944) and Kluckhohn and Leighton (1962, pp. 187-193).
16. It should be mentioned that certain forms of divination used by the Navajo to diagnose illness, such as hand trembling and crystal gazing (Kluckhohn, 1939, pp. 66-71), may have psi-related aspects of their own. They are not mentioned here for matters of brevity, but Reichbart (1976) has pointed out that they may bring about states similar to trance mediumship, and may thus be psi-conducive. The interested reader should consult his article on hand trembling and psi for further discussion.

Healing deity-like spirits and the spirits of deceased tribal members are both called upon during the ceremony for their help in guiding the restoration of the *Diyin* balance, and this may suggest the involvement of the larger tribal longbody (Pratt, 1993, pp. 155-156).

Navajo and Hopi healing ceremonies often consist of a number of rituals that can take anywhere from an hour to several nights to complete.[17] Rituals can include herbal medicine, ceremonial song, smoke fumigation, and group prayer or meditation (Cohen, 1998; Mails, 1988/2003, pp. 81-84). Exclusive among the Navajo is the use of sand-paintings, which depict healing spirits of the underworld and various natural phenomena that represent those same components of *Diyin* (Maryboy & Begay, 2004). Each of these rituals seems to have cognitive and conative aspects associated with them: The ingestion of herbal medicines is thought to bring the patient in touch with the natural healing powers of the earth. The balance and rhythm generated from performing ceremonial song is associated with the cosmic order of the universe (Maryboy & Begay, 2004). Fumigation of people and objects with smoke allows spiritual cleansing, aside from a common tribal belief that smoke carries one's prayers up to the heavens. Sand-paintings are thought to heal through contact with the spirits (Kluckhohn & Leighton, 1962).[18] Group prayer and meditation are associated with the summoning of underworld healing spirits through the use of *pahos*, or prayer sticks (Mails, 1988/2003, pp. 85-89; Waters, 1963, pp. 131-134). Mistakes in any of these rituals are thought to have a negative effect on *Diyin* (Maryboy & Begay, 2004).

The communal group nature of the ceremony, with its shared focus toward healing and restoring *Diyin* balance, may perhaps make it conducive to a group PK effect. In terms of healing, this group effect may be a physiological one similar to that seen in studies of bio-PK and distant mental influence on living systems (DMILS) that have received growing attention in recent years (e.g., Braud, 2003; Delanoy, 2001; Schlitz & Braud, 1997; Targ, 1997). Within other contexts, the focus of the group may have influence on the surrounding environment, an influence interpreted as human effects on *Diyin*. This latter influence may be analogous to the PK-related effect seen in studies of 'field consciousness' (Nelson et al., 1996, 1998). In these studies, random data collected during group workshops focused on distant healing or meditation have shown notable

17. A Navajo healing ceremony is often called a 'Chantway'.

18. Spirit contact healing is thought to be achieved by having the patient sit directly on the sand-painting during the ceremony, and then having the coloured sand poured and rubbed on their body afterwards.

non-random patterns (Nelson & Radin, 2003; Rowe, 1998). So far, at least one such study has been conducted in relation to Native American tradition: data collected during a sacred site healing and preservation ceremony conducted by a Shoshone Indian shaman at Devil's Tower in Wyoming had shown significant deviations from randomness throughout the ceremony (Nelson et al., 1998, pp. 432-433; Nelson & Radin, 2003, pp. 53-54). The concepts of both DMILS and field consciousness seem to suggest some form of interconnectedness through partnership (e.g., Braud, 2003, pp. xliii-xliv) and shared group experience (e.g., Nelson et al., 1996, pp. 136-137), respectively, and this may be another basis for their relevance within the context of healing.

Kachina ceremonies are also thought to have a healing-related purpose underlying them (Adams, 1991), in that they too may be perceived as a contribution to maintaining a harmonious balance in the natural world through positive, focused ritual (Dozier, 1970/1983, p. 200). Thompson and Joseph (1944, cited in Dozier, 1970/1983) note:

> ...to carry out a rite successfully, the participants must not only follow the prescribed ritual behavior, perform all the proper acts and observe the tabus [*sic*], but they must also exercise control over their emotions and thoughts. They must keep a 'good heart.' A 'good heart' means that one must not feel fear, anger, sadness, or worry. In other words, one must be inwardly tranquil and of good will. (p. 200)

In other words, analogous to the Navajo tradition of human effects on *Diyin*, participants must keep a positive focus during a ceremony in order to ensure success of the kachina ceremony. If such an outlook is shared among all the participants, then this too might facilitate a kind of shared group 'coherence' analogous to the kind that is thought to underlie field consciousness effects (Nelson et al., 1996, 1998).

The large group nature of a kachina ceremony might itself suggest the possibility of a group PK effect. Such ceremonies often involve large group dances that are rhythmic and synchronized, with a mass focus of attention upon them by the numerous pueblo villagers in attendance. Tribal members regularly work together to ensure that the ceremony goes smoothly,[19] and families regularly invite each other to their homes for visits and a meal during the ceremony, both of which promote social gathering and cohesiveness (Adams, 1991; Kealiinohomoku,

19. This communal ceremonial aid usually comes about through individual clan functions for a kachina ceremony. For details, see Parsons (1923, pp. 219-224).

1989). With regard to this group nature of a Hopi kachina ceremony, Joann Kealiinohomoku (1989) writes:

> Both dancers and non-dancers are mesmerized by the rhythmically pleasing patterns, and the collective thoughts and energies magnetically attract the katsina spirits. This [spiritual energy] vortex is intensified by the accumulation of rhythms that systematically and insistently beat together with some combination of drums, rattles, bells, and moving bodies.... A feeling of closeness and caring envelops the people who sit or stand quietly together while surrounding the dancers in the plaza. (pp. 58-59).

This seems akin to the kind of social atmosphere reported in some of the group situations that have displayed field consciousness effects (Nelson et al., 1996, 1998), and it may perhaps entail the formation of a short-lived ceremonial longbody. Kachina ceremonies also have the purpose of bringing rain, and a group focus towards this purpose may lead to a possible PK effect on the surrounding physical atmosphere. This possibility is suggested in a natural 'group consciousness' study by Nelson (1997), which found that there tended to be less rain over time on days of large outdoor group ceremonies held at Princeton University. In one sense, this might be seen as the opposite effect of the stereotypical Indian 'rain dance'.

Place Memory and Sacred Sites

There is one other aspect of HNLZ culture that may be relevant to the longbody, and that is sacred Indian sites as possible harborers of 'place memory.' The concept comes from the Oxford philosopher H. H. Price (1939, 1940), who had initially proposed it as a way to account for psychometry and veridical haunting apparitions. Roll (1989, 1993, 2005) later expanded on the concept by providing a logical basis for it: The mind, which holds memories, is embodied. In turn, the body is emplaced, which means the mind is also emplaced. If that is so, then this further means that memories are emplaced. In addition, Roll (1988) has argued that memory can be seen as mind stretched out in space and time, and may therefore serve as both a basis and a limiting factor for the reach of the longbody. Considering this, one could argue that historical and sacred sites may harbor the personal history of a given tribe in the form of place memory as one way to preserve the tribal longbody over time.

Reflecting on recording her second album in Taos, New Mexico, in 1993, musician Tori Amos (Rogers, 1994) had stated:

> When I went to New Mexico I felt the past from the Pueblo nation. You stand out on those plains, and you just see them coming over the hill, you see the horses coming over the hill, and that land is still alive with those memories, the Southwest, that's one reason that I was drawn to go record there. (Rogers, 1994, p. 73)

Anecdotal accounts like these of people 'feeling the history of the tribe' or a 'deep sense of tranquility or peace' at a sacred site or a place of tribal inhabitance may be akin to reports of place memory as it relates to psychometry and haunting. Regarding the latter, Price (1939) had written:

> Persistent and dynamic images, which when once formed may have a kind of independent life of their own, and may escape more or less completely from the control of their author.... An image or a group of images may get itself localized in a particular region of Physical Space.... Once localized there, they might continue to be so localized for a considerable period, retaining the telepathic charge which they had at first, though this might gradually diminish in intensity. (pp. 325-326)

From this perspective, one might argue that sacred tribal places like *kivas* might be most susceptible to place memory given the persistent annual celebration and ritual repetition of ceremony, as well as the dynamic nature of such events (e.g., drumming, rattling, and dancing), the memories of which might be experienced by others visiting the site with time. In discussing place memory, Pamela Rae Heath (2004, 2005) suggested that there may be two ways in which the memories become localized: they may be done so passively through repetitive action, and they may be done so actively through PK.[20] If that is so, then ceremonial action in a *kiva* would seem to be most in line with the former, but it may also involve the latter to some degree if activities that produce sympathetic nervous system arousal (such as dancing) are also conducive to PK (Roll, 1987, p. 20).

The sensibility of sacred sites harbouring place memory is also suggested by a metaphorical statement by Steve McDowell (1990, cited in Hieb, 1992) in relation to historic New Mexican religious architecture: "Architecture is a form

20. There may be some preliminary evidence to support Heath's hypothesis that PK takes an active role in the formation of place memory; see the review by Williams and Roll (2006).

of memory, less similar to the structured mechanisms of history than it is a life form, with a growth, adaptation and life span that resemble those of an ancient tree" (p. 76). This perspective would seem to suggest that architecture can be seen as more dynamic than static, much in the same way that place memory may be seen as dynamic. Louis Hieb (1992) then notes: "In societies without a written language—like the Hopi . . . architecture becomes an enduring embodiment of ideas expressed in symbolic form" (p. 76). Architecture can also be a defining part of place, and in some sense, memories associated with a place might represent an enduring embodiment of ideas expressed in dynamic form.

There may be some suggestion of psi-related experience of persistent place memory within the traditions of a few of the Southwest tribes. Mails (1988/2003) had written that, according to the Hopi tradition,

> The place where one worships and petitions is extremely important. Closeness to the deities, the very warmth and power of their beings, must be felt. When this is so, people hear the powers speak, motivation comes, and amazing things happen. The dead return, magic and miracles occur, and *believers are simultaneously transported back into ancient time and forward into the future. Consciousness is expanded.* (p. 91, emphasis added).

This suggests that experiences of spiritual vision at a Hopi worship site may in part involve the experience of place memory in the same sense as one might experience it when seeing a veridical haunting apparition (Roll, 1981a).

Similar perceptions about the home (called a hogan) are held by the Navajo in relation to bad dreams. Kluckhohn and Leighton (1962) note: "If bad dreams keep coming, the hogan will be torn down and a new one will be built some distance away, because the bad dreams are supposed to come from ghosts who are frequenting their old haunts and trying to draw their relatives into ghostland with them" (p. 204). This too suggests ESP impressions of place memory and apparitions as it relates to hauntings (Roll, 1981a). It also seems to be in line with a slight difference in dream content observed at sacred sites in the UK as compared to home dream reports, though this observed difference is tentative and still needs to be studied further (Krippner, Devereux, & Fish, 2003).

Rina Swentzell (2001) states that Santa Clara Pueblo homes are also viewed in a similar fashion, noting that "Many different kinds of energies flowed through the structures because they shared in the energies of the people who lived and died within them" (p. 89).

Anecdotal Examples of Psi and Longbody Connections

As a way to illustrate how the longbody may tie into tribal psi experiences, three anecdotal examples suggestive of the latter are presented here. The first comes from Navajo researcher Willard W. Hill (1938, cited in Kluckhohn, 1939), who noted in a discussion of the tribe's Rain Chant:

> During a ceremony, the individuals in a hogan were supposed to sit and think hard, stare straight ahead, and be very quiet. If the chanter were [*sic*] performing the ceremony in the right manner some one of the audience would get a vision pertaining to the chanter and his objective. This would be a sign that the ceremony was being properly conducted and that it would be successful (p. 66).

One might note that this ceremonial setting is quite similar to that of a spiritual séance, and might be conducive to group ESP interpreted as spiritual vision. According to Roll, one of the factors that may facilitate psi among a closely-knit group is the formation of a group longbody (Duncan & Roll, 1995, p. 152).

The second example is described by Duncan and Roll (1995), in which an archaeologist challenges a psychic to pick up psychometric information from pueblo artifacts in order to tell where they came from:

> "One tiny piece of shell gave me a picture of a civilization to the west of me," she says. "I got the styles of houses, decorations and styles of pottery, and the name *Zuni*. From a fragment of a pot I got entirely different styles of dwellings, pottery, and decoration, and the word *Aztec*. I identified three more fragments, one of them *Hopi*." The archaeologist verified that all these impressions were accurate and said he did not believe that any professional archaeologist could have done better unless he had spent a lifetime with Indian artifacts from those particular civilizations. (p. 65)

This example may illustrate how the conative aspects of an object, when it is persistently imbued with meaning in ceremony, may be psychically perceived as place memory. Similar cases in which historical artifacts and sites were used as psychometric sources have been described in detail by Schwartz (1978/2001, Ch. 2, 4-6), and they may further illustrate how place memory associated with objects and sites might allow psychics to 'reconnect' with the persisting tribal longbodies of existing or extinct cultures across space and time.

The third was an experience related to me by my father, which had occurred in relation to the passing of my great-uncle:

> I was in Albuquerque the weekend Uncle passed away. I was not there when he did. I was on my way back to California. But on Monday, the day after he passed, I was in Winslow, Arizona. While I was there, I had this feeling to go back to Laguna. Why I had this feeling, I don't know. Or I guess I knew where it was coming from. When I pray in Laguna, I ask the spirits to whisper in my ear, things I need to know. It is my belief that Uncle had sent the spirits to tell me to come home for him that day. I went on to Lancaster. I was there an hour when I got the call that Uncle had passed. I should have gone back while in Winslow. Three-hours later I was on my way back home.

While interpreted within a native context, this experience seems to be suggestive of either precognition or retrocognition, depending on which cognized event is focused on (the phone call or the passing, respectively). My father was known to have a close connection to my great-uncle, visiting him whenever he could, and this might have given rise to a personal longbody connection between them that was maintained at a distance through psi. Alternatively, my father's interpretation suggests a close personal connection to the larger tribal longbody.

DISCUSSION

> "*My people once hunted for buffalo—*
> *now we hunt for knowledge*"[21]

The suggestions from HNLZ tradition of a unity among people, place and spirit; of cognitive and conative aspects within tribal society, and of a possible link between sacred sites and place memory all seem to metaphorically suggest a close interconnection between mind and matter that is akin to that proposed

21. Lakota Chief Joseph Chasing Horse in a press release for a meeting exploring connections between astronomy and traditional Lakota star knowledge (*Science*, 283, p. 2007).

for the longbody in a parapsychological context (Roll, 1987, 1989, 2005). What might the deeper implications of this be for psi and the longbody? Roll (1966, 1975, Ch. 4) has previously proposed a theory in which (long-term) memory traces play an important role in ESP. Given that HNLZ use a memory-based oral tradition as the prime method of preserving their culture, ESP may play a supplemental role in maintaining the traditions over time for the benefit of the survival of the larger tribal longbody. In addition, by remembering them through their oral traditions, the four tribes might keep very close longbody ties to their deceased tribal members. This might at times be conducive to the experience of survival-related phenomena that is often interpreted within the context of underworld spirit connections. Survival after death in this context would more seem to represent a longbody persisting across space and time rather than the survival of individual minds.

To help preserve the history of the tribal longbody, PK might have a role in defining the conative aspects of ceremonial objects and sacred sites that become part of their respective place memories. In this case, the conative aspects might be achieved primarily through group PK effects during a ceremonial event, with the latter carrying strong spiritual meaning for Indian tribes in terms of their survival (Adams, 1991; Dozier, 1970/1983; Kealiinohomoku, 1989; Waters, 1950, 1963). As an object or site is continually used over time in large group ceremonies, it might be subject to place memory formation through repetitive action and PK as proposed by Heath (2004, 2005). As with ceremonial healing, the form of group PK involved might be akin to the 'field consciousness' effects observed in relation to other spiritual techniques, such as meditation (Nelson & Radin, 2003; Rowe, 1998).

It is possible that some tribal psi experiences at sacred sites could be similar to haunt experiences, in that some locations deemed as sacred by Indian tribes may display geophysical properties very similar to those found at reported haunt sites (Roll & Persinger, 2001). Another reason for thinking this is that physical measurements taken at various archaeological sites in Europe suggest that these sites can have unusual geophysical properties (Devereux, 1990). Similarly, some sacred Indian artifacts may have some unique physical properties of their own (e.g., an artifact that is materially composed in part of radioactive elements).

The geophysical properties most likely to be associated with tribal psi experiences among HNLZ are ionizing radiation and geomagnetism, based on the geology of the American Southwest (Adams, 1999). Within New Mexico and Arizona, there is frequent mining for radioactive elements such as Uranium-238, the decay products of which can contribute to background radiation levels if considerable concentrations are present in rock formations surrounding tribal sites. Dry desert winds, such as those produced by the Santa Ana winds, can also affect radiation levels by producing excess positive ion counts (Assael, Pfeifer, & Sulman, 1974; Charry & Hawkinshire, 1981; Persinger, 1979). Some studies seem to suggest that atmospheric ionization can affect brain wave patterns (Assael, Pfeifer, & Sulman, 1974), as well as behaviour and mood (Frey, 1961).

In relation to radiation, radon gas might be a possible secondary factor. Radon is often a decay product of uranium, and is known to be toxic when inhaled in large amounts (Kerr, 1988). Concentrations of radon gas could build up within rock formations and seep into enclosed tribal sites like *kivas*, where it may concentrate. Without proper ventilation, the gas could be frequently inhaled by tribal people occupying the space, leading to hypoxia and its associated hallucinatory effects. Radon toxicity could be one contributing factor behind a Hopi tradition warning non-Indians not to trespass on a sacred tribal site, the consequences of which might be deadly (Marriott & Rachlin, 1968, pp. 243-245).

Electromagnetic and geomagnetic fluctuations within the Southwest region could be another contributing factor. Certain regions, such as the Tucumcari Basin in New Mexico, have been found to have transient geomagnetic variation anomalies in the areas around deep sedimentary basins with conductive properties (Persinger, 1987, p. 97; Porath & Dziewonski, 1971). Anomalies arising from thermoremanent magnetization as a result of excessive heat in room fire hearths and pits may be a further source of magnetic field fluctuation in sacred sites (Sternberg, 1987). The activity associated with geological processes in the area around a sacred site, such as the movement of water in an underground aquifer or volcano-related seismic activity, may also contribute to anomalous magnetic field variations and gas emissions (Persinger, 1979, 1985, 1987).

The effects of these magnetic fluctuations may be similar to those proposed for haunt cases, in that they might affect the brains of people present at the site, leading to subjective experiences similar to the sensed presence, apparitions, and other haunt-related phenomena (Persinger, 1979, 1985, 1987, 1993, 2001; Roll & Persinger, 2001). Certain brain areas particularly sensitive to magnetic fields, such as the temporal lobes and the limbic system, may perhaps affect the content of such experiences if influenced by anomalous magnetic fields. Persinger (1983, 1993, 2001) has suggested that religious and mystical experiences may be a function of temporal lobe microseizuring, a neuroelectrical phenomenon that may be facilitated by exposure to complex magnetic fields. The two main structures of the limbic system, the hippocampus and the amygdala, are known to be centrally involved in memory and emotion, respectively. Electrical stimulation of these structures has been associated with the experience of memory- or dream-like hallucinations of scenes, *déjà vu*, various bodily sensations, and negative emotions, among others (Halgren, Walter, Cherlow, & Crandall, 1978). Activation of these structures through electrical induction by an anomalous magnetic field may perhaps generate similar transient experiences in people visiting sites that contain such a field.

In addition, there might be some aspects of the ceremonial process itself that might facilitate psi-conducive altered states of consciousness, such as the rhythmic beats of ceremonial drumming. Drum beats seem to produce acoustic sound waves that at times can modulate and produce brain wave patterns that 'follow' the same frequency as the waves, a process called 'auditory driving' (Vaitl et al., 2005, p. 107). A similar process may be involved in the technique of binaural beating, which is often used to induce altered states (Atwater, 1997). Sound waves from unified ceremonial singing and chanting that become localized within an enclosed space (like a *kiva*) may also create a standing sound wave within the space that could have an auditory driving-related effect over time. Sound measurements taken in European archaeological sites by Devereux and Jahn (1996) and by Jahn, Devereux, and Ibison (1996) seem to indicate the presence of such standing sound waves, hinting at the sensibility of the idea.

Aside from geophysical properties, there might also be certain psychological factors that could influence the experience of tribal psi. Some studies suggest that certain contextual variables, such as cultural beliefs, rumours, and cues embedded in the surrounding environment, could influence one's perception in a haunt experience (Harte, 2000; Lange, Houran, Harte, & Havens, 1996). Certain environmental factors which might give one the sense of a mysterious atmosphere, such as lighting levels, have also been found to correlate with reported experiences at haunt sites (Wiseman, Watt, Stevens, Greening, & O'Keeffe, 2003). Similar to haunts, these factors might predispose one to an expectation of mystical experience within sacred sites, given their known history, intended use, and spiritual decoration.

In terms of psychological factors that may relate to healing, McClenon (1997) has claimed that suggestions embedded in shamanic rituals may have therapeutic effects, perhaps analogous to a placebo effect. Such claimed could come from contextual variables as well, as argued by Houran, Lange, and Crist-Houran (1997) in relation to shamanic trance. In addition, McClenon (1994) has proposed that anomalous experiences (including psi) may have in part given rise to belief in souls, spirits, and an afterlife, forming the basis for religion. If some anomalous experiences are the result of geophysical factors and/or psychological factors, then this, combined with McClenon's hypothesis, could possibly account in part for the presence of strong spiritual aspects in tribal societies like the ones described here.

CONCLUSION

Some of the ideas relating to longbody aspects of HNLZ tradition and their implications for tribal psi that have been discussed here seem open to further exploration. Possible directions for future research might include:

1. examining through survey study the frequency of psi-related experiences among Indian tribes that rely strongly on a memory-based oral tradition in order to further explore the relation between ESP and memory among Indians;
2. further field exploration of the geophysical properties of sacred Indian sites using measuring instruments, with a comparison to the measurements recorded at traditional haunt sites;
3. field measurements of possible group PK effects during Native American tribal ceremonies through the use of portable random number generators.[22] Similar measurements can be taken for healing ceremonies as they might relate to bio-PK and DMILS;
4. collecting, and making a closer examination of the phenomenological aspects of reported psi experiences among Native Americans to see what they might tell us about tribal psi experience as compared to psi experiences among Anglos. This, along with (1) above, might help to estimate the frequency and type of psi experiences of Native Americans, which can also be compared to Anglo reports.

And of course, psi testing with Native Americans might be worth consideration, provided that willing subjects can be found. To date, it appears that only one

---

22. I have recently made a preliminary effort in this direction by collecting random data during the 2005 Gathering of Nations Powwow (Williams, 2006). Analysis revealed that the data were at chance. It was noted, however, that the psychological atmosphere of this public event was quite different than that for private tribal ceremonies.

study with an Indian population (children from a Canadian Plains tribe) has been conducted, with mixed results (Foster, 1943). Findings from these research directions might be useful in further supporting or disproving some of the ideas suggested here, as well as possibly deriving more refined perspectives on psi and the longbody within the Native American tradition.

» References

Aanstoos, C. M. (1986). Psi and the phenomenology of the long body. *Theta, 13-14*, 49-51.

Aanstoos, C. M. (2005). Phenomenology of embodiment. In *The Parapsychological Association 48th Annual Convention: Proceedings of presented papers* (pp. 12-23). Raleigh, NC: Parapsychological Association.

Adams, E. C. (1991). *The origin and development of the Pueblo Katsina cult.* Tucson, AZ: University of Arizona Press.

Adams, M. H. (1999). Physical anomalies at sacred sites. Paper presented at the 18th Annual Meeting of the Society for Scientific Exploration, University of New Mexico, Albuquerque, NM, June 10-12.

Assael, M., Pfeifer, Y., & Sulman, F. G. (1974). Influence of artificial air ionization on the human electroencephalogram. *International Journal of Biometeorology, 18*, 306-312.

Atwater, F. H. (1997). Accessing anomalous states of consciousness with a binaural beat technology. *Journal of Scientific Exploration, 11*, 263-274.

Braud, W. (2003). *Distant mental influence: Its contributions to science, healing, and human interactions.* Charlottesville, VA: Hampton Roads Publishing Company.

Broughton, R. S., & Alexander, C. H. (1997). Autoganzfeld II: An attempted replication of the PRL ganzfeld research. *Journal of Parapsychology, 61*, 209-226.

Charry, J. M., & Hawkinshire V, F. B. W. (1981). Effects of atmospheric electricity on some substrates of disordered social behavior. *Journal of Personality and Social Psychology, 41*, 185-197.

Cohen, K. B. H. (1998). Native American medicine. *Alternative Therapies in Health and Medicine, 4*, 45-57.

David, N. (1993). *Kachinas: Spirit beings of the Hopi.* Albuquerque, NM: Avanyu Publishing, Inc.

Delanoy, D. L. (2001). Anomalous psychophysiological responses to remote cognition: The DMILS studies. *European Journal of Parapsychology, 16*, 29-40.

Devereux, P. (1990). *Places of power: Measuring the secret energy of ancient sites.* London: Blandford.

Devereux, P., & Jahn, R. G. (1996). Preliminary investigations and cognitive considerations of the acoustical resonances of selected archaeological sites. *Antiquity, 70*, 665- 666.

Dozier, E. P. (1970/1983). *The Pueblo Indians of North America*. Prospect Heights, IL: Waveland Press.

Duncan, L., & Roll, W. (1995). *Psychic connections: A journey into the mysterious world of psi*. New York: Delacorte Press.

Erdoes, R. (1976). *The Rain Dance People: The Pueblo Indians, past and present.* New York: Alfred A. Knopf, Inc.

Feather, S. R., & Schmicker, M. (2005). *The gift: ESP, the extraordinary experiences of ordinary people*. New York: St. Martin's Press.

Fewkes, J. W. (1914/1990). *The Mimbres: Art and archeology*. Albuquerque, NM: Avanyu Publishing.

Foster, A. A. (1943). ESP tests with American Indian children: A comparison of methods. *Journal of Parapsychology, 7*, 94-103.

Frey, A. H. (1961). Human behavior and atmospheric ions. *Psychological Review, 68*, 225-228.

Halgren, E., Walter, R. D., Cherlow, D. G., & Crandall, P. H. (1978). Mental phenomena evoked by electrical stimulation of the human hippocampal formation and amygdala. *Brain, 101*, 83-117.

Harte, T. M. (2000). Contextual mediation of perceptions during hauntings and poltergeist-like experiences: A replication and extension. *Perceptual and Motor Skills, 91*, 451-459.

Heath, P. R. (2004). The possible role of psychokinesis in place memory. *Australian Journal of Parapsychology, 4*, 63-80.

Heath, P. R. (2005). A new theory on place memory. *Australian Journal of Parapsychology, 5*, 40-58.

Hieb, L. A. (1992). The kiva and the evolution of symbol systems. In B. H. Morrow & V. B. Price (Eds.), *Proceedings: The Mesa Verde symposium on Anasazi architecture and American design* (pp. 67-84). Albuquerque, NM: Landscape Architects, Inc.

Houran, J., Lange, R., & Crist-Houran, M. (1997). An assessment of contextual mediation in trance states of shamanic journeys. *Perceptual and Motor Skills, 85*, 59-65.

Jahn, R. G., Devereux, P., & Ibison, M. (1996). Acoustical resonances of assorted ancient structures. *Journal of the Acoustical Society of America, 99*, 649-658.

Lange, R., Houran, J., Harte, T. M., & Havens, R. A. (1996). Contextual mediation of perceptions in hauntings and poltergeist-like experiences. *Perceptual and Motor Skills, 82*, 755-762.

Kealiinohomoku, J. W. (1989). The Hopi katsina dance event "doings." In S. B. Vane & L. J. Bean (Eds.), *Seasons of the Kachina: Proceedings of the California State University, Hayward conferences on the Western Pueblos 1987-1988* (pp. 51-63). Ballena Press Anthropological Papers No. 34. Hayward, CA: Ballena Press/California State University, Hayward.

Kerr, R. A. (1988). Indoor radon: The deadliest pollutant. *Science, 240*, 606-608.

Kluckhohn, C. (1939). Some personal and social aspects of Navaho ceremonial practice. *Harvard Theological Review, 32*, 57-82.

Kluckhohn, C. (1944). *Navaho witchcraft*. Boston, MA: Beacon Press.

Kluckhohn, C., & Leighton, D. (1962). *The Navaho* (Rev. Ed.). Garden City, NY: Anchor Books/American Museum of Natural History.

Krippner, S., Devereux, P., & Fish, A. (2003). The use of the Strauch Scale to study dream reports from sacred sites in England and Wales. *Dreaming, 13*, 95-105.

Mails, T. E. (1983). *The Pueblo children of the Earth Mother, Volume II.* New York: Doubleday & Company, Inc.

Mails, T. E. (1988/2003). *Secret Native American pathways*. Tulsa, OK: Council Oak Books.

Marriott, A., & Rachlin, C. K. (1968). *American Indian mythology*. New York: Mentor Books/New American Library.

Maryboy, N. C., & Begay, D. H. (2004). Ceremonial healing: Traditional ways of healing expressed through Navajo consciousness. *Shift: At the Frontiers of Consciousness, 3*, 25-29.

McClenon, J. (1994). *Wonderous events: Foundations of religious belief.* Philadelphia: University of Pennsylvania Press.

McClenon, J. (1997). Shamanic healing, human evolution, and the origin of religion. *Journal for the Scientific Study of Religion, 36*, 345-354.

Nelson, R. D. (1997). Wishing for good weather: A natural experiment in group consciousness. *Journal of Scientific Exploration, 11*, 47-58.

Nelson, R. D., Bradish, G. J., Dobyns, Y. H., Dunne, B. J., & Jahn, R. G. (1996). FieldREG anomalies in group situations. *Journal of Scientific Exploration, 10*, 111-141.

Nelson, R. D., Jahn, R. G., Dunne, B. J., Dobyns, Y. H., & Bradish, G. J. (1998). FieldREG II: Consciousness field effects: Replications and explorations. *Journal of Scientific Exploration, 12*, 425-454.

Nelson, R. D., & Radin, D. I. (2003). FieldREG experiments and group consciousness: Extending REG/RNG research to real-world situations. In W. B. Jonas & C. C. Crawford (Eds.), *Healing, intention, and energy medicine: Science, research methods and clinical implications* (pp. 49-57). Edinburgh, UK: Churchill Livingstone.

Parsons, E. C. (1920). Notes on ceremonialism at Laguna. *Anthropological Papers of the American Museum of Natural History, 19*, 85-131.

Parsons, E. C. (1923). Laguna genealogies. *Anthropological Papers of the American Museum of Natural History, 19*, 133-292.

Peckham, S. (1989). Prehistoric pottery of New Mexico. In A. H. Whiteford, S. Peckham, R. Dillingham, N. Fox, & K. P. Kent (Eds.), *I am here: Two thousand years of Southwest Indian arts and culture* (pp. 29-45). Santa Fe, NM: Museum of New Mexico Press.

Persinger, M. A. (1979). Geophysical models for parapsychological experiences. In S. Krippner (Ed.), *Psychoenergetic systems: The interaction of consciousness, energy, and matter* (pp. 239-250). New York: Gordon and Breach.

Persinger, M. A. (1983). Religious and mystical experiences as artifacts of temporal lobe function: A general hypothesis. *Perceptual and Motor Skills, 57*, 1255-1262.

Persinger, M. A. (1985). Geophysical variables and behavior: XXII. The tectonogenic strain continuum of unusual events. *Perceptual and Motor Skills, 60*, 59-65.

Persinger, M. A. (1987). Geopsychology and geopsychopathology: Mental processes and disorders associated with geochemical and geophysical factors. *Experientia, 43*, 92-103.

Persinger, M. A. (1993). Vectorial cerebral hemisphericity as differential sources for the sensed presence, mystical experiences and religious conversions. *Perceptual and Motor Skills*, 76, 915-930.

Persinger, M. A. (2001). The neuropsychiatry of paranormal experiences. *Journal of Neuropsychiatry and the Clinical Neurosciences, 13*, 515-524.

Porath, H., & Dziewonski, A. (1971). Crustal resistivity anomalies from geomagnetic deep-sounding studies. *Reviews of Geophysics & Space Physics, 9*, 891-915.

Pratt, K. J. (1993). Some Navajo relations to the past. In J. Piper (Ed.), *Papers from the third, fourth, and sixth Navajo studies conferences* (pp. 151-157). Window Rock, AZ: Navajo Nation Preservation Department.

Price, H. H. (1939). Haunting and the "psychic ether" hypothesis: With some preliminary reflections on the present condition and possible future of psychical research. *Proceedings of the Society for Psychical Research, 45*, 307-343.

Price, H. H. (1940). Some philosophical questions about telepathy and clairvoyance. *Philosophy, 15*, 363-385.

Reichbart, R. (1976). The Navajo hand trembler: Multiple roles of the psychic in traditional Navajo society. *Journal of the American Society for Psychical Research, 70*, 381-396.

Rhine, L. E. (1961). *Hidden channels of the mind.* New York: William Sloane Associates.

Rice, G. E., & Townsend, J. (1962). Agent-percipient relationship and GESP performance. *Journal of Parapsychology, 26*, 211-217.

Ricks, J. B., & Anthony, Jr., A. E. (1993). The Hopi. In N. David, Sr. *Kachinas: Spirit beings of the Hopi* (pp. 6-11). Albuquerque, NM: Avanyu Publishing, Inc.

Rogers, K. (1994). *Tori Amos: All these years: The authorized illustrated biography.* London, UK: Omnibus Press.

Roll, W. G. (1966). ESP and memory. *International Journal of Neuropsychiatry, 2*, 505-521.

Roll, W. G. (1975). *Theory and experiment in psychical research* [M.Litt thesis, Oxford, 1959]. New York: Arno Press.

Roll, W. G. (1978). Hypnosis and object association. In M. Ebon (Ed.), *The Signet handbook of parapsychology* (pp. 327-353). New York: Signet/New American Library.

Roll, W. G. (1981a). A memory theory for apparitions. In W. G. Roll & J. Beloff (Eds.), *Research in parapsychology 1980* (pp. 5-7). Metuchen, NJ: Scarecrow Press.

Roll, W. G. (1981b). "External mystical powers." In W. G. Roll & J. Beloff (Eds.), *Research in parapsychology 1980* (p. 13). Metuchen, NJ: Scarecrow Press.

Roll, W. G. (1987). Memory and the long body. *Theta, 15*, 10-29.

Roll, W. G. (1988). Psi and the phenomenology of memory. In D. H. Weiner & R. L. Morris (Eds.), *Research in parapsychology 1987* (pp. 131-134). Metuchen, NJ: Scarecrow Press.

Roll, W. G. (1989). Memory and the long body. In L. A. Henkel & R. E. Berger (Eds.), *Research in parapsychology 1988* (pp. 67-72). Metuchen, NJ: Scarecrow Press.

Roll, W. G. (1993). Mind and method. In L. Coly & J. D. S. McMahon (Eds.), *Proceedings of an international conference: Psi research methodology: A Re-examination* (pp. 274-294). New York: Parapsychology Foundation, Inc.

Roll, W. G. (1997). My search for the soul. In C. T. Tart (Ed.), *Body mind spirit: Exploring the parapsychology of spirituality* (pp. 50-67). Charlottesville, VA: Hampton Roads Publishing Company.

Roll, W. G. (2004). Early studies on psychometry. *Journal of Scientific Exploration, 18*, 711-720.

Roll, W. G. (2005). Psi and the long body. In *The Parapsychological Association 48th Annual Convention: Proceedings of presented papers* (pp. 149-162). Raleigh, NC: Parapsychological Association.

Roll, W. G., & Persinger, M. A. (2001). Investigations of poltergeists and haunts: A review and interpretation. In J. Houran & R. Lange (Eds.), *Hauntings and poltergeists: Multidisciplinary perspectives* (pp. 123-163). Jefferson, NC: McFarland & Company, Inc.

Rowe, W. D. (1998). Physical measurement of episodes of focused group energy. *Journal of Scientific Exploration, 12*, 569-581.

Schlitz, M., & Braud, W. (1997). Distant intentionality and healing: Assessing the evidence. *Alternative Therapies in Health and Medicine, 3*, 62-73.

Schwartz, S. A. (1978/2001). *The secret vaults of time: Psychic archeology and the quest for man's beginnings*. Charlottesville, VA: Hampton Roads Publishing.

Scully, V. (1975). *Pueblo: Mountain, village, dance*. New York: Viking Press.

Sternberg, R. S. (1987). Archaeomagnetism and magnetic anomalies in the American Southwest. *Geophysics, 52*, 368-371.

Stuart, C. E. (1946). GESP experiments with the free response method. *Journal of Parapsychology, 10*, 21-35.

Swentzell, R. (2001). Remembering Tewa Pueblo houses and spaces. In A. G. Melendez, J. Young, P. Moore, & P. Pynes (Eds.), *The multi-cultural southwest: A reader* (pp. 86-90). Tucson, AZ: University of Arizona Press.

Tapahonso, L. (2001). Ode to the land: The Diné perspective. In A. G. Melendez, J. Young, P. Moore, & P. Pynes (Eds.), *The multi-cultural southwest: A reader* (pp. 97-101). Tucson, AZ: University of Arizona Press.

Targ, E. (1997). Evaluating distant healing: A review. *Alternative Therapies in Health and Medicine, 3*, 74-78.

Vaitl, D., Birbaumer, N., Gruzelier, J., Jamieson, G. A., Kotchoubey, B., Kübler, A., Lehmann, D., Miltner, W. H. R., Ott, U., Pütz, P., Sammer, G., Strauch, I., Strehl, U., Wackermann, J., & Wiess, T. (2005). Psychobiology of altered states of consciousness. *Psychological Bulletin, 131*, 98-127.

Waters, F. (1950). *Masked gods: Navaho & Pueblo ceremonialism.* Athens, OH: Swallow Press.

Waters, F. (1963). *Book of the Hopi.* New York: Penguin Books.

Williams, B. J. (2006). Field RNG exploration during a public Native American powwow. In *The Parapsychological Association 49th Annual Convention Proceedings of presented papers:* (pp. 237-247). Petaluma, NC: Parapsychological Association.

Williams, B. J., & Roll, W. G. (2006). Psi, place memory, & laboratory space. In *The Parapsychological Association 49th Annual Convention*: *Proceedings of presented papers* (pp. 248-258). Petaluma, NC: Parapsychological Association.

Wiseman, R., Watt, C., Stevens, P., Greening, E., & O'Keeffe, C. (2003). An investigation into alleged 'hauntings.' *British Journal of Psychology, 94*, 195-211.

Wright, B., Gaede, M., & Gaede, M. (1988). *The Hopi photographs—Kate Cory: 1905-1912.* Albuquerque, NM: University of New Mexico Press.

Chapter 12

Reincarnation Beliefs of the Gumini People of the Simbu Province of Papua New Guinea[1]

Joan D. Johnstone[2]

The Gumini people live in the southeast of the Simbu Province,[3] in the Highlands of New Guinea. They speak one of a variety of mutually comprehensible dialects of Kuman, the main language of the Province. They see themselves as culturally distinct from the Kuman speakers in a number of important ways. This contrasts with the view of many expatriates who tend to see the similarities rather than the differences between Simbu tribal cultures. I am unaware how widespread the reincarnation beliefs of the Guminis, as described in this chapter, are among the other peoples of Simbu or neighbouring provinces (Johnstone, 1995).

Today the use of the name Gumini is flexible, depending upon the context. Originally it was the name of a hamlet situated near where the Gumini Patrol Post, now Gumini station, is situated. Gumini station is the administrative centre

1. [This chapter was originally published in *Australian Journal of Parapsychology* (2006, vol. 6[1], pp. 21-34). Permission to reprint has been granted by the author and the journal.—Editors.]

2. I did not go to Gumini in 1962 in order to study their reincarnation beliefs. The information presented in this chapter was learnt serendipitously, simply as a consequence of my interaction with the local people during my six months of research into eating habits.

3. After Papua New Guinean Independence in 1975 the name Chimbu was changed to Simbu.

for what is now the Gumini sub-district, an area of hills and deep ravines with scattered small hamlets, and having but one dirt road, which for much of its length is suitable only for four-wheel drive vehicles. Expatriates, and Guminis outside the sub-district, refer to the whole sub-district as Gumini, and the people living there as Guminis. This is the manner in which I use the name.

Gumini was a relatively densely populated area of the Simbu Province. The people live in hamlets comprised of a men's house, in which live a group of close kinsmen and their older sons, situated beside a cluster of women's houses where the wives, daughters and young sons of the kinsmen live. Each wife had her own house. In addition, wives had their own houses in their gardens situated some distance from the hamlet. Today this is changing. Men's houses are becoming redundant. Husbands live with their wives and children in their wives' houses in the hamlet. Men with more than one wife move from one to another. Land is being used to grow coffee (as a cash crop) and vegetables for local consumption.

Guminis, like Papua New Guineans in general, are not a people with a highly developed sense of curiosity. As children, they are discouraged from asking questions of their elders, being told that it is rude to do so, and that they will understand everything when they grow up. As a result, as adults they have become accepting of what they are told, and of the way that things have always been done, without questioning. For a person to think or behave or think differently to their kinsfolk, would endanger losing the cooperation of kinsmen and women that is so essential for many of the day to day and ceremonial tasks that every man and woman needs to carry out.

This explains why I was unable to obtain clear answers to some of my questions. People simply had not thought about many of the issues that seem significant to a social researcher. Added to this was the reticence that those people who claimed to be Christian felt talking about the spirit world. They had been told by missionaries that belief in their traditional spirits was wrong. To talk about spirits might, the Guminis believed, anger their new Christian god. It might indicate that they still believed in these spirits. Talking about reincarnation was easier because it had not been expressly forbidden by missionaries who may not have been aware of the Guminis' traditional reincarnation beliefs.

Reincarnation

Guminis believed that only some people were reincarnated. They were unable to predict who would be, and who would not be, reincarnated. Nor could they explain why some people were reincarnated and others not. It seemed to be arbitrary, depending upon whether an appropriate living person became available for the spirit of a deceased person to enter.

When reincarnation took place, the spirit of the deceased was transferred into the body of a living person of the same age, and probably, perhaps always, of the same sex. Age would be an approximation as no birth records were kept. The people who spoke to me were not sure whether reincarnation only took place between people of the same sex, but this would seem likely. Until I asked, they had not given any thought to the matter. If a young man died, his spirit might be transferred to the body of another young man. This young man would be a stranger to the kinsmen and women of the man who died. A stranger would have no existing genealogical or social relationships with the kin group of the deceased person prior to the recognition of the reincarnation.

I found it difficult to determine when reincarnation was believed to take place—immediately after death, or when the kinsmen of the deceased person became aware of the presence of a person (a stranger) the same age as the deceased at the time of death, whom they believed was the reincarnation of the deceased person. I knew a Gumini woman, Nol, whom several years after the death of her son was still looking, hoping, to meet the man who she could identify as being the reincarnation of her son. She had lived in Port Moresby for many years. She returned to Gumini a few months after her son died in Port Moresby in 1993, from liver failure. There she waited, hoping that her son's reincarnation would come and look after her.

Spirits

The people of Papua New Guinea—and the Guminis are no exception—lived, and still do to a large extent, in a world full of spirits. Many, but not all, of these spirits are those of deceased ancestors and kinsmen, but are not identified individually. They have no physical form. They exist in the minds of people as a collection of influences. In rural life these spirits were, and still are to a very large degree, closely integrated into the lives of the living.

There is an absence of any sharp distinction between the human world and the spirit world. In the urban situation the influence of spirits on Gumini migrants is widely felt even among those people who are devout Christians. This is partly a consequence of towns-people maintaining close links with their rural kinsfolk and *vice versa*. There is a continual coming and going of Guminis, mainly men, between town and country, in spite of the high cost of airfares. Flying is the only means of transport between Port Moresby and the major towns of Papua New Guinea, including Kundiawa, the only town in Simbu Province.

The Guminis believe that spirits can, and do, but not in large numbers, travel from their home area to other parts of Papua New Guinea, to places where other Guminis are living. They do not travel to Australia. This may be because there are few, if any, Guminis living in Australia. More importantly, for Guminis living outside of the Gumini area, is the belief that the spirits of the people into whose area they have migrated will have harmful effects upon them if they offend these local people, or other people who have migrated to the same town, and who may have a reputation for strong and aggressive spiritual powers.

Ancestor spirits are believed by the Guminis to be benign, always provided that time-honoured rituals are carried out at appropriate times. It is believed that these rituals give the ancestor spirits pleasure. Pig feasts of various kinds are the most common example of rituals that please the spirits. The sight and smell of cooked pig, and other edible delicacies, make the spirits happy. They are able to absorb, on a spiritual level, something of the essence of the pig meat and other cooked foods. Food is not set aside for these spirits who, it is believed, will become angry and cause trouble for people if their living descendants do not behave according to Gumini tradition and put on pig feasts at appropriate times.

An essentially evil spirit, which demonstrates the close integration of spirits and humans in Gumini society, is the *sanguma*, or witch. These are people, men or women, believed to be possessed by a spirit that causes people to do outrageous things that no ordinary human would ever do; in particular, to do harm to their own kinsfolk by, for example, making them ill, or even causing their death. A sudden, unexplained death is likely to be attributed to a *sanguma*, one who is a kins-man or -woman of the deceased. Male *sanguma* are kept with their kinsmen where they will be given every consideration so that they will not want to harm any of their kinsfolk. Female *sanguma* are banished to the hills with their young children.

After death, during the mourning period of a few days, the body is kept in the house of a wife, mother or kinswoman. It is then buried near to this wife's, or kinswoman's house. The spirit of the deceased leaves the body and either remains in the area, joining a collectivity of existing spirits hovering around a collection of houses, or enters the body of a person, a stranger to the kinsfolk of the deceased, a person who is then believed to be the reincarnation of the deceased.

Reincarnation and Social Identity

Reincarnation was not expected to replace the deceased person physically, but some physical similarities between the deceased and the living person believed to be a reincarnation may be noted and may be of help in identifying the person as the reincarnation of a dead kinsman or kinswoman. In some respects, at least initially, there would seem to have been two spirits in the one person, but this was not something that the Guminis thought about. Over time, it seems, the original spirit of the living person either faded away or became dominated by the new, reincarnated spirit. This without there being any physical change of the living person. Thus a new social identity was established for the reincarnated person, one that had been adopted into the kin group of the deceased because of the group's recognition that this person, this physical identity, contained the reincarnated spirit of a deceased member of their kin group. But he, or she, was not expected to act or have the knowledge of the person they were believed to have been in a previous life, but they were expected to take on the role of that person within the kin group and behave accordingly.

Given such a close integration and interaction between spirits and the daily lives of Guminis, it seems very plausible to the Guminis that these spirits, when released from a human body at the time of death, might enter the body of another human being, rather than hover in spirit form in the physical environment of the dead person and his/her kinsfolk. After all, the Gumini consider human spirits and the spirits in the physical environment as being essentially the same. (Note that the concept of a human spirit might well be experienced and referred to as human consciousness.)

To cite my own experience as the believed recipient of the spirit of a deceased Gumini woman: In 1962, soon after I arrived to live in a hamlet, Obil, ten minutes walk from the Gumini Patrol Post, my neighbour, to whom I was a stranger, recognised me as the reincarnation of her younger daughter who had died some weeks before I arrived in Gumini. At the time, and for some years after, I was quite unaware of this. All that was said to me in 1962 by this neighbour, Mon, was that she felt sorry for me being on my own, without any relatives nearby. She was now my Mother, she told me. I regarded this as simply a friendly act, an informal and temporary adoption. Sometime later I realised, from their behaviour, that all her other members, Mon's kin group, and the men in the nearby men's house, and their wives in the surrounding houses, had accepted me as their kinswoman. I do recall that a casual remark had been made to the effect that my nose was similar to that of the deceased woman, but I had placed no particular significance on this comment. The dead woman's name was never mentioned.

Still later, after I had left Gumini and was living in Port Moresby, I found out that my relationship with Mon's kin group was not one simply of adoption. I was believed to be the reincarnation of Mon's younger daughter. The thing that had convinced her that I was her daughter was the fact that I had some scars on my left arm (in fact, vaccination scars). Her daughter had fallen into a fire as a child, and sustained scars on her left arm as a result. This was never explained to me at that time. No doubt they would have assumed I understood the entire situation once Mon had told me that I was her daughter.

Forty years later I am still regarded as a kinswoman of the group, but the younger, educated Christian urban members see it as a relationship based on adoption only, rather than one of reincarnation. But these younger members live in urban centres, in contact with people from all over Papua New Guinea. They are not involved in tribal fighting. There is an unwritten agreement that tribal fights in Gumini will not be duplicated in the urban environment (Whiteman, 1973).

Twenty years later, in 1994, I made a return visit to Gumini. A small ceremony was held to mark the occasion, and I was given the woman's name, Drikori. It had been too painful for the close relatives to mention her name until now.

Adoption

Adoption was, and is, a common practice in Gumini society, for a variety of reasons. It takes place mainly within kin groups as a means of distributing children more evenly among the women of each kin group. Children belong to their father and his kinsmen. It was believed that only men were responsible for conception. His wife simply looked after the child for her husband and his kinsmen both *in utero* and after birth. A conscientious mother and wife might be given some rights due to her children, but she had to earn them. She looked after her daughters until they married, and her sons until puberty. No formal procedure was required when a child was adopted within its own kin group, but some compensation might be given to the birth parents by the adopting parents. Birth parents maintain some rights in the child they give up, even after compensation has been paid. They would routinely be in regular contact with the adopting parents when involved in group activities if both sets of parents remained in Gumini.

Adoption of a male born into a kin group different to the one he was to be adopted into was more complicated than the adoption of a girl child because social ties within a group are based on male genealogy. All kin groups, except those that have become unviable due to the loss of most of its male members, want to increase, rather than reduce their numbers. Reincarnation, simultaneously with adoption, was a way of giving a stranger (an outsider) a new social identity within the group that adopts him. Adoption was an essential part of the reincarnation process, but not all adoptions involve reincarnation. There was no need for adult women to be reincarnated in order to join another kin group. This happens routinely after marriage, and women from decimated kin groups are taken as wives in this polygamous society, without a brideprice having to be paid.

Interpersonal relationships based upon kinship and conjugal ties are of major importance in the structure of Gumini society. It would be almost impossible for a person to live as an individual without kinship ties. So much of Gumini life is organised on a kingroup basis, as was ownership of land. Reincarnation occurred with strangers who had become physically estranged from their kin group of birth, and were therefore free to take on the social identity of a deceased man or woman of the same age. This was facilitated by the fact that there was little variation in the life-style of Gumini people. All people of the same sex had more or less the same skills and degree of knowledge.

There are some details relating to Gumini reincarnation, beliefs of which I do not have knowledge. This is due in part because they relate to matters that were not raised by the Guminis themselves, and in part because I did not undertake a formal study of Gumini reincarnation beliefs. The information I have presented here was collected incidentally, mainly as a consequence of my own changed identity within Gumini society. Unfortunately I do not know whether reincarnation may occur after the death of an infant, or whether they are simply adopted with their mothers when they are taken into the conquering kingroup as wives if their husband had been either killed or his kingroup disintegrated due to lack of sufficient male members. If they did have children, would they become members of a new kin group by means of adoption or reincarnation? Kingroups are always looking for new members in order to strengthen their fighting ability.

I do not know how widespread the type of reincarnation beliefs of the Guminis were held outside of Gumini. The ethnographies of Papua New Guinea that I am familiar with make no references to reincarnation. This does not mean that Papua New Guineans other than the Guminis do not believe in reincarnation. This would seem unlikely. There may simply be no records of such beliefs because the ethnographer, linguist or missionary working with a group of people had no particular interest in the topic, or had no interest in publishing their findings on the subject.

Cannibalism and Reincarnation

To the south of the hilly and relatively densely populated land of Gumini lies The Bomai, a wide open plain traversed by many deep river ravines. It is sparsely populated with people, but contains considerable wildlife, which does not exist in Gumini. The Bomai people, known collectively as the Bomai, live mainly from hunting and gathering rather than from vegetable gardening and caring for domesticated pigs, as do the Guminis. Gumini men from time to time braved the potentially harmful spirits of The Bomai to go on trading expeditions for Bird of Paradise and other feathers, cassowaries, and possum skins.

According to the Guminis, who were incensed if asked whether they used to be cannibals, the Bomais were still practising cannibalism in the 1960s. At that time there had been very little contact between expatriates and the people of The Bomai. The Bomai, Guminis told me, ate some of the flesh of well respected, recently deceased, leaders or sorcerers, in the belief that some of the mental characteristics, some of the deceased's spirit that had made the man a great leader or sorcerer, or enabled a woman to become a respected sorcerer, would enter the person consuming his/her flesh. This spirit would endow the consumer with some of the qualities that had made the deceased a great leader or respected sorcerer.

I suggest that such a belief could be classified as a reincarnation belief, the more so when considered in the context of Gumini reincarnation beliefs. It presents reincarnation as a method of direct spiritual transference from the deceased to the body of a living person. Whether, in addition to knowledge and mental qualities, physical characteristics were also believed to be transferred, I cannot say, but I consider it unlikely.

CONCLUSION

The following functional interpretation of Gumini beliefs in reincarnation was not made or suggested to me by the Guminis themselves, although my trend of thought may have been initiated by remarks made in a different context. "We are always looking for new members for our group, to make it stronger," I was told. Stronger for fighting in tribal warfare was their main concern. I have already stated that Guminis, like many of the Highlands people of Papua New Guinea, live in small groups based on genealogy and specific geographical localities. Within any given neighbourhood there are groups traditionally considered to be friends and others to be enemies. It seems that there were no means by which enemy groups could become friendly groups or *vice versa.*

Disputes between friends were resolved by compensation being paid either by both parties, or by the offending party, according to circumstances; disputes between enemies resulted in warfare and a continuing system of tit for tat, or pay-back. Consequently a continual state of friction and fighting existed between groups that were enemies. From time to time one group would be wiped out and disintegrated, its land and surviving women and children taken over by the conquerors and integrated into one of the conquering kin groups. The few remaining male members might also be absorbed into the conquerors' group through reincarnation. The Guminis were, and still are in their homeland, in an almost continuous state of warfare, a situation which continues, in spite of government attempts to stop it. In the past, these little wars were fought with bows and arrows; today guns are used (see also, Brown, 1973, pp. 29-32).

This continual state of warfare meant that the number of able-bodied men belonging to a group was very important. The larger the number of men in a kin group, the more likely the group was to win its fights with enemy groups. Men were continually being killed in these fights, from one or two, to up to six, in a single incident. Consequently all groups were always looking for new members. The most important source of new members, apart from the birth of children, was from defeated groups.

Gumini reincarnation beliefs facilitate the absorption of a person into a new group of kinsmen. They defined his/her social relationships with those of the individual who had accepted him/her as the reincarnation of a kinsman or woman. Consequently other members of the group also accepted the reincarnation and took in a replacement member of their kin group. In addition men who no longer had a functioning kin group might simply be accepted into a new group without prior reincarnation, and over a period of time were regarded as members of the group, but this was a more hazardous route to full acceptance. And with this acceptance came land from the defeated group. The death of any kinsman or woman from any cause might give rise to the hope of their spirit being reincarnated. And the underlying cause for the desire for a reincarnation by individual members of a kin group may not always be, particularly in the modern situation, to bring an enlargement to a kin group.

Gumini beliefs relating to reincarnation have advantages for all those concerned. The kinsmen and women of the deceased, both the individual and the group, have a replacement for their lost one, a replacement who is able to perform the duties and activities that would have been the role of the deceased, including participating in tribal fighting.

The man, whose kin group has disintegrated, probably as a consequence of tribal fighting, is able to take on a new social identity with new kinsmen and women. He is no longer alone in the world. It would probably be impossible to survive for any length of time without membership of a kin group. And finally, the spirit of the deceased has another chance of life in this world with his/her own kinsfolk.

Could reincarnation beliefs such as those held by the Gumini and people of the Bomai have been the precursors of the more sophisticated reincarnation beliefs of some of the Asian peoples to the north and north-east of Papua New Guinea? Be that as it may, the Gumini beliefs are a demonstration of the fact that in the very early days of the development of human societies (i.e., the Stone Age), mankind had a belief in what today we call reincarnation. The Guminis' first contact with Europeans was during the early 1940s and there can be no doubt that the beliefs I have described were a part of their pre-contact social and belief system.

Stevenson (1974) writes that the different reincarnation types that he describes may be consequences of different cultures, and in particular of different religions of these cultures. He suggests that Hinduism is conducive to occurrence of many children who provide insights into what is claimed to be their previous life. The data presented in this chapter is very different in purpose, methodology and findings to that of Stevenson's comprehensive research into suggestions of reincarnation exhibited in various cultures. This makes comparisons difficult. However, I would suggest that the information I have gathered from the Guminis and Bomais indicates that a belief that there is a human force that can, after death, be transformed into spirits or transferred to another human being, goes a very long way back into the development of the human psyche. Could this be the cause, rather than the effect of religions such as Hinduism and, to a lesser degree, Buddhism?

* * *

Postscript: As of mid-2006, I have found no reports of beliefs in any way similar to those of the Guminis, including those of the Igbo of Nigeria. This does not necessarily mean that such beliefs do not exist either amongst other peoples of Papua New Guinea or amongst other peoples worldwide. Researchers, notably, Stevenson, have been looking in a variety of societies, specifically at cases of children claiming to have memories of previous lives. Other types of reincarnation beliefs could have existed concurrently with the type reported in the present chapter, but which went unnoticed or unreported. Similarly, there may have been children with memories of previous lives amongst the Guminis, but they did not come to my attention.

» References

Brown, P. (1973). *The Chimbu: A study of change in the New Guinea Highlands.* In A. Kuper (Ed.), *International library of anthropology* (pp. 29-58). London: Routledge & Kegan Paul.

Johnstone, J. D. (1995). *The Gumini Bisnis-Meri. A study of the development of an innovative indigenous entrepreneurial activity in Port Moresby in the early 1970s.* Unpublished Ph.D. thesis. Department of Anthropology and Sociology, University of Queensland.

Stevenson, I. (1974). *Twenty cases suggestive of reincarnation* (2nd ed., revised and enlarged). Charlottesville, VA: University Press of Virginia.

Whiteman, J. (1973). *Chimbu family relationships in Port Moresby. New Guinea Research Bulletin No. 52.* Australian National University Monograph, Canberra.

PART 3: PSI AND SCIENCE

Chapter 13

Why Parapsychology Is Amongst the Most Important of the Sciences[1]

Vernon M. Neppe

Let me show in allegory how far our nature is enlightened or unenlightened. The truth may be nothing but the shadows of images. If told this were an illusion, would Man not fancy that the shadows he formerly saw were truer than the objects now shown to him? He will take refuge in the shadows, which are clearer to him than the truth.
(Plato, 1998)

The Problem

It is with the full realization of my own inadequacies, that I examine the implications for scientific endeavour of a subject that I believe to be of the utmost importance, both philosophically and in its possible practical application. So

1. This paper is an adaptation of the First Prize paper for Great Scholarship in Dr. Alexander Imich's 20th International Essay Contest: "Why Parapsychology Is Among The Most Important Sciences." [This chapter was originally published in *Australian Journal of Parapsychology* (2005, vol. 5[1], pp. 4-22). Permission to reprint has been granted by the author and the journal.—Editors.]

much and yet so little is known: so much because a vast body of evidence has accumulated over more than a century; and so little because of this knowledge base's limited ability to withstand critical scientific analysis. The discipline is, of course, a subject originally with philosophical and theological bases, a metaphysical concept and a religious exercise, that Max Dessoir in 1889 termed the science of 'parapsychology' (Hövelmann, 1987). Despite the American Association for the Advancement of Science controversially making the official body of this discipline, the Parapsychological Association, an Affiliate of their Association in 1969, many mainstream scientists reject parapsychology and its contributions out of hand:

> If there were a tenth the evidence for any other subject as there is for telepathy, I would accept it immediately, but even if there were ten times more evidence for telepathy, I could never accept it (Chaplin, 1960).

Such prejudice amongst scientists reflects the irrational scientific approach. The basic tenets of how parapsychology functions are disputed by many in the more conventional scientific community. To them, questions as to parapsychology's basic legitimacy will always remain.

Parapsychologists continue trying to prove the same phenomena over and over again to satisfy the critics that so-called extra-sensory perception (ESP; Pagenstecher, 1924), and psychokinesis (PK; J. B. Rhine, 1943; L. E. Rhine & Rhine, 1943), or compositely 'psi' (Wiesner & Thouless, 1942), exist, or to argue the evidence in controversial areas such as survival. And yet as far back as 1959, a doyen of psychology, H. J. Eysenck, argued that if fraudulent experimentation is the answer to the positive evidence for ESP, it implies that there is "a gigantic conspiracy involving some thirty University departments all over the world and several hundred respectable scientists in various fields" (Eysenck, 1957, p. 131). We can feel comfortable there is a place for such research.

The Perspective

It is not the mission of this chapter to attempt to prove that anomalous phenomena exist. Nor do I aim to prove the extent of anomalous behaviour (slight and comprehensible within our worldview, or radical requiring profound perspective changes). Like Eysenck, I strongly maintain that the summary dismissive attitude of the major science dealing with the anomalous is incorrect and inappropriate, and that the area not only deserves rigid scientific scrutiny, but could contribute enormously to our knowledge base and methodology: Parapsychology, where applicable, uses conventional scientific methods and scientific principles of deduction, induction, and data examination; it formulates hypotheses, tests hypotheses empirically, and applies where applicable, theoretical mathematical realities. It is a science that has accumulated solid research data over a century. But that data has been subject to a scrutiny and skepticism unparalleled in any other area of scientific endeavour. Parapsychology could, *ipso facto*, be argued to be amongst the most important of the sciences for the very reason that it evokes such emotional attention: its research is not 'silent'; it thunders through controversy because the consequences of its ostensible findings are literally mind shattering. This is because the domain of parapsychology impacts, interfaces, and extends to cosmological theories.

However, cosmological scientific data by its very properties does not involve control of the experiments by humans. Therefore, certain exact experiments cannot be replicated, either because the situation of the experiment never again exists in that exact form, or because the results require examination through the limited scientific instrument of our conventional three-dimensional space and one-dimensional time universe. Cosmologically, such results may reflect the Platonic shadow and not the whole perspective of data extending beyond these four dimensions.

Imagine: Imagine an area of scientific endeavour that is so important that it changed the perspectives of other sciences. All sciences are important and all sciences use similar methodology in that one is looking at possible information and trying to test hypotheses to improve knowledge. Very often science involves deductive and inductive reasoning, and often repetitive phases of these, like verification or retesting, or the postulation of new hypotheses as further information becomes available.

I maintain that parapsychology is one of the most important of all the areas of scientific endeavour for five major reasons: (i) at the very least its implications broaden our worldview, and are so profound in its more radical framework; (ii) it allows the development of cosmological theories and new scientific endeavours may develop as a consequence; (iii) its methodology serves as a model for both the physical and humanistic sciences to adopt; (iv) it extends the methodology issue because the subjective approach in parapsychology extends its usefulness even further in the social and medical sciences; and (v) partly as a synthesis of the above, it should be accepted as a major legitimate scientific endeavour as the implications of the findings are so fundamental, ubiquitous, and versatile for almost all our sciences (i.e., it is not a narrow endeavour). It potentially implies extremely broad impacts on almost every other discipline. Any of these five reasons would be sufficient to elevate it to such a lofty status.

The discussion below is not intended to provide cogent proof of the area. The purpose is not to provide factual evidence or analyze the strengths and weaknesses of specific research, but to allude to the scientific methodology that has developed and can develop, and by so doing, demonstrate the potential breakthroughs and potential implications of an ongoing scientific area that has been, is being, and will be explored.

The Implications of Parapsychology Broaden Our Worldview

Imagine: Imagine being at a single point in a three dimensional spatial box and being able to obtain information in another remote area of this enormous box without using any of our conventional 'sensors' (e.g., seeing, hearing, any forms of electronic communication). That metaphorical box could be our Earth. If we are able to replicate such apprehension of information by ostensibly paranormal means, we would demonstrate contemporaneous ESP, or what I would prefer to call *contemporaneous anomalous cognition.* This imaginary research could demonstrate the extension of the nature of space either beyond or differently from our perspective of three-dimensional spatial realities.

Imagine: Imagine being able to manipulate other objects in that box or events occurring remotely, ostensibly without using appropriate motor or known physical apparatus (like electromagnetism or light waves). If sufficiently controlled and replicated, we would demonstrate PK (Rhine, 1943; L. E. Rhine, 1970; Rhine & Rhine, 1943), or what I would prefer to call *contemporaneous anomalous influence.*

Imagine: Imagine someone at a single point in time being able to look forward towards the future, or backwards at the past. Imagine someone apprehending this information by means other than our usual conventional physical senses or logic. Imagine demonstrations of this experience being replicated repetitively by others. This imaginative example is different from real-time ESP because it would potentially demonstrate the scientific veridicality of *precognition* or *retrocognition,* and would argue cogently for a concept of time beyond our current point-to-point present concept in which we do not even know what will happen a second in advance unless there are sensorimotor or logical or electrical or other conventional physical or psychological clues. Time to us, in our current world, is not even linear; it is a series of discrete moments! Our imaginary events, moving across time, would illustrate that movements along a linear or other dimension are occurring.

However, the conventional scientific reality of parapsychological research is not so optimistic, for these imaginary events appear to be rare. They are very difficult to apprehend or influence in the conventional, small, worldly, physical framework of our three dimensions of space and one of time. We use a tiny portion of our one-dimensional, unidirectional 'linear' time that we specifically call the 'present'. That present does not allow glimpses into the future except by using logic and deductive reasoning. We can make logical predictions and even have meaningful correct 'guesses' of spontaneous events, but we cannot easily quantify such meaningful coincidences. Such quantification and replication is a challenge for the important scientific discipline of parapsychology, but when demonstrated, it would extend our breadth of thinking in the sciences.

Using the examples above, with us at a single point in the box, obtaining or manipulating contemporaneous information elsewhere or even into the future or past, it could be that we could examine time and space purely from within and yet somehow jump to another point in time and space in that box. But we may not see the whole picture, just glimpses and this may be what sometimes happens when we apprehend or influence information, objects or events. This may imply an approach that still is radical in that it defies conventional scientific endeavour, but it may still be explained within the conventional framework of laws requiring only some modification, not a total revamping. I call this approach "*minimalistic parapsychology*" (Neppe, 2003a). Physicists may be intrigued by the implications, and attempt explanations using, for example, modified models of quantum physics. In essence, scientists may be able to accommodate such theorizing within the natural laws of our current scientific base.

Nevertheless, before this theorizing stage comes the conventional methodology of replication. This has proven a major difficulty, even at this minimalistic level, although there are areas where major experimental designs have demonstrated replicability and extensions of hypotheses, with such results being generated worldwide by dozens of researchers and appropriately repeated. Areas such as remote viewing, Ganzfeld research, and biological healing at the microscopic level, broadly referred to as DMILS (Direct Mental Interaction in Living Systems, a.k.a. Distant Mental Influence on Living Systems, or bio-PK), micro-PK and the potentially more radical macro-PK (e.g., psychokinetic metal-bending; PKMB) are promising examples of current forms of research. These areas have created new, fertile, and provocative areas for research, making parapsychology an ongoing modern science full of new ideas and extensions to previous concepts.

Some findings of psi research could be argued to be anomalous in the context of our current materialistic worldview, but because of the difficulty of replicating them in lab situations, they may still be explained within this worldview. While there is the suggestion that our carefully constructed materialistic edifice may collapse, we need not fear that it will be shattered. We invoke, instead, explanations ranging from statistical aberrations, to new theories of quantum physics, or new perspectives on mathematics and dimensional physics; or if none of these work, conventional scientists, in desperation, can use the ultimate backhanded compliment to parapsychologists, and explain results simply as the "result of plain fraud".

Imagine: Imagine this approach of minimalistic parapsychology attempting to solve problems that do not quite fit into the fabric of our physical worldview. Imagine results that were statistically relevant and the research was untouchable. This would require alterations or modifications of our basic laws of physics and reality, but would still fit well into our fabric of natural law. However, this is only if minimalistic parapsychology was enough.

The Implications of Parapsychology are Profound in its More Radical Framework

It is extremely difficult to 'perceive' the full three-dimensional box from within the three dimensions itself: As a parallel, it is easier to see the one side (two dimensions) of a three dimensional box from the standpoint of being located at another point in our three-dimensional world than having just a two-dimensional fabric, and being contained in that. Similarly, we would have enormous difficulty trying to conceive of the whole three-dimensional box if we were located in a two-dimensional mirror or TV tube. Using our conventional world, the observer in a four-dimensional (4D) space-time universe would perceive a fifth dimension as extra-dimensional. Yet an observer in that fifth dimension could potentially more easily perceive the lower four dimensions because he would be observing from without. The psi process would become much easier to understand as the whole picture would be seen.

Similarly, it may be that in order to look outwards in time, we may need to 'look in' to perceive a reality across past, present, and future, instead of discrete blips of the present. That 'looking in' implies seeing time not as a point in space, but made up of multiple points along at least one dimension. 'Looking in' could be done more easily from the outside, implying a linear dimension of time (moving from a point in time to a line) at what should in our physical reality be a single moment in time.

Similarly, the three dimensions of space in the box example could require a conceptual jump to another area of spatial reality in order to apprehend or manipulate multiple, or complex, information or event sources. Examples could conceivably be the so-called 'cross-correspondences'[2] and other alleged forms of communication with the dead. This would imply a further dimensional shift in space.

In our mythical box, we could imagine a point out beyond that box. In order to see that whole box, the earth and the cosmos, one needs a further dimension. Using similar reasoning for time as for space, one may need a further dimension in time. This implies we could need a fifth dimension to have cogent anomalous awareness of our four-dimensional world. But if a fifth dimension is possible, we could look from the outside into those five dimensions. This implies a sixth dimension. We could look from the outside again into the sixth dimension from the standpoint of a point that is an extra dimension away. Logically, we can extend this observational theory ad infinitum, producing an N-dimensional universe or cosmos of time and space—what I describe as '*N-dimensional pluralism*'. I have not commented here on the nature of this N-dimensional framework, but such studies involve significant implications for parapsychological research. There would be enormous philosophical implications and scientific endeavours that would need a whole new base to extend beyond the limitations of the conventional 4-D concepts.

These speculations go beyond our conventional 4D universe and clearly have radical implications because mathematicians, physicists, chemists, physicians, psychologists, and many other scientists heavily committed to a monistic, one-brain/one-body/physicalistic view, would have to change their whole framework of thinking. *They would have to unthink thoughts they have thought before!* This is

2. [Cross-correspondence is defined as "a highly complex series of independent communications delivered paranormally (and ostensibly from one or more discarnate entities) to two or more geographically separate mediums such that the complex message is not clear until the separate fragments are pieced together into a meaningful whole" (Thalbourne, 2003, p. 24).—Editors.]

what I call the "*radical parapsychological approach*" (Neppe, 2003a). It is radical because the implications force scientists to fundamentally modify their worldview. Such 'radicality' is even uncomfortable for many parapsychological researchers, possibly because their tenuous attempts at scientific respectability may be more distanced as established scientific knowledge becomes even more threatened.

Imagine: Imagine a very different world of new science that required a radical parapsychology. The whole fabric of our current perception and worldview would change. Imagine an awareness of more than four dimensions of space-time and even an N-dimensional cosmology or reality. Again, the impacts for science are radical. Reaching to ostensibly deeper dimensions, if true, has radical implications for theories that explain all events, including life, as purely (bio)physicochemical. These are examples of ideas that have a cosmological nature. These cannot be tested using our broader physical three-dimensional space universe as a base as they would require radical new hypotheses, which are outside this realm. Clearly, future directions in parapsychological research may assist in supporting theoretical frameworks about our nature in the cosmos. Such theories in their turn may provide better heuristic frameworks for the future of parapsychological research. Conversely, if we were able to find a philosophical paradigm that did not conflict with any of the conventional sciences, we would have advanced enormously in our potential progress towards understanding the cosmos and we would be ready to radically advance our scientific knowledge in other sciences as well.

Imagine: Imagine apparently knowing events that happened in, for example, an operating room while in a coma. This requires radical alterations of conventional thinking in relation to memory. It shakes the entire basis for the *physicalistic presupposition* as the only basis for reality. If such events happen, even if rare, and these can indeed be demonstrated and proved, then we need to re-look at our whole idea of everything being physical. Even such non-survival of bodily death experiences may be radical in their hypothetical needs. But *such experiences can be tested because they still significantly impact on our 4D realm.*

Imagine: Imagine now going beyond easily testing hypotheses in our 4D realm. Imagine if there were scientifically overwhelming data for survival of bodily death. A century of psychical research has focused on the survival after bodily death issue and particularly communication. Imagine if there was demonstrable, cogent scientific evidence of the survival of the human personality after bodily death.

Survival of the human personality after bodily death is certainly a radical concept even in parapsychological research, so much so that many have steered away from it to the more basic ESP and PK research variants. However, there is accumulating, challenging and sometimes even cogent data, particularly given information from scientifically based proxy sitter mediumistic communications, hypnotic regression, reincarnation research, new approaches to xenoglossy, to cross-correspondences, to so-called near-death experiences (NDE) and also (to a lesser extent) even to out-of-body experiences (OBE), and occasionally to ectoplasmic materializations.

However, to encompass the most parsimonious approach, the so-called *super-ESP hypothesis* (so named by Hornell Hart [Hart, 1958, 1959]) has been invoked (see also, Gauld, 1961). But this hypothesis, in and of itself, still involves the 'radical parapsychological approach' as it implies by its very definition that there are no known limits to psi on the part of the living. By so doing it attempts to exclude most elements of survival, but it is radical in that it requires extension across time, space, simultaneous events, and sometimes acquisition of information not known to anyone. And moreover, there are alleged survival cases that cannot even be explained by super-ESP (Neppe, 1973). But these cases are ostensibly not replicable. Certainly many scientists would argue that such events as the very nature of survival of the human personality are not easily demonstrable in a lab situation. This may well be true. *Research here becomes cosmological and goes beyond our 4D verificatory realm.*

However, the implications of survival communication are philosophically remarkable. For example: death as an extinction would be an illusory concept; human entities would survive physical death; these individuals would retain at least some knowledge of their physical experiences; and the 'dead' would, under appropriate conditions, be able to communicate with the living. Possibly, the information would suggest that individuals could continue to learn after physical death. And the most extreme, even more radical stretch of Occam's Razor (i.e., the law of parsimony) would be support for the reincarnation hypotheses.

Even more so, proof of some form of life after death would also have enormous impact on our conventional science. They are the 'dollars' in the 'mint'. And that would mean that the mint exists. The 'mint' here would imply that laws are apparent which contradict, or which occur outside the range of our physical laws of space, time and even mass. Many scientists would find this terrible: They would have to unthink what they had learnt before. Or maybe, they would have to at least realize the limitations of their thoughts in the 4D realm.

Additionally, because parapsychology allows the development of cosmological theories, there are new scientific endeavours that may develop; and parapsychology potentially impacts broadly on almost every other discipline and would require recognition of a whole new body of scientific theory.

Conventional scientific endeavours look at the results in the framework of the four dimensions of our physical realm—three space and one time. They cannot go beyond and need not go beyond. However, beyond these four dimensions, there would be problems applying our physicalistic presuppositions and methodologies for explanatory purposes. When time, instead of being a single, very transient point, becomes linear and can be extended backwards or forwards, one suddenly has a whole new perspective on looking at the world. One has to invoke cosmological theories and hypotheses, and this contradicts the scientific convention of replicability.

Does non-replicability or inconsistent replicability disqualify parapsychology as a science, never mind as one of the most important of the sciences? The answer is a decisive "No!" There are areas of accepted science that are not replicable or not easily proven. To 'replicate', the possibility of replication is needed. Only phenomena controlled or produced by humans can be replicated. Many phenomena cannot be replicated. But replicability does not apply to certain events because they do not appear more than once in that exact form. One cannot replicate the Big Bang, or past events as illustrated by previous evolution. For that matter, theoretical physicists cannot 'prove' 10-, or 11-, or 26-dimensional string theories. Whereas there is support for string theory in that it fits the data, as yet there is no evidence that it is a better theory. For example, M-theory is an extension of string theory but does not yet even have any equations, and any supposed equations would have infinitely many solutions so that they could not define reality. In this context, "it is truly 'vapourphysics', and all that supports it is mathematical elegance" (B. Josephson, personal communication, February 21, 2005). However, these limitations, be they replication failure, or lack of equations, do not negate these areas as being 'sciences'. To quote another physicist, Stephen Hawking: "We have no idea how the world really is. All we do is build up models which seem to prove our theories" (cited in Boslough, 1985).

Similarly, we cannot exactly replicate spontaneously anomalous events, and even if they are recursive, they would never be exactly the same because events, time, space, physics and psychology, all necessarily change from moment to moment. And these are key confounders in parapsychological research: Invariably, apparently *replicated* events in parapsychological research would show minor variations, and because the results relate to rare though quantifiable events, such variance becomes highly clinically and statistically relevant, such that the research situation is compromised. Confounders and variables include progression of time in seconds, sidereal time, time of day, geomagnetic variations, so-called 'experimenter effects', cognitive, affective, conative and physical conditions of the subjects, percipients, agents and observers, as well as the macro- and micro- environments.

The Methodology of Parapsychology

The methodology of parapsychology serves as a model that both the physical and humanistic sciences could adopt. There are two major contributions of parapsychology to methodology; namely, the 'no holds barred approach' and the 'detailed phenomenological' approach. Parapsychology uses what I call the 'no holds barred approach'. It goes flat out to ensure the greatest rigidity and scrutiny of the data.

Imagine: Imagine a need for developing a methodology in science that is so rigid that it takes into account variables that scientific endeavours usually ignore. This approach means every source of possible physical and psychological leakage has been eliminated or controlled or explained. This way, the scientist can be certain he or she is investigating only anomalous experiences, as it means the utmost care has been taken to eliminate both afferent (sensory or perceptual or any other form of communication) and efferent (motor, executive or mechanistic) information transfer. We could conclude, if the research quantitatively demonstrates it, that so-called ESP can be the only explanation at the afferent level, and that so-called PK can be the only explanation at the efferent level. Such research generally involves the minimalist parapsychological approach, so it is quantitatively possible to remain 'inside' our 4D realm.

Examples of such methodological advancements include random number generation to ensure complete randomness, computer generated targets apparently to ensure that human influence may be diminished (except, of course, this may not be so in psi research!), automated recordings to exclude recording errors critical in rare events, Faraday Cages to exclude any sensory leakage or motor communications, noting in detail the psychological and physical states of all researchers including even the attitudes of the subjects (e.g., the percipients, the agents, any volunteers and control subjects), the experimenters and any observers and anyone else who may be involved (as supposedly they all could influence the experiment and its outcome and when rare events are being measured everything needs controlling).

Parapsychological methodology also ranges from direct analytical research, and broad and very complex statistical analyses, to case studies including the personal and trans-cultural, as well as field investigations and analyses of beliefs and practices in different ethnic groups, to theoretical models including phenomenology and mathematical modelling, to conventional experimental and laboratory research. This versatility allows broader applications of the range of this science.

Parapsychology might not have advanced as rapidly as it could have over the past century, and yet it has made great strides in the rigour of its methodology, its statistical analysis, and awareness of confounding variables. And parapsychologists approach their research with considerable scrutiny: What kind of technology is being used? What factors, such as weather and events, are involved? What controls have been implemented that take into account the time of day (even measures of sidereal time may be relevant)? Additionally, the keenest statistical techniques are used, and probability values are set far higher than in any other area of scientific endeavour. Parapsychologists can be proud that this is one of the significant ongoing contributions of parapsychology to science.

In the future, we may see entirely different approaches from experts within parapsychology and across other disciplines. To train any scientist properly, in any discipline, I believe they should be well-versed in the parapsychological scientific method. Yet this is not generally taught even in the social sciences, or in medicine, where such lack of controls, and failure to use valid methodologies, may negate or distort results.

Imagine: Imagine an entirely different approach in psi research that does not try to prove that psi phenomena exist, but looks at, what I term, *subjective paranormal (psi) experience* (SPE). This approach extends the fabric of phenomenology and the methodology of science to an understanding that detailed elaborations are necessary to differentiate phenomena more fully. Again, we need not *imagine* as this work has been performed at least at the pioneering level: The subjective psi approach is what I have emphasized in detail in both my Masters (Neppe, 1979) and Doctoral research work (Neppe, 1981), as well as numerous publications [e.g., Neppe, 1983a,b,c, 1993, 1999, 2002, 2003b; Palmer & Neppe, 2003] and presentations (Neppe, 2003a,b). This work is ongoing and continues.

This theoretical shift from objectification to the subjective approach effectively impinges not only on that psychological portion of parapsychology called anomalistic psychology, but also on what I have called *parapsichiatry*—the discipline that impinges on questions of psychopathology and anomalous brain function (Neppe, 1982). SPE involves the analysis of reported paranormal events from their subjective aspects (Neppe, 1990). This allows a more non-prejudicial interpretation of psi phenomena (Neppe, 1985), But effectively, the approach allows such SPEs to be analyzed in the same context as anomalous cognitive brain phenomena such as hallucinations, flashbacks, and *déjà vu*, or curious other-body distortions. In all these experiences, the distinguishing characteristic is their external non-validation and their subjective nature.

However, experimental and control groups can be formed based on the presence or absence of a cluster of criteria such as quality and quantity of SPEs. This approach allows for the analysis of specific aspects of brain physiology, anatomy, symptoms, and psychological functions such as personality and attitudes. Patients with normal or abnormal brain functioning can be analyzed for such SPEs, just as they are for hallucinations or delusions, which are other kinds of subjective experiences (Neppe, 1982; Neppe & Ewart Smith, 1982). Again, this is a significant contribution to the sciences because it makes parapsychology not only relevant to the potentially objectifiable, but contributes to the humanistic and social sciences by way of phenomenological (subjective) quantification and classification.

The human sciences can learn from the classificatory systems developed for parapsychology. For example, I have proposed a multi-axial classification that describes and characterizes anomalous events, their extent, their certainty, the degree of their verifiability, and their correlated symptoms (Neppe, 1985). This is not only important from the perspective of phenomenological research, but more relevant is the ability to demonstrate links with various areas of the brain. In this regard, multi-axial classification allows us to analyse brain function, such as temporal lobe lability and disease.

Moreover, it impacts on the medical sciences, for example, by making possible the analysis of patients with complex partial seizures. It also has enormous implications for psychology ranging from the examination of attitudes (e.g., levels of paranormal belief and experience), to personality quantification, to measurements of physiological variables. Finally, it also feeds back to locating appropriate research subjects in parapsychological and other research.

Moreover, this subjective approach can diminish the threatening elements of parapsychology substantially. It is more credible: By contrast, an objectively researched psi event necessarily constitutes a threat to the universality of currently accepted scientific theories, introducing entirely different philosophical frameworks.

Finally, in part a synthesis of the above, parapsychology should be accepted as a major legitimate scientific endeavour because it potentially impacts extremely broadly on almost every other discipline and so has generalizable properties. This is because the methodology and consequences are so fundamental, making the findings ubiquitous and versatile for almost all our sciences: In short, parapsychology is not a narrow endeavour.

A medical example illustrates how the parapsychological perspectives differ from conventional scientific approaches, allowing a broadening of attitudes since phenomena are often narrowly perceived from within the framework of one's scientific training:

> A person describes finding himself outside his body such that he "could see his physical body from the outside, and could not move it." He would be described by the parapsychologist as having had an "out-of-body experience" (OBE). The psychiatrist could record the experience as pathological "ego-splitting with sleep paralysis" (Neppe & Ewart Smith, 1982). Both these specialists (i.e., the parapsychologist and the psychiatrist) have described a single experience within the perspective of their respective disciplines. From the parapsychological standpoint, frequent OBEs would be described as normal; the psychiatrist may delve deeper into such frequent episodes: He will generally regard the episodes as a 'symptom' of an underlying abnormality, and may explain them as indicative of an ego-boundary disturbance possibly as a defense against anxiety. Thus, basic terminology in psychiatry often labels SPEs psychopathologically using an all-encompassing medical model. Parapsychological education reconciles these poles. Science should educate psychiatrists.

Similarly, psychologists and neurophysiologists will extend their perspectives, for example, on consciousness research, memory and perception. Biologists may understand more about perceiving and responding to our world. Physicists will appreciate space, time, energy, mass and information transfer differently. And health-care professionals, and social scientists particularly, can apply the basic approaches to parapsychology to their disciplines, allowing us to re-establish diagnostic nomenclature, narrow-down what is regarded as abnormal, and appreciate that ostensibly double-blind studies may be subject to influences of outcome that were previously unappreciated. Once parapsychology becomes part of a routine teaching curriculum in other scientific endeavours such as psychiatry and undergraduate psychology, the potential for others to research their disciplines will increase by an order of magnitude.

So Why is Parapsychology Amongst the Most Important of the Sciences?

Parapsychology is amongst the most important of the sciences because it can significantly modify or totally alter our worldview and philosophical perspectives. Parapsychology has developed a methodological infrastructure, both in its objective measures, and in the analysis of subjective (phenomenological) experiences, both of which could be applied to other scientific fields.

What may currently be lacking, however, is a pragmatic direction. How can parapsychology be applied to better the sciences? Such a question will be answered in due course: I could posit many hypothetical applications, but only solid funding and dedicated research will more solidly demonstrate the utility of parapsychology in understanding and applying its findings to practical life. We need to see to visualize; we need to hear to appreciate sound; we smell to protect us from burning; and ultimately, our prescience may assist in understanding our world. We will appreciate commonalities and differences.

Modern-day parapsychology has seen a movement toward the minimalistic parapsychological approach. Explorations of anomalous or ostensibly anomalous phenomena explained potentially as an extension of physics ('paraphysics'), or more literally an extension of psychology ('parapsychology'), is less threatening to conventional science. Some parapsychologists regard themselves as more likely to join the community of scientists that way. But to ignore the broader frameworks of super-ESP and, even more so, of survival, they are in danger of throwing the baby out with the bath water. The iconoclasts try directly to marry the physics to the psychology. And yet even at that minimalist level, the implications of parapsychological research are enormous, but in keeping the 'baby', and by moving to the area of radical parapsychology, the implications are even more profound. Add in the methodological contributions at an experimental level, and the phenomenological elements of subjective paranormal experience, and parapsychology's essential role in teaching such methodology and broadening the epistemology of the social and medical sciences, parapsychology indeed joins the ranks of the most important of the sciences. We should recognize Arthur Koestler's remarks:

> Innovation is a two-fold threat to academic mediocrities: it endangers their oracular authority; and it evokes the deeper fear that their whole laboriously constructed intellectual edifice may collapse. (Koestler, 1959, p. 427)

We began this chapter and end it with Plato. We should understand our limitations:

> Behold! Human beings living in an underground den…like ourselves… they see only their shadows and the shadows of one another which the fire throws on the opposite wall of the cave. (Plato, 1998, Book 7)

Is it possible that the 'shadows' which humans see are their physical reality alone? This is what the discipline of parapsychology sets out to establish. This is what makes parapsychology such a prime science—and one of the foremost areas of scientific endeavour. (For an update on parapsychology's progress since 2005, see the Appendix in this chapter.)

» References

Boslough, J. (1985). *Stephen Hawking's universe.* New York: Universe Avon.

Chaplin, J. P. (1960). *The unconscious.* New York: Ballantine.

Eysenck, H. (1957). *Sense and nonsense in psychology.* London: Penguin.

Gauld, A. (1961). The super-ESP hypothesis. *Proceedings of the Society for Psychical Research, 53,* 226-246.

Hart, H. (1958). To what extent can the issues with regard to survival be reconciled? *Journal of the Society for Psychical Research, 39,* 314-323.

Hart, H. (1959). *The enigma of survival.* Springfield, IL: Charles C Thomas.

Hövelmann, G. H. (1987). Max Dessoir and the origin of the word "parapsychology". *Journal of the Society for Psychical Research, 54,* 61-63.

Koestler, A. (1959). *The sleepwalkers.* London: Hutchinson.

Neppe, V. M. (1973). Aspects of psychical phenomena. *The Leech, 43,* 27-35.

Neppe, V. M. (1979). An investigation of the relationship between temporal lobe symptomatology and subjective paranormal experience. *Unpublished Thesis for Master of Medical Psychiatry.* Johannesburg, South Africa: University of the Witwatersrand.

Neppe, V. M. (1981). A study of deja vu experience. *Unpublished Thesis for PhD in Medical Psychiatry.* Johannesburg, South Africa: University of the Witwatersrand.

Neppe, V. M. (1982). Psychiatric interpretations of subjective paranormal perception. *Parapsychological Journal of South Africa, 3*(1), 6-16.

Neppe, V. M. (1983a). Anomalies of smell in the subjective paranormal experient. *Psychoenergetics: Journal of Psychophysical Systems, 5*(1), 11-27.

Neppe, V. M. (1983b). *The psychology of deja vu: Have I been here before?* Johannesburg, South Africa: Witwatersrand University Press.

Neppe, V. M. (1983c). Temporal lobe symptomatology in subjective paranormal experients. *Journal of the American Society for Psychical Research, 77*, 1-29.

Neppe, V. M. (1985). A multiaxial classificatory system for anomalous experience. *Parapsychological Journal of South Africa, 6*(1), 57-72.

Neppe, V. M. (1990). Subjective paranormal experiences: A decade later. *Exceptional Human Experience, 8*(1/2), 37-39.

Neppe, V. M. (1993). Clinical psychiatry, psychopharmacology and anomalous experience. In L. Coly & J. D. S. McMahon (Eds.), *Psi and clinical practice* (pp. 145-162). New York: Parapsychology Foundation.

Neppe, V. M. (1999). *Cry the beloved mind: A voyage of hope.* Seattle, WA: Brainquest Press (with Peanut Butter Publishing).

Neppe, V. M. (2002). "Out-of-body experiences" (OBEs) and brain localisation: A perspective. *Australian Journal of Parapsychology, 2*, 85-96.

Neppe, V. M. (2003a). Invited address: Subjective paranormal experience, the brain and the future of parapsychology. Paper presented at the *Parapsychological Association 45th Annual Convention,* Vancouver, BC.

Neppe, V. M. (2003b). Parapsychological approaches to interpreting anomalous brain function and subjective paranormal experience: The out-of-body experience as an example. Paper presented at the *Parapsychological Association 45th Annual Convention, 2003,* Vancouver, BC, Cananda.

Neppe, V. M., & Ewart Smith, M. (1982). Culture, psychopathology and psi: A clinical relationship. *Parapsychological Journal of South Africa, 3*(1), 1-5.

Pagenstecher, G. (1924). *Aussersinnliche wahrnehmung. Experimentelle studie über den sog. Trancezustand* [*Extra-sensory perception: An experimental study of the so-called trance state*]. Halle: C. Marhold.

Palmer, J., & Neppe, V. M. (2003). A controlled analysis of subjective paranormal experiences in temporal lobe dysfunction in a neuropsychiatric population. *Journal of Parapsychology, 67*, 75-98.

Plato (1998). *The Republic VII* (version of the original ancient Greek). Oxford: Oxford University Press.

Rhine, J. B. (1943). Editorial: 'Physical phenomena' in parapsychology. *Journal of Parapsychology*, *7*, 1-4.

Rhine, L. E. (1970). *Mind over matter: Psychokinesis*. Chantilly, VA: Collier.

Rhine, L. E., & Rhine, J. B. (1943). The psychokinetic effect: I. The first experiment. *Journal of Parapsychology*, *7*, 20-43.

Thalbourne, M. A. (2003). *A glossary of terms used in parapsychology (2nd ed.)*. Charlottesville, VA: Puente.

Wiesner, B. P., & Thouless, R. H. (1942). The present position of experimental research into telepathy and related phenomena. *Proceedings of the Society for Psychical Research*, *47*, 1-19.

APPENDIX

The Relevance of Consciousness Research in Today's Science: An Update from V. M. Neppe[3]

My chapter above was pertinent at the time of its original writing in 2004. A short seven plus years later, and we have witnessed events that have changed things dramatically, but justified many of the original points made in 2005. Today there is more awareness of research in areas that cannot be explained using conventional sensory or motor modalities of sentient beings or their machines. And we may have also witnessed a greater antagonism by many so-called 'pseudo-skeptics' who prefer not to believe in the possibility of phenomena that do not fit their models than to rethink their carefully built current materialistic edifice that is threatened and, indeed, awaits collapse.

It may be that these changes have initiated the final, potentially prolonged, phase of acceptance of the new data, but given its radical nature, this could take decades, even with the advent of world-wide Internet communications. What has changed? The challenge to the closed-minded materialist bastion has recently come from several sources that reflect the beginnings of significant breakthroughs. These support the ideas in my original chapter, ranging from:

- neurophysiological psi research demonstrating subtle changes that should not be occurring: possible highlights include Bastyr University and other neurophysiology-of-psi work, and research with presentiment (Achterberg et al., 2005; Radin, 2006; Radin & Nelson, 1989; Richards, Kozak, Johnson, & Standish, 2005);
- controlled survival studies (e.g., Neppe's, 2007, controlled analysis of the Eisenbeiss and Hassler "Maroczy" vs. Korchnoi chess game—see Eisenbeiss & Hassler, 2006; Hassler, 2007);
- research implying backwards causation (e.g., Bem, 2011; Bem, Utts, & Johnson, 2011).

Nevertheless, there is still profound antagonism to any data that may be perceived as compromising or even contradicting the materialistic presupposition that

3. This appendix is an update to Vernon M. Neppe's chapter and original article (Neppe, 2005).

attempts to explain all of reality (Bem, 2011; Bem et al., 2011). The small but important contradictions are simply ignored, or the research derided without justified scientific reasoning, or the researchers involved are attacked *ad hominem* (Neppe & Close, 2012).[4] The current scientific paradigm is taught like the 'flat-earth concept' was. Our current three dimensions of space and one point in time (3S-1t) in a physical world can still explain 99.99% of reality (Neppe & Close, 2012). To the pseudo-skeptic, the 0.01% of data that is contradicted can best be ignored, denied, regarded as artifacts, or scoffed at. At best, such contradictions can be puzzled over, or rationalized. Our current, ostensibly flawed, materialistic physical scientific paradigm implies that the *process* for all key paradigms can be explained, for example, by:

- tendencies towards disorder as in the entropy of the second law of thermodynamics;
- our biology being no more than an epiphenomenon of our physiology and determined purely by our DNA;
- our 'consciousness' being simply the endpoint expression of our nervous system based on chemistry and electrical firing;
- our cosmos consisting purely of space and time, without any 'consciousness' other than it being a neurophysiological epiphenomenon;
- everything evolving by accident, based on a statistical reality of billions of worlds and one or more just happening to have the correct 'mix';
- any implications of psi research being rejected by applying non-frequentist statistics where the null hypothesis cannot be proven because the Bayesian approach for the pseudo-skeptic may require 'prior odds' that approach the transfinite level, and are based on *a priori* assumptions such as psi being a fundamental impossibility to be relegated to pseudoscience.

But the problem is that these implications appear untrue (Neppe & Close, 2012). Consequently, a model that argues for the extreme relevance of the approaches of Consciousness Research, in both the context of its implications of the findings of psi research, and also the profoundly advanced methodologies in psi research

---

4. A series of 12 citations based on chapters in this work were or are being published in the *Dynamic Journal of Exceptional Creative Achievement* in 2011 or in press. These subdivide the topics but the essential reference is Neppe and Close (2012), whereby each citation is covered in more than one section of the book.

that have consequently developed to eliminate sources of leakage, is even more relevant today than it was in 2004 (Neppe, 2005). This relevance has recently been emphasized by a book, we have just launched, *Reality Begins with Consciousness* (Neppe & Close, 2012). In this ostensibly groundbreaking contribution, the importance of the limitations of the current model of materialism (even including the significant breakthroughs in Quantum Mechanics) is pointed out. Even more so, the authors emphasize areas of refutation: Effectively, our current materialistic worldview as the only one that exists, is falsified. For example, there are nine different areas of psi research that generate frequentist statistical odds of greater than one in a billion against chance, also referred to as 'six sigma data' (Neppe & Close, 2012). These nine are: (i) Remote Viewing (RV); (ii) Random Event Generation (REG); (iii) Ganzfeld; (iv) Global Consciousness Project (GCP); (v) Presentiment; (vi) Backward Precognition (Bem Protocol); (vii) survival/super-psi, (viii) Staring Protocol, and (ix) Precognition. Effectively, these facts emphasize the importance of the disciplines of Consciousness Research, Parapsychology, and Dimensional Biopsychophysics (Close & Neppe, in press; Neppe & Close, 2012) because the findings demonstrate the need for a new paradigm.

Similarly, we argue in our book and in its sequel *Space, Time and Consciousness* (Close & Neppe, in press) that any new all-embracing meta-paradigm should solidly be supported by the data. *Inter alia*, this involves a profound challenge. There are needs to explain 'consciousness' mathematically and scientifically; to develop a consistent theory that can explain a paradigm such as Space, Time, and 'Consciousness', all being inseparably tethered from its origins but being able to separate from each other across finite dimensions and into the infinite, yet still be linked; to explain the universe; to reconcile Quantum Mechanics and Relativity; to adequately explain psi; to reconcile entanglement and nonlocal data; to explain if evolution is indeed possible without some kind of meaning; to explain multiple dimensions; to find the role for infinity; to explain how life begins; to explain order as opposed to just generalized disorder; to create a self-consistency across the physical, biological, consciousness and psychological sciences; to provide a mathematics that can support this; to enlarge our Philosophy of Science paradigm beyond pure Popperian falsifiability; to (if necessary) include lower dimensional feasibility as part of the jigsaw puzzle pieces that we see in 3S-1t; and finally to reconcile this philosophically.

Neppe and Close (2012) believe that their model called the Triadic Distinction Vortical Paradigm (TDVP) addresses these issues (see also, Close & Neppe, in press). This is not by magic. It is simply that we incorporated 'Consciousness' (in its broadest sense), Dimensions, and Infinity into our model. We realized the need to recognize multidimensional and infinite order ("ordtropy") (Close & Neppe, in press; Neppe & Close, 2012), as well as the current entropic disorder, and understood that the concept of potential life in the finite, actualizing itself in 3S-1t, and implying survival after bodily death, was profound. We, therefore, vindicate the importance of parapsychology and the consciousness sciences, and amplify the relevance of the Neppe 2004 essay and 2005 publication (Neppe, 2005). Neppe and Close hope that their new TDVP meta-paradigm has contributed even more to this venture.

In conclusion, I (Neppe, 2005) argue that research in Consciousness Science is critical because the data that has accumulated profoundly challenges the scientific worldview of physicalistic materialism. There are areas there that are now falsified requiring new paradigms. This has continued to grow, in the past five years as given by the nine 'six-sigma' domains listed above. Also illustrated here are examples of the advances in methodology developed in the area of consciousness research, particularly in psi research, survival research, presentiment and retrocognition. Because these have impact on every area of science, they remain, as was the case in 2005, fundamental areas to be taught in scientific education irrespective of discipline.

» References

Achterberg, J., Cooke, K., Richards, T., Standish, L. J., Kozak, L., & Lake, J. (2005). Evidence for correlations between distant intentionality and brain function in recipients: a functional magnetic resonance imaging analysis. *Journal of Alternative and Complementary Medicine, 11*(6), 965-971.

Bem, D. (2011). Feeling the future: experimental evidence for anomalous retroactive influences on cognition and affect. *Journal of Personality and Social Psychology, 100*(3), 1-19.

Bem, D. J., Utts, J., & Johnson, W. O. (2011). Must psychologists change the way they analyze their data? *Journal of Personality and Social Psychology, 101*(4), 716-719.

Close, E. R., & Neppe, V. M. (in press). *Space, time and consciousness: The tethered triad.* Seattle, WA: Brainvoyage.com.

Eisenbeiss, W., & Hassler, D. (2006). An assessment of ostensible communications with a deceased grandmaster as evidence for survival. *Journal of the Society for Psychical Research, 70*(2), 65-97.

Hassler, D. (2007). Correspondence. *Journal of the American Society for Psychical Research*, *71*, 53.

Neppe, V. M. (2005). Why parapsychology is amongst the most important of the sciences. *Australian Journal of Parapsychology*, *5*(1), 4-22.

Neppe, V. M. (2007). A detailed analysis of an important chess game: revisiting 'Maróczy versus Korchnoi'. *Journal of the Society for Psychical Research*, *71*(3), 129-147.

Neppe, V. M., & Close, E. R. (2012). *Reality begins with consciousness: A paradigm shift that works*. Seattle, WA: Brainvoyage.com.

Radin, D. I. (2006). *Entangled minds: Extrasensory experiences in a quantum reality*. New York: Simon & Schuster (Paraview Pocket Books).

Radin, D. I., & Nelson, R. D. (1989). Evidence for consciousness-related anomalies in random physical systems. *Foundations of Physics*, *19*(2), 1499-1514.

Richards, T. L., Kozak, L., Johnson, L. C., & Standish, L. J. (2005). Replicable functional magnetic resonance imaging evidence of correlated brain signals between physically and sensory isolated subjects. *Journal of Alternative and Complementary Medicine*, *11*, 955-963.

Chapter 14

Examining the Evidence for Psi in the Context of Scientific Revolution[1]

Hannah Jenkins

"We have done all that we can when the critic has nothing left to allege except that the investigator is in the trick. But, when he [*sic*] has nothing else left to allege, he will allege that" (Sidgwick, 1882, cited in Griffin, 1977, p. 44). These words were spoken by the philosopher Henry Sidgwick in 1882. They were part of his presidential address for the inauguration of the Society for Psychical Research. The remarks are relevant today because in the subsequent 119 years the results of academic investigation into psi phenomena can be seen to have created just such a situation.

Implicit in most mentions of psi in philosophy texts is the assumption that the evidence for psi has been created by either fraudulent means or unintentional self-delusion. This position is founded on a modern interpretation of Hume's miracle argument (about which more below). There is, however, a long and fascinating history of academic inquiry into psi phenomena, and there are a growing number of academics who study the evidence that investigation into psi has produced. It is due to this dedicated and tenacious group of philosophers, psychologists, physicists, biologists and parapsychologists (among others, both past and present) that knowledge of what psi might be—and repeatable evidence for psi—has gained the acceptance it has to date. In fact, even some of the harshest critics of the evidence for psi have acknowledged that recent experiments have

1. [This chapter was originally published as an article in *Australian Journal of Parapsychology* (2001, vol. 1[2], pp. 117-126). Permission to reprint has been granted by the author and the journal.—Editors.]

produced something that at least *appears* to be psi. They are "now of the opinion that repeated demonstrations of psi-effects are no longer of interest, and suggest instead that priority in parapsychology should be given to seeking a theoretical framework for psi in terms of lawful relationships" (Parker, Persson & Haller, 2000, p. 65).

It is the interpretation of the evidence for psi that has given rise to a confusing situation. On the one hand there is a small but dedicated group of academics pursuing studies in the field of parapsychology and a small group of other academics using this information; on the other hand there is virtually no recognition that the evidence for psi should be taken into consideration in modern philosophical speculation. The reasons for this disparate approach to the evidence for psi stem from deep-seated and opposing beliefs about what is possible in this world. In this chapter I will argue that these differences indicate that the evidence for psi has put modern science into the 'crisis stage' of a scientific revolution (as set out by Thomas Kuhn in his book *The Structure of Scientific Revolutions*). In doing so it will answer the following questions: Why is the evidence for psi either not mentioned or dismissed in many mainstream texts? Should this representation be changed? And finally, if so, then how?[2]

The Representation of Psi in Mainstream Philosophy

The following is an example of how the evidence for psi is presented in a text on contemporary philosophy of mind. It is representative of how psi is usually presented when it is mentioned in such texts. Here psi is referred to as 'parapsychological phenomena'.

> Of course, it *could* turn out otherwise, if, say, there were any satisfactory evidence of so-called "parapsychological" phenomena, e.g. telepathy, telekinesis, clairvoyance. If there were such phenomena, then existing

2. This paper does not present a rundown of the available evidence for psi, or psi effects. This has been done numerous times before and to a much more thorough degree than the space available in this chapter would allow. For the reader who is interested in finding out more about the history of the investigation into psi phenomena and the current state of affairs of the evidence for psi, I recommend the book *The Conscious Universe* by Dean Radin (1997). For an in-depth look at the philosophical aspects and implications of psi, I recommend the book *ESP and Psychokinesis: A Philosophical Examination*, by Stephen E. Braude (1979).

> physical theory would certainly appear to be inadequate. But there is no evidence of such phenomena (or so most current philosophers of mind assume). Moreover, even if there were, it is unclear how it would bear upon the explanation of vast amounts of perfectly normal human and animal behaviour when such evidence seems even less likely to arise. (Rey, 1997, p. 72)[3]

The author, Georges Rey, has recognised that psi could be used to solve some of the philosophical problems encountered in the study of the mind; he is unclear exactly how it would help and has doubts about how effective it would be. But psi is at least mentioned and the potential recognised. However, the possibility of using the evidence for psi in this argument is quickly brushed aside when he states with conviction: "But there is no evidence of such phenomena (or so most current philosophers of mind assume)" (Rey, 1997, p. 72). It is important to note that this statement is not referenced, nor is there any subsequent information about who these philosophers are or how they came to this conclusion nor who the philosophers are who do not accord with this view. It is presented as a *fait accompli* and not open to serious questioning despite the ramifications this evidence may have on the issues involved in the study of the mind.

That neither the argument for nor against the evidence for psi is mentioned is important. It is important because it gives the reader a false impression. It gives the impression that there are no contentious issues involved, that it is generally accepted that there is no evidence for psi, and that it would be ridiculous to question this assumption. As mentioned previously there has in fact been over 119 years of serious investigation into the anomalous phenomena now known as psi. The evidence has been accumulated from a huge database of laboratory experiments and, although the statistical analyses are questioned in some quarters, the serious criticisms about methodology and procedure have been addressed over the past 50 years. There is also much evidence that has been collected and studied about spontaneous psi and there is a widespread popular belief that psi is possible. The exact nature of psi and its implications are still to be determined but they would appear to be profound.

---

3. It should be noted that the use of this quote is not a criticism of this book. In fact, the book should be commended for mentioning psi and its possible role in solving contemporary problems in the philosophy of mind. There are many texts that do not even broach the issue. The example from this book is used only to illustrate the way that evidence for psi is often presented in current philosophy texts.

How can these two interpretations of the evidence co-exist? How can the representation of psi in these texts remain without references and further discussion when there are universities that actively support academic inquiry into psi? More questions spring to mind: On what is this assumption based and why is it so dominant? In attempting to answer these questions, we come to the nub of the issue. This is that the representation of the status of the evidence for psi is based on a *belief* of what is possible in this world, as dictated by what is currently known of the workings of it. The next section looks at the nature of the arguments for and against the validity of psi phenomena with this in mind.

The Traditional Arguments For and Against the Evidence for Psi

When he states that there is 'no evidence for psi', what is the author of this book on the philosophy of mind really saying? There is after all ample evidence for what *appears* to be psi. Surely this requires the attention of philosophy if even some of the most ardent critics of psi have acknowledged that the field of parapsychology has produced what appears to be evidence for psi. Underlying this statement is the sentiment that the nature of the evidence for psi and the possibility of the evidence pointing towards the actual existence and operation of psi phenomena is nil.

The basis for the assumption that there is no evidence for psi stems from the modern interpretation of David Hume's argument against miracles. It was first presented by George Price in 1955. In this chapter he maintained that it is better to believe that all evidence for psi has been obtained by fraudulent means or self-delusion than that something can exist that is completely incompatible with modern physics. To support this assertion he showed that psi phenomena were incompatible with modern physics and accordingly he believed that he was justified in concluding that there is no evidence for psi (Flew, 1987, p. 217). He did this by referring to the work of the philosopher C. D. Broad who had analysed how psi effects are incompatible with nine 'basic limiting principles' (Flew, 1987, pp. 37-52). The argument contends that since we do know that fraud has been perpetrated, and we do know that psi transgresses the laws of nature, then it is far more rational to attribute any instance of psi to fraud or illusion (intentional or not) than to maintain that something such as psi exists. It is this conclusion that we see perpetuated in current philosophy texts like the one mentioned at the beginning of this paper. Hume first used this argument as an 'everlasting check' against people who claimed to have witnessed miracles that were in fact produced by fraudulent means (presumably as opposed to those genuinely produced by a God) (Flew, 1987, pp. 204-208). Price modernised the argument to target instances of apparent psi but the formulation of the argument is the same. People who uphold this argument are often referred to as Humean skeptics and this paper will use this label to describe this position.

The person who maintains this argument has become, as Henry Sidgwick predicted, only able to criticise the evidence for psi effects on the basis that they have been produced by tricks (wittingly or not) on behalf of the investigator or the investigator's subjects. This is a perfectly valid stance to take but as the data amass and the weight and standing of the investigators gain more acceptance, the weaker this stance becomes. The question is have we reached this watershed point yet?

The modern interpretation of the Humean miracle argument in regard to psi has its detractors. Shortly after the Price article was published, Paul Meehl and Michael Scriven wrote a reply, in which they made the comment that to maintain this Humean skeptical argument there are two points that must hold. The first is that psi is incompatible with modern science, and the second is that modern science is complete and correct. If either of these is not true then the Humean skeptic is left without a basis for the assumption that all evidence for psi must have been obtained through fraudulent or mistaken means (Flew, 1987, p. 230). It is the second point that poses the best challenge to this argument and I doubt that there are many philosophers who would be willing to uphold such a point of view. It is interesting that hidden behind the assumption that there is no evidence for psi, there lies this assertion. It is also possible to argue that the evidence for psi is valid but that it does not defy the laws of modern science. That is, it challenges them but it does not transgress them. This is a weaker position given what is currently known about the apparent operation of psi; however, it should be recognised as a possibility.

But the purpose here is not to delve too far into the debate between these points of view. It is enough to show that at the basis of the Humean skeptical argument is the belief that modern science is complete and correct enough to maintain that something like psi cannot possibly exist. Instead, two points should be emphasised: first, that the assumption made in the text that there is no evidence for psi is made on the basis of beliefs that would not be upheld by most philosophers if they had knowledge of the foundations of these assumptions and, second, that these arguments are not able to be resolved on rational grounds alone, as they each involve a belief as to what the evidence for psi entails rather than an interpretation of the evidence itself. The second point is explored more fully below.

The argument against the evidence for psi is based on the belief that psi cannot exist. This belief is founded on the basis that modern science cannot accommodate the anomalous phenomena that evidence for psi produces. This argument does not deny that there is what appears to be evidence for psi. What it claims is that it is not possible for this evidence to exist given what we currently know about the workings of the world, which is based on the modern scientific view. It is an argument that reinforces itself once the initial step is taken. In fact it almost ceases to be an argument because it is a statement about what is possible in the world and what is not. No matter how many times it appears as if psi is in operation, for someone who believes it *cannot* exist, it is not until they change that belief that they will be able to accept the possibility that evidence for psi is real and not manufactured by fraud or self-delusion. In other words, according to this view, there is no evidence for psi because there cannot possibly be, given what we know about the world.

Conversely, once it is accepted that there is evidence for psi and that this evidence does indeed challenge modern science, it must be accepted that either some laws will need to be revised, and the anomalous phenomena incorporated into them, or new ones discovered. This is based on a belief that the laws of modern science are able to adapt or change to such an extent that they can contend with the anomalous phenomena that the evidence for the operation of psi has produced.

The arguments for and against the existence of psi are therefore based more on belief as to the state of affairs about what is possible in the world rather than purely on the evidence that the investigation of psi has produced. They acknowledge that the evidence for psi poses a challenge to the modern scientific view of the world, but the Humean skeptic takes this to indicate that psi cannot exist, whereas the proponents of the arguments against this view take it to mean that psi will need to be incorporated into a new, or at least revised, worldview. The fact that only one side of the debate is currently represented in mainstream philosophy is due to this particular characteristic, namely, that these arguments cannot be reconciled as each of them involves beliefs about anomalous phenomena which have arisen under the current worldview. Traditionally the more conservative explanation remains dominant, which is why this is the one being perpetuated in philosophical texts. This indicates that the state of the evidence for psi could be in the crisis stage of a Kuhnian paradigm shift.

The next section will discuss the state of the evidence for psi in terms of this stage. This interpretation will be used to argue that it is beneficial for the evidence for psi to be represented in mainstream philosophical texts as a possibility to be explored to solve current problems, and that this interpretation might make the presentation of this information more palatable to those who wish to maintain the assumption that psi cannot possibly exist.

The Crisis Stage

According to Thomas Kuhn, a change of paradigm will occur in the following stages: first some anomalies will arise that cannot be explained readily by the current scientific worldview. Then, as the anomalies grow larger and become even less explicable in current terms, a crisis stage emerges. This is when it becomes apparent that something is not quite right with the current theories but it is not known in exactly what way they should be changed or refined in order to explain the anomalies that have arisen. At this stage there will be a small number of scientists who will accept that the current worldview is not sufficient to explain the amount of anomalous phenomena that has been obtained. A small number of people will be found working with the anomalous phenomena who believe that eventually the anomalies will somehow be used to create a new paradigm based on a revised or new worldview. The situation will continue until a problem in the current paradigm is solved by an explanation using the anomalous phenomena. This will show that the anomalies can be used to refine our understanding of the world even if they challenge previously accepted beliefs. After this has happened, the new paradigm will gradually be accepted until a majority of scientists are operating using the new worldview as old laws have been revised or new ones created by the explanation of the anomalies that threw the last paradigm into a state of crisis. Those who continue to maintain that the new paradigm is not workable even when a large majority of their profession is using it will cease to be able to work constructively in their field (Kuhn, 1996, pp. 158-159).

In 2001 we still have the situation where a handful of professionals are actively working with psi, but the rest of mainstream science and philosophy appears to be oblivious to it. This is because it is still the case that the anomalous phenomena, with which researchers into psi are dealing, raise more problems than they solve. Psi challenges our basic notions of time, space and causality, and it is far from clear how psi might fully be explained or what ramifications it may have for theories of consciousness. It will not be until the anomalous phenomena are used to solve a contemporary problem (or problems) in the sciences that the possibility of a new paradigm will be in serious contention with the existing one. Only once this has happened will the evidence for psi be used more widely as a problem-solving tool rather than a problem-creating one. This will bring us into the resolution stage of a scientific revolution in which the paradigms will contend for dominant position based on their respective ability to best explain how the world works. This is why it is important for the evidence for psi to gain entrance into mainstream scientific and philosophical problem-solving areas.

But where do we start? Science textbooks will not start to present the evidence for psi when the evidence challenges so many of the theories already present in those textbooks. It would be akin to getting somebody to toll their own death bell. Instead, I propose a solution based on two of Kuhn's observations of previous scientific revolutions. Kuhn points out two things that happen during the response to the crisis stage of paradigm changes. First, that "the decision to reject one paradigm is always simultaneously the decision to accept another, and the judgment leading to that decision involves the comparison of both paradigms with nature *and* with each other" (Kuhn, 1996, p. 77). It is not a matter of being right or wrong, it is a matter of which paradigm is more successfully used that will ensure both its survival and wider acceptance, but the two need to be in contention with each other. If one is invisible then it cannot be used in this constructive manner. He also comments that in the past philosophy has been the discipline most able to cope with analysing the anomalies that have given rise to the crisis. In this stage thought experiments and philosophical analysis are more useful tools than those of traditional scientific inquiry because the current worldview can no longer be used to explain them but a new workable worldview has yet to emerge (Kuhn, 1996, p. 88).

A Solution

One of the first steps that should be taken is to address the issue of a fairer representation of the evidence for psi in philosophical texts, and that this should be done in the light of a Kuhnian crisis stage. Hopefully this will enable those who wish to maintain the dominant view that there is no evidence for psi to accept the possibility that psi could be used to solve current problems. This is because it will not be presented as an outright challenge to the dominant view, which previous rational debate has failed to resolve, but rather as an option open to investigation. This is an appeal to the spirit of philosophical fair play where once it is recognized that we have a situation in which conflicting paradigms, rather than arguments, are at issue, it is only right to let them fight it out fairly with all sides represented by a full team. This will enable future students of philosophy to start using the evidence for psi as a problem-solving tool and if this is successful then it will filter down into the mainstream sciences.

To go over briefly how this conclusion has been reached, this is a synopsis of the paper so far: We have seen that the competing beliefs about what the evidence for psi entails are incompatible. They are representations of beliefs about what is possible in the world, not about the evidence itself. The dominant one is the traditional argument as represented in the text that was quoted at the beginning of the paper, namely, that psi cannot exist because the evidence for it poses too many challenges to the current worldview. Despite this prevailing perspective, parapsychology has continued to grow and produce results, and a handful of other academics are investigating the evidence. There still is, however, a massive resistance to the possibility of psi, as anyone who has done work in this area will be fully aware. The evidence for psi is unlikely to be presented in mainstream scientific textbooks at this stage because it challenges too many of the tenets of modern science without providing enough answers or another working paradigm.

Areas where psi could be used as a problem-solving tool are many. Attempts have already been made which use psi to postulate new theories of the mind and explain some of the mysteries that quantum physics has thrown up such as nonlocality (Radin, 1997, p. 282). As Rey recognised, *if* psi were considered a possibility its application to theories of the mind would be profound. Consciousness studies, particularly the study of how a person's will and intention affect the body, could benefit from a look at how psi might explain things like psychosomatic illnesses. All of our current notions of what information is accessible from the world around us are challenged by the possible existence of psi and, at this stage, we can only guess what the implications are on theology, technology and space/time theories.

What this paper argues is for philosophy to provide a neutral boxing ring where the contenders that the arguments for and against the existence of psi have produced can parry and spar, with the analytical tools of philosophy as umpire. In this arena the Humean skeptic, the proponents for a new worldview, and those for a revised worldview, will be able to discuss, compare, and analyze the implications that the evidence for psi has for our understanding of the world. Eventually one will be deemed the winner because of its superior capability to explain some of the conundrums that are now faced in modern science. The first step is for philosopher/scientists and scientist/philosophers to have access to the arena by presenting the three possibilities in philosophical texts that deal with these issues. (For a more up-to-date perspective on parapsychology's progress since 2001, see the Appendix in this chapter.)

» References

Braude, S. (1979). *ESP and psychokinesis. A philosophical examination.* Philadelphia, PA: Temple University Press.

Flew, A. (1987). (Ed.) *Readings in the philosophical problems of parapsychology.* New York: Prometheus Books.

Griffin, D. (1997). *Parapsychology, philosophy, and spirituality. A Postmodern Exploration.* Albany, NY: State University of New York Press.

Kuhn, T. (1996). *The structure of scientific revolutions.* Chicago, IL: University of Chicago Press.

Parker, A., Persson, A. and Haller, A. (2000). Using qualitative ganzfeld research for theory development: Top-down processes in psi mediation. *Journal of the Society for Psychical Research, 64*, 65-81.

Radin, D. (1997). *The conscious universe.* New York: HarperCollins.

Rey, G. (1997). *Contemporary philosophy of mind.* Cambridge, England: Blackwell.

APPENDIX

This chapter was based on an article that I (Jenkins, 2001) wrote over ten years when I was a Masters student in philosophy at the University of New South Wales. My understanding of scientific laws, explanation theory and anomalous phenomena has deepened since this time as I went on to complete a PhD at the University of Tasmania. However, the core ideas in this chapter are, unfortunately, still relevant to philosophy today. The results of parapsychology are *still* as invisible in mainstream philosophical discussions and there are only a handful of philosophers working on how to develop an understanding of psi effects.

Though I am not as convinced as I was then that the Kuhnian scenario will play out exactly as Kuhn's theories would have anticipated, in recent years the evidence for psi *is* making it out into mainstream journals where it has caused an all too predictable ruckus (e.g., Daryl Bem's 2011 paper "Feeling the Future" in *Journal of Personality and Social Psychology*, and the ganzfeld meta-analysis in 2010 by Storm, Tressoldi and Di Risio in *Psychological Bulletin*). At the very least these publications have provided a wider platform from which to disseminate information about the current goings on in psi research.

However, despite these advances the dominant voices heard in the academy and media are still those who continue to dismiss the evidence for psi out of hand, oddly sometimes contrary to what they privately disclose. This is an indication that there is still an awfully long way to go. It seems that, barring a few small pockets sprinkled around the world, careers are still in jeopardy for anybody who publicly indicates they take the evidence for psi seriously.

My focus now is to investigate psi, not just in relation to philosophical speculation, but with a view to solving informational problems in the real world that are applicable and useful. Continued problems in gaining funding and support from the academy for research into psi dictates that this will most likely need to be a commercial success as well as one which should feed back into the philosophical and scientific discussions about the phenomena (more about this progress can be found at www.qipp.com.au).

The commercial aspect of scientific endeavour does not loom large in Kuhn's theories. University research funding structures have changed enormously since his day. Perhaps the development of commercially viable applications for psi, and the growing need for universities to prove their worth in financial terms, will force the change that is needed to prompt a wider acceptance of the evidence for psi which will encourage further investigation.

» References

Bem, D. (2011). Feeling the future: experimental evidence for anomalous retroactive influences on cognition and affect. *Journal of Personality and Social Psychology, 100*(3), 1-19.

Jenkins, H. (2001). Examining the evidence for psi in the context of scientific revolution. *Australian Journal of Parapsychology, 1*, 117-126.

Storm, L., Tressoldi, P. E., & Di Risio, L. (2010). Meta-analyses of free-response studies 1992-2008: Assessing the noise reduction model in parapsychology. *Psychological Bulletin, 136*(4), 491-494.

Chapter 15

Looking into Higher Dimensions: Research with Joseph McMoneagle[1]

RONALD BRYAN

In elementary-particle physics, one of the most difficult problems is detecting neutral particles, like photons, neutrons, and neutrinos. Neutrinos are the hardest of all to measure. Those emitted by nuclear reactors can travel as far as 25 light-years in *solid lead* before being deflected.

Another problem is seeing down to small distances. It takes larger and larger accelerators to see down to smaller and smaller distances because the accelerated particles that we use to see with must have wavelengths as small as the structure that we want to study, and smaller wavelengths call for higher energies. Nowadays our most energetic electron and proton accelerators cost billions of dollars.

A third problem is that our scientific devices, like their creators, can only look in the lower four dimensions: the three of space and the one of time. Yet modern theories point to the possibility of extra dimensions, possibly of great extent. How can we see in these directions?

In 1998 I gave a talk at an annual meeting of the Society for Scientific Exploration, and sitting in the audience was one of the world's best remote viewers, if not the best: Joseph McMoneagle.[2] In my talk I described a model for elementary particles that I had developed (Bryan, 1986, 1998). It required four

1. [This chapter was originally published as an article in *Australian Journal of Parapsychology* (2008, vol. 8[1], pp. 58-88). Permission to reprint has been granted by the author and the journal.—Editors.]

2. Joe McMoneagle has published four interesting and informative books on remote viewing (see McMoneagle, 1995, 1998, 2000, 2002).

dimensions in addition to the ordinary four of space and time to accommodate the 48 elementary Dirac particles (quarks and leptons) of the Standard Model. Furthermore my extra dimensions were infinite in extent. How could I determine if these extra dimensions really exist?[3]

After my talk, Joe and his publisher, Frank De Marco, invited me to go to a nearby restaurant to get acquainted. We went to the Baja Bean in the middle of the University of Virginia campus in Charlottesville where the scientific meeting was being held. As I described the problems in detecting elementary particles, Joe got interested and volunteered to 'look' at elementary particles for me. I was delighted.

I had worked with another gifted psychic, Janet Jackson of Victoria, Texas. I found that she could see down to nuclear dimensions, slow the rate of atomic and nuclear processes so that she could get a better look at them, see neutral particles, and even obtain information on higher dimensions: "The higher dimensions are just like the lower dimensions," said Jackson. So when Joe offered to do research with me, I immediately accepted. I thought that between us, we might discover some pretty interesting stuff.

As luck would have it, I had a chance conversation with another person attending the conference and discovered that he was the treasurer of the Lifebridge Foundation of New York City. Charles Overby thought that the Foundation might support my travel expenses to see Joe at his home from time to time to carry out our program. And so it came to pass. The Lifebridge Foundation gave me enough funds to visit Joe eight times over the next three years.

Within a few months (i.e., on March 20, 1999), my wife Mary and I were visiting Joe and his wife Nancy in their home near Charlottesville. Joe had designed and built the house himself. It is nestled in the foothills of the Blue Ridge Mountains about two miles up the road from The Monroe Institute where Joe is a frequent speaker.

I was ready to ask Joe some questions to begin our research when Nancy explained to me how I should pose them. Having directed The Monroe Institute for nearly ten years for her step-father, Robert Monroe, Nancy was familiar with intuitive intelligence and knew how to present the questions:

> You don't just ask him the question right out. Instead you write your question on a piece of paper, put the paper in an envelope, and seal the envelope. On the outside of the envelope you write just enough to

3. An extended version of this talk is published in Bryan (2000).

identify the question. Joe answers your question in due time without ever opening the envelope.

"How will he know what I asked?" I inquired. Later Joe himself explained. He uses his inner senses to go to the spacetime point where I posed the question, and reads my intent. He says that he gets the question right about 70% to 80% of the time. "People have a hard time believing that I can do this", he said, but in our research that followed, he indeed got the question right about 70% to 80% of the time.

"Why can't I just ask you the question straight out?" I queried. "Wouldn't that be a lot simpler?" He explained with an example. A few years ago, the US military was interested in an up-coming Chinese nuclear test shot. His military interrogators put the latitude and longitude of the test-site on a slip of paper, sealed it in an envelope and just wrote on the outside, "This is a test." Joe took up the question and in time reported that he saw a chemical explosion; that was all. This disappointed his questioners because they thought that he had not given them any useful information. However a few weeks later, the Chinese carried out the test and indeed it was a dud. The nuclear material never detonated. Only the chemical explosive went off. Joe said that if he had been asked outright to describe an upcoming nuclear test shot (this is called 'front-loading'), he probably would have told them everything he had ever learned about nuclear tests. Instead, just using his inner senses, he went forward in time and reported what he saw. Just the chemical explosion.

Three Questions

To initiate our research, Nancy helped me put my questions in the format that Joe wanted. I thought of three questions and put them in sealed envelopes.

My first question was, "Look deep inside an electron. What do you see?"

For my second question, I drew on the fact that Joe had told me at the Baja Bean that he could see active phenomena more easily than passive phenomena. Therefore I put a small harmless radioactive sample in envelope #2 and asked him to tell me what he saw.

With my third question, I really tested his abstract ability. I asked him to "describe a wavefunction." We theoretical physicists know that to understand the nature of a particle, we really have to look at its wavefunction, or what might better be termed its 'waveform' (since the wave might not necessarily be parameterized by a mathematical function). It is the waveform that we use to make our predictions. I wondered what Joe would come up with, since he is neither a physicist nor a mathematician.

In about three months (June 13, 1999) I returned to the McMoneagles and Joe gave me his answers in text and drawings. I was amazed at what I read. Here is his report:

> **Verbal Description—Target A 32199 [March 21, 1999] (Sealed Envelope) [Joseph McMoneagle]**
>
> The object of interest as depicted on [Figure 15.1], is either an elemental [*sic*] particle, or something more exotic. I think it's probably an elemental particle of some type, as my sense is that it is circling a nucleus.
>
> The red-square drawn around it, signifies a cut or plane across its direction of flight or path.
>
> Figure 15.2 depicts a close-up of what this elemental particle looks like in relationship to the plane across its path of direction. I get a strong sense though that there are mirror images of this same particle, which are ghosted off to all sides (only two depicted in the drawing), some of which are traveling in opposite directions with regard to spacetime.
>
> In relationship to the plane across the particle, there are at least three rotational directions that might be affecting the particle, but I say that only because I've been forced to show this on a two dimensional paper. I think there is also a fourth relative to our reality, but I would have to bring the particle off the paper in order to show it.
>
> This particle also probably has weight and a charge, but my sense is that it is hypothetical so comments on these factors would not be relevant here. [End of report.]

So in response to my first question, Joe drew a particle in orbit about a heavier particle. His drawing is reproduced in Figure 15.1. It could well be a picture of a hydrogen atom, that is, an electron in orbit about a proton.

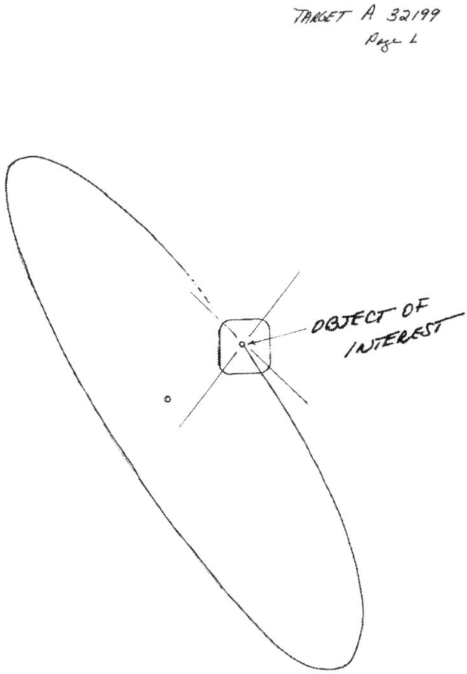

Figure 15.1. McMoneagle's first drawing in response to "Look deep inside an electron."

Then he gave a detailed picture of the orbiting particle which is reproduced in Figure 15.2. He sketched a spherical particle "ghosting off in two directions, but in reality in six directions." This is exactly right. He should not have seen a particle, but rather a waveform or wavepacket peaking at a central point and dying out in all directions. This is the correct description of an electron localized in a high orbit.

Joe went on to report that portions of the particle were moving backwards in spacetime. Right again. The electron's waveform is mathematically generated by the Dirac equation and is characterized by four wavefunctions, not one, with a pair of them telling the direction of the axis of spin (see below), and a different combination saying whether the particle has positive energy moving forward in time, or negative energy moving backward in time. (The latter is mathematically identical to its anti-particle, the positron, moving forward in time, and is usually identified as such.)

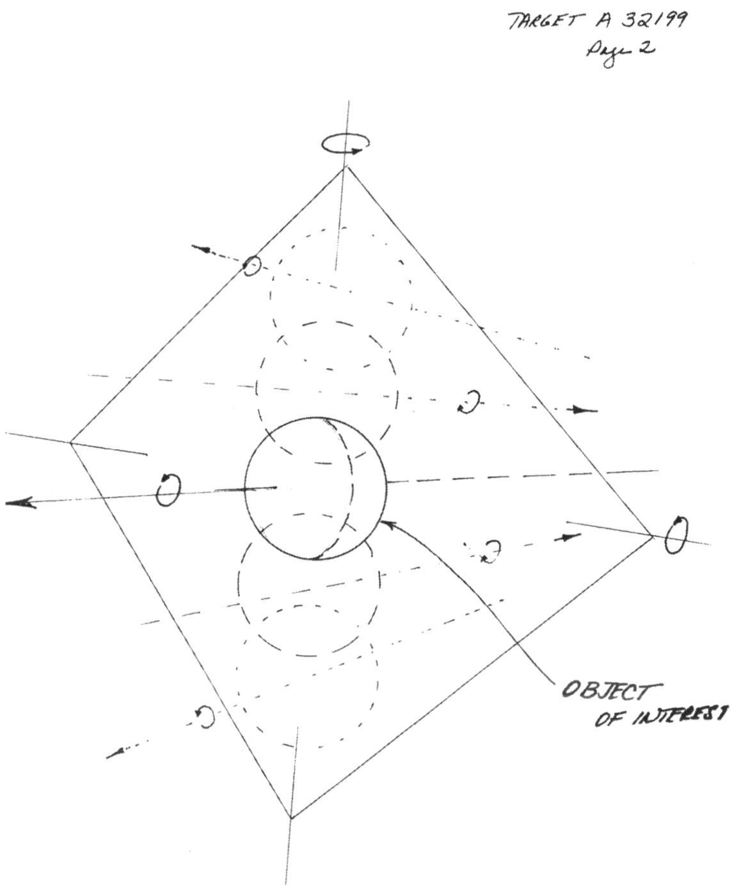

Figure 15.2. McMoneagle's second drawing in response to "Look deep inside an electron."

Finally, in his picture of the electron, Joe showed each portion of the electron-waveform rotating about an axis through its centre. Correct again. A fundamental feature of the electron is this intrinsic spinning motion. Its axis of rotation can be oriented in any direction in three-dimensional space. This may be what Joe meant when he wrote that "There are at least three rotational directions that might be affecting the particle."

Note that Joe did not answer my first question precisely. I had wondered if he would see any structure in the electron, since a popular model a decade or two ago predicted that quarks and electrons were composed of sub-particles. Joe spoke not at all about any internal structure. Instead he described the electron as we currently understand it. If it has internal structure, it has not been seen. According to present-day experiment, the electron is a 'point-particle' consistent with Joe's report.

The fact that Joe did not answer my exact question must be the 70% to 80% accuracy with which he says he perceives the questions. But the information that he did come up with was quite correct. He described the electron about as well as one can, using just words and pictures. As I said, Joe is neither a physicist nor a mathematician.

There was also a tantalizing bonus. Joe saw the axis of spin of the electron oriented in a fourth direction as well as the three of ordinary space. This might be one of the extra dimensions that I proposed in my elementary-particle model (Bryan, 1986, 1998).

If my first question was a bit general ("Look deep inside an electron"), my second question was more specific. I asked Joe to describe what he saw in the envelope. It held a button consisting of a few grams of non-radioactive material plus about two nanograms of radioactive thallium; that is, about 10^{22} non-radioactive atoms and about 6.0×10^{12} radioactive thallium atoms. About 40,000 of the thallium nuclei were decaying each second *via* the reaction,

$$ {}^{204}_{81}\mathrm{Tl} \rightarrow {}^{204}_{82}\mathrm{Pb} + e^- + \bar{\nu}_e \, , $$

where e^- is the electron, $\bar{\nu}_e$ is the anti-electron-neutrino, ${}^{204}_{81}\mathrm{Tl}$ is a thallium nucleus of charge 81 and atomic weight 204, and ${}^{204}_{82}\mathrm{Pb}$ is a lead nucleus of charge 82 and atomic weight 204. About 0.8 MeV kinetic energy was released in each decay, with most of the energy going to the neutrino and the electron.[4]

I had expected that Joe's attention would be drawn to the decaying thallium nuclei, since the electrons and anti-neutrinos from the decay were emerging with far more kinetic energy than the ordinary electrons had. Instead, Joe drew a picture of a stable atom with a small inner nucleus, two heavier particles orbiting near the center and two very light particles orbiting much farther out. See his drawing in Figure 15.3.

4. [MeV = Mega (10^6) electronvolts.— Editors.]

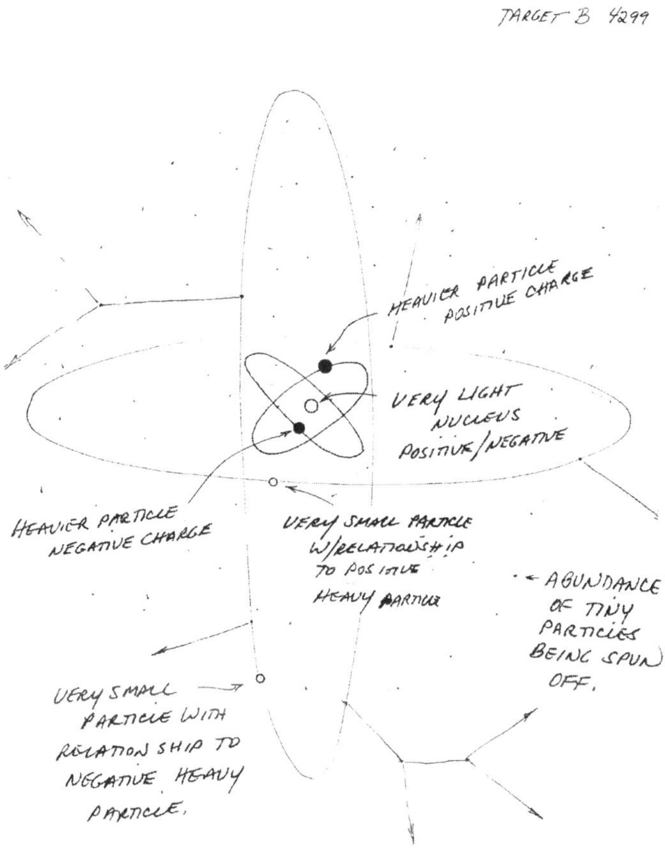

Figure 15.3. McMoneagle's drawing in response to "Describe what you see in the envelope."

His report is as follows.

Verbal Description—Target B 4299 [April 2, 1999] (Sealed Envelope) [Joseph McMoneagle]

This is probably a real extant object in time-space. My sense is that it is a simple one however, that consists of a core (nucleus), which is lighter than most. It [is] either negatively charged or doesn't have much of a positive charge to it. I would guess the latter.

Circling the nucleus, are two larger particles (they actually seem larger than the core), one is positively charged and one is negatively charged. If

> the core was about the size of a basketball, I would say these two particles were circling at about the distance from the basketball as the Moon's orbit—just to give a comparison.
>
> Following the same example, if you were to go on out to about where Saturn's orbit lies, you would find two more particles circling there. Each of those particles having a separate relationship to one of the heavier moon-orbit particles—one being related to the positively charged particle and one being related to the negatively charged particle. These are also much smaller than the moon-orbit particles, on the magnitude of about a thousand to one. If these outermost particles weighed in at around a pound, the moon-orbit particles would weigh in at about half a ton each.
>
> These outer orbital particles are racing through an almost empty space, but that almost empty space is filled with even smaller particles that have a positive charge. However, I do not see them having a major relationship to any of the other particles. Now and then the outer orbital particles will strike one of these positively charged smaller particles and it sends the smaller particle off into space. Where it goes I have no idea. There is a good chance that eventually it is either annihilated or absorbed—my bet being the latter. [End of report.]

Again, McMoneagle intuited the main intent of my question, this time to look at objects ten orders of magnitude or more smaller than the envelope. However instead of reporting on the radioactive nuclei, he seemed to be seeing electrons and stable nuclei, or portions of stable nuclei.

We know that nuclei are composed only of neutrons and protons, so perhaps in McMoneagle's report, the heavy positively charged particle was a proton, and the heavier negatively charged particle was a neutron, although neutrons actually have zero charge. (On the other hand, he may have been observing the *isotopic spin* of the proton and neutron; the isotopic spin of the proton is +½ and that of the neutron is –½, and these quantum numbers are just as important as the charges.)

Possibly he was looking at a deuterium nucleus. The two light particles farther out could be electrons, since Joe said that they weighed about 1/1000th as much as the heavy particles, and we know that electrons weigh about 1/1840th as much as a nucleon (i.e., neutron or proton). Furthermore Joe said that the light particles were about 4000 times farther out from the center than were the heavy particles (which Joe described in terms of the ratio of the Earth-Saturn distance to the Earth-Moon distance), and we know that the electrons in an atom are about 25,000 times farther out from the center than the nucleons in the nucleus. So Joe's estimates of the relative orbital distances and masses of his particles were within an order of magnitude of the known relative orbital distances and masses of electrons and nucleons.

However, the atom that Joe described could not be deuterium because deuterium has only one orbiting electron. Perhaps the heavy particles in Joe's picture were *representative* of the many neutrons and protons in a typical nucleus and the light particles were representative of the many electrons in a complete atom. This would agree with the atoms in the sample that he was viewing.

Joe also remarked that these light particles "are racing through an almost empty space, but that almost empty space is filled with even smaller particles that have a positive charge." During debriefing he told me, "My sense is these are not in circular orbits, but sparkles of light popping in and out of reality. They have like a finite time of existence, but they are never in the same space." Although in his report he called them "even smaller particles," Joe may have been referring to copious electron-positron pairs which constantly appear out of nowhere in the vacuum and then quickly self-annihilate and disappear. This is a well-understood feature of quantum electrodynamics, known as polarization of the vacuum. The fact that Joe apparently saw vacuum polarization made it even more likely that he was observing nature down at the scale of elementary particles.

However, there was one feature of Joe's viewing which did not agree at all with our current understanding of the nucleus. He wrote of a core "which is lighter than most. It [is] either negatively charged or does not have much of a positive charge to it. I would guess the latter." If, as Joe said, the core's size was in the same ratio to nuclear dimensions as a basketball is to the Moon's orbit, then the core had a diameter of about 10^{-24} meter. According to the Heisenberg Uncertainty Principle, to see something this small using a conventional beam (electron or proton) in an accelerator would call for the bombarding particle to have an energy,

$$E \approx \hbar c / \lambda = 2 \cdot 10^{-7}\,\text{eV} \cdot \text{m} / 10^{-24}\,\text{m} = 2 \cdot 10^{8}\,\text{GeV},$$

or about 100,000 times greater than the energy of the beams of the most powerful accelerator on Earth, FermiLab near Chicago.[5] And observing such an object using such an accelerator beam would blow the nucleus to smithereens

5. [GeV = Giga (10^9) electronvolts.— Editors.]

and create millions of secondary particles. If Joe actually saw this core, he did not disturb it . . .

What could this core be? Then I remembered giving a talk before a gathering on a Sunday morning where I likened an atomic nucleus to an orchestra. The neutrons would be the strings (violins, violas, cellos, basses) and the protons would be the brass instruments (never mind the woodwinds). Then someone asked, "What about the conductor?"

Of course there is no 'conductor' in current models of the nucleus. But I wondered if Joe had seen a conductor even so. In a previous paper (Bryan, 2002), I have given arguments that, just as a person has a consciousness, and major organs may also have consciousnesses (a person receiving a heart transplant suddenly has a craving for foods that the donor was fond of) (Pearsall, Schwartz & Russek, 2002), so perhaps consciousness goes all the way down to individual nuclei. Perhaps Joe has seen the seat of *consciousness* of a nucleus.

This gets very interesting because the Heisenberg Uncertainty Principle tells us that there is no way for us to know when a particular radioactive nucleus is going to decay. At a given moment we can only know the *probability* with which it will decay. But if the nucleus has a consciousness, then perhaps this consciousness determines when the nucleus decays. And if we could learn more about this consciousness, then perhaps we could stimulate it to decay upon *our* command. It might be possible to detonate radioactive waste in a safe, controlled manner rather than wait for it to decay on its own, a time that can stretch into thousands of years.

My third question to Joe, "Describe a wavefunction," was without doubt the most abstract of my questions. A wavefunction or waveform is not a physical entity; it is more like a thought, expressed in mathematics. I wondered if Joe could even comprehend the question, since he is not a mathematical physicist. In fact, he gave a good example of a wavefunction. His report appears below:

Verbal Description—Target C 4299 [April 2, 1999] (Sealed Envelope) [Joseph McMoneagle]

The target of interest is in constant motion, which is very difficult to demonstrate. It appears that there is a minimum of four planes of motion that are all going on simultaneously. I have chosen to depict actually only two.

On page one [Figure 15.4] there is a circle, which represents the particle at rest, which actually it isn't. Out to either side I've drawn overlaying lines depicting sort of what I could call a wave apex, or front wall.

The particle is sort of painting shadows of itself across and within the interior portion of this front wall. Unfortunately, I also have an impression that the wave is mobile through spacetime, which I've depicted in drawing number two [Figure 15.5]. Again, this is difficult to show because while I can depict what appears to be three directions of movement, I cannot depict the fourth, or at least have not found a way of doing that yet.

I have a suspicion that dependent upon how you look at the motion determines the direction in which it appears to be flowing. The wall therefore changes with the motion as well.

Of the bunch [of questions], this is probably the most difficult to depict. As I also get a feeling that the wall can be moving in both directions through spacetime as well, forward and backward relative to time anyway. [End of report.]

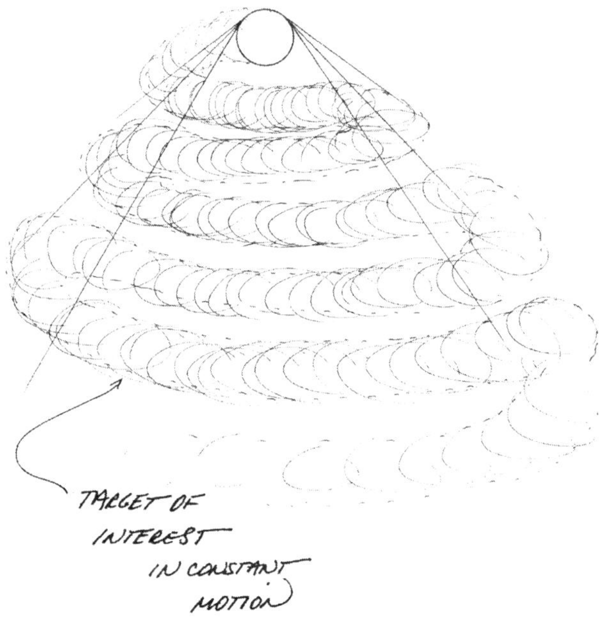

Figure 15.4. McMoneagle's first drawing in response to "Describe a wavefunction."

In McMoneagle's diagrams, the wavefunction looks like a spherical wave-packet circling about a magnetic field line, or perhaps the trajectory of a wave-packet in a Penning trap, which can be used to trap single ions. In Figure 15.5 we see the trajectory in a side view. In Figure 15.4 we may be looking at it more from on top. The particle's oscillations appear to be getting larger with time, but this might just be due to the fact that the particle is getting closer to the viewer.

Figure 15.5. McMoneagle's second drawing in response to "Describe a wavefunction."

Note that Joe again refers to a fourth space-like dimension ("I cannot depict the fourth"). He also reports that the "wall can be moving in both directions through spacetime as well, forward and backward relative to time anyway." This report, like his report to my first question, could be a description of an elementary particle, perhaps an electron, moving in higher-dimensional spacetime.

I followed up on each of my three questions with three further inquiries on July 20, 1999. Joe completed his responses within a couple of months. His reports were consistent with his earlier reports (i.e., he did not go off in radical new directions). As I was to observe in later reports, his first impressions were also the most informative. These, plus debriefings, appeared to make the best use of his special abilities.

I was very pleased with McMoneagle's responses to my questions.[6] He gave an excellent description of an electron, right down to its spin states and anti-matter components. He was also able to sketch a wavefunction, an abstraction if there ever was one. His take on the radioactive source did not correspond to any known nucleus, but did contain the essential features of an atom. Also he apparently picked up on vacuum polarization. I found all of this to be convincing evidence that he really was "making himself small" as it were, and seeing physics on the atomic and also nuclear scale.

Joe also reported several times that he saw a fourth space-like dimension. Perhaps the 'extra dimensions' of current elementary-particle theories really do exist. Joe could be my telescope to peer into these higher dimensions. And if the higher dimensions stretch off to infinity as they do in my elementary-particle model (Bryan, 1986, 1998, 1999, 2000) and that of Rubakov and Shaposhnikov (1983), then perhaps he could look off into that distance too.

Original Research with Joseph McMoneagle: The Utah Event

McMoneagle had done so well answering questions to which I knew some of the answers that I felt that we could go ahead and examine an event that had (and still has) the astrophysics community perplexed.

On a moonless night in October, 1991 a thin streak appeared high in the sky over Dugway Flats, Utah. It was seen by a device called the Fly's Eye Detector, an array of 67 five-foot-diameter concave mirrors spaced several feet apart defining a large circle on the ground. About a dozen photo-multiplier tubes were mounted above each mirror at its focal plane. The mirrors were aimed toward the sky and

6. Note that Joe answered my three questions in the order I gave them. The odds of which are 1/6 by chance alone.

were used to record atmospheric events on clear moonless nights such as this one. (These occur about 10% of the time.) The streak was a thin, bright, fluorescent line whose tip had travelled thousands of times faster than a typical meteorite. This indicated that the line was not caused by a bit of space debris, but probably by a high energy particle moving with a velocity close to the speed of light, c. As the particle hit the oxygen and nitrogen molecules in the upper atmosphere, it ionized them to produce a shower of particles, and electrons recombining with the ions emitted photons producing the visible streak seen by the Fly's Eye. Short-lived particles like pi-mesons were also produced when the shower-particles hit atomic nuclei; these decayed to produce more particles and electromagnetic radiation, some visible.

The experimental group which recorded the event (Bird et al., 1995) reported that the particle arrived at our atmosphere with an apparent energy $E = (3.2 \pm 0.9) \times 10^{11}$ GeV. This was (and is) the highest energy of a particle ever recorded, over 100,000,000 times the energy of protons accelerated at Fermilab.

The particle might have been a hypothetical super-massive particle left over from the Big Bang whose mass turned into the shower's energy, but more likely, it was an extremely energetic light particle (see the review by Bhattacharjee & Sigl, 2000). The problem is that if it was indeed a light particle coming from a great distance, then it should never have arrived with so much energy. When a particle is travelling very fast through the cosmos, the three-degree Kelvin photons left over from the Big Bang begin to look like high-energy gamma (γ) rays to the particle in its rest frame, due to the Doppler effect. If the particle is charged, say a proton (p), and has energy $E > 5.0 \times 10^{10}$ GeV, then the gamma rays are energetic enough to produce neutral pi-mesons (π^0) *via* the reaction:

$$\gamma + p \rightarrow p + \pi^0$$

After the particle travels a few hundred million light-years producing these neutral pi-mesons, its energy degrades to about $E = 5.0 \times 10^{10}$ GeV, the GZK bound (after Greisen, 1966; Zatsepin & Kuzmich, 1966).[7] The Utah projectile came in with *six times* this energy.

If a particle has this much energy, then the inter-galactic magnetic fields (the order of 10^{-9} gauss) are too weak to deflect it very much, so one should be able to look back along its arrival direction and see the active source that produced it.

7. [The Greisen-Zatsepin-Kuzmich (GZK) bound limits the amount of cosmic rays entering the Earth's atmosphere.—Editors.]

This source should be less than a few hundred million light years away, else the particle should not have arrived with so much energy. But when scientists look back over the 3.0×10^{10} GeV particle's path, they see no such source. So how did the particle get here?

This looked like an interesting problem for McMoneagle and me to examine. I knew that Joe could look forward and back in spacetime (e.g., McMoneagle, 1998), but I was not sure that he could zero in on an upper atmospheric elementary-particle event that occurred eight years before and two thousand miles away. Even if he could, then could he come up with useful information? I decided that it was worth a try.

On October 2, 1999, I e-mailed Joe's wife Nancy the following query to put in a sealed envelope for Joe:

> An ultra high-energy cosmic-ray particle entered our atmosphere in Utah, USA on October 15, 1991 at 7:34:16 Universal Time, and was detected by the Fly's Eye Array. The shower of particles that the incoming particle created pointed to Galactic Latitude = 9.6 degrees and Galactic Longitude = 163.4 degrees. Trace the incoming particle back to its source.

On the outside of the envelope, Nancy wrote: "An event occurred on October 15, 1991 in Utah at 7:34:16 Universal Time. 1. Describe the event. 2. Describe where and how the event originated." She then gave the envelope to Joe.

Joe's report follows. I first read this report while visiting the McMoneagles on January 2, 2000.

McMoneagle's Report on the Utah Event

> 7:34:16 UT, Utah, Oct. 15, 1991 [Joseph McMoneagle]
>
> 1. Describe the event:
>
> Actually the event took place over a period of time that began roughly at the time noted above. I believe it probably went on for some seconds, perhaps a little over a minute. My sense is that there was a huge wave impact on the face of the planet that took place at this position on the planet. My impression is that the impact looked very much like a teardrop of energy of some kind coming into contact with the Earth. What is interesting about it, is that it was generally localized and then

sort of peters out as you go away from the epicenter or initial point of contact. The energy was apparently particles of some kind that are customarily seen only sporadically on the planet. My sense is that while they had some mass, which is measurable, they did not contain any form of specific charge. The other interesting thing is that it appears the impact of the teardrop was in reverse of how one might think it would occur. (See the attached drawings [Figures 15.6 and 15.7] for state-by-state effect.) Particles were extremely and unusually dense at point of impact and occurred with a measurable rise in density and then falling off to normal. (See attached drawing of density profile [Figure 15.6].)

2. Describe where and how the event originated:

The generator of this event lies in deep space. My sense is that it is really huge. A very large and dense cloud of energy, that for all intensive [*sic*] purposes appears to be a star to us from our vantage point. But, it seems to be a star that has pretty much expended most of its ability to radiate. It's probably been expanding for in excess of [15×10^9] years. It has essentially consumed most of its energy and become a cloud of gas with mass but not energy.

At some point in time, the core stops expanding and begins to suck matter back into it at an astounding rate. Sort of like a vacuum cleaner. As the matter is sucked back in, it begins to build heat at the point of convergence, which initiates a large spike of power, sort of like a power surge. This speeds up the process that begins to actually feed on itself. As the cloud begins to re-consolidate, the core becomes heavier and heavier, and eventually begins to put off an enormous output of energy waves—much like a bulb as it converts electrical energy into heat energy. But, this wave is not visible to the naked eye. It appears to be something more electrical than visual.

Eventually, the star is able to consume all that it contained in the first place, wherein it collapses into itself and emits a huge burst of energy with no charge, as no charge can escape from its core any longer. I get a sense that this is the formation or the beginning of what we call a black hole in space. This incredibly dense and heavy part of what appears to be otherwise empty space then begins to search for and suck other energy into it as it grows in power.

I believe that event is generated at the precise point where the collapsing star becomes a black hole or begins to actually trap light. It releases a huge burst of energy that is of great mass but with no charge. It is a portion of that blast that struck Utah in 1991.

Remote viewing: 8 hours
Joseph W. McMoneagle,
November 10-December 31, 1999.

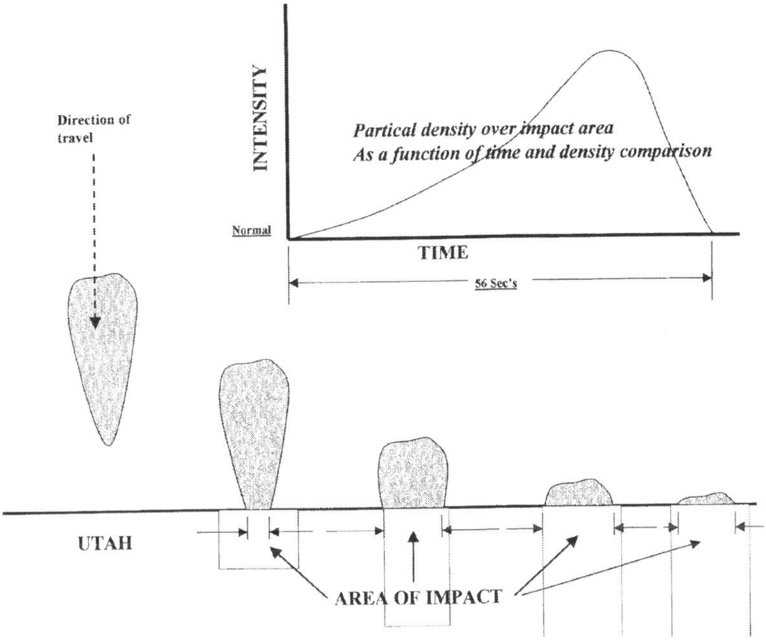

Figure 15.6. McMoneagle depicts the development of the 1991 Utah cosmic-ray shower.

Analysis of McMoneagle's Report

"1. Describe the event." Amazingly, McMoneagle perceived not an explosion or some such on the ground as one might have expected, but something high in the sky. And he did not see a chemical or nuclear explosion at this altitude because the debris did not flow out spherically. Rather the event propagated with a pointed shape. It was apparently comprised of "particles of some kind that are customarily seen only sporadically on the planet." Could Joe have zeroed in on the Utah event? For what he was seeing was no ordinary cosmic-ray event. One would have expected a shower with a flat front end shaped like a pancake several hundred feet in diameter (as explained below), not the arrowhead shape that McMoneagle saw as in Figure 15.6. (In fact, the Fly's Eye apparatus did not have the resolution to determine the shape of the front end of the shower. The time that the actual Utah shower took to reach the ground must have been of the order of tens of milliseconds, not tens of seconds as Joe reported, but it is common for remote viewers to see events unfolding much more slowly than in real time.

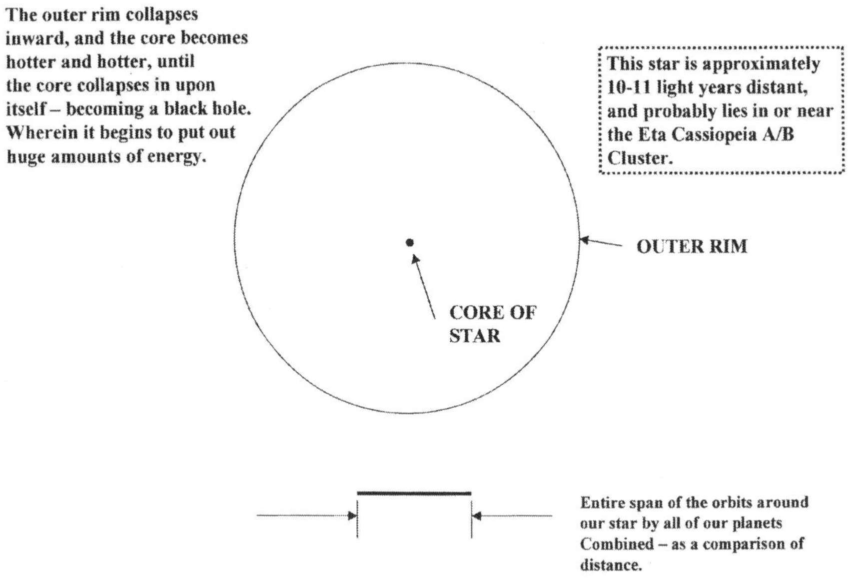

Figure 15.7. McMoneagle depicts the generator of the 1991 Utah cosmic ray.

"2. Describe where and how the event originated." Although he is neither a physicist nor an astronomer, McMoneagle is clearly describing and drawing a huge Type II Supernova. If it had been centered at our Sun's position, then the Supernova would have reached out beyond the orbit of Pluto. It culminated in the formation of a black hole (as he states) and the release of an incredible flux of neutrinos. ("It releases a huge burst of energy that is of great mass but with no charge.") Indeed, neutrinos are electrically neutral, and although recent measurements of neutrino oscillations indicate that individual neutrinos have very little mass, the neutrino flux of a supernova is so stupendous that it carries a huge amount of energy and mass. Joe estimates that the star which ended its life as the supernova began 15×10^9 years ago. This is only slightly longer than current estimates of the age of the universe, about 13.7×10^9 years.

The event that McMoneagle reported sounds like a cosmic-ray event all right. He finds the primary particle or particles originating in a Type-II Supernova, travelling to Earth and creating a shower of particles of some kind. The shape of the shower is a little strange, though.

The shower measured by Bird et al. (1995) points to an "apparent source" with celestial coordinates right ascension $\alpha = 85° \pm 1°$ and declination $\delta = 48° \pm 6°$. McMoneagle reports the primary came from the direction of celestial coordinates right ascension $\alpha = 12.3°$ and declination $\delta = 57.8°$—i.e., the direction of Eta Cassiopeia, a binary star in our local universe labeled A/B. A short calculation shows that McMoneagle's reported source subtends an angle fully 57° with respect to the Utah group's "apparent source."

In fact, there were no reported sightings of a Type-II Supernova in *any* direction during October 1991 (R. Schorn, personal communication, 2004). So what to make of this?

One clue may be that McMoneagle's cosmic-ray shower has the shape of a pointed shock wave, whereas one would expect it to look more like a pancake in front, as stated above. See Figure 15.8, where I show shock waves created by objects travelling faster than ordinary waves in a given medium. In the upper atmosphere, ordinary light waves travel at a speed perhaps 1% less than their speed in a true vacuum. A highly energetic cosmic ray will nonetheless travel essentially at the vacuum speed of light in the upper atmosphere. Thus it will create a shock wave like the one labelled $v = 1.01c$ in Figure 15.8. However, Joe's shower looks more like the shock wave of a particle travelling at a velocity $v = 4c$ (see the shock waves labelled $v = 1.4c$ and $v = 4.3c$ in Figure 15.8).

How could McMoneagle have seen a particle moving with a speed greater than the speed of light in a vacuum? Such particles, called tachyons, have been looked for over the years but never seen (E. C. G. Sudarshan and others have predicted the properties of tachyons in a definitive series of papers; e.g., Bilaniuk & Sudarshan, 1969). If, on the other hand, McMoneagle's particle came from outside our local four dimensions of space and time M^4 (where 3D-space + 1D-time = 4D 'manifold' to represent spacetime M^4) then it might indeed have entered with a speed greater than the speed of light. Nobody knows what laws govern speeds outside M^4. Indeed, speed = (distance covered)/(time elapsed), and time outside M^4 might be quite different from time inside M^4, if it exists at all there.

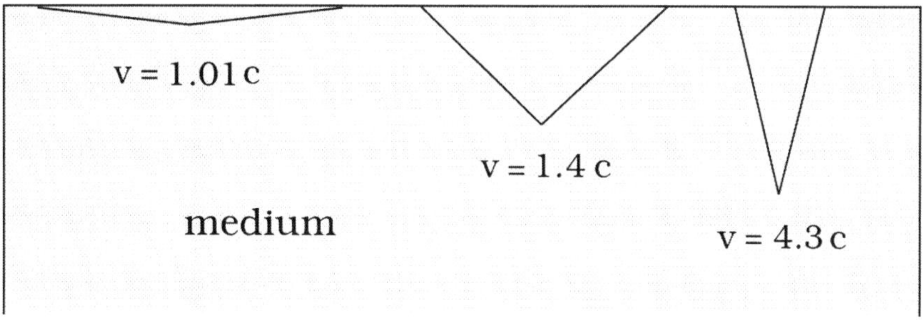

Figure 15.8. Shock waves produced by projectiles travelling with velocity v greater than the velocity c of normal waves in a given medium.

If the cosmic-ray particle did enter our local spacetime from higher-dimensional spacetime, then it might have penetrated our space with speed ~$4c$ (i.e., approximately four times the speed of light), creating the pointed shock wave that McMoneagle saw. This could explain how it arrived with kinetic energy six times the GZK bound. Travelling outside our local spacetime, it never encountered the 3K photons. It may have entered our spacetime right over Utah.

After a little thought, though, one realizes that even if the cosmic ray did enter our M^4 directly over Utah, it probably would have punched right through our local spacetime and continued on in the extra dimensions. How could it have initiated a shower over Dugway Flats?

To explain this point, I would like to use a simplified model of lower and higher dimensions. Imagine that our local space had just two dimensions, say the horizontal x- and y-dimensions. This reduced space would still be adequate to describe a lot of physics, e.g., the orbit of the Earth around the Sun, or a high localized orbit of an electron around a proton. See the plane labeled "portion of lower universe" in Figure 15.9. This slab is a portion of a plane which stretches out to infinity in the x and y directions. Now in place of the ordinary z-axis perpendicular to the x- and the y-axes, let us draw a new axis and call it $\tilde{z}$. (The tilde over $\tilde{z}$ indicates that it is an extra dimension.) These x - y - $\tilde{z}$ axes are sketched in Figure 15.9.

We can now use this extra dimension $\tilde{z}$ to make space for another universe. Make a copy of "portion of 'lower' universe" and place it parallel to "portion of 'lower' universe" only higher along the $\tilde{z}$-dimension, as sketched in Figure 15.9. Call it "portion of 'upper' universe". It too is just a portion of a horizontal plane which stretches out to infinity in both directions. "Upper universe" might contain an electron orbiting a proton also.

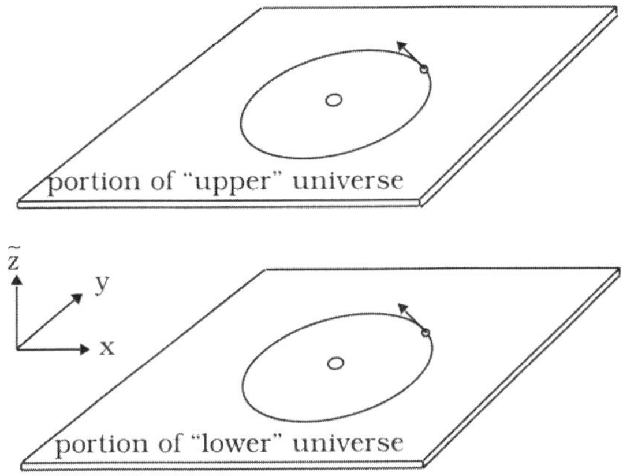

Figure 15.9. Two parallel universes, each depicted with just two ordinary x- and y-dimensions, spaced a distance apart along a vertical extra dimension $\tilde{z}$.

Now we are ready to tackle the problem of how a particle from outside our local spacetime could initiate a shower over Utah (see Figure 15.10). Again I consider just two dimensions of our local universe M^4. Earth now appears as a very thin disk. The surface of real Earth is now just the circumference of this disk. Earth's atmosphere coats the circumference.

The illustrated thickness of "our universe" is not the thickness in the ordinary z direction, but rather the thickness in the direction of the extra dimension $\tilde{z}$, and is probably less than 10–19 meter, a thickness of Earth's elementary particles in the $\tilde{z}$ direction suggested by Rubakov and Shaposhnikov (1983) and Bryan (1986, 1998, 1999).

Now imagine, as in Figure 15.10, that the Utah cosmic-ray primary actually was accelerated by a supernova in an "upper universe." Suppose that it escaped and sped on to reach our universe M^4 near Earth. What might have happened when it hit our local spacetime? Usually I suppose that it would just have gone straight through the 10^{-19} meter of "our universe" and continued on in the extra dimension. However if it had entered with a speed greater than c, then it might have set up a shock wave in M^4, as such a speed is strictly forbidden by Einstein's Theory of Special Relativity. This shock wave might have proceeded to Earth and created the shower. The primary wave would have been deflected slightly and continued on to a "lower" universe, as sketched in Figure 15.10. Alternately, the wave might have ricocheted off a molecule high in Earth's atmosphere, with the molecule initiating the shower. In either case, the shower would have pointed back to the "apparent source" of Bird et al., as indicated in Figure 15.10.

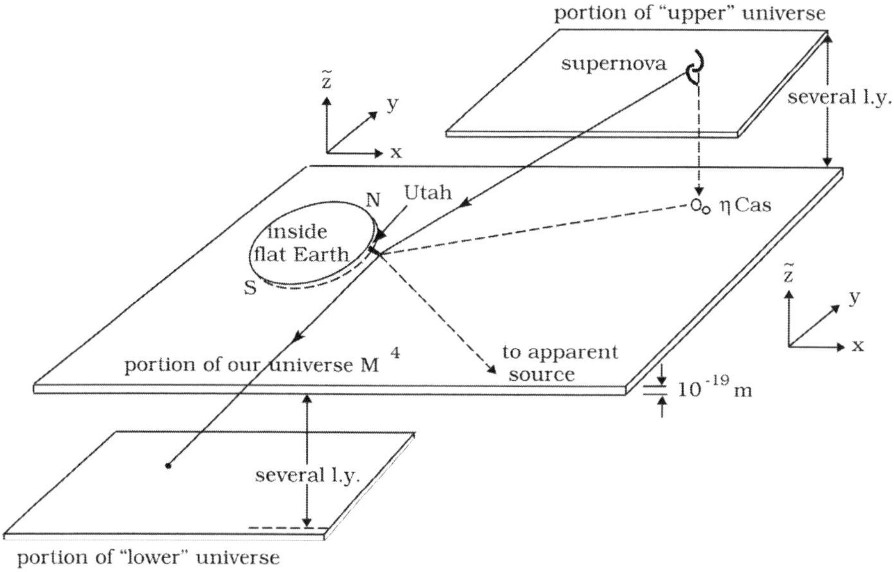

Figure 15.10. Scenario in which a Type-II Supernova in an "upper" universe accelerates a cosmic-ray particle to ultra high energy. The particle escapes and propagates to our universe M^4*, entering with a speed in excess of the speed of light. There it hits a secondary particle (or creates a shock wave simply by encountering our spacetime) and proceeds on to a "lower universe." The secondary heads toward Earth and creates the shower seen by the Fly's Eye Detector in Dugway Flats, Utah in 1991.*

If the primary had already been travelling some distance *within* M^4, then Special Relativity dictates that any particles that it hit or created would have travelled right along with the primary in nearly the same direction. However for a primary entering from *outside* our local spacetime, we do not know what rules apply at the boundary of M^4, so perhaps the primary *could* hit another particle and send it off at right angles into M^4 as suggested in Figure 15.10.

Note that just from the geometry, a primary reaching Earth would be much more likely to materialize somewhere in the middle of the planet rather than in its atmosphere. If it had entered M^4 inside Earth, then it would have then passed right on through the 10^{-19} meter and disappeared in the extra dimension and we would never have known about it.

Of course Earth is three-dimensional, not two-dimensional, so for a more realistic picture of lower and higher dimensions, consider what an observer would see as he or she moved along the $\tilde{z}$-axis starting from above the "upper universe" and passing on through "our universe." Before the observer entered the "upper universe," s/he would see nothing except perhaps a few stray elementary particles. However as soon as the observer entered the "upper universe," s/he would see the supernova in all three dimensions. Upon leaving the "upper universe," s/he would again see nothing, as the (assumed) elementary particles of that universe only exist inside the universe. Light, for example, could not inform the observer what was going on inside the "upper universe" for photons would not be able to leave that universe.

Travelling along $\tilde{z}$ would be something like travelling through time. Three-dimensional scenes would unfold each time the observer entered the thin plane of a universe with its population of elementary particles. When the observer entered our universe M^4, s/he would see Earth, the solar system, our galaxy, all galaxies in three-dimensional glory. The instant that the observer passed on through along, our universe would disappear again.

This, incidentally, explains how an elementary particle from outside our universe could first enter Earth at *any* point within its interior, $\tilde{z}$-direction included. The $\tilde{z}$-direction would open up the instant that the particle entered our slab in the (extra) $\tilde{z}$-direction.

Regarding McMoneagle's report of a Type-II Supernova in the direction of Eta Cassiopeia, if it did occur in a "higher universe," then it would not have been observable on Earth, as photons (if such exist in that universe) would have been trapped there and unable to reach Earth, as noted above. McMoneagle's Supernova might exist above Eta Cassiopeia in a higher dimension, a few millimeters in $\tilde{z}$ above our universe, or maybe a few light-years as suggested in Figure 15.10.

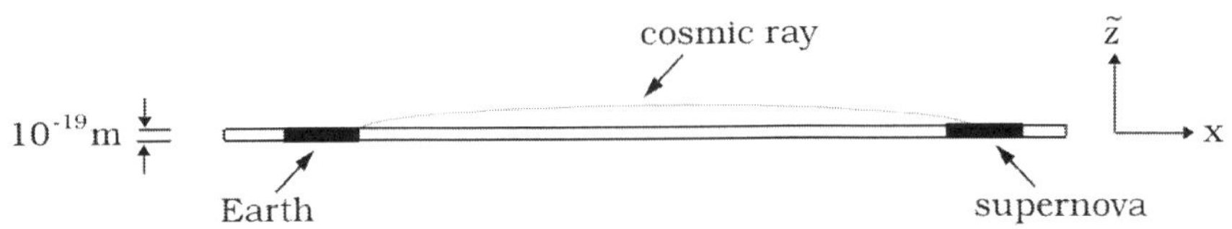

Figure 15.11. A Supernova-generated cosmic ray escaping M^4 *and travelling slightly "higher" in an extra dimension* $\tilde{z}$ *before returning to* M^4 *in the vicinity of Earth. Our lower three dimensions are represented by a single ordinary dimension* x.

I would be remiss if I did not point out another possible scenario for the Utah event. In this picture, the parent Supernova exists somewhere in our *own* universe M^4, while the cosmic ray travels at superluminal speed just outside M^4, as sketched in Figure 15.11.

The speeding ray leaves M^4 by moving slightly in the direction of the higher dimension $\tilde{z}$, grazes M^4 (represented by a single dimension x), and returns to Earth's surface over Utah. (If the "density" of the vacuum just above M^4 were less than that in M^4, then redirection of the cosmic ray back into M^4 might occur the same way that light in a fibre-optic strand is trapped in the strand due to total internal reflection each time it grazes the wall of the fibre.) Meanwhile the normal outburst of photons and neutrinos travels conventionally within our lower four dimensions and simply has not reached us yet. These photons and neutrinos from the Supernova might be a few light-years, or perhaps millions of light-years, behind the cosmic ray. The as yet unseen Supernova might indeed be in the direction of Eta Cassiopeia as McMoneagle says. Or perhaps along the line-of-sight reported by the University of Utah group (Bird et al., 1995).

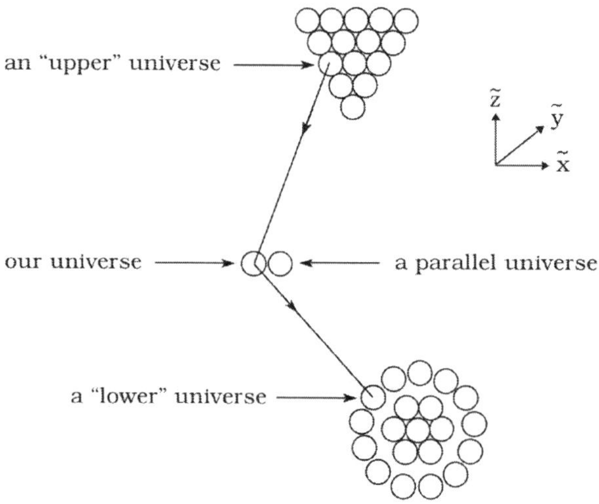

Figure 15.12. Universes depicted as spheres in three extra dimensions $\tilde{x}$, $\tilde{y}$, and $\tilde{z}$. The spheres have diameters of 10^{-19} meter or less in the extra dimensions. The ordinary dimensions x, y, and z exist also, but are suppressed so that the higher dimensions can be shown. The upper cluster of universes resembles a bunch of grapes; the lower, seeds of a pomegranate. Our universe is shown alongside a parallel universe. Additional universes may be as common as grains of sand on Earth.

With regard to the number of extra dimensions, we probably need to extend the parallel-planes picture of one higher dimension to one with several higher dimensions: to accommodate the 48 elementary particles, not one but at least four extra dimensions are needed (Bryan, 1998). I show three extra dimensions in Figure 15.12. Each small sphere represents another universe with a small diameter (10^{-19} meter or less) in the extra dimensions. The three ordinary dimensions are suppressed in Figure 15.12 to permit showing three extra dimensions. In this picture, a particle leaving the "upper" universe need not travel through our universe to reach the "lower" universe. It might not hit any universes at all.

DISCUSSION

It appears that Joseph McMoneagle uses his 'inner senses' to gain information otherwise inaccessible to most of us. I think that his description of the electron is particularly striking. And drawing a quantum-mechanical wavefunction when he has no background in physics or mathematics is remarkable. McMoneagle not only determined the question in the sealed envelope, but oftentimes, if not always, answered it as well. Some manner of information transfer is clearly taking place, and certainly not through the four fields that we physicists are currently conversant with: electromagnetic, weak, strong, and gravitational. There is something waiting to be discovered here.

McMoneagle does not give precise quantitative answers as a rule. He gives impressions, verbal and visual. These comprise a wonderful storehouse of ideas, invaluable to 'right-brained' researchers receptive to new concepts. As in any era, some ideas have immediate applications, others may be years ahead of their time. And some may not relate to our universe at all. But there are, no doubt, some gems awaiting our perusal.

For example, the Heisenberg Uncertainty Principle is a cornerstone of present-day quantum mechanics. Yet McMoneagle seems to be blissfully unaware of its limits. How can he examine the interior of a nucleus, down to 10^{-15} meter without disturbing it? To see this structure with a particle beam requires the particles to have quantum-mechanical wavelengths of 10^{-15} meter or less. Protons of this wavelength would have kinetic energies of over 600MeV. Since the protons and neutrons in a nucleus are bound together with an average energy of about 8MeV, such a beam would disturb the nucleus, most likely knocking several nucleons out of it.

It is true that McMoneagle did not describe a nucleus and electron cloud corresponding to any known atom, but he may have seen a generic form. Most interesting was his seeing a nucleus *within* the nucleus, of a size about 10^{-24} meter. This inner nucleus may have no bearing with reality, but what if it actually does exist? Joe has been correct on many counts where he could not have known the answer (the four-component Dirac form of the electron-wavefunction, the Chinese test shot, etc.). It appears that his inner senses give him correct information. So perhaps he has correct information here too.

The implications for nuclear physics are astounding. If such an inner nucleus exists, and if we can learn to manipulate it, then a whole new era in nuclear science could begin. Perhaps we can use this hint to put us on track to learn how to make radioactive nuclei disintegrate at *our* command. Again the Heisenberg Uncertainty Principle does not seem to be coming into play. It says that we cannot know when any particular radioactive nucleus will decay.

Note, incidentally, that if Joe indeed saw a nucleus *within* a nucleus, and it is as small as 10^{-24} meter, then he saw detail that would have required a particle beam with an energy of 200,000TeV, or 100,000 times more energy than the most energetic beams currently available on Earth, the Fermilab proton and anti-proton beams.[8] And dumping this much energy in a nucleus would not only cause it to disintegrate completely, but would produce millions of short-lived elementary particles. If his reports are accurate, then Joe has found a way to get information in a way not permitted by the Heisenberg Uncertainty Principle.[9]

If Joe can see far smaller structure than our current accelerators and other instruments can, then perhaps he can also see neutral particles. He reported seeing beams of neutral particles streaming out of a Type-II Supernova which were clearly neutrinos, particles notoriously difficult to detect. Physicists might be very interested to know the means by which he sees these neutral, barely interacting particles. In a typical Fermilab secondary beam pulse of 10^{13} neutrinos, only about one neutrino interacts with the target.

Also of great interest to physicists is the possibility that extra space-like dimensions exist. Joe reported seeing the electron spinning about a fourth dimension (a dimension in addition to the usual three). He also described the wavefunction proceeding in a fourth direction. And when he showed the

8. [TeV = Tera (10^{12}) electronvolts.—Editors.]

9. Alexander Imich has credibly argued that conjectured psychic observation of subatomic particles may not be subject to limitations of the Heisenberg Uncertainty Principle (Imich, 1996).

cosmic-ray shower comprising what appears to be a shock wave, again he may have given evidence of an extra dimension, perhaps light-years in length. Joe knew of my great interest in extra dimensions (Bryan, 1986, 1998, 2000), but for over twenty years he has demonstrated an ability to use his 'inner' senses to report information independent of what his collaborators might expect to hear (McMoneagle, 1995, 1998, 2000, 2002).

So I would recommend to cosmic-ray physicists that they measure the speed of incoming ultra-high energy cosmic-ray particles to see if they are entering our atmosphere faster than the speed of light. (For a recent survey, see the Appendix in this chapter.) This would suggest the existence of extended higher dimensions and explain how particles could enter our space with energies in excess of the GZK bound. And it would alter our view of our place in the cosmos just as surely as the Copernican model forced our ancestors to relinquish the belief that Earth sat peacefully at the center of the universe.

What is of particular interest about McMoneagle's extra dimension(s) is that they are (presumably) straight lines macroscopic in length. The whole string-theory effort is focused on extra dimensions that are basically little circles within circles of the order of 10^{-32} meter in diameter (although some physicists have suggested that one of these extra compact dimensions might be a straight section the order of 10^{-6} meter in length). *Macroscopic* extra dimensions bring the peculiar features of theoretical particle-theory right into every-day life.

For if extra dimensions are an unproved hypothesis for scientists, they may be reality for millions of people who have had a near-death or out-of-body experience. Travelling down a dark tunnel and arriving at the light to meet deceased relatives in new surroundings might be explained as leaving our lower four dimensions and tunnelling to a higher dimensional universe.

McMoneagle may well have described such a universe when he reported seeing the Type-II supernova. There is no record of astronomers' seeing such a supernova anywhere in the sky in October 1991 (R. Schorn, personal communication, 2004). Joe may have had to go outside our universe to see the event leading to the Dugway Flats shower. (Although I have also suggested another scenario where the Supernova is sited in our universe and the cosmic ray skims along in the extra dimension at greater than light-speed; meanwhile the conventional particles travelling in ordinary space are still on their way here.)

If higher dimensional space exists in addition to our lower three dimensions of space, then our concept of time may have to be modified if it is to hold in these higher dimensions. A possible clue might be that an observer moving along an extra dimension $\tilde{z}$ sees whole three-(normal)-dimensional universes open up each time he or she crosses a "slab" containing the particles that make up that universe. This moving along $\tilde{z}$ appears to be akin to moving along in time, where again one sees a three-dimensional panorama unfold as time proceeds.

I would like to close with a comment on higher dimensional universes. If they exist, then they are probably quite numerous, not just a few scattered about like I used to model the Utah event in Figure 15.10. They may sometimes come in clusters, such as I have sketched in Figure 15.12. In this figure I have suppressed the three ordinary dimensions so that I could show three extra dimensions, measured by coordinates $\tilde{x}$, $\tilde{y}$, and $\tilde{z}$. I show an "upper" universe in Figure 15.12 as part of a cluster of universes resembling a bunch of grapes (each small sphere representing a distinct universe, with the ordinary dimensions suppressed) and a "lower" universe as part of a pomegranate-like cluster. For our own universe I suggest a companion parallel universe. Note that probably no universe anything like our own could keep a 3.0×10^{11} GeV particle from breaking loose and travelling through higher-dimensional spacetime, if such exists.

» Acknowledgments

First of all, I want to thank Joseph McMoneagle for the essential role he played in our joint effort to study some of the universe about us, large and small. Our research was funded in part by the Lifebridge Foundation of New York City. I want to thank Charles Overby for informing me about the Foundation, and especially Lifebridge's president, Barbara Valocore, for her encouragement and financial assistance. Nancy McMoneagle was helpful throughout our research, including instructing me how to present my questions to Joe. I would also like to thank Ronald Schorn for information on astronomical matters, and Nelson Duller for information on cosmic-ray showers. Also I would like to thank Linda Young for a confirming observation. Finally, I would like to thank my philosopher wife Mary Lind for her encouragement and keen appraisal of the metaphysics that Joe and I were engaged in.

» References

Bhattacharjee, P. & Sigl, G. (2000). Origin and propagation of extremely high energy cosmic rays. *Physics Reports, 327*, 109-247. [Available at http://lanl.arXiv.org/pdf/astro-ph/9811011]

Bilaniuk, O. M., & Sudarshan, E. C. G. (1969). Particles beyond the light barrier. *Physics Today, 22*(5), 43-51.

Bird, D. J., Corbató, S. C., Dai, H. Y., Elbert, J. W., Green, K. D., Huang, M. A., Kieda, D. B., Ko, S., Larsen, C. G., Loh, E. C., Luo, M. Z., Salamon, M. H., Smith, J, D., Sokolsky, P., Sommers, P., Tang, J. K. K., & Thomas, S. B. (1995). Detection of a cosmic ray with measured energy well beyond the expected spectral cutoff due to cosmic microwave radiation. *Astrophysical Journal, 441*, 144-150.

Bryan, R. (1986). Isoscalar quarks and leptons in an eight-dimensional space. *Physical Review D, 34*, 1184-1193.

Bryan, R. (1998). Are quarks and leptons dynamically confined in four flat extra dimensions? *Nuclear Physics, B523*, 232-242.

Bryan, R. (1999). Are the Dirac particles of the Standard Model dynamically confined states in a higher dimensional flat space? *Canadian Journal of Physics, 77*, 197-210. [Available at http://faculty.physics.tamu.edu/bryan]

Bryan, R. (2000). What can elementary particles tell us about the world in which we live? *Journal of Scientific Exploration, 14*, 257-274. Reprinted in electronic-journal *NeuroQuantology*, 2003, *4*, 375-392. [Available at http://faculty.physics.tamu.edu/bryan]

Bryan, R. (2002). Consciousness and quantum-mechanical wavefunctions. *unpublished.* [Available at http://faculty.physics.tamu.edu/bryan]

Greisen, K. (1966). End to the cosmic ray spectrum? *Physical Review Letters, 16*, 748-750.

Imich, A. (1996). The indeterminacy principle. *The Scientific and Medical Network Review, 60*. [This article has been reprinted by the Aroostook Mental Health Center and is available online at http://www.amhc.org/poc/view_doc.php?type=doc&id=296].

Kersting, N. (2006). The GZK bound in discrete space. Retrieved, May 17, 2012, from: http://arxiv.org/find/astro-ph/1/au:+Kersting_N/0/1/0/all/0/1.

McMoneagle, J. (1995). *Mind trek.* Charlottesville, VA: Hampton Roads.

McMoneagle, J. (1998). *The ultimate time machine.* Charlottesville, VA: Hampton Roads.

McMoneagle, J. (2000). *Remote viewing secrets.* Charlottesville, VA: Hampton Roads.

McMoneagle, J. (2002). *The Stargate chronicles.* Charlottesville, VA: Hampton Roads.

Pearsall, P., Schwartz, G. E. R. & Russek, L. G. S. (2002). Changes in heart transplant recipients that parallel the personalities of their donors. *Journal of Near-Death Studies, 20,* 191-206.

Rubakov, V. A. & Shaposhnikov, M. E. (1983). Do we live inside a domain wall? *Physics Letters, B125,* 136-138.

Zatsepin, G. T., & Kuzmich, V. A. (1966). Upper limit on the spectrum of cosmic rays. *JETP Letters, 4,* 78-80 [*Pis'ma Zh. Eksp. Teor. Fiz., 4,* 114-117].

APPENDIX

Survey of Ultra-High-Energy Cosmic Rays

There are two main collaborations that have looked at incoming ultra-high-energy cosmic rays in the past 20 years, the Utah group (Fly's Eye, Hi-Res I & II) and the Pierre Auger Collaboration, using the observatory in Argentina. Both groups find that the number of incoming particles with energies *above* the GZK bound sharply decreases with increasing energy, as predicted by Greisen (1966), and Zatsepin and Kuzmich (1966). The Pierre Auger Collaboration (Abraham, Snow, et al., 2008) paper pretty much sums up both groups' data. They list just four particles with energies above 100 EeV,[10] with the most energetic at 220 EeV (see Figure 3 in their paper).

Interestingly enough, PAC does *not* list the "Fly's Eye" event measured in 1991 (see Bird et al., 1995). I think that the energy of this event is too high to fit the predicted statistical drop-off of events with energies above the GZK bound. Yet I have not seen any disclaimer of this event in the literature. I may be the only one who has suggested that this particle does not fit the GZK physics and might have come from higher dimensional space. As such it *might* have arrived with a speed exceeding that of light.

—R. A. Bryan (May 21, 2012)

» References

Abraham, J., Snow, G., & The Pierre Auger Collaboration (2008). Observation of the suppression of the flux of cosmic rays above 4×10^{19} eV. *Physical Review Letters, 101*(6), 061101-1-061101-7.

Bird, D. J., et al. (1995). HIRES collaboration. *The Astrophysical Journal, 441*, 144-150.

Greisen, K. (1966). End to the cosmic ray spectrum? *Physical Review Letters, 16*, 748-750

Zatsepin, G. T., & Kuzmich, V. A. (1966). Upper limit on the spectrum of cosmic rays. *JETP Letters, 4*, 78-80 [*Pis'ma Zh. Eksp. Teor. Fiz., 4*, 114-117].

10. [EeV = Exa (10^{18}) electronvolts.—Editors.]

Chapter 16

Avoiding the Intervention Paradox[1]

COLIN MITCHELL

The aim of this chapter is simply to show that there are models of time for which the 'Intervention Paradox' is not an obstacle to the possible existence of a type of precognition which results in action removing or changing the event precognised. That is the sole aim. I make no attempt to argue for the existence of any type of precognition or to propose a mechanism for the operation of precognition, although I do mention the possibility of 'backward causation'. It is not the aim of this chapter to propose or advocate any particular theory of precognition—the sole aim is to show that it is possible to construct models of the universe which would allow the existence of the type of precognition for which the Intervention Paradox is considered to be a problem.

In discussing this I will also go a little broader to consider the whole idea of 'changing the future', not just a particular precognised event.

The Intervention Paradox is defined by Thalbourne in his *Glossary of terms used in parapsychology* as follows:

> If a person has a precognitive impression of an event E, and as a result of this information takes action such that E subsequently fails to occur, then the Intervention Paradox is the question of what it was that caused the precognitive impression in the first place, since the putative cause, viz. the future event E, never came into being. (Thalbourne, 2003, p. 57).

1. [This chapter is based on an article that was originally published in *Australian Journal of Parapsychology* (2004, vol. 4[2], pp. 81-104). Permission to reprint has been granted by the author and the journal.—Editors.]

I would prefer to use the term 'occurs' rather than "came into being" in the above definition, to remove any metaphysical assumptions.

Problems with talking about time arise with the very nature of the language we use because our language embodies assumptions about the nature of time and is itself conditioned by our experience of being 'in' time. We want now to try to 'objectify' time and consider it as an entity in itself—in other words we will try to be 'outside' time rather than 'in' it. In order to do this we must separate the notion of existence (or 'being') from time itself. Normally we consider that for something to exist it must have duration for a certain length of time, no matter how short, but we will assume that existence is a separate matter to time. We need to do this because we are going to consider the existence of time itself.

In fact the term 'exists' has more than one use. It can be used in a purely time or place dependant sense to indicate something that is present at a particular time(s) or place(s) (implied in Thalbourne's definition above). Or it can be used in a more general sense to indicate reality regardless of its presence in time or not. I will be using it in the latter sense in this chapter.

I will be arguing that the Intervention Paradox itself embodies a number of assumptions about the nature of time which imply a particular model of time. I will show that there are other possible models of time which circumvent the Intervention Paradox.

Precognition

First a word about precognition itself. I am assuming a meaning of precognition which implies some sort of psi, not a forecasting of the future that could take place by means of normally acquired knowledge of present or past conditions. Thalbourne defines precognition as "a form of extrasensory perception in which the target is some future event that cannot be deduced from normally known data in the present" (Thalbourne, 2003, p. 90).

One theory of precognition would have it that the precognised event is *deduced* or *extrapolated* from data about the world acquired in the present by ESP or super-ESP (clairvoyance and/or telepathy) (Irwin, 2004, pp. 99-100). Under that theory of precognition the Intervention Paradox need not be a problem. In this chapter I will be considering the type of precognition for which the Intervention Paradox is considered a problem—precognition which involves the direct sensing by some unknown mechanism of future events or possible futures which in some sense exist. When I say precognition from now on I mean this type of precognition.

Block Space-Time

The nature of time is a great mystery. Philosophers have found that some of our everyday assumptions about time do not stand up under scrutiny, and physicists have found the same thing. One of these everyday assumptions is that time itself 'flows' or that we ourselves 'move through time'.

There are different ways of thinking about time, but embodied within the idea of precognition is the idea that future events exist or that 'possible futures' have some kind of existence. In contrast with this notion of time at least one modern physical theory of which I am aware (Chown, 2000, pp. 24-28)) operates within the paradigm of 'presentism'—the philosophical position that the present moment is all there is and there is no such thing as the future or the past (Dainton, 2001, pp. 79-82). Still other notions of time embody a 'growing universe' where there is a present and a past, but not a future (Dainton, 2001, pp. 68-69). It is difficult to see how precognition could operate at all in these latter models.

Since Einstein's time, the dominant way of viewing time amongst philosophers and physicists is in terms of geometry. Representing time as an extension in space has been around since cave-people carved notches along the length of a bone to measure the passage of the days. But Einstein came up with a much more sophisticated bone—a 4-dimensional one. Einstein's Special Theory of Relativity united space and time into a single entity: 4D spacetime.

Previously space and time had not been considered as physical entities in themselves, but were merely the background arena in which physical entities did their thing. Now space and time were brought into the fold and considered to be physical entities just as much as anything else in physics. They were also joined together into space-time. Time was conceptualised as an extra dimension like the three space dimensions—the so-called fourth dimension. Physicists do tell us that the time dimension is in fact different from the other (space) dimensions for reasons to do with the finite limit on the speed of light (Delsemme, 1998, pp. 281-283). However for our purposes we can conceptualise the time dimension as a fourth dimension of space at right angles to the others. This model can also be used for a 'Newtonian' universe (without relativity).

Einstein's General Theory of Relativity explained gravitation in terms of the curvature of space-time (Barbour, 1999, pp. 147-181; Dainton, 2001, pp. 287-289; Hawking, 1988, pp. 32-36; 2001, pp. 30-41). Gravitation was explained in terms of the curvature of this 4-D space-time and according to some physical theories even sub-atomic particles of matter may be viewed as 'knots' in space-time. Note that physicists do not consider that space-time is curved *into* any higher dimension of space—the 4-D universe is not 'embedded' in any other space. This is hard (impossible) to visualise because as human beings we operate using a mental 3-D model of the world around us in which anything that is curved is curved in space. But mathematicians and physicists assure us it is not a requirement of curvature that this be so, at least not for space-time itself (Martin, 1988, pp. 89-90).

The discoveries of quantum physics indicate that space may not be smooth and continuous but have a fine (and dynamic) structure (Smolin, 2004, pp. 56-65). Time may also not be continuous and there has been speculation about "chronons"—the quantum unit of time (Davies, 1995, p. 187; Smolin, 2004, p. 62). Also quantum physics is indicating that space and time may not themselves be fundamental properties of the universe but secondary derived phenomena from more fundamental realities (for example quantum properties) (Chown, 2000, pp. 24-28; Smolin, 2004, pp. 56-65).

We will not need to worry unduly about this—for our purposes it will be sufficient to model time as the 4th dimension of a 4-D universe. What we end up with is what is called in philosophy "block space-time" (also called the 'B-series') (Barbour, 1999, p. 143; Dainton, 2001, pp. 6-11; Davies, 1995, pp. 71-72). I shall call it the "block universe" because it includes not only space and time, but everything else as well, all incorporated into a 4-D sculpture of incredible complexity. I am going to use this model to talk about time even though it is destined to be qualified in the future by the findings of quantum physics and/or a totally new theory. Even if space and time turn out to be derived properties from more fundamental phenomena, this model will hopefully still have validity as a depiction of the large-scale structure of the universe.

The block universe is illustrated in Figure 16.1—the rectangular shape is arbitrary. The illustration does not show any of its complex structure: all it shows is the relationship between the three dimensions of space, represented in the diagram by a square 2-dimensional surface, and the 4th dimension of time at right angles to it. Each 2-dimensional section through the 'block' can be thought of as an instant of time in our 3-D universe.[2] The key feature is that time is being modelled as an extension along the 4th dimension, like a space dimension.

One can see that in this model every position along the time dimension has equal status of existence. There is no 'preferred' position which is picked out as

2. Strictly speaking, this is so only in a 'Newtownian' universe without relativity. In the pre-Einstein Newtonian view, a universal instant of time applies across the whole universe, which is modified with Einstein's relativity (more on this point shortly).

the 'present moment' as compared with any other 'moment' (or position along the time dimension). Any position along the time dimension could be taken as the 'present moment' under consideration. And at any of these positions along the time dimension the future exists just as surely as the past and the position that we are designating as the present moment. So the block model supports the notion that the future exists.

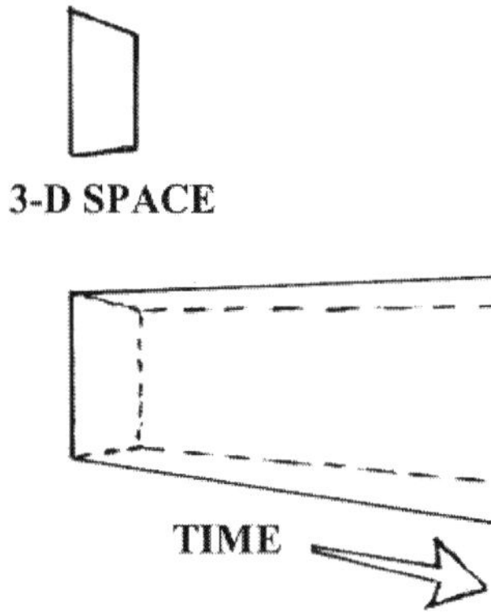

Figure 16.1. The Block Universe.

We are not going to worry about the complications of Special Relativity, which tell us that there are in fact no global 'universal' instants of time across the entire universe. Special Relativity tells us that different observers in relative motion measure time and distances differently (Dainton, 2001, pp. 254-268; Thorne, 1994, p. 71-84). However, we are conceptualising the impossible—to get outside the entire universe and view the structure as a whole from outside. The reason we are doing this is that we want to free ourselves from being trapped within time and model its structure. From our god-like perspective we are no longer subject to the limitations of observers within the universe. This includes their differing perspectives on times and distances. Observers within the universe experience motion and change. From our perspective we can see that there is in fact no change and no motion. The 'block universe' is a gigantic and incredibly complex 'static' piece of sculpture.

I need to expand just a little further on Special Relativity. Special Relativity tells us that there is no such thing as a universal time scale applicable to all observers. This is not just a limitation of the perspective of observers—there *really isn't* any universal time.[3] This is so as long as you are in the universe. But from the 'impossible perspective' we are adopting where we are outside the whole structure of space-time we can see that there is an objective reality to what we call time.

The other thing to bear in mind is that the block universe does not float in any other space or dimension. There is in reality no 'outside' to it. Even though, due to the limitations of our minds, we must visualise it as existing in a space, in reality it is not 'embedded' in any higher space—it encompasses all there is. Also, modern cosmologists speculate about 'other universes' and 'parallel universes' and other dimensions. We can regard all these as forming part of the total structure of the block universe. 'Universe' here is taken to be the sum-total of all there is including any 'other universes' and 'parallel universes'.

The objection may be raised that if there is no possibility of any observer getting outside the universe to attain such a view (since by definition any observer forms part of the universe) the model has no validity. My answer is we need to construct the model to 'objectify' time in order to understand how the future could be 'changed'—it is a *tool* to help understanding and remove us from a perspective where we are imprisoned 'within' time.

Time and Motion and the 'Now' Moment

I am now going to expand further on the nature of the block model to convince the reader that it can provide a satisfactory account of the universe we live in. I want to 'sell' the reader on the block model so that I can then use it to show how the Intervention Paradox can be circumvented.

One problem long recognised by philosophers and physicists is that the block model of space-time does not have anything in it which picks out any special moment (or 'position' along the 4th dimension) as 'now', and has nothing which parallels our experience of 'moving through time' or a 'travelling present'. There is no privileged position along the time axis that can be designated as 'now'—past, present and future have equal status.

---

3. To accommodate this supposition we would need to modify our understanding of the Block Universe model so that time is not simply one universal extension along a 4th dimension. Rather, according to relativity the 'Block' is a block of spacetime which can be divided up differently into space sections and time sections according to the perspective of differently moving observers.

Another noticeable feature of the model is that it is 'static'. The problem is that motion is something that is subject to time, so if we were to incorporate anything moving into our model (such as a 'travelling consciousness' or a 'moving present') then we would have to posit yet another time dimension within which that motion could take place (a 5th dimension to act as that time dimension). However, then we run up against the same problem because that total system of five dimensions is static—the motion of 'something' along the 4th dimension is depicted as a static extension in the 5th dimension. To reintroduce motion we have to introduce yet another time in the 6th dimension and so on to infinity. We end up with an infinity of 'times'—what is called an 'infinite regression'. Physicists do not like infinities—they try to eliminate them from their equations. Also it never really solves the problem—it just pushes the problem further and further away without ever really solving it. So infinite regressions are to be avoided if possible.

By the way, J. W. Dunne, known to parapsychologists for his book *An Experiment with Time* (in which he tried to explain precognition) constructed a theory of time based on extra time dimensions incorporating a 'moving consciousness'. He ended up with an infinite regression of time dimensions (and lived with it). He was trying to put 'motion' in his model of time. That always results in an infinite regression (Dunne, 1927/1958, pp. 105-159). Dunne also explained how the Intervention Paradox could be avoided within his scheme (Dunne, 1927/1958, pp. 184-188). So one way of circumventing the Intervention Paradox is to accept an infinite regression of time dimensions. We are going to do it without an infinite regression.

Motion within the universe can be depicted quite adequately within our 'static' block model. The motion of any entity in 3-D space is incorporated within the structure as its 'world-line' through space-time like a strand of spaghetti (see Figure 16.2) (Barbour, 1999, pp. 139-140; Dainton, 2001, pp. 182-183; Davies, 1995, pp. 75-76). 'World-line' is a term associated with Relativity theory—it describes the motion of an entity or observer through space over time. But the line itself does not move. Again there is no preferred position picked out as the present moment along this line. All positions along the world-line of an observer have equal status of existence, so the future of any observer exists as surely as their present and their past.

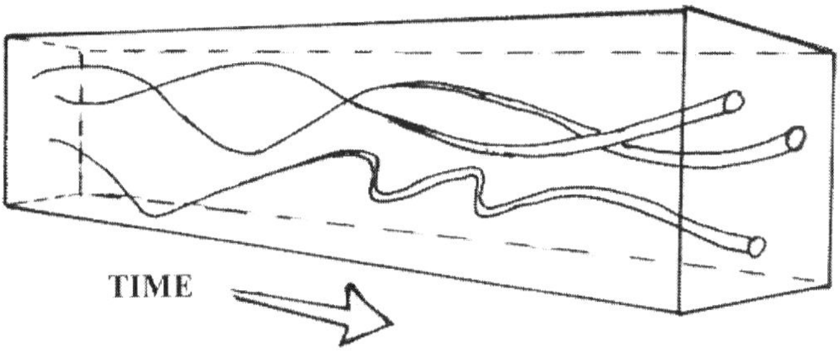

Figure 16.2. "World Lines" of three particles in the Block Universe.

But how do we depict our experience of a changing 'present moment' in this model? One way of doing it is illustrated in Figure 16.3. In this illustration the 3 dimensions of space are represented by the vertical axis (a single line) and the time dimension by the horizontal axis—making a 2-D representation of 4-D space-time. An individual mind is represented at A, B, C, and D—at successive times along the time axis. At each of these positions there is a 'static' structure which is the experience within this brain or mind of feeling that they are in the 'now' moment. Also at each position is a record of the past states (memories) so that B remembers A, but has no structure representing knowledge of C or D which are in B's future. C remembers A and B, but has no knowledge of D, etc. In this way the experience of a mind at each point in the block universe is that it is in the present moment and that it can remember the past, but does not know about the future.

The memories can also include the memory of an experience of the 'now' from the previous time so that the individual, at each point, has the experience of a changing 'now' and motion through time (for a graphic illustration and accompanying discussion which may help illuminate this scenario see Dainton, 2001, pp. 38-40).

Some physicists and philosophers are not willing to accept this scenario and feel that there must be some special process within the physical universe, or within the brain, or associated with consciousness which somehow creates a dynamic present moment. On the other hand, all the dynamism, motion and experience of the present moment that you could wish for can be incorporated within the structure of our block model of the universe. Remember that all observers are within the block universe and are part of it. No one can ever actually get outside of it to observe the 'static' structure—it is just a model. As far as all observers are concerned the universe is inherently dynamic and is full of change and motion over time. This change, motion and the experience of time are *real* in any sense of the word—it is the block model which if anything is 'unrealistic'. Once an appreciation of this is gained it can help in accepting the block model as a useful tool.

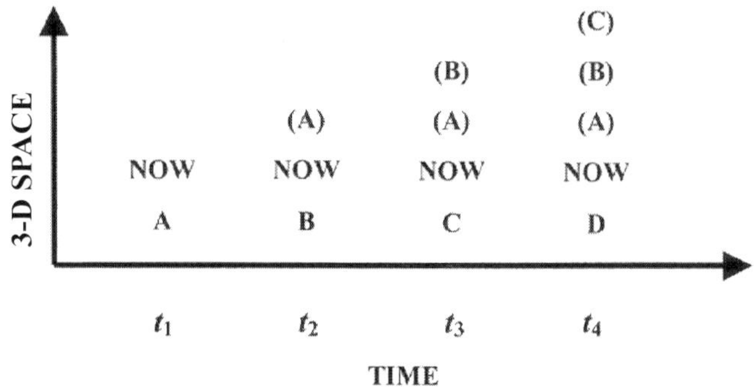

Figure 16.3. The history of a mind in the Block Universe (NOW = experience of being in the 'Now Moment').

In fact the standard solution by physicists to the problem of our experience of the 'now' has been to pass the problem off to psychology and neurophysiology. This is the solution which has been illustrated in Figure 16.3. This does not mean that we have to describe this experience as an 'illusion' in my view. The solution may *seem* very contrived, but it describes the features of the world that we observe. Our conscious perception of the passage of time is generated through our perceptions, memories, etc.—mental activity. This is exactly what is depicted in Figure 16.3. At each point in time the mind of the conscious observer feels that "I am in *this* unique moment and no other". This happens at A and B and C and D—at each point the observer thinks (correctly) that they are in that one particular moment. From the viewpoint of our block model we can see all these moments displayed in series together—but this is from a viewpoint 'outside' the universe and 'outside' of space and time itself. It would be inappropriate to describe the experience of observers within the universe (of the passage of time and motion and change) as illusion—it is a concrete reality built into the complex actual structure of this 'block universe'.

For the same reason in my view the block universe model should not be interpreted as meaning that the universe is necessarily completely deterministic and that freewill cannot exist. Any indeterminism (such as quantum indeterminism) or freewill (if it exists) is 'built into' the block universe as part of its structure. But this does not mean we have to call these features an illusion. From the point of view of observers within the universe (and that is *all* observers) these features (if they exist) are a reality.

I will now use the block model to portray the Intervention Paradox and ways around it.

The Intervention Paradox

Embodied within the Intervention Paradox is the notion that future events exist. This assumption is consistent with our block model.

Figure 16.4 depicts the incompatible conditions involved in the Intervention Paradox. In this figure, 3-D space is again represented by a vertical line and the time dimension by the horizontal axis. In Condition 1, an observer O has a precognitive perception P of event E in the future. O carries the memory of this perception with them into the future towards E. In Condition 2, O has recognised the lead-up to event E and taken action to avoid it, so E does not appear at *t4*.

Note: we assume that the precognition is the type of story in which say a person dreams of being involved in an accident at a bend in the road around which they normally never slow down. In the dream a truck comes around this corner on the wrong side of the road and there is a head-on collision. When the person finally finds themselves at that corner in the future they remember the dream and as a result of that dream slow down to a crawl. The truck of the dream comes around that corner on the wrong side of the road, but as a result of their slow speed they are able to swerve off the road and avoid the otherwise inevitable collision. In this type of scenario the action is such that the *event depicted in the dream* (a head-on collision) *would certainly have taken place but for the avoiding action* taken as a result of the precognitive dream.

Let us take the event of the head-on collision as event E in Condition 1. We assume that the event E and the precognitive perception P are linked in some causal or acausal way. I am not going to get into speculating how this is so, except to mention that backward causation from the future to the past is not ruled out by modern physics. In Condition 2, O has taken action to avoid E, and E is not there. Instead the event E is replaced by events other than E. The paradox is the *logical contradiction* between the event E being both there and not there.

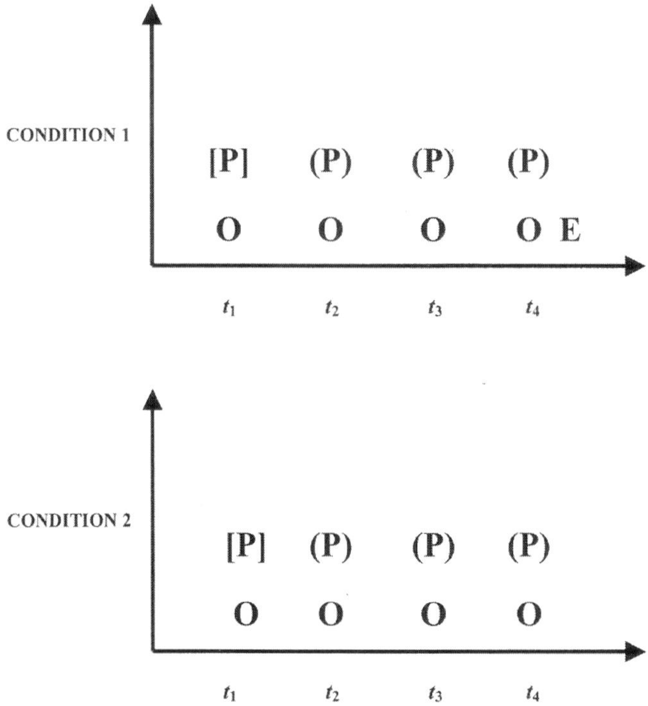

Figure 16.4. Incompatible conditions involved in the Intervention Paradox.

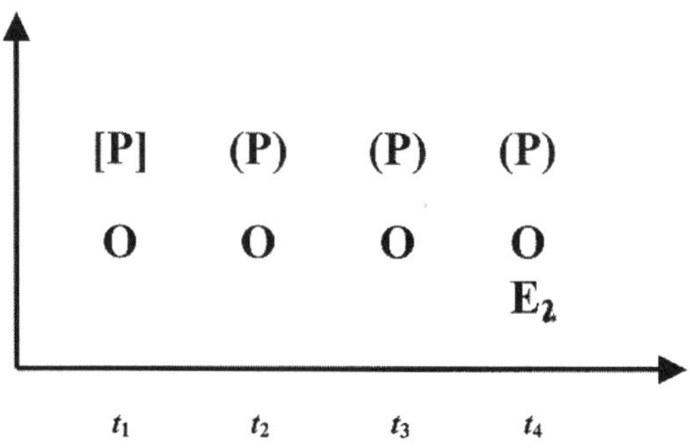

Figure 16.5. Precognition without E.

Note that we are also assuming that it is the event E that causes or is linked to the precognitive perception P and that therefore P would not be there if E is not also there. If that is not the case then it is possible that the observer O could have had P which then results in O slowing down at the curve in the road and missing the truck, but the event E (the head-on collision) does not exist. We would have to explain P as an imaginary construction of what would have happened if O had not slowed down. But the actual event which would have been the consequence of not slowing down is not there. This would be a perplexing state of affairs because O would seemingly have had divine intervention in the form of P to manipulate O into staying alive. But *no logical contradiction* would be involved in this state of affairs and therefore no paradox over existence. The story under this scenario is self-consistent (see Figure 16.5).

Or if one wants to avoid 'divine intervention' in the above scenario one could assume that the *cause* of P is the act of slowing down and the startling event of seeing a truck come around the corner on the wrong side of the road and being able to swerve off the road and miss it. This event (E_2) causes, or is linked to, a precognitive dream P which incorporates an imaginary construction of what *would have* happened if O had not slowed down. P then causes O to slow down at the bend in the road and as a result E_2 occurs (see Figure 16.5). As above there is no logical contradiction here and the story is self-consistent. So this scenario also does not involve the Intervention Paradox. The strange aspect would be "what caused the deviation from normal behaviour in the first place?" It is a chicken and egg problem. Who laid the original egg? There is a closed causal loop in which P causes E_2 which causes P, but how did this cycle come to be in the first place, given that under normal conditions of habitual behaviour O would have speeded around that corner and been involved in a head-on collision? However, in spite of this perplexing aspect, there is no logical contradiction here and the scenario is therefore allowed by physics. There is no paradox involving a contradiction about existence and non-existence.

Now back to our 'hard-core' Intervention Paradox—here the event E is straightforwardly depicted in the precognitive perception P. The action taken to avoid it results in not-E. Condition 1 and Condition 2 are on the face of it mutually incompatible. How can we avoid the logical contradiction of E both existing and not existing?

Many Futures

One way to avoid the logical contradiction of E both existing and not existing would be by allowing both worlds to exist. Have a bifurcation at some point which will still allow E to cause P (by some as yet unknown mechanism), but will result in two futures—one in which E is placed, the other in which action is taken to avoid E and E is not placed. This situation is illustrated in Figure 16.6. In this illustration we have to reduce 3D space to a point so that we can use the vertical axis to illustrate bifurcation. The time dimension extends along the horizontal axis as before.

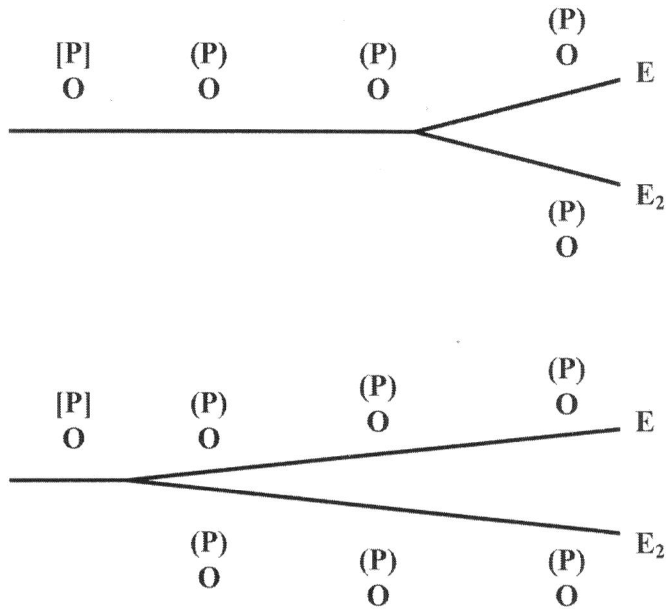

Figure 16.6. Two futures.

There are two possible points of bifurcation illustrated, but this could happen anywhere between when O receives the precognitive perception, to just before E and E_2 occur. Both these points of bifurcation (and any in between) allow for backwards causation from E to P (if that is how they are linked) but two different courses of action take place at some point which lead to two different results. We would have to explain these different courses of action. Perhaps O forgets about the precognitive dream in one path and keeps it in conscious mind in the other (I have still shown P as stored in the brain somewhere in both paths). Perhaps O becomes distracted by other things in life in one path.

There is a way to avoid the problem of O ignoring P. It is illustrated in Figure 16.7.

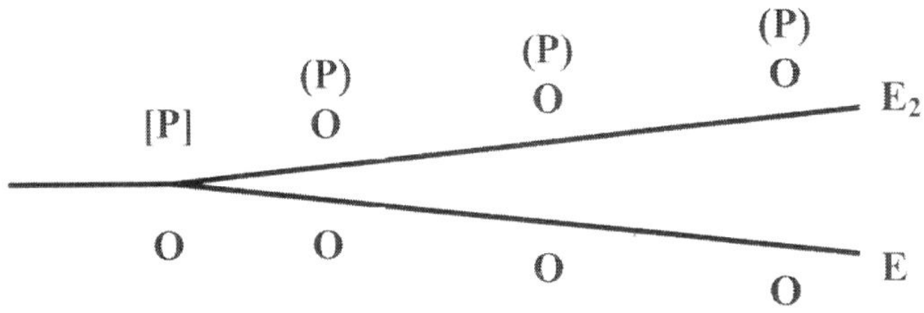

Figure 16.7. Precognition only carried into one future.

Here, although receiving the precognitive perception is related to E in one future, the perception is only remembered and carried with O in another future. Another way of saying it could be that when O receives precognition of E the universe immediately splits off another future in which that precognitive impression exists. In the future with E the precognitive impression does not exist.

There is yet another way. Strictly speaking with the block universe model there is no reason why communication between different futures cannot be built into the system short-circuiting the actual paths taken by O. This is illustrated in Figure 16.8. By some as yet unknown mechanism E in one future influences or causes a precognitive impression P in another future *after* a bifurcation in the history of O has taken place. This takes place across the space between the paths O takes through the block universe (later we will see that this can be regarded as a 5th dimensional space—the block universe in this case is a 5-dimensional structure). We may suppose that the bifurcation in the history of O is minor enough that it will not affect the fact that O will still be driving around the corner and encountering the truck due to O's habitual driving schedule. This scenario also allows the precognitive impression to affect only the future without E in it, the future with E in it has no precognitive impression.

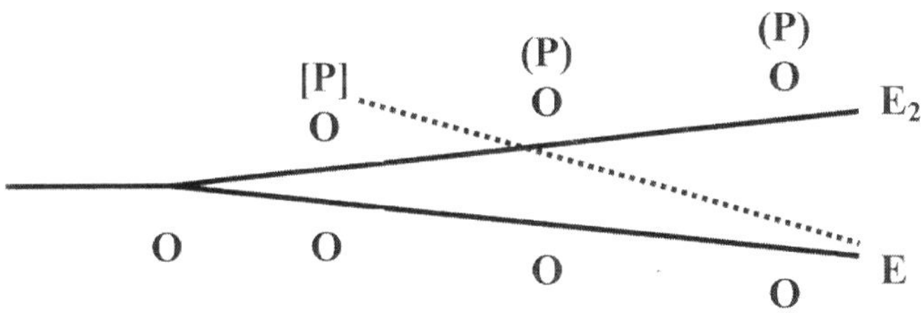

Figure 16.8. Precognitive perception 'across futures'.

There is no need to worry unduly about what may 'cause' these bifurcations. A block model can incorporate bifurcations as needed—they are simply 'there'. As long as there is a chain of cause and effect from the viewpoint of each observer within the block universe then causality reigns supreme for that observer. I could however point out that some quantum processes are thought to be 'random' and without any specific cause. We do not know how the block universe may be constructed. It may be perhaps that bifurcations happen according to definite 'laws' in a regular pattern (e.g., every time a precognitive impression occurs). In the case of the situation illustrated in Figure 16.8 we would need another reason apart from a precognitive impression. Perhaps a bifurcation in O's history occurs when O comes to a knife-edge decision which goes both ways. Or some quantum event happens in one of O's neurons and sends O's life off in two different directions.

Obviously the actual picture may be much more complicated than in Figure 16.6. There may be many different futures and a very complex branching 'tree' of paths corresponding to all sorts of minute variations in the future of O between when O receives P and the encounter with the truck (see Figure 16.9).

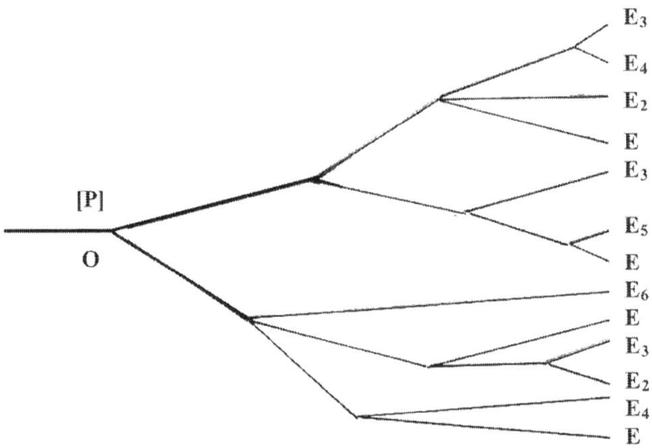

Figure 16.9. Many futures as a complex branching 'tree'.

The block model can accommodate as many futures as we want—it just makes the structure more complex, that's all. All futures co-exist from our god's eye viewpoint outside the block universe—they are not 'possible' futures, they are all there. But from inside the structure to O they may be regarded as 'possible' futures, even though they all actually happen. They are 'possible' because O does not know which future he or she will end up in. The observer O is split into two very similar individuals in each of the two futures, or in the case of a multitude of futures a multitude of differing individuals. Each individual experiences themselves as the only individual and is unaware of the others (unless perhaps they could receive a precognitive perception by backward causation from another self).

What I have just described resembles the many-worlds interpretation of quantum mechanics (or more exactly one interpretation of the many-worlds interpretation). In the conventional (i.e., Copenhagen) interpretation of quantum processes the wavefunction of a process, which embodies within it many different possible states, 'collapses' when observed or measured into one particular state (the exact state cannot be predicted although there are probabilities attached to the various states) (Davies & Brown, 1986, pp. 26-34; Tegmark & Wheeler, 2001, p. 7). In the many-worlds interpretation of quantum mechanics when a measurement or observation is made (or when equivalent quantum processes take place in the universe), the universe splits into a multitude of paths corresponding to all the possible states. Which one we observe depends on which one of these worlds we end up being in. The observers also split so in each world there is an observer to observe the particular result (Barbour, 1999, pp. 221-227; Davies & Brown, 1986, pp. 34-38; Tegmark & Wheeler, 2001, pp. 57-58).

One objection to the many-worlds interpretation is parsimony (or Occam's Razor)—there are an *awful* lot of many worlds (depending on the interpretation this could be an infinite number or just a very large finite number). On the other hand supporters of the many-worlds interpretation argue that the 'collapse of the wave-function' is an arbitrary imposition on quantum mechanics (to force theory to fit observation), which does not follow from the mathematics describing the evolution of the wave-function. They say that it follows naturally from the evolution of the wave-function that all possibilities should manifest. Therefore, they say, their interpretation involves less assumptions than the Copenhagen interpretation and is more parsimonious in that respect (Davies & Brown, 1986, p. 37). In any case our block model can certainly accommodate many futures—it just makes the structure much more complicated (but a lot richer).

However, we should note that Quantum Mechanics and General Relativity have not yet been married together. Physicists are currently searching for a new theory that will do that. The block model fits more easily into a perspective that comes from General Relativity. General Relativity is a theory which proposes space-time and explains phenomena in the universe in terms of the geometry of space-time. From this has arisen the block model, which has been elaborated on by philosophers. Exactly how the phenomena of quantum physics would fit into this model, or how the model itself may have to be modified, is not yet clear. Quantum physics is probably going to undermine the continuity of time and space and also the view that time and space are *fundamental* properties of the universe. That will not necessarily invalidate the block model on the large scale—it will just put a new perspective on it. The model may still help us to understand the conundrums of time.

We should also note that there has been no indication from quantum physicists that I am aware of that any of the many worlds of the many-worlds interpretation could communicate with each other or affect each other with forces. I do not know whether this rules out backward causation from 'another world'. But this would still not affect the fact that 'many futures' can be used to circumvent the Intervention Paradox. What it may be problematic for is the mechanism for the operation of precognition. There would have to be some way of linking an event in one of many possible futures with a precognitive perception. If influences could act in reverse through the branching tree of worlds this could perhaps do the job.

At this point it may be a good idea to remind the reader that talk about 'influences acting' or causation does not conflict with the 'static' nature of the block model. All motion, forces, etc., are to be viewed as incorporated within the marvellous intricacies of the 'static' sculpture of the block universe.

Regardless of whether the many-worlds interpretation of quantum mechanics fits the bill for a branching block universe with many futures, such a block universe with many futures is still a perfectly valid hypothesis in itself. I want to emphasise this point. The idea of 'many futures' is not tied to the validity or otherwise of the many-worlds interpretation of quantum mechanics. A block universe with a branching 'tree' of futures is hypothesised as a way of circumventing the Intervention Paradox.

The great thing about the block model is that you can twist it and mould it and build anything you like into it. This includes closed causal loops, even ones that appear to have no prior reason for their existence (such as the situation illustrated in Figure 16.5). Closed causal loops that are self-consistent involve no logical contradiction and therefore no paradox which would ban their existence. Time-travel is not ruled out by physics for this reason.

One concern may be the 'cause' for the bifurcations illustrated in Figures 16.6, 16.7, 16.8, and 16.9. The block model itself does not have to explain or justify itself—it just 'is'. But as observers within the universe, we notice patterns in the construction, which we interpret as 'cause and effect'. Could observers going into different futures maintain a consistent account of their history in terms of cause and effect? We normally think of each cause as having only one outcome, especially on the macro-level. How could this diverge into different outcomes?

It would seem that the only way this could happen would be for it to be possible for one cause to give rise to alternative results. The only level at which we observe this to be possible is at the quantum level. We could perhaps speculate that quantum level effects could multiply to produce macro-level effects. There has been some speculation that quantum processes could be important at the level of neuronal function in the brain. If so, perhaps a precognitive impression in the brain could be the 'cause' for a divergence of futures. Or any mental knife-edge decision to be made by O, depending on properties at the quantum level of a particular neuron, may act as the 'cause.'

Whichever way it might happen, the alternative results that may come from a single cause must *all* actually exist, not just one of them. At the quantum level this is the many-worlds interpretation. According to the Everett version of the many-worlds view (Everett was the originator of the many-worlds interpretation) the effect of this constant splitting of the universe with each quantum interaction is to create versions of the observer which gradually become more and more different to each other over time (Bryce De Witt, 1973, cited in Barbour, 1999, p. 225). In this way, quantum-level effects could indeed build up rapidly over time to create observers who are different (in different futures) on a macro-level. This could perhaps explain how a small cause (a quantum event) giving rise to a number of different small results could result eventually in macroscopically different futures, without violating causality as it operates within quantum processes. Speaking of each branch of the Everett many worlds 'tree', Julian Barbour says "there is nothing within the branch as such to indicate that it alone does not constitute the entire history of the universe" (Barbour, 1999, p. 225). In other words, there is a completely consistent causal chain of events in each branch of the tree and the answer to our question above is that observers going into different futures can indeed maintain a consistent account of their history in terms of cause and effect.

So, we could speculate that diverging futures, although they go their separate ways on a very small scale initially, build up over time and over many more such small divergences into futures which are macroscopically different. This could give us our original cause for 'bifurcations' but the 'bifurcations' in this picture would be a gross simplification of a vastly more complex branching tree. We should be aware also that some quantum processes are regarded as spontaneous and without a cause, so causality does not reign entirely supreme in our world. This may open up the possibility of branching futures without a cause.

Changing the Future—Two Times

There is another way of circumventing the Intervention Paradox, which involves introducing another time dimension. Because this is relevant to the general issue of 'changing the future', I want to consider this as well and kill two birds with one stone.

So far we have assumed that since there is only one time dimension if an individual has a precognitive perception then this means that in the future history of that individual there 'already' exists (from the viewpoint of the block model) the memory of that perception in that individual's mind. This was depicted in Figures 16.4, 16.5, and 16.6. The closed causal loop is 'already' in place. But a common view of time is that although the future may be set given the present circumstances if we change those conditions then we can change the course of the future. How could this be modelled?

The only way is to introduce another 'higher' time dimension within which our time dimension operates. That way our future could be one way at one time in the 'higher' time dimension and another way at a later time in the 'higher' time dimension. In terms of the block model this is depicted in Figure 16.10, where 3D space is represented as a point, our time (Time 1) is the horizontal axis and the 'higher' time (Time 2) is the vertical axis. Time 2 is a 5th dimension at right angles to Time 1 which is the 4th dimension.

The illustration shows how our precognition scenario from before could be laid out in this type of block universe. There are different ways it could be laid out and I show two of them. They have the common feature of circumventing the Intervention Paradox because both E and E_2 exist. As to which O is the real observer—they all are and they all feel that they are the only one. In one part of the block universe O is involved in a head-on collision. In another part due to a precognitive perception O avoids the head-on collision.

This two-time model has the advantage that we do not have to invent reasons why, in one future, O did not act on P to avoid E (as we had to for some types of the multiple futures model). In some types of the multiple futures model one of the futures has E in it even though O has precognition of it. But in the two-time model that need not be the case. If O has precognition O avoids E. If O does not have precognition O does not avoid E.

Remember when we tried to add extra time dimensions before to account for a 'moving present moment'. We ended up with an infinite regression of time dimensions. That is not happening in this case because we are using the block model—there is no 'moving present'. We have a 'static' model with two time dimensions only.

It may be objected that there is no evidence in physics for another time dimension. My reply would be that the nature of time is far from settled within physics and that I feel free to speculate to account for any data suggesting the existence of the type of precognition mentioned in the Intervention Paradox. Any such data can themselves be regarded as evidence and it is a normal process in science to generate hypotheses to account for data. Physicists have hypothesised the existence of many extra space dimensions to account for the phenomena of the universe (e.g., String Theory).

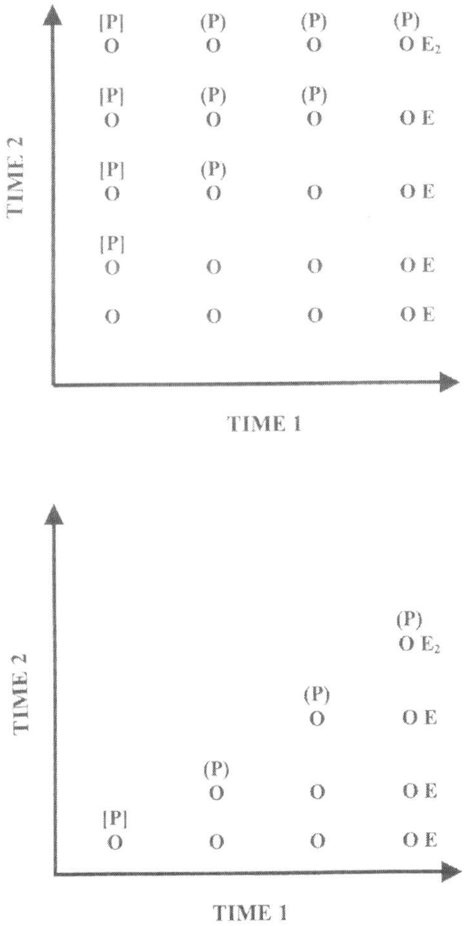

Figure 16.10. The Two-Time Block Universe.

If it is objected that we only experience one time dimension this is easily answered. There is no reason *per se* that human beings should be constructed to be aware of another time dimension—our awareness of time is a function of how our memories and mind are configured in the block universe. Human beings are not automatically aware of all the features and properties of the universe. We are not aware of the hypothesised extra space dimensions, but this does not mean they cannot exist.

A two-time block universe can resolve another issue about 'changing the future'. Intuitively it may be felt that precognition is a problem because it is changing a future which otherwise would have gone in a different direction. And in fact precognition 'changes the future' regardless of whether the precognitive impression is acted on or not. Why? Because the precognitive impression has changed the individual's mind. But in the two-time universe, changing the future is no problem. There can still be a future in which the individual's mind has no precognitive impression. That future remains unchanged. Then there is another future (a 'later' future in Time 2) in which there is a precognitive impression and that future is different. All this is shown in Figure 16.10.

Further thought reveals the possibility that both these alternative models of time, many-futures and 'two-times', may really be describing the same thing. Notice that in drawing the splitting of time into multiple futures in Figures 16.6, 16.7, 16.8, and 16.9, I have used the vertical axis, representing a fifth dimension. This could be regarded as equivalent to the time-2 dimension in Figure 16.10. So the splitting into multiple futures may be equivalent to extension into another time dimension. For example Figure 16.7 is equivalent to one of the alternatives I have drawn in Figure 16.10, if you join up the Os along the horizontal and diagonal in that alternative. I have shown this in Figure 16.11. Figure 16.7 depicts an interpretation of a splitting into two futures in which the precognitive impression from E is only carried forward into one of the futures (resulting in E_2) and the other future with E remains without the precognitive information. This is equivalent to the situation depicted in Figure 16.10 for a two-time universe.

Finally, I have not said anything about 'possible futures'. It has been speculated that precognition could be a process of accessing one of a number of 'possible futures', and action may be taken to select another future than the one precognised. What kind of status of existence would 'possible futures' have? From the point of view of the block universe model, I do not see any status for existence other than 'full-on' existence. There are no half-measures or 'ghostly realities'. But multiple futures (or 'many worlds') could fit the bill as possible futures perhaps. The qualification is that all the possible futures do actually exist.

They are 'possible' in the sense that you do not know which one you are going to end up in (and which your other 'split-off selves' are going to end up in). But perhaps if you had precognition from one future, you could take action to make sure you take an alternative path into another future.

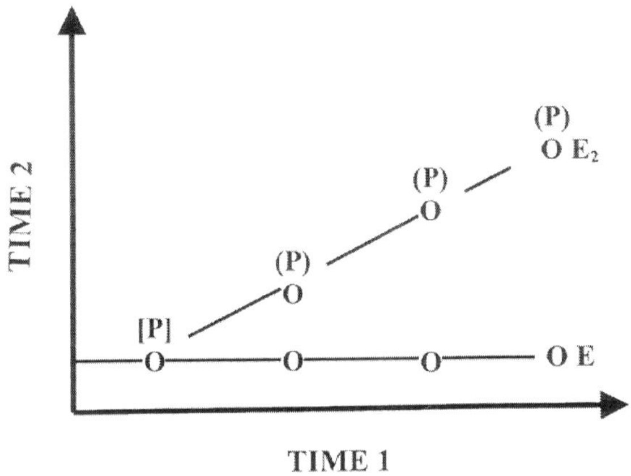

Figure 16.11. Two-times model equivalent to multiple-futures model.

I suppose another possibility is that the block universe structure incorporates (as a really existing structure) a kind of 'map', which approximates or mirrors the multiple futures. Precognition could then be accessing part of this map.

In summary, here are what I think are three assumptions contained within the Intervention Paradox and the response of a block universe model to them:

ASSUMPTIONS	BLOCK UNIVERSE MODEL
The future exists	Confirmed
There is only one future	Not necessarily
There is only one time dimension	Not necessarily

I hope I have shown that there are possible models of time in which the Intervention Paradox is not a paradox—it ain't necessarily so.

» References

Barbour, J. (1999). *The end of time.* London: Weidenfeld & Nicolson.

Chown, M. (2000). Random reality. *New Scientist*, February, 24-28.

Dainton, B. (2001). *Time and space.* Chesham, UK: Acumen.

Davies, P. (1995). *About time.* New York: Touchstone.

Davies, P. C. W., & Brown, J. R. (1986). *The ghost in the atom.* Cambridge: Cambridge University Press.

Delsemme, A. (1998). *Our cosmic origins.* Cambridge: Cambridge University Press.

Dunne, J. W. (1927/1958). *An experiment with time.* London: Faber and Faber.

Hawking, S. W. (1989). *A brief history of time.* Moorebank, NSW, Australia: Bantam.

Hawking, S. W. (2001). *The universe in a nutshell.* London: Bantam.

Irwin, H. J. (2004). *An introduction to parapsychology.* Jefferson, NC: McFarland.

Martin, J. L. (1988). *General relativity: A guide to its consequences for gravity and cosmology.* Chichester, UK: Ellis Horwood.

Smolin, L. (2004). Atoms of space and time. *Scientific American*, January, 56-65.

Tegmark, M., & Wheeler, J. A. (2001). 100 Years of quantum mysteries. *Scientific American*, February, 54-61.

Thalbourne, M. A. (2003). *A glossary of terms used in parapsychology (2nd ed.).* Charlottesville, VA: Puente.

Thorne, K. S. (1994). *Black holes and time warps: Einstein's outrageous legacy.* London: Picador.

Chapter 17

Social Psi and Parasociology[1]

ERIC OUELLET

In this chapter, a review of the sociologically-oriented literature dealing with the paranormal is presented to show that fundamental conceptual gaps exist in the social study of such phenomena. To provide at least some elements for filling these conceptual gaps, a discussion on the concepts of social psi, parasociology, and socially relevant anomalies is offered. Then, some methodological considerations are put forward on how to study the possibility of uncovering social psi events. Finally, a short case study of the Unidentified Flying Saucers (UFO) Wave of 1954 in France is proposed as an illustration of what parasociological research could offer to the study of anomalistic events.

The Social Study of Anomalistic Events

Social sciences in general and sociology in particular have a history of studying paranormal beliefs. From the early days, there was an intense interest in studying magical practices in the so-called 'primitive' societies. For instance, the classical French sociologist and anthropologist Marcel Mauss, nephew of Émile Durkheim, the founder of sociology, wrote a now classical piece on the topic in 1902, *Esquisse d'une théorie générale de la magie* (Mauss & Hubert, 1902), and it was followed by a series of other ethnographic studies on magic (Hubert & Mauss, 1929; Mauss, 1909, 1910). In all cases, however, Mauss never considered that there was anything

1. [This chapter was originally published as an article in *Australian Journal of Parapsychology* (2011, vol. 11[1], pp. 73-88). Permission to reprint has been granted by the author and the journal.—Editors.]

objective beyond the actual practice of magic. For him, magical practices were important to maintain social cohesion in pre-modern communities, and from that standpoint it is the socially shared belief in magic that remains the key to understanding the social effectiveness of magic. In other words, Mauss considered magic beliefs and magical practices as social facts suited to sociological analysis, to be studied without judging the actual content.

This detached and analytical attitude became the dominant one in sociology and anthropology with respect to the study of the paranormal. Overtime, similar topics were studied in a similar way like beliefs in astrology, New Age practices, parapsychology, reincarnation, UFOs, etc. (Goode, 2000). As the parapsychologists Caroline Watt and Richard Wiseman eloquently noted recently, "anthropologists and sociologists, in contrast, are not concerned with the ontological reality of paranormal beliefs. Rather, their interest focuses on the social and cultural function that such beliefs serve" (Watt & Wiseman, 2009, p. vii).

There are, however, some exceptions to this detached attitude among sociologists and anthropologists. There are some sociologists who actually took a position against the beliefs themselves as they studied them, such as Bridgstock (1982), and Eve and Harold (1986). Others, coming from the field of sociology of science analyzed the knowledge construction and discursive structure of parapsychology and other so-called 'pseudo-sciences' and found that in several instances it was not possible to draw any significant distinction between them and the socially sanctioned scientific knowledge and discourse (Collins & Pinch, 1979; 1982; Pinch, 1979). The influence of such research can be observed in more recent sociological research where the possibility of the ontological reality of paranormal phenomena is presented in a more positive way, as something at least open for discussion (Davies, 2007; Emmons, 1997; Goode, 2000).

In the field of anthropology, some like Winkelman (1982) have even attempted to introduce the parapsychological notion of psi into their research. Susan Greenwood, in a recent book (Greenwood, 2010), went as far as to practice magic in order to understand it better; something that Marcel Mauss would never have dreamed of doing. While others, like David Hess (1991), are more prudent, but work with the assumption that there are more than just beliefs involved in the paranormal.

There is one notable exception in the work of the French sociologist Bertrand Méheust (1978), who established a direct link between the narrative content of older science fiction stories (mid-nineteenth to early-twentieth century) and UFO reports from the second half of the twentieth century. For Méheust, there is more than just a belief in UFOs. According to him, there is an objective reality taking shape and form out of social representations.

This rapid tour of the status of the paranormal in the social sciences shows that this notion is a topic of study, but mostly looked at as belief systems. The analysis is rarely done by assuming the possibility that paranormal events may be real or have a degree of reality. However, it is important to point out that there is research conducted outside the social sciences that integrate the possibility of the paranormal into social-level analyses.

Early psychical researchers noted that telepathy appears to have a social component and could be 'contagious' (Warcollier, 1928, 1962). The psychoanalyst Carl Jung's interpretation of UFO sightings as a sign of social tensions, while being unclear about the ontological status of UFOs, is another early example (see Jung, 1958/1979, p.110). More recently, some group psychoanalysts also noted the possibility of group anomalistic effects (Powell, 1991).

The philosopher and theologian Theillard de Chardin (1959) developed a notion of a collective consciousness that he called the noosphere, where he noted that humanity seems to be developing a common and enlarged consciousness, and such consciousness seems to be shared through mystical processes. His ideas were expanded through the 'Global Consciousness Project' (mostly composed of parapsychologists and physicists), and lead to some interesting publications about global precognition of the 9/11 events (Nelson, 2002).

Some psychologists proposed that a population practicing Transcendental Meditation would produce measurable improvements in the quality of life for the whole population (Assimakis & Dillbeck, 1995; Dillbeck, 1990; Orme-Johnson et al., 1988). The neurophysiologist Allan Combs and psychologist Stanley Krippner (Combs & Krippner, 2008) developed the idea that there are subtle levels of connectivity between people so as to establish a form of collective consciousness akin to psi effects. The system theoretician Erwin Laszlo (2003) is well-known for developing the notion of psi-field, later renamed Akashic field, which represents a universal way for memory to be stored and used, including collective memory acting in non-local ways. The biologist and disciple of Laszlo, Attila Grandpierre (1997), went as far as proposing a 'Physics of Collective Consciousness'. Lastly, the biologist Rupert Sheldrake (1987) developed the concepts of 'morphic field' and 'morphic resonance' with obvious applications to the social sciences. He also applied these concepts to telepathy and other psi-related phenomena (Sheldrake, 1995, 1999, 2003). Although he did not explicitly connect social science applications and psi phenomena together, his concepts clearly offer such a possibility.

Although the above description does not pretend to constitute a fully comprehensive review of what has been done, it is broad enough to show two key tendencies. First, social scientists tend to ignore the possibility that anomalistic events may be more than mere make-belief. Second, a number of non-social scientists, with the lenses and implicit assumptions of their respective disciplines, have tried to understand the social dimension of anomalistic events. In light of such an intellectual context, it is clear that a common denominator is needed to bridge the intellectual resources of the social sciences and the rigorous research on anomalies.

Social Psi and Parasociology

A first necessary step to building such a bridge is to use some common concepts. The most obvious one is the notion of 'social psi' proposed by Dean Radin when discussing the Global Consciousness Project (Radin, 2006, p. 295). This notion implies that when many people are engaged in a common experience, they collectively contribute to, and are affected by, psi effects that have a dynamic of their own, irreducible to individual psi dynamics.

Beyond the Global Consciousness Project, the notion of a psi dynamic acting in ways independent of individual psi effects, and yet still emanating from the human mind, has some experimental bases in Batcheldor's research on group séance (Batcheldor, 1984; Reihart, 1994), in the famous Philip Experiment by Owen and Sparrow (1976), and more recently in collective remote viewing (Storm, 2003). Even earlier, is the notion of a collective gestalt proposed by Fodor to describe collective psi effects that he noted in his empirical research. He wrote of...

> ...death coaches driven by ghost drivers, and many other human, semi-human, and animal apparitions that in old English families are the heralds of impending death. They add 'body' to the Family Gestalt. The older the family, the stronger the Gestalt. Nebulous and ill-defined as it necessarily must be, the concept of the Family Gestalt unites a variety of ill-assorted phenomena of folklore with psychical research. (Fodor, 1959, p. 51)

Psi effects noted during all these empirical observations could be qualified as 'impersonal' in that they are interpreted as being made of an amalgamation of several individual intents and unconscious processes. As Scott Rogo noted:

> There is another psychological factor which comes into play during group PK practices which I felt Batcheldor fails to appreciate. As Maxwell and others have argued, group-PK effects are often directed by a collective mind created by the sitters. By joining forces, several people may actually form some sort of semiautonomous will or mind which directs the PK. Now this "entity" is not "owned" by or dependent upon any single group member. It is, on the contrary, semi-independent of all of them. A PK group, therefore, can overcome ownership inhibition because the PK is really being architectured by an ego-alien personality. (Rogo, 1978, pp. 195-196).

The experimental research on social psi remains limited in scope at the present time, but it offers more than mere inductive leads for further research. To look at psi effects as an 'impersonal' force is not fundamentally different in its explanatory structures from the classical definition of social institutions found in sociology. As Émile Durkheim wrote about social institutions in his classic book *The Rules of Sociological Method* (1895/1938), social institutions are "collective ways of action and thinking" (p. 52) that exist in their own right, outside the individuals, and which have a coercive influence over individuals' consciousness, acting from the outside in.

From both an empirical and conceptual point of view, the notion of social psi can be quite useful in understanding anomalies. This usefulness can be further expanded if it is properly integrated into a common approach using existing knowledge produced by the social sciences and parapsychology. It is in this context that 'parasociology' is defined as the study of social psi phenomena using sociological theories, models and methods. In other words, parasociology is to sociology what parapsychology is to psychology.

Socially Relevant Anomalies

Usually, one of the first methodological questions asked about any new way of looking at an object of study concerns its fundamental unit of analysis. Although the existence of social psi remains a central assumption of parasociology, psi is not directly observable (as parapsychologists have long discovered). The concept of psi is built on the notion that it is a manifestation of 'something' without observable cause-and-effect, where information is acquired, or matter altered, without using known means of information exchange or matter modification. There are no logical reasons to approach social psi differently.

Parapsychologists have devised two generic classes of objects for study of what seem to express the presence of psi effects, namely extra-sensory perception (ESP) and psychokinesis (PK). In both cases, they describe phenomena that are observable. In the case of parasociology, a proper research object would be something combining a socially observable event, in order to be a social object, which has some elements that are considered as defying conventional explanations, in order to be considered an anomaly. Hence, it is proposed, as a heuristic conceptual tool, the notion of the 'Socially Relevant Anomaly' (SRA) for the main unit of analysis for parasociology.

Under the concept of SRA, many phenomena can be studied, such as UFO waves, Marian apparitions, sea and lake monsters, etc. Such concept can also include phenomena that are more localized such as haunting and poltergeists, as part of the social life of a particular community.

This concept may differ on the surface from what some parapsychologists are used to; namely that psi effects are often no more than statistical anomalies such as those found in the Global Consciousness Project (GCP). But the aim of the GCP, concerned with collecting data about potential psi effects surrounding socially relevant events like 9/11, is not fundamentally different. Whether an anomaly becomes socially relevant *on its own*, or through the efforts of researchers looking for it, the end result is the same. Once such an anomaly is found, it becomes inseparable from the social event that was used to investigate the possible psi effect. Sociology has long accepted that the social world is made of complex adaptive systems constantly reacting and integrating experimenter's effects.

Parasociological Methodology—A First Approximation

Given that the social sciences in general have ignored the concept of psi in its analysis, and that the notion of social psi was mostly investigated by researchers outside the social sciences, a parasociological method remains to be established. In light of the parapsychological literature (particularly concerning spontaneous macro-psi effects like poltergeist phenomenon, also known as Recurrent Spontaneous Psychokinesis [RSPK]), and putting an emphasis, at least as a starting point, on SRA cases, a few methodological criteria can be proposed. To be sure, these criteria still remain broad and allow competing analyses to emerge without being able to determine firmly which one is the most accurate. However, it should be seen as a step forward in that it provides some rigor and discipline to parasociological analysis, and can open the way to finding additional criteria that would narrow down the number of possible competing analyses to explore the genesis of SRA events.

It is important to remember, however, that the aim of these criteria for investigating possible parasociological effects (or social psi effects) is to help circumvent the significant problem of the absence of observable causal relationships between the social and the physical realm (Shewmaker & Berenda, 1962), and the fundamental elusiveness of psi (Kennedy, 2001). They are:

1. The Observation System is Social

That the observation system is social means that the SRA received enough attention from the general public to be noted, usually through the mass media. This criterion is based on a number of findings and theories emerging from parapsychology. Psi phenomena are considered to be the outcome of emotional intentions and meaningful events (Heath, 2003; Von Lucadou & Zahradnik, 2004). The key question is, meaningful for whom? The visible range of psi phenomena can be a good indicator for assessing to whom the psi effect is directed—that is, to whom the information is directed. Hence, a social psi event would be directed to society at large.

2. Geographical Proximity

Geographical proximity means that SRA events are more likely to be observed in geographical areas around particularly meaningful actions or events that would carry an important emotional charge (Roll, 1972/2004; Roll & Persinger, 2001). This criterion is based on the same notion that psi effects are information directed to 'someone', and that 'someone's' attention needs to be grabbed where that 'someone' can be found.

3. Chronological Proximity

Chronological proximity means that SRA events are more likely to be observable around the same time as a meaningful social event. It can be a few days before or after a particularly meaningful action or event, and an important emotional charge would be present. But such an event is usually not known publicly at the time. In most cases, chronological proximity can only be noted after the fact. This criterion is based on a number of findings and theories from parapsychology where psi effects are believed to be emerging from the unconscious (Eisenbud, 1983), which is by definition not observable; like the feeling of 'something will happen' but not knowing what it is. At the social level, there are individual actions that will have a significant social impact, although their scope and nature cannot be known, but only 'felt' intuitively.

4. Symbolic Relationship

SRA events oftentimes carry symbolism that can be related to particularly meaningful actions or events that would carry an important emotional charge. Such symbolism, however, emerges from the unconscious and can be quite subtle in nature, oftentimes only comprehensible through lateral forms of thinking, and usually long after the fact. This criterion is based on a number of findings and theories emerging from parapsychology where psi effects are the outcome of unconscious processes, and that the language of the unconscious is fundamentally symbolic (Fodor, 1958; Von Lucadou & Zahradnik, 2004).

5. Internal Validity Through Mutually Reinforcing Criteria

The four criteria just described should reinforce each other, and thus emerges the fifth criterion. The yet unknown meaningful action or event that would carry an important emotional charge should be considered as being such (i.e., meaningful and emotional) by the people who are part of the social observation system. The symbolism found in the event can also be found in the chronology (e.g., a particular anniversary in the same timeframe), and the geography (e.g., name of the place where observations are made). The 'message' carried through symbolism is meaningful for the observation system if that system allows for the decipherment of that message.

A Short Illustration—The 1954 French UFO Wave

In 1954, France and many parts of Western Europe were experiencing a rash of UFO reports. These were reported in the news, and the authorities were contacted many times to investigate what was happening. A book that would become famous in ufological circles was written about the events by Aimé Michel (1958). It was clearly a social event stemming from a number of individual events that were considered anomalous. Hence, *the observation system is social.*

Donald A. Johnson (2009) reanalysed the data about the 1954 Wave using the UFOCAT catalogue, a commonly used UFO sightings catalogue created and maintained by the Chicago-based Center for UFO Studies, and noted that the number of UFO sightings for the year 1954 was 3,015, of which about 58% occurred in Europe. The Wave was in fact worldwide, but it had a particular peak in October with nearly a third of all sightings (961) in Europe. Of those 961 European cases, 750 occurred in the skies of France, with one particular peak on October 3, and another one on October 15, with about 80 sightings for each date. Although the wave was not exclusively a French UFO Wave, it is fair to say that it was indeed centred over France. Hence, *geographical proximity.*

When an anomalous phenomenon is reported in the general press, an accumulation of news clipping can create a sense that there is something going on. Then, one can expect that natural phenomena are reported as UFOs, and hoaxers feel compelled to do their part as well. This effect is well known in communication studies, referred to as the 'bandwagon effect'. The mass media can create a snow-ball effect, but also can bring about the demise of the phenomenon by expecting more and more until it cannot 'give' anymore, and then the press and its readership lose interest. This can lead to a quick decline in sightings. Hence, *chronological proximity.*

In spite of non-anomalous social dynamics at play, the real question is whether the noted anomalies can be described as expressions of social psi. Given that the causes of psi are non-observable, this raises a significant methodological challenge. However, a number of elements can be taken into consideration. The geography and chronology for the Wave's peak are certainly interesting. On October 10, 1954, between the French UFO sightings peaks of October 3 and October 15, the *Front de Libération Nationale* (FLN) was informally created by a small group of anti-colonial insurgents in Algeria. As we now know, the FLN waged an extensive political and armed struggle to free Algeria from French colonial rule. This led to a bitter conflict involving more than 500,000 French soldiers, countless victims in Algeria, and something that deeply shocked French society. Although the

French Army won on the ground (Zervoudakis, 2002), the FLN won the political battle based on the immorality of colonialism and, in 1962, Algeria gained its independence. Over one million French citizens of European descent living in Algeria sought refuge in France to avoid brutal retaliations from the newly formed Algerian authorities. The creation of the FLN in October 1954 was not known to the French public, and even the FLN terrorist actions of November 1954 did not appear to be anything threatening at the time (Pickles, 1961). Hence, the strength of the emotional affect to come provides some additional internal validity by linking the geographical and chronological proximities.

Some would argue that this could be a coincidence, though probably an unlikely one. UFO waves are relatively rare events, and when they have a clear peak period, they rarely last more than a few days. The events that the foundation of the FLN set in motion had a very deep political, social, and cultural impact on French society (Girardet, 1964)—such events are also very rare. Hence, there is a *symbolic relationship* between these events in the form of a 'synchronicity' of events in France and in Algeria. The notion of synchronicity developed by Jung seems here more appropriate than coincidence (Main, 1997, 2006). This view of UFO sightings as synchronistic events has been explored by Jung himself (1958/1979), where UFO sightings are construed as representations of the Self which manifest during times of distress, and especially when there is collective anxiety. Finally, this synchronicity can be construed in ways similar to the collective premonition of the very significant and tragic event of 9/11, which the Global Consciousness Project unravelled.

As noted above, in its present state the parasociological method is still young and might lead to competing interpretations of events. However, it opens the possibility of considering the case of the French UFO Wave of 1954 as an anomaly within an anomaly. This is no proof that we are facing something of a social psi-like nature (collective premonition), but it certainly provides further arguments for pursuing such a hypothesis. Furthermore, this possibility is consistent with the presence of psi-like anomalies within UFO events that have been noted through some systematic analysis of individual-level UFO experiences (Cassirer, 1988; Randles, 1983; Vallée, 1969), and at the local community level (Keel, 1975). Hence, in light of other research on the paranormal dimension of UFO events, this possible interpretation of the 1954 Wave is not groundless.

The greater question as to whether UFO events are themselves grand scale (social) psi events (Clark & Coleman, 1975; Viéroudy, 1977; 1978) remains unanswered at this time. Similarly, it is not possible to determine if UFO waves and social psi are interdependent phenomena (Philips, 1993; Spencer, 1994), or if they are eventuate through similar but unknown enabling conditions (Budden, 1995; Persinger, 1979, 1987, 1990; Persinger & Lafrenière, 1977).

CONCLUSION

This chapter has presented a few key concepts (such as social psi, the socially relevant anomaly [SRA], and parasociology) to establish bridges between the realms of social science and the rigorous study of anomalies found in parapsychology. As well, it proposed a few key methodological indicators and a short empirical illustration about how the study of social psi can be conducted in ways that are consistent with the findings of both the social sciences and parapsychology.

As the brief illustration on the 1954 French UFO Wave has shown, these concepts and methodologies have the potential to provide a wider understanding of psi effects. More research is obviously necessary to better ground a parasociological approach. Hence, the parasociological hypothesis remains, for the time being, just that, a hypothesis, but there are a number of other reasons that justify pursuing it. Not only do several studies in parapsychology point towards a collective dimension to psi, but also the social sciences suffer from a serious limitation in that they are only able to explain certain social phenomena, such as religious miracles, by ignoring the substance of the events (Claverie, 1990) and focusing only on the narrative and symbolic dimensions. Yet, this attitude found in the social sciences is not entirely true to the fundamental nature of what symbolism is. As Carl Jung once wrote,

> ...symbols, I must point out, do not occur solely in dreams. They appear in all kinds of psychic manifestations. There are symbolic thoughts and feelings, symbolic acts and situations. It often seems that even inanimate objects cooperate with the unconscious in the arrangements of symbolic patterns. There are numerous well-authenticated stories of clocks stopping at the moment of their owner's death...(Jung, 1964, p. 41)

A number of SRAs, such as UFO sightings, are also symbolic manifestations that cannot be described solely as subjective experiences, but are well-authenticated for also involving 'participation' from inanimate matter (Budden, 1998; Devereux, 1982; Poher & Vallée, 1975; UK Ministry of Defence, 2000), whether it be through synchronicity, extra-sensory perception or psychokinesis. Hence, to have a fuller understanding of symbolic relations in a given society—a key social science task—parapsychology *and* the social sciences may benefit from taking a wider perspective that includes social psi and an approach like parasociology.

» References

Assimakis, P. D., & Dillbeck, M. C. (1995). Time series analysis of improved quality of life in Canada: Social change, collective consciousness, and the TM-Sidhi program. *Psychological Reports*, *76*, 1171-1193.

Batcheldor, K. J. (1984). Contributions to the theory of PK induction from sitter-group work. *Journal of the American Society for Psychical Research*, *78*(2), 105-122.

Berger, P. L., & Luckmann, T. (1966). *The social construction of reality*. New York: Anchor Books.

Bridgstock, M. (1982). A sociological approach to fraud in science. *Journal of Sociology*, *18*, 364-383.

Budden, A. (1995). *UFOs psychic close encounters: The electromagnetic indictment.* London: Blandford.

Budden, A. (1998). *Electric Ufos: Fireballs, electromagnetics and abnormal states.* Darby, England: Diane Publishing.

Cassirer, M. (1988). *Parapsychology and the UFO*. London: Cassirer.

Clark, J., & Coleman, L. (1975). *The unidentified*. New York: Warner.

Claverie, E. (1990). La Vierge, le désordre, la critique: Les apparitions de la Vierge à l'âge de la science. *Terrain*, *14*, 60-75.

Collins, H. M. & Pinch, T. J. (1979). The construction of the paranormal: Nothing unscientific is happening. In R. Wallis (Ed.). *On the margins of science: The social construction of rejected knowledge* (pp. 237-269). *Sociological Review Monograph*, *27*. Keele, England: University of Keele.

Collins, H. M., & Pinch, T. (1982). *Frames of meaning: The construction of extraordinary science*. London: Routledge.

Combs, A., & Krippner, S. (2008). Collective consciousness and the social brain. *Journal of Consciousness Studies*, *15*(10-11), 264-276.

Davies, O. (2007). *The haunted: A social history of ghosts*. Basingstoke, England: Palgrave Macmillan.

Devereux, P. (1982). *Earthlights*. Wellingborough, England: Turnstone Press.

Dillbeck, M. C. (1990). Test of a field theory of consciousness and social change: Time series analysis of participation in the TM-Sidhi program and reduction of violent death in the U.S. *Social Indicators Research, 22,* 399-418.

Durkheim, É. (1895/1938). *The rules of sociological method.* Chicago, IL: University of Chicago Press.

Emmons, C. (1997). *At the threshold: UFOs, science and the New Age.* Mill Spring, KY: Wild Flower Press.

Eisenbud, J. (1983). *Parapsychology and the unconscious.* Berkeley, CA: North Atlantic Book.

Eve, R. A., & Harrold, F. B. (1986). Creationism, cult archaeology, and other pseudoscientific beliefs: A study of college students. *Youth & Society, 17,* 396-421.

Fodor, N. (1958). *On the trail of the poltergeist.* New York: Citadel Press.

Fodor, N. (1959). *The haunted mind: A psychoanalytical look at the supernatural.* New York: Garrett.

Girardet, R. (1964). *La crise militaire française 1945-1962: Aspects sociologiques et idéologiques.* Paris: Armand Colin.

Goode, E. (2000). *Paranormal beliefs: A sociological introduction.* Long Grove, IL: Waveland Press.

Grandpierre, A. (1997). The physics of collective consciousness. *The World Futures. The Journal of General Evolution, 48*(1-4), 23-56.

Greenwood, S. (2010). *The anthropology of magic.* Oxford, England: Berg Publishers.

Heath, P. R. (2003). *The PK zone: A cross-cultural review of psychokinesis.* Bloomington, IN: iUniverse.

Hess, D. J. (1991). *Spirits and scientists: Ideology, spiritism and Brazilian culture.* University Park, PA: Penn State University Press.

Hubert, H. & Mauss, M. (1929). Étude sommaire de la représentation du temps dans la religion et la magie. *Travaux de l'Année sociologique* (pp. 189-229). Paris: Félix Alcan.

Johnson, D. A. (2009). The Worldwide UFO wave of 1954. Retrieved June 3, 2011, from: http://www.ufoinfo.com/onthisday/papers/Worldwide%20 UFO%20Wave%20of%201954.pdf.

Jung, C. G. (1958/1979). *Flying saucers: A modern myth of things seen in the skies.* Princeton, NJ: Princeton University Press.

Jung, C. (1964). *Man and his symbols.* New York: Dell.

Keel, J. (1975). *The mothman prophecies.* New York: Tor.

Kennedy, J. E. (2001). Why psi is so elusive? A review and proposed model. *Journal of Parapsychology, 65*, 219-246.

Laszlo, E. (2003). *The connectivity hypothesis: Foundations of an integral science of quantum, cosmos, life, and consciousness*. Albany: State University of New York Press.

Main, R. (1997). *Jung on synchronicity and the paranormal.* Princeton, NJ: Princeton University Press.

Main R. (2006). The social significance of synchronicity. *Psychoanalysis, Culture and Society, 11*, 36-53.

Mauss, M. (1909). L'origine des pouvoirs magiques dans les sociétés australiennes. Étude analytique et critique de documents ethnographiques. In M. Mauss & H. Hubert (Eds.) *Mélanges d'histoire des religions* (pp. 131-187). Paris: Félix Alcan.

Mauss, M. (1910). La démonologie et la magie en Chine. *Année sociologique, 11*: 227-233.

Mauss, M., & Hubert, H. (1902). Esquisse d'une théorie générale de la magie. *Année Sociologique, 7*, 1-146.

Méheust, B. (1978). *Science-fiction et soucoupes volantes*. Paris: Mercure de France.

Michel, A. (1958). *Flying saucer and the straight-line mystery*. New York: Criterion Books.

Nelson, R. D. (2002). Coherent consciousness and reduced randomness: Correlations on September 11, 2001. *Journal of Scientific Exploration, 16*, 549-570.

Orme-Johnson, D. W., Alexander, C. N., Davies, J. L., Chandler, H. M., & Larimore, W. E. (1988). International peace project in the Middle East: The effects of the Maharishi technology of the unified field. *Journal of Conflict Resolution, 32*(4), 776-812.

Owen, I. M., & Sparrow, M. (1976). *Conjuring up Philip: An adventure in psychokinesis*. Toronto, Canada: Harper & Row.

Persinger, M. A. (1979). ELF field mediation in spontaneous PSI events: direct information transfer or conditioned elicitation? *Psychoenergetic Systems, 3*, 155-169.

Persinger, M. A. (1987). Spontaneous telepathic experiences from Phantasms of the Living and low global geomagnetic activity. *Journal of the American Society for Psychical Research, 81*, 23-36.

Persinger, M. A. (1990). The tectonic strain theory as an explanation for UFO phenomena: A nontechnical review of the research, 1970-1990. *Journal of UFO Studies, 2*, 105-137.

Persinger, M. A., & Lafrenière, G. F. (1977). *Space-time transients and unusual events*. Chicago, IL: Nelson-Hall.

Phillips, K. (1993). The psycho-sociology of ufology. In D. Barclay & T. M. Barclay (Eds.). *UFO: The final answer?* (pp. 40-64). London: Blandford.

Pickles, D. (1961). The seven-year struggle in Algeria: Retrospect and prospect. *The World Today*, *17*(11), 479-489.

Pinch, T. (1979). Normal explanations of the paranormal: The demarcation problem and fraud in parapsychology. *Social Studies of Science*, *9*(3), 329-348.

Poher, C. & Vallée, J. (1975). Basic patterns in UFO observations. *American Institute of Aeronautics and Astronautic Annual Conference*, Pasadena, California, 20-22 January.

Powell, A. (1991). Matrix, mind and matter: From the internal to the eternal. *Group Analysis*, *24*(3), 299-322.

Radin, D. *Entangled minds: Extrasensory experiences in a quantum reality*. New York: Paraview.

Randles, J. (1983). *UFO reality: A critical look at the physical evidence*. London: R. Hale.

Reihart, P. B. (1994). PK induction: An extension of Batcheldor approach. *Journal of the American Society for Psychical Research*, *88*, 137-145.

Rogo, S. (1978). *Minds and motion: The riddle of psychokinesis*. New York: Taplinger Publishing.

Roll, W. G. (1972/2004). *The poltergeist*. New York: Paraview.

Roll, W. G., & Persinger, M. A. (2001). Poltergeists and hauntings. In J. Houran & R. Lange (Eds.). *Hauntings and poltergeists: Multidisciplinary perspectives (pp.* 123-163*)*. Jefferson, NJ: McFarland & Company.

Sheldrake, R. (1987). *The presence of the past*. New York: Bantam.

Sheldrake, R. (1995). *Seven experiments that could change the world: A do-it-yourself guide to revolutionary science*. New York: Riverhead.

Sheldrake, R. (1999). *Dogs that know when their owners are coming home: And other unexplained powers of animals*. New York: Crown.

Sheldrake, R. (2003). *The sense of being stared at: And other aspects of the extended mind*. New York: Crown.

Shewmaker, K. L., & Berenda, C. W. (1962). Science and the problem of psi. *Philosophy of Science*, *29*(2), 195-203.

Spencer, J. (1994). *Gifts of the gods? Are UFOs alien visitors or psychic phenomena?* London: Virgin Books.

Storm, L. (2003). Remote viewing by committee: RV using a multiple-agent/multiple-percipient design. *Journal of Parapsychology, 67*, 325-342.

Teilhard de Chardin, P. (1959). *The phenomenon of man*. New York: Harper & Row.

UK Ministry of Defence. (2000). *Unidentified Aerial Phenomena (UAP) in the UK Air Defence Region* (Scientific & Technical Memorandum 55/2/00). London: Ministry of Defence.

Vallée, J. (1969). *Passport to Magonia: From folklore to flying saucers*. Chicago, IL: Regnery.

Viéroudy, P. (1977). *Ces ovnis qui annoncent le surhomme*. Paris: Tchou.

Viéroudy, P. (1978). Vagues d'Ovnis et psi collectif. *Revue de Parapsychologie* 6 (July). [http://gerp.free.fr/PA06_VAGUEOVNIS.htm]

Von Lucadou, W., & Zahradnik, F. (2004). Predictions of the Model of Pragmatic Information about RSPK. In *Proceedings of the 47th Annual Convention of the Parapsychological Association* (pp. 99-112). Petaluma, CA: Parapsychological Association.

Warcollier, R. (1928). L'accord télépathique. *Revue métapsychique, 4*, 286-306.

Warcollier, R. (1962). La contagion mentale au groupe télépathique. *Revue métapsychique*, (sole issue of 1962), 37-43.

Watt, C. & R. Wiseman. (2009). Foreword. In H. J. Irwin (Ed.). *The psychology of paranormal belief: A researcher's handbook* (pp. *vii-viii*). Hatfield, England: University of Hertfordshire.

Winkelman, M. (1982). Magic: A theoretical reassessment. *Current Anthropology, 23*(1), 37-66.

Zervoudakis, A. (2002). A case of successful pacification. In M. Alexander & J. F. V. Keiger (Eds.). *France and the Algerian War: Strategy, operations and diplomacy* (pp. 54-64). London: Frank Cass.

PART 4: CONCLUSION

Chapter 18

In Search of Psi: Destination Unknown or Destination Nowhere?

Adam J. Rock and Lance Storm

This anthology has provided various contemporary views concerning ESP, PK, and postmortem survival. So, in the final analysis, what can one say about psi? Does the study of psi have a future? In this chapter we will examine the key issues raised in the preceding chapters that impinge on our search for psi.

Extra-Sensory Perception, Psychokinesis, and Survival

Challenging the Prevailing Paradigm

In Chapter 1 (Imagery Cultivation and Extra-Sensory Perception), the editors, Lance Storm and Adam Rock, challenged the *noise-reduction model*, which is typically considered the prevailing paradigm in parapsychology. Indeed, Storm and Rock argued that the parapsychological preoccupation with the signal-to-noise ratio "has created a paradigmatic block that has blinkered parapsychologists to the degree that they have not entertained alternative, even antithetical, methodologies that encourage fantasy, imagination and other active cognitive processes" (p. 3). Surveying the literature concerning shamanism, Storm and Rock emphasised the link between mental imagery cultivation and ESP, arguing that a shamanic journey to the 'lower world' is a journey into the unconscious, which is a well-spring of psi-images.

Thomas Kuhn (Kuhn, 1962), the distinguished philosopher of science, was particularly interested in the development of scientific knowledge. Kuhn contended that science approaches a topic like psi from the perspective of the dominant paradigm—in our case, the noise reduction model—until sufficient evidence for an alternative paradigm is amassed. Storm and Rock (2009) referred to their new paradigm as the *Imagery Cultivation* (IC) model. This model has received empirical support (see Storm & Rock, 2009, 2011), but it is still early days (see the Appendix for Chapter 1, pp. 29-31).

We suggest that, if any science is to have a future, parapsychologists must look back at the past—they must consider our ancestral beginnings, and observe how psi and related phenomena have been treated in the past, which is reflected in the cultures of today that still adhere to the practices that hail from that historic and pre-historic past. We speak of the relevant indigenous cultures, and it is from the shamanic traditions in particular that we draw our ideas for the IC model. We do not expect that we have unearthed anything world-shattering (and certainly our *shamanic-like* model is an extremely modest approximation of the real thing), and we are yet a long way from providing a solution to one of parapsychology's ongoing dilemmas (namely, a consistent and reliable proof of psi), but readers must also realise that we are attempting to serve that objective of heeding and giving obeisance to our distant ancestors whose voices are echoed today in those extant indigenous groups. We will have more to say on that point later in this chapter.

Parapsychology Goes 'Neuronal'

In Chapter 2 (Telepathy as a Process Mediated by Quantum Teleportation Between Remote Neurons), Richard Blumenthal highlighted the important contributions that physics and neuroscience can potentially make to our understanding of the nature of psi. Indeed, Blumenthal's neuronal theory underscores the 'slippery' dynamics of telepathy, and Blumenthal explains why neuroscientific studies are preferable to experiments that quantify "success and failure on the basis of exact or nearly exact content replication from agent to percipient" (p. 45). In this context we might consider Laughlin and Rock's (2013) contention that:

> At this point in the history of social and behavioral science a discussion of methods that is not grounded upon both a neuroepistemology and a neurophenomenology soon will not be worth considering. Why? Because

> it is now known that the consciousness is a function of the internal organization of the brain. (p. 261)

Perhaps the same can be said for parapsychology. Are we standing at the forefront of the emergence of a *neuro*parapsychology? Here we remind the reader of Blumethal's contention that, "the neuronal view of telepathy not only helps to explain its mechanics, but also its imperfection as a method of communication" (p. 41).

It is also noteworthy that, throughout his chapter, Blumenthal implicitly suggested that telepathy might conform to the natural laws of the prevailing scientific world-view. This is consistent with what Neppe, in Chapter 13, referred to as a 'minimalistic parapsychology' approach. Moreover, Blumenthal's outline of a neuronal research prospectus suggests that there is a place for further research into parapsychological phenomena that may extend our understanding of the world.

'Slippery' Psi Information Sources

In Chapter 3 (The Possible Role of Psychokinesis in Place Memory), Pamela Rae Heath suggested that psychokinesis might aid in the creation of some cases of "place memory". Heath argued that living beings leave an ostensibly energetic imprint in the environment (i.e., *place memories*), which might be retrievable paranormally by some individuals. Heath's chapter highlights the difficulty in isolating place memory from other sources of ESP. In fact, Heath emphasised that, "we currently have no way of distinguishing between sources of ESP information—whether the environment, living minds, the future, the past, discarnate sources, or even other dimensions of existence" (p. 55).

This ambiguity is an enduring methodological problem for parapsychologists. For example, parapsychologists have been unable to design an experiment that distinguishes between the possible sources of mediums' anomalous information about deceased individuals. Indeed, the results of mediumship studies (e.g., Beischel, Boccuzzi, Biuso, & Rock, 2012) continue to support multiple hypotheses including: (a) the super-psi or super-ESP hypothesis (see, for example, Braude, 2003); (b) the psychic reservoir hypothesis (i.e., somewhere in the universe there exists a cosmic store of all information since the commencement of time, and mediums obtain their anomalous information from this cosmic store rather than the deceased; see Fontana, 2005), and (c) survival of consciousness (i.e., postmortem continuation of at least aspects of one's individual consciousness or personality). We do, however, appreciate Heath's other comment that the intentional creation of place memories may be possible. If we learn how to do this in a controlled way, we may also be able to distinguish two categorically different psi sources—the one as the sole source of the (psychometric) 'reading' at the 'site' of the place memory *per se*, and the other as efficacious normal and paranormal psi sources (e.g., living and discarnate agencies, and even other inanimate material sources).

Altered States and Anomalous Motor Activity

In Chapter 4 (Human Levitation), Simon Harvey-Wilson examined the link between altered states of consciousness (ASCs) and human levitation:

> The capacity to enter certain ASCs, therefore, seems to be the most likely explanation for such a small percentage of the groups' members levitating, despite many of them having the same spiritual beliefs and regularly carrying out the same physical activities. (p. 79)

Similarly, in Chapter 1 of the current anthology, Storm and Rock (citing Bem & Honorton, 1994, p. 5) noted that, "Historically, psi has often been associated with meditation, hypnosis, dreaming, and other naturally occurring or deliberately induced altered states of consciousness."

Arguably one of the limitations of the field of parapsychology is its inability to operationalize the altered states of consciousness construct. Tart (1975) argued that terms such as *states of consciousness* and *altered states of consciousness* "have come to be used too loosely, to mean whatever is on one's mind at the moment" (p. 5). Consequently, Tart (1975) developed the term *discrete states of consciousness* (d-SoC) in an attempt to rectify this terminological problem. A d-SoC may be defined as:

> a unique configuration or system of psychological structures or subsystems...that maintains its integrity or identity as a recognizable system in spite of variations in input from the environment and in spite of various (small) changes in the subsystems. (p. 62)

Pekala (1985) asserted that, from Tart's (1975) perspective, it is the pattern or configuration of these different structures or subsystems (i.e., phenomenological elements) that constitutes a d-SoC. In contrast, Singer (1977) argued that it is the intensity of these different elements, rather than the pattern, that defines a d-SoC. Pekala and Wenger (1983) synthesized the essential aspects of Tart's (1975) and Singer's (1977) conceptions to define a SoC as the "particular intensity and pattern of associated phenomenological parameters that characterise one's subjective experience during a given time" (pp. 252-253).

What does Harvey-Wilson offer or suggest when he relates ASCs to levitation—the latter surely being the most compelling evidence yet of PK? Given the well-established psychosomatic link between the mind/brain complex and the rest of the body, one answer to that question is that, probably, it should be no great leap of the imagination to realise that levitation is merely another form of PK, for the same 'PK-rules' apply, whether we speak of *micro-PK* or *macro-PK* (see Chapter 13 for definitions). We stress that the only other problem we have with levitation, beyond its causal factors, is its rarity. Of course it behoves parapsychologists, and even interested anthropologists (since many of the most intriguing levitation claims come from the more remote and relatively inaccessible parts of the world), to search high and low for such evidence. For too long we have endured the false claims of charlatans, but perhaps one day, in a controlled environment like the humble university laboratory, we may yet find substance to these claims.

Further Down the 'Slippery' Slope

In Chapter 5 (A Discussion of the Evidence that Personal Consciousness Persists after Death with Special Reference to Poltergeist Phenomena), William Roll examined the notion of survival after death with regards to poltergeist phenomena. Roll considered two interpretations of recurrent spontaneous psychokinesis (RSPK); RSPK is due to PK by living people or discarnate entities. He concluded that, "there is little evidence that RSPK is due to spirits other than the corporeal spirit of the RSPK agent" (p. 88). Roll's interpretation of RSPK is parsimonious relative to the discarnate entity interpretation and, therefore, does not violate Occam's Razor because it does not posit the existence of an afterlife.

Subsequently, Roll critically appraised various assumptions about personality that, in his view, have influenced survival research. Roll asserted that:

> If we are to conclude that a medium or a rebirth subject incorporates the personality of someone deceased, we have to be certain that the

> information about the deceased could not have been derived by ESP from the minds of living survivors or from physical sources, such as obituaries. (p. 92)

Roll's sentiment echoes a theme from Chapter 3 whereby Heath lamented the ostensible inability of the scientific method to distinguish between the various sources of ESP information. Clearly, stringent controls are needed to eliminate competing sources of ESP.

If, however, scientists take psi seriously, then this ambiguity problematises the notion of 'blinding' participants and experimenters. For example, let us recall the picture identification task used to test the IC Model described by Storm and Rock (see Chapter 1 of the current anthology). Imagine that a participant is handed a target picture necessarily wrapped in aluminium foil, and then concealed in an envelope, to avoid sensory leakage. The target picture is randomly selected from a set of four pictures that were randomly selected from a pool of picture sets. The participant focuses on the concealed target picture and is, subsequently, presented the set of four pictures (i.e., the target and three decoys). The task for the participant is to identify the target from amongst the four pictures. By parapsychological convention, we might describe success in this task as evidence of clairvoyance, thus ruling out telepathy. For if the experimenter is 'blind' to which picture is the target, then the participant cannot use ESP to 'read' the mind of the experimenter to ensure a 'hit' on the task. However, someone was, by necessity, required to randomly select the target and wrap it in aluminium foil. Consequently, the participant might telepathically communicate with the distant target-setter.

Alternatively, a psi-gifted participant might obtain information about the target picture precognitively from the future moment when they are debriefed regarding which picture is the target and which are the decoys. Of course, if the participant is never debriefed, then this may eliminate precognition as an ESP information source; however, telepathic communication with the target-setter remains an issue. And while we are still theorising, might we not propose that correct target identification could be based on picture-to-brain (or brain-to-brain) perturbations, which are surely PK effects since only physical systems are involved?

It is for the very reason of this variety of 'explanations' of the psi process that we must consider the discourses we use in describing psi as either ESP or PK. Clearly, there is a great discursive dependence on thinking about psi phenomena *as if* they might yield to normal rules, and all we need do is fill in the gaps so that psi might conform. We see the very instance of this approach when Roll, by the evidence, shifts the causal source from the 'other' world to this world. In Storm and Rock's IC model, a similar discursive shift in thinking may be possible—perhaps we should not think of paranormal (i.e., telepathic, clairvoyant, or precognitive) picture identification as *identifying* a picture, since the word *identification* suggests a kind of 'seeing' that might not be seeing at all. Reading between the lines, Roll's chapter suggests we steer a new course in our thinking.

The Prognosis for Survival

In Chapter 6 (Is the Scientific Investigation of Postmortem Survival an Anachronism? The Demise of the Survival Hypothesis), Harvey Irwin addressed the scientific merit (or lack thereof) of the survival hypothesis. Irwin's contention that the survival hypothesis occupies a "central conceptual position in parapsychology" (p. 106) is perhaps an overstatement. Indeed, Beischel and Rock (2009) noted that parapsychological research is focused on the 'big Four' (i.e., telepathy, clairvoyance, precognition, and PK), with only "an occasional nod toward survival and afterlife topics" (Braud, 2005, p. 40). This suggests that survival topics are peripheral to parapsychology and, therefore, exert far less influence on the discipline than Irwin would have us believe.

Irwin asserted that survival is an untestable hypothesis. He reviewed séance phenomena, NDEs, OBEs, poltergeist and apparitional experiences, and reincarnation experiences and concluded that "the operation of such processes" as super-ESP are "impossible to exclude" and, thus, the aforementioned phenomena "cannot be conclusive for the survival hypothesis" (p. 100). Again, we observe the scientific method's apparent inability to distinguish between psi information sources.

In Chapter 7 (The Demise of the Survival Hypothesis, or the Errors of Harvey Irwin?), Montague Keen critically appraised the previous chapter by Harvey Irwin. Keen stated that, "I accept that the evidence from mediumistic communications for survival of consciousness is not conclusive; but it is the only viable alternative to a super-psi explanation which for most informed observers would be considered less persuasive" (p. 111).

There are at least two issues here that warrant our attention. First, one may, of course, wonder on what grounds Keen feels qualified to speak on behalf of "most informed observers" (p. 111). Second, Keen makes little attempt to justify *why* he considers the survival of consciousness explanation to be superior to the super-psi explanation in the case of ostensible mediumistic communication. Keen briefly cited three cases, which he stated are all "…in theory susceptible to an explanation which confines a psychic faculty to the living mind, but only by postulating the most improbable, speculative and evidentially unsupported extensions of psi" (p. 110). However, Keen does not elaborate on these "most improbable, speculative and evidentially unsupported extensions of psi" (p. 110).

What do we conclude? Who of the two, Irwin or Keen, presents the best argument? Unfortunately, neither settles the debate, and many have tried since, and made little or no progress (for example, see the essays in Storm & Thalbourne, 2006). The real issue? The evidence, or what passes as evidence! If afterlife research is to have a future, whichever discipline chooses to take it on, researchers must break new ground, and venture into new territory. How that is to be accomplished is up to the researchers of that same future.

Belief and Culture

Believe It or Not

In Chapter 8 (Scepticism and Credulity), Peter Delin gave us a thoughtful and thought-provoking essay on a dichotomy that he traces back to the scientific thinking of the seventeenth century. Since that time, the beginning of the so-called Age of Enlightenment, many of us have laboured under the apprehension that superstition and myth have been put to rest once and for all. In fact, paranormal ideas, claims, and experiences still prevail; they have not been swept under the carpet; nor have they escaped the scrutiny of the scientific eye. Delin tells us that scientific thinking is a minority view, and is essentially skeptical. The vast majority, however, takes a credulous attitude towards natural phenomena no matter how unbelievable those phenomena may be to the conventional scientist. On the strength of that difference, the skeptical scientist and the credulous believer might be considered discernable and distinguishable types, but Delin points out that those who are sceptical, and those who are credulous, so long as they represent extreme forms of their respective types, are very similar psychologically. Thus Delin's words concerning the typical scientist are worth repeating here in full:

> One might have thought that to the scientist, striving to obtain an objective view of the universe, a piece of evidence for a proposition would have a status independent of his previous opinions, but this is not so. What he in fact does is to weight the evidence according to his current

> state of belief about the phenomenon or theory it relates to. In other words he attaches a certain probability to the phenomenon or theory, and demands stronger or weaker evidence in accordance with this a priori probability. (p. 123)

Might we not substitute the word "scientist" with the words 'paranormal believer'?

The best evidence to date that supports Delin's proposition is the recent trend of applying Bayesian statistical analysis to the psi databases. If ever there was an opportunity for the subjective factor to enter into science as Delin describes it, it is this Bayesian chimera born of statistical mind-play. There is now a steady stream of papers that draw attention to this problem in parapsychology (see for example, Bem, Utts, & Johnson, 2011; Tressoldi, 2011; Wagenmakers, Wetzels, Borsboom, & van der Maas, 2011). As statistician Jessica Utts has stated: "Bayesian methods utilize [a] 'degree of belief' interpretation of probability to model all uncertainty" (Utts, Norris, Suess, & Johnson, 2010, p. 2). On Bayesian statistics, statistician Andrew Gelman (2008) puts it this way: "as scientists we should be concerned with objective knowledge rather than subjective belief" (p. 2).

Beyond Belief?

Why do some people believe in the paranormal, whereas others do not? Parapsychologists of distinction, such as Dr. Dean Radin, argue that there is overwhelming evidence supporting the existence of psi; however, the debate still rages between proponents of psi and skeptics. In Chapter 9 (The John Edward Phenomenon: "I Want to Believe"), Sue-Ellen Kjeldal applied contemporary decision-making theory to belief in the paranormal. In this chapter, Kjeldal posited numerous variables that might contribute to skeptical and non-skeptical mental sets. Kjeldal appeared to suggest implicitly that perhaps the rational cognitive processes of skeptics are, relative to believers, less affected by variables such as time pressures, ambiguous circumstances, overload of information, and visceral factors. Thus, the skeptic is able to maintain his or her ideological position regarding psi despite these environment stressors, whereas for the believer, intuitive cognitive processes are induced.

It is also important to consider personality traits (e.g., sheep-goat trait, positive schizotypy, transliminality) when examining belief in psi (see, for example, Irwin, 2009; Jinks, 2011). One might consider, for instance, positive schizotypy, which is characterised by unusual perceptual experiences and magical thinking.

Perhaps the effect of positive schizotypy on one's assessment of the validity of a John Edward public performance is mediated by information processing on the 'Cognitive Continuum'. In other words, one might hypothesise that high positive schizotypy enhances intuition which, in turn, facilitates a positive appraisal of John Edward.

Schizotypal or not, we must also draw attention to the fact that suspicion or doubts (i.e., skepticism) about the alleged paranormal skills of psychics like John Edward may be "biologically unnatural, and only possible in a culture where connections must carry the burden of proof before becoming fact" (Bressan, 2002, p. 30), whereas paranormal belief is a "byproduct" of the normal genetically determined process of searching for "bonds, pattern, [and] meaning" (p. 30). Let us suppose that, for…

> …some number of skeptics, their reasoning ability may be developed to the point where they feel compelled to rationalise their experiences more than is required in the circumstances. This line of argument would also explain why believers more readily resort to paranormal explanations of their coincidences—not only are they philosophically bound to accept paranormal explanations; they are also engaging in a basic human function. (Moore, Thalbourne, & Storm, 2010, p. 162)

This line of argument is a sobering thought for those bent on a sceptical view on all-and-sundry putatively paranormal phenomena, but we must bear in mind Delin's views (just discussed), which critique the hard-line approach taken by scientists on both sides of the debate.

Appropriately, we now move on to a closer consideration of the differences between believers and skeptics, or as parapsychologist Gertrude Schmeidler (1943, 1945) called them, 'sheep' and 'goats', respectively.

Of 'Sheep' and 'Goats'

In Chapter 10 (The Australian Sheep-Goat Scale: Development and Empirical Findings), Michael Thalbourne discussed a self-report measure, The Australian Sheep-Goat Scale (ASGS), that he developed to quantify belief in psi and scepticism. The development of the ASGS is bound-up with a philosophical problem referred to as the fallacy of reification. Reification is variously referred to as the fallacy of misplaced concreteness (Whitehead, 1946) and substantialisation or hypostatisation of abstracta (Reichenbach, 1951), and may be defined as "the accidental error of mistaking the abstract for the concrete" (Whitehead, 1946, p. 66). That is to say, reification consists of confusing an abstract noun (e.g., the 'sheep-goat' trait) with a thing-like entity (Reichenbach, 1951). If one were to attempt to, for example, use a self-report measure (e.g., the ASGS) to quantify an ostensible trait or disposition, then one would be attributing numerical values to a nonmaterial variable and, thus, committing the fallacy of reification. Rather than implicitly conceptualising the sheep-goat trait as a thing-like entity via quantification, it may be more accurate to regard it as a process or function. Of course, this issue of reification also applies to a great deal of orthodox psychology.

While previous studies of the ASGS have typically focused on, for example, personality correlates of the ASGS, and whether the ASGS predicts success on ESP and PK tasks, phenomenological correlates of the ASGS have been neglected. Indeed, this trend is widespread within parapsychology where attention is focused on replicating psi effects rather than investigating the phenomenological process underlying the psi effect.

Phenomenology "is a term that refers to a philosophy, a research approach, and, in a more general way, the study of experience" (Pekala & Cardeña, 2000, p. 59). The phenomenological investigator examines "the way things are experienced by the experiencer, and...how events are integrated into a dynamic, meaningful experience" (Hanson & Klimo, 1998, p. 286). With this type of analysis, the researcher is able to identify the essential aspects of the experience under investigation (Fischer, 1998). Previous phenomenological research has investigated, for example, the experience of meditation (Gifford-May & Thompson, 1994), being unconditionally loved (Matsu-Pissot, 1998), and shamanic journeying (Rock, 2006). It is noteworthy that phenomenological research may be qualitative (e.g., Gifford-May & Thompson, 1994) or quantitative (e.g., Pekala, 1991), and numerous scholars argue that these two approaches are reconcilable and may inform one another (e.g., Abussabha & Woelfel, 2003; Burke-Johnson & Onwuegbuzie, 2004; Crawford, Weever, Rutter, Sensky, & Tyrer, 2002; Foss & Ellefsen, 2002).

In recent times, parapsychologists (e.g., Rock & Storm, 2010) have emphasised the value of a phenomenological analysis of psi. Indeed, the future of psi research may be a methodological pluralism whereby qualitative and quantitative approaches are used in a complementary or integrated fashion in order to investigate the phenomenological processes that may underlie psi phenomena. Thus, as the field of parapsychology matures one might expect a shift away from studies aimed at the mere replication of a psi effect towards attempts to understand the nature of psi.

Parapsychology Goes 'Tribal'

In Chapter 11, (Pueblo Parapsychology: Psi and the Longbody from the Southwest Indian Perspective), Bryan J. Williams introduced us to the concept of the *longbody*, which denotes "the larger web that connects people, object, and place across space and time" (p. 183). Throughout this chapter Williams hinted at the contribution anthropology can make to parapsychology. This is particularly salient in light of the fact that one of the limitations of laboratory-based parapsychology is that the experimental procedures used often lack ecological validity—"the extent to which research can be generalized to real-life situations" (Jackson, 2009, p. 418). The danger is of course that, as psi researchers design and implement increasingly rigorous experimental protocols, these protocols become progressively poorer approximations of real-life situations. We thus run the risk of 'killing-off' any psi that might be associated with natural purposeful activity. By conducting field investigations of tribal psi we can begin to restore ecological validity.

However, there is a 'flip-side' to this coin. That is, enhancing ecological validity results in less stringent methodological controls. A poorly controlled study has the potential to allow extraneous variables to become confounding variables. In other words, the internal reliability of the study is compromised so that one can no longer ascertain whether or not the psi effects are due to the experimental manipulation of an independent variable (e.g., being administered a Ganzfeld stimulus or no stimulus). Clearly, a more measured approach is to implement rigorous experimental protocols that exhibit high internal validity coupled with naturalistic or participant observation that demonstrates high ecological validity. The results of these approaches could be triangulated to enhance our understanding of psi.

In Chapter 12 (Reincarnation Beliefs of the Gumini People of the Simbu Province of Papua New Guinea), Joan D. Johnstone described the results of her field research with the Guminis. Interestingly, the objective of Johnstone's research was to examine eating habits. However, she was serendipitously exposed to the Guminis' beliefs concerning reincarnation and spirits. Johnstone emphasised that the Guminis lived in a 'world full of spirits' (p. 214), and this world is "closely integrated into the lives of the living" (p. 214). Here one is reminded of shamanic cultures where the shaman "journeys" to the "spirit world" in order to serve members of his or her social group (Rock & Krippner, 2011). Thus, the ontological reality of spirits is an integral component of shamanic and Gumini culture.

It is clear that Johnstone's rich data could only be obtained through the researcher's lived experience of a particular cultural milieu; the laboratory is simply not going to 'cut it' in this instance. Thus, Johnstone's chapter underscores the value of naturalistic observation as a methodology that has been largely ignored by parapsychologists. Indeed, as we saw in Chapter 11, parapsychology's preoccupation with internal validity comes at the cost of generalisability to the real world.

Psi and Science

Minimalism, Radicalism, and the Scientific Enterprise

In Chapter 13 (Why Parapsychology is Amongst the Most Important of the Sciences), Vernon E. Neppe argued that parapsychology is one of the most crucial areas of scientific enquiry, because the implications of its findings have far-reaching consequences for almost all other sciences. Neppe referred to the *minimalistic parapsychology* approach whereby scientists are able to accommodate the implications of parapsychology within the current scientific worldview. In contrast, according to Neppe, the implications of a *radical parapsychological* approach are that scientists would be required to "fundamentally modify their world-view" (p. 232). The adoption of a radical parapsychological approach suggests that science is in the midst of what Thomas Kuhn referred to as a "crisis" stage that precedes a "resolution" stage in the context of the development of science. However, a critical mass of evidence is required to catalyse a scientific revolution. Thus, the question becomes "What constitutes evidence?" As we stated in our Preface to this anthology, "It is unclear just what it would take to convince skeptics that psi exists, but they would wonder what it would take to convince believers that the opposite is true" (p. xi). Moreover, as we observed in Chapter 14, the dominant ideology plays a crucial role regarding how one interprets "evidence".

Neppe emphasised the rigorous nature of parapsychological methodology which uses what he referred to as a "no holds barred approach"; that is, "it goes flat out to ensure the greatest rigidity and scrutiny of the data" (p. 235). For example, while double-blind protocols appear to be the standard in orthodox experimental psychology, parapsychologists are known to implement triple-blind (e.g., Beischel & Schwartz, 2007), and quintuple-blind protocols (e.g., Beischel, Boccuzzi, Biuso, & Rock, 2012). Methodological rigor is paramount in parapsychology because, to paraphrase Dean Radin loosely, when one investigates psi everything is an extraneous variable; even the Moon (D. I. Radin, personal communication, 2005).

Despite the rigors of parapsychological research, one might wonder, with some justification, to what extent the scientific method is equipped to investigate psi. For example, as we have already pointed out, we are not aware of the results of a single study in the field of survival that allows one to distinguish between living agent psi and survival psi information sources. Moreover, if one takes the super-ESP hypothesis seriously and, thus, entertains the possibility that psi has no limits, then is it logically possible to design, for example, a mediumship protocol that eliminates all non-survival explanations of anomalous information reception?

Putting the Psi Into Science

In Chapter 14 (Examining the Evidence for Psi in the Context of Scientific Revolution), Hannah Jenkins provided a Kuhnian analysis of the current evidence for psi. Jenkins tackled head-on the philosophical problem science has with parapsychology. She targeted the entire epistemological venture that is collectively maintained by the various disciplines—a worldview with which scientists identify, resulting in a marginalisation of parapsychology. Jenkins argued that mainstream science dismisses psi on ideological grounds rather than on the basis of an assessment of the evidence for or against psi. In other words, the representation of the evidence for psi in mainstream academic texts is "based on a *belief* of what is possible in this world, as dictated by what is currently known of the workings of it" (p. 251). In the social world, what passes for "reality" is determined by the power elite or, to use Marxist terminology, the bourgeois (ruling class). These power structures are reproduced in the scientific disciplines where mainstream academia determines what constitutes the dominant discourse and, thus "legitimate" subject matter and modes of inquiry.

In 2001, Jenkins argued that we have entered the "crisis stage" of a scientific revolution whereby the growing evidence for psi is proving problematic for the current scientific worldview. It is noteworthy, however, that 10 years later Jenkins lamented that, "The results of parapsychology are *still* as invisible in mainstream philosophical discussions and there are only a handful of philosophers working on how to develop an understanding of psi effects" (p. 258). Jenkins speculated that the growing demands of academic capitalism (academics forced to engage in market-like behaviour) may precipitate the development of "commercially viable applications for psi" (p. 258), which may, in turn, promote a wider acceptance of the existence of psi. However, Jenkins neglected to mention the various obstacles to harnessing psi for commercial gain. First, psi is not well understood by parapsychologists. The often-mentioned "source of psi" problem is a case in point. In addition, Michael Thalbourne's (Thalbourne, 2004) theory of psychopraxia, which collapses the ESP-PK dichotomy, calls into question parapsychology's current taxonomy of psi processes (see also, Storm & Thalbourne, 2000).[1] We emphasise the fact that the important *discursive* claims made by Thalbourne in regard to psychopraxia may help pave a new way forward for parapsychology, for it may be that the entrenched *discourse* currently used by parapsychologists is actually misleading us. Second, psi effect sizes are typically small and, thus, difficult to detect with statistical procedures. Finally, given the 'slippery' nature of psi it is difficult to identify genuinely psi-conducive stimulus conditions. It is arguable that the transition from a Kuhnian 'crisis' stage to a 'solution' stage will not occur until these obstacles are overcome.

Higher Dimensions and a Human Telescope

In Chapter 15 (Looking into Higher Dimensions: Research with Joseph McMoneagle), Ronald Bryan proposed a model for elementary particles that he attempted to empirically verify by soliciting the help of a world-class remote viewer: Joseph McMoneagle. Bryan was unable to determine the nature of the anomalous information transfer that occurred when McMoneagle engaged in Remote Viewing (RV). If McMoneagle was genuinely using RV then clearly the psi process is clairvoyance. However, it is possible that McMoneagle was using telepathy to "read" Bryan's mind in order to obtain answers to questions such as "Look deep inside an electron. What do you see?" As we know, Bryan himself would not need to have any conscious knowledge of even his more speculative notions about the sub-atomic world, for telepathy would work just the same. Alternatively, McMoneagle may have used precognition to view the future event in which Bryan debriefed him regarding the model for elementary particles. Again, we are faced with the "source of psi information" problem (see for example Chapters 3, 5 and 6 in the current anthology).

Bryan stated that if McMoneagle's perceptions are veridical, then the "implications for nuclear physics are astounding" (p. 286). More specifically, according to Bryan, if McMoneagle's reports are accurate, then he is able to

1. Psychopraxia Theory has received empirical support (see, for example, Storm, 2010).

access information in a way that violates Heisenberg's Uncertainty Principle. If nuclear physicists are able to accommodate McMoneagle's findings within their current scientific worldview, then this is consistent with what Neppe (see Chapter 13 in the current anthology) dubbed the *minimalistic parapsychology* approach. Alternatively, a *radical parapsychological* approach becomes necessary if McMoneagle's observations necessitate a radical reconsideration of nuclear physics' current worldview. In any event, McMoneagle's ostensibly anomalous information reception contributes to evidence in support of psi and, thus, exacerbates what Jenkins (see Chapter 14 in the current anthology) observed as the current Kuhnian "crisis" stage.

'Razors', 'Blocks', and the Structure of the Universe

In Chapter 16 (Avoiding the Intervention Paradox), Colin Mitchell addressed the Intervention Paradox, which, as we discovered, states that precognitive information might lead one to 'change the future' and, thus, eliminate the future event that caused the precognitive impression. Mitchell argued that it is possible to construct models of the universe, alternatively referred to as "block-space-time", the "B-series", and the "block universe", that allow one to dissolve the Intervention Paradox.

One might argue that Mitchell's *block model* lacks parsimony because, for example, in one scenario he needed to 'invent' an additional time dimension in order to dissolve the Intervention Paradox. However, perhaps the structure of the universe does, in fact, consist of two temporal dimensions and, thus, Mitchell's block model is a more accurate representation of the universe than the commonly accepted four-dimensional space-time construct. At any rate, Mitchell's ability to eliminate the "*logical contradiction* between the event E being both there and not there" (p. 301) provides implicit support for the existence of precognition and, thus, for a dimension that extends beyond the reality we sanction as normal. Mitchell's chapter highlights the important contributions that can arise from disciplines such as philosophy and physics in our search for psi.

Parapsychology Goes 'Social'

In Chapter 17 (Social Psi and Parasociology), Eric Ouellet defined *parasociology* as "the study of social psi phenomena using sociological theories, models and methods" (p. 319). The subject matter of parasociology is what Ouellet referred to as *socially relevant anomalies* (SRAs), which include Marian apparitions, UFO waves, and cryptozoological entities (e.g., the Loch Ness monster, Sasquatch). Essentially, once a psi phenomenon becomes a socially relevant event it may be conceptualised as *social psi*. Given parapsychology's preoccupation with laboratory experimentation and the resultant issues around ecological validity, parasociology's focus on SRAs and, thus, a form of psi that is associated with natural purposeful activity, may provide new insights regarding the nature of psi phenomena. Here one is, of course, reminded of Williams' "Pueblo parapsychology" and Johnstone's field research with the Guminis (see Chapter 11 and 12 of the current anthology, respectively).

Ouellet's proposal that the investigation of psi phenomena might form the basis of a new sub-discipline (in this case in sociology) is not an isolated one. For instance, the journal *Paranthropology* publishes articles focusing on anthropological approaches to psi. The disadvantage is that in each of these aforementioned disciplines, psi research is relegated to the "fringe" and is often perceived as an illegitimate "scientific" inquiry.

Here one is reminded of the field of shamanic studies, which is scattered across the disciplines of, for example, anthropology, psychology, and even cognitive science. In 2010 at the *17th International Transpersonal Conference* in Moscow, the distinguished psychologist Stanley Krippner proposed that a future generation of academics might witness the fragmented field of shamanic studies coalesce in to a unified discipline that might be referred to as *shamanology*. Krippner's musings could be readily applied to psi research. Indeed, perhaps the study of psi will one day be integrated to form a unified discipline where variants of psi (e.g., social psi) will constitute sub-disciplines under the umbrella of *psi-ology*.

CONCLUSION

Psi is certainly a 'slippery' phenomenon. In this anthology we have seen parapsychologists struggle to use the scientific method in order to distinguish between the various psi information sources. We have discovered that if one takes the full ramifications of psi seriously, then it appears impossible to design a genuinely 'blinded' experimental protocol. We have also observed that some parapsychologists consider certain psi hypotheses (e.g., the survival hypothesis) untestable (see the chapters by Harvey Irwin and Montague Keen).

After re-hashing this coroner's report, the reader may well wonder if psi research has a future. But that would be jumping the gun. We must not forget that we stand at the forefront of many exciting developments within the field. For instance, we introduced a new paradigm (the IC Model), based on psi-conducive active cognitive processes, that may one day supersede the prevailing paradigm that focuses on mental quietude (see Chapter 1). Moreover, Richard Blumenthal's neuronal research prospectus for parapsychology suggests alternative explanatory models for telepathy.

Apart from the main arguments set out in the chapters by Pamela Rae Heath, Simon Harvey-Wilson, and William Roll, we have also come across subtler references to the ways in which parapsychologists are discourse-dependent. As good as their science is, they must allow themselves the freedom to consider the language they are using when they describe and depict paranormal processes. This will surely open doors to a science that sees psi in a new light. Such advice, and such a vision for the future, is exemplified in those chapters. We have just said that certain psi hypotheses, such as life after death, are untestable, and it is clear that ESP and PK are ambiguous and mercurial in nature, but even with the survival question, a more satisfactory answer may only come once the question is reframed.

And then we come to another big issue in parapsychology; one that has dogged the field since its inception, though in fact it traces back to the dawn of time—belief vs. skepticism. In truth, Peter Delin gives skeptics a taste of their own medicine, but Sue-Ellen Kjeldal and Michael Thalbourne take things a step further. Both Kjeldal and Thalbourne show us how different are the mind-sets of believers and skeptics. Can we beat some sense into either one, or both of them? That all depends on how hard-wired belief or non-belief is. But we also have a choice in the matter—choice that must be tempered with reason and open-mindedness.

Then there are the chapters by Hannah Jenkins and Ronald Bryan. First, Jenkins targets a ruling scientific paradigm that has brushed parapsychology to the side, and she gives some philosophical insight into this problem. In turn, Bryan provides a solid basis for Jenkins's philosophical finger-pointing, thus entitling believers to do a little eyebrow-raising of their own.

Finally, we considered the social issues pertaining to parapsychology. Bryan Williams's Pueblo parapsychology, Joan Johnstone's observations in New Guinea, and Eric Ouellet's 'parasociology', offer new ways forward that promise to free parapsychology from the straightjacket of laboratory experimentation and enhance the external validity of the resultant findings. It seems that there remains a vast distance to traverse on our journey in search of psi, but it is a journey with a destination.

» References

Abussabha, R., & Woelfel, M. L. (2003). Qualitative vs quantitative methods: Two opposites that make a perfect match. *Journal of the American Dietetic Association, 103,* 566-569.

Beischel, J., Boccuzzi, M., Biuso, M., & Rock, A. J. (2012). Anomalous information reception by certified research mediums. *2012 Bial Foundation Symposium*, Casa do Médico, Portugal.

Beischel, J., & Rock, A. J. (2009). Addressing the survival vs. psi debate through process-focused mediumship research. *Journal of Parapsychology, 73*, 71-90.

Beischel, J., & Schwartz, G. E. (2007). Anomalous information reception by research mediums demonstrated using a novel triple-blind protocol. *EXPLORE: The Journal of Science & Healing, 3*, 23–27.

Bem, D. J., & Honorton, C. (1994). Does psi exist? Replicable evidence for an anomalous process of information transfer. *Psychological Bulletin, 115*, 4-18.

Bem, D. J., Utts, J., & Johnson, W. O. (2011). Must psychologists change the way they analyze their data? *Journal of Personality and Social Psychology, 101*(4), 716-719.

Braud, W. (2005). The farther reaches of psi research: Future choices and possibilities. In M. A. Thalbourne & L. Storm (Eds.), *Parapsychology in the twenty-first century: Essays on the future of psychical research* (pp. 38–62). Jefferson, NC: McFarland.

Braude, S. E. (2003). *Immortal remains: The evidence for life after death*. Lanham, MD: Rowman & Littlefield.

Bressan, P. (2002). The connection between random sequences, everyday coincidences, and belief in the paranormal. *Applied Cognitive Psychology, 16*(1), 17-34.

Burke-Johnson, R., & Onwuegbuzie, A. J. (2004). Mixed methods research: A research paradigm whose time has come. *Educational Researcher, 33,* 14-26.

Crawford, M. J., Weever, T., Rutter, D., Sensky, T., & Tyrer, P. (2002). Evaluating new treatments to psychiatry: The potential value of combining qualitative and quantitative research methods. *International Review of Psychiatry, 14,* 6-11.

Fischer, C. (1998). Being angry revealed as self-deceptive protest: An empirical phenomenological analysis. In R. Valle, (Ed.), *Phenomenological inquiry in psychology* (pp. 111-122). New York: Plenum Press.

Fontana, D. (2005). *Is there an afterlife? A comprehensive overview of the evidence.* Oakland, CA: O books.

Foss, C., & Ellefsen, B. (2002). The value of combining qualitative and quantitative approaches in nursing research by means of method triangulation. *Journal of Advanced Nursing, 20,* 242-248.

Gelman, A. (2008). Objections to Bayesian statistics. Retrieved, March 13, 2011, from: *ba.stat.cmu.edu/journal/2008/vol03/issue03/gelman.pdf.*

Gifford-May, D., & Thompson, N. (1994). "Deep states" of meditation: Phenomenological reports of experience. *Journal of Transpersonal Psychology, 26,* 117-138.

Hanson, D., & Klimo, J. (1998). Toward a phenomenology of synchronicity. In R. Valle, (Ed.), *Phenomenological inquiry in psychology* (pp. 281-307). New York: Plenum Press.

Irwin, H. J. (2009). *The psychology of paranormal belief: A researcher's handbook.* Hatfield, UK: University of Hertfordshire Press.

Jackson, S. L. (2009). *Research methods and statistics: A critical thinking approach* (3rd ed.). Belmont, CS: Wadsworth.

Jinks, T. (2011). *An introduction to the psychology of paranormal belief and experience.* Jefferson, NC: McFarland.

Kuhn, T. S. (1962). *The structure of scientific revolutions.* Chicago: University of Chicago Press.

Laughlin, C. D., & Rock, A. J. (2013). Neurophenomenology: Enhancing the experimental and cross-cultural study of brain and experience. In H. Friedman & G. Hartelius (Eds.), *The Wiley-Blackwell handbook of transpersonal psychology* (p. 261-280). Oxford, UK: Wiley-Blackwell.

Matsu-Pissot, C. (1998). On the experience of being unconditionally loved. In R. Valle, (Ed.), *Phenomenological inquiry in psychology* (pp. 321-334). New York: Plenum Press.

Moore, T., Thalbourne, M. A., & Storm, L. (2010). A study on coincidences. *Australian Journal of Parapsychology, 10,* 154-176.

Pekala, R. J. (1985). A psychophenomenological approach to mapping and diagramming states of consciousness. *Journal of Religion and Psychical Research, 8,* 199-214.

Pekala, R. J. (1991). *Quantifying consciousness: An empirical approach.* New York: Plenum Press.

Pekala, R. J., & Cardeña, E. (2000). Methodological issues in the study of altered states of consciousness and anomalous experiences. In E. Cardeña, S. J. Lynn, & S. Krippner, (Eds.), *Varieties of anomalous experience: Examining the scientific evidence* (pp. 47-82). Washington, DC: American Psychological Association.

Pekala, R. J., & Wenger, C. F. (1983). Retrospective phenomenological assessment: Mapping consciousness in reference to specific stimulus conditions. *Journal of Mind and Behavior, 4*, 247-274.

Reichenbach, H. (1951). *The rise of scientific philosophy*. Berkeley: University of California Press.

Rock, A. (2006). Phenomenological analysis of experimentally induced visual mental imagery associated with shamanic journeying to the lower world. *International Journal of Transpersonal Studies, 25*, 45-55.

Rock, A. J., & Krippner, S. (2011). *Demystifying shamans and their world: A multi-disciplinary study*. Exeter, UK: Imprint Academic.

Rock, A. J., & Storm, L. (2010). Shamanic-like journeying and psi: II. Mental boundaries, phenomenology, and the picture-identification task. *Australian Journal of Parapsychology, 10*(1), 41-68.

Schmeidler, G. R. (1943). Predicting good and bad scores in a clairvoyance experiment: A preliminary report. *Journal of the American Society for Psychical Research, 37*, 103-110.

Schmeidler, G. R. (1945). Separating the sheep from the goats. *Journal of the American Society for Psychical Research, 39*, 47-49.

Singer, J. L. (1977). Ongoing thought: The normative baseline for alternate states of consciousness. In N. E. Zinberg (Ed.), *Alternate states of consciousness* (pp. 89-120). New York: Free Press.

Storm, L. (2010). *A parapsychological investigation of the theory of psychopraxia*. Saarbrücken, Germany: Lambert Academic Publishing.

Storm, L., & Rock, A. J. (2009). Shamanic-like journeying and psi: I. Imagery cultivation, paranormal belief, and the picture-identification task. *Australian Journal of Parapsychology, 9*(2), 165-191.

Storm, L., & Rock, A. J. (2011). *Shamanism and psi: Imagery cultivation as an alternative to the ganzfeld protocol*. Adelaide, SA: AIPR, Inc.

Storm, L., & Thalbourne, M. A. (2000). A paradigm shift away from the ESP-PK dichotomy: The theory of psychopraxia. *Journal of Parapsychology, 64*, 279-300.

Storm, L., & Thalbourne, M. A. (Eds.). (2006). *The survival of human consciousness: Essays on the possibility of life after death*. Jefferson, NC: McFarland.

Tart, C. T. (1975). *States of consciousness.* New York: Dutton.

Thalbourne, M. A. (2004). *The common thread between ESP and PK.* New York: The Parapsychology Foundation.

Tressoldi, P. E. (2011). Extraordinary claims require extraordinary evidence: The case of non-local perception, a classical and Bayesian review of evidences. *Frontiers in Psychology, 2*(117), 1-5.

Utts, J., Norris, M., Suess, E., & Johnson, W. (2010). The strength of evidence versus the power of belief: Are we all Bayesians? Plenary Paper, *8th International Conference of Teaching Statistics.*

Wagenmakers, E. J., Wetzels, R., Borsboom, D., & van der Maas, H. (2011). Why psychologists must change the way they analyze their data: The case of psi: Comment on Bem (2011). *Journal of Personality and Social Psychology, 100*, 426-432.

Whitehead, A. N. (1946). *Science and the modern world* (2nd ed.). London: Cambridge University Press.

About the Contributors

Richard Blumenthal is a counsellor, lecturer, author and inventor. He holds a Master of Science Degree in Counseling from Long Island University (New York, USA). He is a New York State Licensed Mental Health Counsellor and is certified by the National Board for Certified Counselors. Mr. Blumenthal earned a certificate from the Institute for Rational-Emotive Therapy in New York City, where he studied with Dr. Albert Ellis, as well as a certificate from the Milton Erickson Institute of Hypnosis of New York, where he studied with Dr. Daniel Araoz. He is the author of numerous peer-reviewed articles in such publications as *Medical Hypnoanalysis, The British Journal of Clinical and Experimental Hypnosis, The Journal of Human Behavior and Learning, The International Journal of Psychosomatics*, and the *Australian Journal of Parapsychology*. He co-authored (with Dr. Joseph A. Despres) the book *Major Decisions: A Guide to College Majors* (1992). He is the originator of Rational Suggestion Therapy and inventor of "Method and apparatus to create and induce a self-created hypnosis" for which he was awarded United States patent 6,565,504.

Ronald Bryan PhD is professor emeritus of the Department of Physics and Astronomy at Texas A&M University, College Station, Texas, USA. His field of expertise is theory of elementary particles and medium energy physics. Chapter 15 in this anthology is Bryan's first (but not last) publication in the physics of parapsychology. Currently he is participating in an experiment to see if a person using only his/her mind might be able to reverse the direction in which a single electron is spinning.

Peter S. Delin was educated at Midhurst Grammar School in Sussex, UK. At school, an interest in mental magic (conjuring) became transmuted into an interest in the putative phenomena being simulated in that activity. This led to a relationship with the Society for Psychical Research in London, and for a number of years he carried out investigations on behalf of that organisation. He won a scholarship to Corpus Christi College, Oxford, where he obtained his BA in Psychology and Philosophy, followed by an MA. He then moved to the University of Adelaide, where he taught and researched in the Psychology Department for forty-two years, obtaining his PhD along the way, while becoming, among other things a frequent contributor to research and public discussion on parapsychology. In the course of this extended discussion, he became less interested in paranormal phenomena *per se*, and more interested in the difficulty that mainstream scientists had in remaining scientific when confronted by scientifically controversial claims. 'Scepticism and Credulity' (see Chapter 8 above) was one paper reflecting that interest.

Pamela Rae Heath has doctorate degrees in medicine and parapsychology and worked as an anaesthesiologist for nearly thirty years before retiring from medical practice to write full time. She has over 16 years experience performing haunting investigations, and has appeared as a paranormal expert on multiple television and radio shows. Dr. Heath is currently a member of the Parapsychological Association, the Society for Scientific Exploration, and the Society for Psychical Research. Her books include *The PK Zone* (2003), *Suicide: What Really Happens in the Afterlife?* (2006); *Handbook to the Afterlife* (2006); and *Mind-Matter Interaction: A Review of Historical Reports, Theory & Research* (2011). (For more information, please visit her website at www.pamelaheath.com.)

Harvey J. Irwin (PhD, 1978) has an international reputation in research on the psychology of parapsychological experiences and paranormal beliefs. His publications include over a hundred papers in academic journals and four books, including the highly praised and widely used text *An Introduction to Parapsychology* (2007). Dr. Irwin was a member of the School of Psychology, University of New England (Armidale, NSW, Australia) for over 30 years, teaching a variety of courses from parapsychology to psychopathology, and serving as Head of the School for some years. Since his formal retirement from academia in 2003 he has remained active in research and remains an Adjunct Research Fellow in his former university. In 2002 the Parapsychological Association accorded Dr. Irwin its Outstanding Research Contribution Award in recognition of his empirical and theoretical work in parapsychology over 25 years.

Hannah Jenkins completed an undergraduate degree (Honours) in Philosophy at the University of Sydney, NSW, Australia, where her interest in parapsychological literature developed at the university's Fisher Library. She eventually went on to complete a Masters (UNSW) and PhD (University of Tasmania). Both degrees focused on the evidence for psi and philosophy of science. She is now working on a book called *Secret Science* which aims to entice a wider audience into the intriguing world of psi research. She has also founded the self-funded, research institute Quality Investigative Psi Projects (QIPP). The research aims of QIPP can be found at www.qipp.com.au.

Joan D. Johnstone is a retired independent scholar and researcher, formerly a lecturer and researcher at the University of Sydney. She practiced as an anthropologist and conducted fieldwork in 1962 in New Guinea where she "serendipitously" observed the reincarnation beliefs (amongst other anthropological issues) of the Gumini People of the Simbu Province in Papua New Guinea. Dr. Johnstone points out that she did not go to Gumini expressly to study reincarnation beliefs—what she learnt was a consequence of her interaction with the local people during her six months of research into their dietary habits.

Montague Keen (1925-2004) thought of himself as a positive agnostic. He started a writing career as a journalist at the age of 16. Intrigued by claims made by Irish clairvoyant, Tom Corbett and some famous UK mediums, he became convinced that there was some truth to psychic prediction. He joined the Scole group of physical mediums, and regarded the cross-correspondence cases as the best evidence for the survival of human personality. He also investigated crop circles and macro-PK phenomena. He was a member of the Society for Psychical Research (SPR) for nearly 60 years, became an SPR council member in 1992, and was the SPR's Honorary Media Officer. Having a long-time interest in survival, he was instrumental in forming the SPR's Survival Research Committee, and was elected its first Secretary. He published many books and parapsychological papers, including *The Scole Report*. He passed away on January 15, 2004.

Sue-Ellen Kjeldal, PhD, is Senior Lecturer in Organisational Behaviour at the New England Business School at the University of New England (Armidale, NSW, Australia). Her areas of research interest cover organisational behaviour and change, psychological research methods, evolutionary psychology and consumer behaviour. In 2005, she gave a lecture at the *Fifth International Conference on Knowledge, Culture and Change in Organisations* in Greece.

Colin Mitchell completed a BA at the University of Adelaide in 1984. He has studied at the University of Adelaide (South Australia), Flinders University (South Australia), and Melbourne University (Victoria). His fields of study include philosophy and physics. Currently, he is working as a Research Assistant in the Department of Philosophy, University of Adelaide. Colin Mitchell has had a long-term interest in parapsychology; he has investigated many claims of parapsychological phenomena Australia-wide, and he has contributed to the *Australian Journal of Parapsychology*, of which he is a member of the editorial board in the capacity of specialist consultant.

Vernon M. Neppe is Director of the Pacific Neuropsychiatric Institute (Seattle, Washington, USA). He is also Adjunct Professor of Psychiatry and Human Behavior, St. Louis University School of Medicine (St. Louis, Missouri, USA), and Clinical Faculty (and formerly Director, Division of Neuropsychiatry), University of Washington (Seattle, Washington). He has acted as a referee for more than a dozen scientific journals, and has over 200 publications. His published books include *The Psychology of Déjà Vu* (1983), *Innovative Psychopharmacotherapy* (1989), and *Cry the Beloved Mind* (1999). He has served as guest editor of the *Journal of Clinical Psychiatry* and founding editor of a South African scientific journal and on the editorial boards of several others. He is a specialist consultant for the *Australian Journal of Parapsychology*. His major research areas include developing neuropsychiatric instruments and inventories, evaluating anomalistic psychology and pharmacological areas.

Eric Ouellet is an Associate Professor with the Department of Defence Studies at the Royal Military College of Canada, but physically located at the Canadian Forces College (Canada's Staff and War College) in Toronto. He has a PhD in sociology from York University, Canada. His research focuses on the social dimension of psi effects, and how the concept psi could be used in sociological research. Lately, his research has emphasized the UFO phenomenon, as it is an anomaly more amenable to sociological analysis. Eric Ouellet is also a consultant for the not-for-profit organization Paranormal Studies and Investigations Canada (PSICAN) and maintains a blog where he explores informally various ideas about psi and social dynamics at: http://parasociology.blogspot.com.

Dean Radin has an MS in electrical engineering and PhD (1979) in educational psychology, both from the University of Illinois (Champaign-Urbana, USA). For sixteen years, he conducted experimental studies of psi phenomena in academia and industry, including appointments at Princeton University, University of Edinburgh, University of Nevada, and SRI International. Prior to becoming President of the Boundary Institute, he was in charge of a psi research program at Interval Research Corporation in Palo Alto, California. Dr. Radin was elected President of the Parapsychological Association, an affiliate of the American Association for the Advancement of Science (AAAS), in 1988, 1993, and 1998.

His research awards include the Parapsychological Association's 1996 Outstanding Achievement Award and the Rhine Research Center's Alexander Imich Award for advances in experimental parapsychology, also presented in 1996. He has appeared in dozens of television programs, most recently PBS's Closer To Truth. Radin is author of the award-winning books, *The Conscious Universe* (1997), and *Entangled Minds* (2006), and is author or co-author of over 175 peer-reviewed journal articles and technical reports. He is currently Senior Scientist at the Institute of Noetic Sciences in Petaluma, California.

Adam J. Rock has a BA (Honours) and PhD in Psychology (2005) from Charles Sturt University Sydney (NSW, Australia), and is currently a lecturer in psychology at the University of New England (Armidale, NSW, Australia). He is President of the Australian Institute of Parapsychological Research, Inc., a Founding International Board Member of the International Transpersonal Association, a Special Topics Editor and Editorial Board Member of the *International Journal of Transpersonal Studies*, an Associate Editor of *Anthropology of Consciousness*, and a specialist consultant for the *Australian Journal of Parapsychology*. He has published dozens of scholarly articles in prestigious academic journals such as the *Journal of Scientific Exploration*, *Transpersonal Psychology Review*, and the *Journal of Parapsychology*. He is the author of *Constructivism and Shamanic Experiences* (2010). In addition, he co-authored (with Dr. Lance Storm) *Shamanism and Psi* (2011) and co-authored (with Professor Stanley Krippner) *Demystifying Shamans and Their World* (2011).

William G. Roll (1926-2012) received his BA from the University of Berkeley (California, USA), a BLitt and an MLitt from Oxford University (England), and a PhD from Lund University (Sweden). The MLitt thesis was about Roll's ESP experiments; the PhD thesis was an examination of parapsychological findings suggestive of the survival of human personality after death. Dr. Roll has written four books, including *The Poltergeist* (1972), and *Unleashed: Of Poltergeists and Murder* (2004), which he co-wrote with Valerie Storey. He has also written several book chapters and more than 200 research papers. Dr. Roll has appeared on the television series *Unsolved Mysteries*, and other television documentaries. He received the Distinguished Career Award from the Parapsychological Association in 1996, and the Tim Dinsdale Memorial Award from the Society for Scientific Exploration in 2002. He passed away January 9, 2012.

Lance Storm earned a BA (Honours) in psychology (1998) and a PhD in parapsychology (2002) at the University of Adelaide, South Australia. He has published in a number of major peer-reviewed journals, including *Psychological Bulletin*, *Explore*, *Journal of Parapsychology*, *Journal of Scientific Exploration*, *International Journal of Jungian Studies*, and *Quadrant*. He is a full member of the Parapsychological Association, and the Australian Institute of Parapsychological Research, Inc., of whose journal the *Australian Journal of Parapsychology* he is current editor. He was awarded the Gertrude R. Schmeidler Student of the Year Award for 2003 by the Parapsychological Association, the Frances P. Bolton Fellowship by the Parapsychology Foundation in 2007, and the Parapsychological Association Outstanding Contribution Award in 2012. Dr. Storm is the author of two books: *The Enigma of Numbers* (2008), and *A Parapsychological Investigation of the Theory of Psychopraxia* (2010), and he co-authored (with Dr. Adam J. Rock) the monograph *Shamanism and Psi* (2011). He co-edited two books with Michael Thalbourne: *Parapsychology in the Twenty-First Century* (2005), and *The Survival of Human Consciousness* (2006); and he edited the book *Synchronicity: Multiple Perspectives on Meaningful Coincidence* (2008). As a research fellow, he conducts psychological and parapsychological research at the School of Psychology, University of Adelaide.

Michael A. Thalbourne (1953-2010) obtained his BA (Honors) degree at the University of Adelaide (South Australia) in 1976, and his PhD in Parapsychology at Edinburgh University (Scotland) in 1981. He has been published in all the major English-speaking parapsychological journals, and wrote the widely used book *A Glossary of Terms Used in Parapsychology* (1982). He was a member of the American and British Societies for Psychical Research, and the Parapsychological Association. Dr. Thalbourne was president of the Australian Institute of Parapsychological Research, Inc., and founding editor of its journal, the *Australian Journal of Parapsychology*. His most recent publications are the second edition of the above-mentioned *Glossary* (2003), and the parapsychological monograph *The Common Thread Between ESP and PK* (2004). He is co-editor with Dr. Lance Storm of the book *Parapsychology in the Twenty-First Century* (2005), and *The Survival of Human Consciousness* (2006). He was a research fellow at the University of Adelaide, where he was director of the Anomalistic Psychology Research Unit. He passed away on May 4, 2010.

Bryan J. Williams is currently a research associate with the Psychical Research Foundation, a non-profit organization dedicated to research and education in parapsychology. A co-recipient of the Parapsychology Foundation's Eileen J. Garrett Scholarship Award for 2008, he previously received his education at the University of New Mexico, and had studied under the late Dr. William G. Roll of the University of West Georgia from 2004 to 2012.

Simon Harvey-Wilson (1951-2006) devoted the latter part of his short life to the formal study of parapsychology, and earned himself a PhD in the process. The topic of his PhD thesis was Human Levitation (see Chapter 4). He lectured, contributed articles to peer-reviewed journals, and acted as editor of the *West Australian Journal of the Society for Psychical Research*. In the last three years of his life, before succumbing to motor neurone disease, he became an avid reader. He passed away on September 3, 2006.

Index

B

C

D

L

M

N

S

Pari Publishing is an independent publishing company, based in a medieval Italian village. Our books appeal to a broad readership and focus on innovative ideas and approaches from new and established authors who are experts in their fields. We publish books in the areas of science, society, psychology, and the arts.

Our books are available at all good bookstores or online at
www.paripublishing.com

If you would like to add your name to our email list to receive information about our forthcoming titles and our online newsletter please contact us at
newsletter@paripublishing.com

Visit us at **www.paripublishing.com**

Pari Publishing Sas
Via Tozzi, 7
58045 Pari (GR)
Italy

Email: info@paripublishing.com